PENGUI

DESTINY

Born in 1925, John Burnett was educated at High Pavement School, Nottingham, and at Emmanuel College, Cambridge, where he was an Exhibitioner and Sizar. After reading history and law at Cambridge, he researched in social history at the London School of Economics and was awarded a Ph.D. in 1958. He has had a varied teaching career in primary schools, technical colleges, polytechnics, extra-mural departments and universities, and is now Professor of Social History at Brunel University.

His main research and writings have been in the history of the standard of living, particularly in the nineteenth and twentieth centuries. Previous publications include *Plenty and Want: A Social History of Diet in England from 1815 to the Present Day* (1966, revised edition 1979), *A History of the Cost of Living* (Pelican 1969), *The Challenge of the Nineteenth Century* (1970), *Useful Toil: Autobiographies of Working People from the 1820s to the 1920s* (Pelican 1977; reissued in Penguin, 1984) to which this book is a sequel, and *A Social History of Housing 1815–1970* (1978, paperback 1980). He is now editing a bibliography of nineteenth-century working-class autobiographies.

DESTINY OBSCURE

Autobiographies of childhood,
education and family
from the
1820s to the 1920s

*Edited and Introduced
by John Burnett*

PENGUIN BOOKS

Penguin Books Ltd, Harmondsworth, Middlesex, England
Penguin Books, 40 West 23rd Street, New York, New York 10010, U.S.A.
Penguin Books Australia Ltd, Ringwood, Victoria, Australia
Penguin Books Canada Ltd, 2801 John Street, Markham, Ontario, Canada L3R 1B4
Penguin Books (N.Z.) Ltd, 182–190 Wairau Road, Auckland 10, New Zealand

First published by Allen Lane 1982
Published in Penguin Books 1984

Copyright © John Burnett, 1982
All rights reserved

The illustrations on Part titles One and Two
are from the Mary Evans Picture Library;
that on Part title Three is from the BBC Hulton Picture Library

Printed in Great Britain by
Richard Clay (The Chaucer Press) Ltd,
Bungay, Suffolk

Let not ambition mock their useful toil,
Their homely joys, and destiny obscure;
Nor grandeur hear with a disdainful smile,
The short and simple annals of the poor.

'Elegy Written in a Country Churchyard,'
Thomas Gray

CONTENTS

Contents

PREFACE
AUTOBIOGRAPHIES AS HISTORY

This collection of autobiographies follows *Useful Toil: Autobiographies of working people from the 1820s to the 1920s*, first published by Allen Lane in 1974. Since then, much more material has come to light and other social historians have begun to work on what is still a neglected source of evidence about life in past time. While 'oral history' has now been recognized as a respectable academic enterprise for at least a decade, autobiographical history, which can carry the researcher back much further than living memory, is still at the infant stage of scholarly development.

This is not for any lack of material. In his doctoral thesis Dr David Vincent analysed the contents of forty-nine published working-class autobiographies relating to the period 1800–1850 and has subsequently discovered more.[1] For the later nineteenth and early twentieth centuries, the material becomes increasingly abundant and it is clear that the only available bibliography, edited by William Matthews in 1955, is far from complete.[2] In addition, my own researches have already revealed several hundred unpublished autobiographies by men and women of all social classes, and more extensive search would undoubtedly yield many more.

After letter-writing, autobiography was, and probably still is, the most common form of personal literary expression. It is sometimes said that the one person we all really know is ourself, and the one book we can all write is our own autobiography, but, however debatable either statement may be, the fact is that for at least the last three hundred years very many people have, for various reasons, considered that their life histories were worth recording. Perhaps the earliest examples of this form of writing, dating from the seventeenth century, are the memoirs of nonconformists, especially Puritans and Quakers, in which the authors describe their conversion from sin, their persecutions, and hopes for ultimate salvation. Though written as personal testimonies, their message was clearly propagandist – a call to other sinners to repent and follow in the paths of righteousness. Spiritual autobiographies of this kind continued to be a popular genre well into the nineteenth century[3] and represent an important stage in the growth of identity and consciousness among an underprivileged minority.

During the nineteenth century the economic and social upheavals associated with the growth of industrialization produced a set of auto-biographies by radicals of a different kind. A number of men who played some part in the development of the early labour movement left records of their struggles against oppression through their involvement in trade unionism, co-operation, the campaign for a free press and the reform of parliamentary representation. It is memoirs of this kind – by Thomas Cooper, Alexander Somerville, William Lovett, Samuel Bamford, James Burn and others[4] – which have been best known to historians and have attained the rank of minor classics. In these the dominant theme is the wrongs of the working man rather than his sins: the message is proclaimed that power lies in the hands of the people, and that through organization, self-help and education the new Jerusalem can be built in this world.

Though usually of humble origin, such men who stood up to oppression and often suffered trial and imprisonment for their views were clearly exceptional, and became important and acknowledged in their lifetimes for their contribution to the labour movement. But, as literacy spread in the later nineteenth century, autobiographical writing became increasingly common among ordinary people who never attained to any position of power or leadership. As this selection illustrates, they are to be found among all ranks of society, written not only by the middle classes and the 'aristocrats' of skilled labour but over the whole occupational range of the working class, and by women as well as men. Most were written only in manuscript form and with no thought of publication. Usually the reason the author gives is simply to set down a record of a very different kind of life for the amusement or edification of grandchildren. Occasionally there is a moral purpose – to demonstrate the triumph of fortitude, hard work and education over poverty, deprivation or disability; sometimes an autobiography is undertaken to improve writing skills or merely to pass the time during unemployment, convalescence or retirement. Although the keeping of a daily diary by working people, at least in any detail, seems not to have been common, no doubt from lack of time or opportunity, the writing of autobiography was evidently a widespread and popular form of self-expression. It enabled the author to give himself identity, to place himself in the context of history, geography and social change, and so to make a kind of sense out of an existence which might otherwise seem meaningless. Many authors begin with an account of their parentage and more distant lineage, so far as this is known, almost in the way that an aristocrat might trace his descent; nearly all, as we shall see, give a more or less detailed account of their childhood, recognizing this as a crucial period when character and personality are formed. In such ways autobiographers seek to establish themselves in time and to leave behind a testimony that the significance of a life does not end at death.

To the historian attempting to reconstruct the past 'as it really was', the outstanding merit of autobiography lies in the fact that it is the direct, personal record of the individual himself – the actor or eye-witness – without the intermediary of another person who may change the situation or misread the experience. The autobiographer's version of what happened to himself possesses a personal validity which is different in kind from any second-hand account, however skilled the reporter may be in techniques of observation and analysis. The auto-biographer, writing at a distance after the event, may forget or mis-remember details, but the essence of his task is to record what, to him, have been the most important and significant occurrences which have shaped his life. The very partiality of the account is, therefore, part of its value, for the author has chosen his own ground, patterned his own experiences, and has painted a self-portrait which is more revealing than any photograph.

In this way the author can take us into realms of experience which have usually evaded the historian. 'Official' history is primarily con-cerned with public events, autobiography with private experiences. These may not always be recorded in the depth or detail we may wish, either because the author is reticent to expose his innermost self or because he may not possess the skill necessary to do so, but in all such writings the hopes and fears, joys, sorrows, ambitions and frustrations of ordinary people are revealed to a greater or lesser extent. In reading these accounts we take a journey into largely unknown territory where feelings sometimes lie too deep for words, and where what is not said may be as significant as that which is. To the conventional skills of his craft – judgement, the ability to weigh evidence, to detect inconsistency and insincerity – the historian of autobiography needs to add a good measure of sympathy and sensitivity.

The limitations of such material as historical evidence have also to be recognized and, as far as possible, guarded against. Autobiographers may suppress or misrepresent the truth, may exaggerate or sensational-ize, may tell only half the story and thereby make the part that is told misleading. They may do these things accidentally, because time and memory can play strange tricks, or deliberately, because they have something to conceal or a false image to project. Where an autobi-ography is written for publication, the needs of the market or the type of

readership may influence the form and content of the writing in ways
difficult to detect. In this respect the unpublished autobiography which
was never written with an eye to the 'market' has the advantage, though
even here an author who is leaving a record for future generations of his
family may wish to present himself to advantage. But such limitations
are common to any kind of evidence: absolute truth is never available to
the historian, who has to make the best use he can of his material,
prodding and probing to the best of his ability with his own imperfect
tools.

It has also to be recognized that however wide the 'sample' of
autobiographies may be, they will never be completely 'representative'
of the whole of society. To write one's life story must always be an
untypical activity, requiring time, ability, energy and, above all, a degree
of literacy, and the further we go back in time the less frequently these
requisites existed among ordinary working people. More autobiographies were written in the nineteenth century by professional people than
by manual workers, more by skilled craftsmen than by labourers, more
by men than by women. As the century advances the sample becomes
wider, but the poorest classes are always least represented, and we must
accept that there remain some sections of society whose voices cannot
yet be heard by the historian.

Although autobiographies naturally vary much in length, content and
style, writers generally address themselves to a fairly specific set of
major themes. Not surprisingly, working men and women often devote
substantial space to their experiences of work itself: the nature and
rewards of their labour, their search for work and reactions to it – a
theme which formed the subject of *Useful Toil*. Beyond this, the major
preoccupations of autobiographers are with their childhood, education,
home and family relations, subjects with which almost all deal in different degrees, and which in a good many accounts form almost the entire
content of their memoirs. In some accounts working life is passed over
with perfunctory notice, while early experiences are given pride of place
and recorded with a vivid detail which advancing years seem only to
heighten.

In recent times the phase of life which we know as childhood has
come to be of increasing interest to historians, and the tantalizing
question posed by Peter Laslett about the 'crowds and crowds of little
children [who] are strangely absent from the written record'[5] has begun
to be answered in a variety of ways. In his pioneering study Philippe
Ariès argued that the separate status of the child did not suddenly

emerge in modern times, but was the culmination of processes which began in western Europe in the later Middle Ages and gained particular momentum in wealthier households in the sixteenth and seventeenth centuries. In support of this thesis he pointed to changes in the vocabulary describing children, to the portrayal of children by sculptors and painters, the development of distinctive children's dress, games and toys, and to advances in schooling which gradually extended the categorization of children and the length of dependence. Thus he argues that the indifference with which children had been regarded in earlier times gradually changed to a privileged status in the nineteenth century, particularly within the privatized life of the bourgeois family, though to a much smaller extent among the families of the poor.[6] Developing this theme in terms of psychohistory, Lloyd de Mause has emphasized the maltreatment of children and cruelty towards them in centuries before the nineteenth – the extent of infanticide and abandonment, the early separation of children from parents, the prevalence of wet-nursing and the use of dangerous opiates as 'quieteners', and the violation of children by excessive corporal punishment and sexual abuse.[7] And, by contrast with earlier centuries, when in law the child was regarded as the property of its parents to be used as they directed, Pinchbeck and Hewitt have charted the development of protective legislation in the nineteenth and twentieth centuries which has recognized the child as having independent legal status with rights of its own.[8] Important examples of growing public concern for the welfare of children can be traced through legislation dealing with their hours and conditions of work (Factory Acts from 1802 onwards), juvenile delinquency (Youthful Offenders' Act, 1854), education (compulsory from 1880), cruelty and neglect by parents (Custody of Children Act, 1891) and the nutritional status of schoolchildren (School Meals Act, 1906), as well as in the remarkable growth of voluntary philanthropic agencies formed to ameliorate the sufferings of destitute, disabled and neglected children. These changes in public attitudes and legislation laid the foundations of twentieth-century social policy (e.g. the Children's and Young Persons' Act, 1933, and the Children's Act, 1948) in which the welfare of the child becomes paramount.

So much may be regarded as historical fact and largely uncontroversial, but lively debate has recently surrounded the work of Lawrence Stone and his concept of the development of 'affective individualism'. Stone distinguishes six types of child-rearing practices which are in part chronological and in part class-specific. He argues that the Early Modern family was characterized by high mortality and low affect. Among the aristocracy, the attitude towards children had been largely one of indifference once the needs of succession has been met by the birth of a male heir: children were abandoned to nurses, tutors and other surrogates and little direct care or affection was evidenced. During the seventeenth and eighteenth centuries there was a marked growth of civility, polite manners and language, campaigns against cruelty and a decline in formality of relations between parents and children; greater privacy was introduced into family life and greater concern for children's health and education. These new forces came into full development in the third type of family pattern, among the wealthy bourgeoisie of the eighteenth century where family life was now child-oriented, affectionate and permissive; traditional practices such as swaddling, wet-nursing and severe punishment declined, and more education took place at home rather than at boarding-schools. But, although affection had now largely superseded neglect, a further change occurred in the closing decades of the eighteenth century associated with the Methodist Revival – the concept of the child as naturally sinful and requiring his will to be broken by stern discipline. In many middle-class households there was therefore a reversion to a more patriarchal, authoritarian family type, though involving intense emotional and religious concern for children's welfare, which held sway roughly from the 1770s to the 1870s. Among the working classes, it is argued, these changes did not reach very far. Here, ignorance and lack of resources still caused heavy infant mortality, drove children out to work at a tender age, and brutalized relationships between spouses and between parents and children. Until real incomes rose in the later nineteenth century, until family size began to decline and more infants survived, there was little time or space in working-class life for strong emotional investment, and children had to take their share in the common struggle for survival. The final stage of Stone's model is reached in the late nineteenth century, when there is a gradual return to permissiveness, child-centredness and emotional affect, again beginning in the middle-class intelligentsia but caused by a variety of new influences – the decline of strict religiosity, women's emancipation, family limitation and the new psychological theories of child development. These trends ultimately affected all social classes in the twentieth century in one way or another, resulting in the small modern family characterized by a high concentration of affection and attention, a decline in paternal authority, more 'natural' child-rearing practices and more democratic sharing of roles. In the modern family, where infant death is exceptional, where the length of children's dependence is increased by extended education, and where marriage itself now often endures for fifty or more years, love and affection have become increasingly important as the primary bonds of family life.[9]

In this view, then, a small but close and strong nuclear family has emerged in post-industrial society, whatever may have been the disruptive influences of early industrialization and urbanization. Even the 'traditional' theory, derived from Engels and other opponents of industrial capitalism, that the advance of the factory system destroyed family relationships and parental responsibility by forcing husbands, wives and children out into separate employment, has recently been challenged. In his study of the cotton town, Preston, during the industrial revolution, Michael Anderson has argued that in some respects the factory system increased the interdependence of the family, and that most young people remained at home longer than before.[10] In part-support of the Engelian theory of moral decline during early industrialization, Edward Shorter has claimed a marked increase in illegitimacy rates and pre-marital pregnancy in the period 1750–1850 sufficient to warrant the description of a 'sexual revolution',[11] though alternative explanations of these phenomena are not difficult to suggest. In rural society marriage was frequently delayed until there was evidence of the intended spouse's fertility, when local sanctions usually brought the couple to wedlock; in the more mobile and anonymous towns and cities of the nineteenth century the same sexual values may well have obtained, but without the social controls to enforce marriage.[12] In this interpretation the 'sexual revolution' was a non-event.

Sufficient has been said to indicate that childhood and family relationships have become a major debating-ground among social historians in recent years, calling support from a variety of other disciplines including psychology, sociology and demography. It seems important, therefore, to take account of the direct experiences of ordinary people themselves as expressed in their autobiographies. In the following pages autobiographical extracts illustrate a wide variety of experiences from different periods of time, different social classes, occupations and regions, while in the introductions to the three major sections of the book some analysis and interpretation of the contents is attempted. It is important that the people should speak for themselves, but also important that the historian should try to understand what they say. It is notable that in describing their childhoods writers generally address themselves to a fairly restricted set of themes which, by inference, they regard as of particular significance – for example, their earliest memories, their first realization of identity, their fantasies and religious beliefs, their discipline and duties within the home, the extent of child-care, the end of childhood and their first entry to full-time work and the adult world. Similarly, major themes in autobiographers' accounts of home and family include the physical structure and contents of the home, family size, household tasks, relationships within the family and within the local neighbourhood and community.

No single or simple consensus emerges from these considerations. There is no general agreement, for example, that childhood or school life was either a specially happy or specially unhappy period, that parents always loved their children or children their parents. People are individuals, their life experiences are to an extent unique and not to be confined within statistical categories. Nevertheless, some relevant generalizations emerge from the writings which bear on the recent debate. Contrary to what has been argued, the care and affection of parents for their children does not appear to be related directly to social class – there were neglectful and unaffectionate parents among the well-to-do as there were loving ones among the poor. Economic resources obviously limited what could be spent on children, but concern for their welfare and the misery which illness or death frequently caused suggests that 'affective individualism' was not, at least in this period, specific to a particular social class and that emotional investment in children is not to be equated with the economic. In other respects social class clearly had major consequences for childhood experiences – for instance, in determining the length of dependence and the age at which children became wage-earners, and in the degree of control which parents exercised over children's behaviour. In general it seems that the extent of restraint increased in the middle class and the severity of punishment in the working class, though exceptions may immediately be cited. But children's happiness at home bore no direct relationship to wealth or poverty, to possessions or the lack of them, to overcrowded or inadequate housing conditions. This is not to deny that there was an economic limit below which the struggle for existence cast a blight on the lives of all, and there are not a few hungry, miserable children, over-strained, nagging mothers and drunken, brutal fathers in the following pages. Yet the happiest memories of child life generally came from large working-class families which, by modern standards, had no luxuries and few comforts, but which stood somewhat above the level of the very poor.

Not surprisingly, many autobiographies originate from this section of the 'respectable' working class, where the virtues of education, hard work and self-improvement were respected but not usually at the expense of a close, affectionate family life. In many such households, 'family' extended into neighbouring houses where grandparents or other kin lived and into the nearby streets which served as an extension of 'home' into the open air. Although it would be easy to over-romanticize it, the accounts which many autobiographers give of local community life – equally in rural areas, in mining villages and in working-class districts of towns and cities – suggest that it held a significance in their lives which was largely absent in the privatized homes of the middle classes. In such communities there was no lack of 'affect' for children by aunts and uncles, neighbours, shopkeepers and the numerous hawkers and pedlars who brought colour and excitement into the streets. As children grew into adolescents and young adults the streets became the venue for 'larking' and courtship rituals, but the autobiographies do not support the case for a 'sexual revolution' in the early and mid-nineteenth century. The fact that sex was a taboo subject, as many writers record, may account for the silence of almost all autobiographers on pre-marital or extra-marital relations though the part which sexual attraction played in marriage is evident in some of the writings.

On such intimate subjects as their loves and sorrows the auto-biographers often leave us asking for more. Sometimes we can 'read between the lines' to fill out the emotional gaps: sometimes we can recognize that the simple words and phrases in an author's limited vocabulary have to stand for deeper feelings that he is unable to express. The following accounts describe lives which are sometimes almost unimaginably different from our own, yet which constantly touch on human experiences that are timeless and universal. We see ourselves in past time, less educated, less sophisticated, perhaps less trammelled with worldly goods or desires, but with thoughts and feelings that we can immediately recognize and share. In that sense we ourselves are their 'destiny obscure'.

ACKNOWLEDGEMENTS

This book is based on the autobiographies of what are commonly described as 'ordinary' men and women whose lives spanned the century from the 1820s to the 1920s; the reader may come to feel that 'ordinary' lives often contain much that is extraordinary. A few of the autobiographies exist in published or privately printed form, but the great majority are unpublished and came in response to requests for such material in the press and in a BBC programme. I am deeply grateful to more than eight hundred people who sent me manuscript accounts of their own lives or autobiographies previously written by ancestors and without whose help and forbearance over several years this book could not have been composed. It has been possible to quote only a few lengthy extracts, and it should be said that these find a place not necessarily because they are the 'best', most interesting or well written, but because they illustrate key themes which it was important to include. Many more contributors are represented only by brief quotation and, regrettably, more still are denied even this small acknowledgement, but from all I have learned and profited, not least in humility.

I wish also to thank very warmly Valerie Radford, who not only coped enthusiastically with the problems of unfamiliar manuscripts, as well as with the more familiar difficulties of my own, but also kept careful control over the documents and the complicated correspondence. If there are errors or omissions in acknowledgement the responsibility, of course, is mine.

PART ONE

Childhood

INTRODUCTION

1. Almost all autobiographers write of their childhood, often at length, and some continue their life stories no further than this. Childhood is clearly seen as an important – perhaps the most important – phase of development, a time when identity and personality are formed and when crucial influences are brought to bear which shape the character and destiny of the individual. Yet there is, as the following pages will show, no single or simple view of childhood expressed by the authors – no consensus that it was an especially happy or unhappy period, that parents always loved their children or children their parents; still less is there agreement about when and how childhood ended, when innocence was lost and the realities of the adult world broke through. These differences are partly accounted for by time, by class and economic status, but also by a variety of individual familial circumstances which defy classification. Nevertheless, it is evident from a wide reading of autobiographies, both published and unpublished, that in accounts of their childhood writers generally address themselves to a limited number of themes which, inferentially, they regard as being of particular importance. An examination of these themes will therefore indicate not a collective experience of childhood in the past, but at least some of the aspects of childhood which were of particular interest or concern.

2. Many autobiographers record their earliest memories, and these immediately suggest an astonishing variation in the powers of mental recall. The earliest of all appears to be that of Margaret Cunningham, who remembers what must have been an exciting and emotional experience at the very early age of seven months:

> I remember being carried out into a shining sea, clinging to my father's wet brown neck, and aware of his fair curly hair and very blue eyes. That must have been on a holiday in Weymouth when I was only seven months old.[1]

Memory, as is well known, can play strange tricks, and some very early 'memories' may not be such at all, though this one seems particularly well authenticated. Averil Thomas rightly observes:

> Certain personal happenings I remember well, but how much I remember through having experienced them, or what part I remember because they were often recounted in my childhood, I am not sure.[2]

Very early memories are often connected with a dramatic, even traumatic, event, which left a deep and lasting sensation of fear, disaster or rejection. Few can have been so scarring as that experienced by one autobiographer at the age of fourteen months:

My earliest memory . . . has recurred again and again, and its constant resuscitation leaves no doubt, it seems to me, of its authenticity . . . It had been my habit for some time to wake up early, as nearly all young children do, and creep in beside my mother in the big bed. She was drowsy and affectionate and warm, and I liked looking at her . . . It did not occur to her to hide her breasts from me: I had always been free of them . . . I still regarded that territory as mine by right. Suddenly, my father's voice, thick with anger, broke in upon my morning scene: 'Back to your own bed at once!' he growled at me. And to my mother: 'Making a fool of the boy!'[3]

By contrast, other autobiographers record that they have no clear memories until a much later age – quite often at around the age of five. James Carter wrote that he had no recollections until the end of his fifth year – then they became very sharp.[4] Similarly, Christopher Thomson's earliest memory was of being left at the age of five in the care of his grandparents when his mother went to join her husband who was serving in the navy during the Napoleonic Wars.[5] And for W. J. Linton, born in 1812, 'my real recollections begin with the year in which George III ceased to be nominal King of England' – that is, 1820, when he was eight years old; he was in the garden of their house in the Mile End Road with his father when they heard the great bell of St Paul's Cathedral, used only for solemn State occasions, and his father remarked, 'The old King is dead.'[6]

Most early memories fall between these two extremes, the age of two or three being the most common time. Occasionally they are connected with a particularly happy event such as a birthday:

The first thing I remember was standing on a table in the nursery in a red frock and being told that it was my birthday and that I was three years old. I can see that red frock still. Perhaps one recollects earliest the things that one cares for most: certainly I have always had a love for colour.[7]

Many early memories have this quality of capturing a particular moment in time, isolated photographs not yet set in a sequence or perspective. Nor are the pictures always visual, for one of Jack McQuoid's first memories is of smell – the smell of a column of soldiers who had stopped for a rest, and whose uniforms, rifles, boots and webbing all had distinctive scents which he noticed as he handed round a basket of pears:

I was moving out of the phase of the nursery, and my senses were keen. I could even smell the earth and the dust they had picked up while tramping rough Northumbrian roads . . .[8]

Often, as here, early recollections are of an event which marks a stage in development – a birthday, or, from the frequency with which the event is recorded by autobiographers, the 'breeching' of a boy when he was promoted from a dress to trousers. Historically, boys and girls had both worn frocks until the age of five or six, and through the nineteenth century the practice survived for male infants, though the age of breeching gradually fell to between two and three years. It seems that mainly in the north of England and in rural areas the act of putting a boy into trousers was still a ritual event marking the transition from baby-hood to boyhood and was often attended by relatives and neighbours in a similar way to a christening. Samuel Mountford, one of twelve children born to a poor Birmingham family in 1907, writes:

I think without any doubt my first recollection of life was when I was breeched . . . It was the usual thing to make a fuss, and I was no exception. I remember standing on the table all dressed up in white blouse, velvet trousers with shoulder straps, white ankle socks, patent black shoes and bow tie. My word, I did look posh, and I felt posh. All the folk in the terrace came in to inspect and wish me all happiness in life, and of course presented me with presents and, as was customary, a silver coin (in those days, a silver threepenny bit). I think my age would be two to three years, but still I am sure it stuck in my mind from that day onwards.[9]

In this family, clothes were normally made from other people's cast-offs. For Charles Esam, breeching was made to coincide with his second birthday; until then, he had worn a pleated, grey serge frock which came to just below the knee, with a cap of the same material.[10]

But the majority of earliest memories recorded by autobiographers are of an unhappy experience, often of an accident, shock or trauma. For James Burn, the illegitimate 'Beggar Boy' who was 'born in poverty, nursed in sorrow' in a garret in Dumfries, his first memory was of being held up by his mother to witness a public hanging.[11] Frank Wensley's earliest memories were of fear – of a big, black dog and of being pitched out of his baby-carriage.[12] Thomas Cooper remembered nearly drown-ing in the river Leate at the age of two,[13] while James Hopkinson first remembered cutting his fingers severely on his father's razor when he was three, 'so that I speak feelingly when I say my first knowledge was of pain and suffering'.[14] One of Eleanor Hewson's first memories is of her mother weeping at the death of her brother:

This frightens and appals me. It is the first time I have seen my mother cry, and for the moment she is a stranger to me. No longer the source of all comfort and security, but herself in need of protection, and therefore a human being and not merely 'Mother'. It is my first experience of the ultimate loneliness of every human spirit.[15]

Writing his memoirs seventy years after the event, Jack Goring remembered a Christmas 'party' at which the refreshment consisted of one chestnut for each child.[16] Averil Thomas remembers her fear of a stampeding horse as she was being pushed along a narrow country lane in her pram, and her near escape as her sister snatched her up and ran for shelter.[17] Incidents of this kind may seem unimportant, almost trivial, yet the fact that they are remembered many years later indicates the deep impression which they made. Usually they are of some 'internal' event which happens to the individual within the home or the family circle, rather than an 'external', national event. James Burn's memory of the public execution is an exception to this, as are those writers who record witnessing Queen Victoria's funeral procession or 'Mafeking Night' celebrations at a very early age. Two autobiographers record first-hand memories of railway disasters, one at Abergele in North Wales in 1868, in which thirty-three people died and which, at that time, was the worst accident to have occurred on British railways. George Grundy, aged seven, and an older friend were the only eye-witnesses when two trains, each travelling at sixty miles an hour, collided about fifty yards from where they sat watching on an embankment:

Anyone who has ever seen such a sight as we two boys saw then will understand that every detail of it will abide in the memory through life. At the moment impact took place the engine rose like a horse taking a fence, and came down on the fourth truck. The three first coaches of the mail were reduced to matchwood . . . We promptly ran down the embankment to where the engine lay. The bodies of the driver and fireman were lying face downwards about ten yards from the engine, from which steam was pouring . . . We were not going to miss a scene of such absorbing interest for a mere trifle such as the bursting of a boiler . . . I was taken to the funeral at Abergele. All that remained of those who had been killed was buried in one grave in minute coffins, only a few fragments of bones in each, so the sexton told my father. The fierce heat had consumed all else. It was not till then that I realized the tragic side of what I had seen, and I wept freely at the funeral.[18]

3. Frequently in the autobiography of childhood some event is mentioned which clearly marks a turning-point in the development of the individual. This may be the first consciousness of identity – the realization of self as having thoughts, emotions and desires distinct from those

of the adults who have hitherto constituted the child's world; sometimes it takes the form of recognizing that those adults are not perfect, but frail and mortal; again, the first recognition of self is, for some, the experiencing of deep emotion which is individual and not shared by others. Whatever form it takes, the essence of the experience is the recognition by the child that it is an independent personality and, usually associated with this, that it is not the centre of the universe. Such a momentous discovery is often hard to reconstruct and, as the examples will show, its articulation may be concealed in an incident of seeming unimportance.

Several writers describe this growth of consciousness in terms of the physical expansion of the child's universe – the realization of a larger, stranger world, sometimes ugly and frightening, sometimes mysterious and beautiful, beyond the confines of the domestic hearth. Jack McQuoid recalls this dawning realization of a distinct environment:

. . . outside my little world of gas-lighted bedrooms, the kitchen with the blazing coal fire, the parlour, which was seldom used, with its creaking floorboards that set the china on the dresser jingling . . . there was the street outside, where children played round lamp-posts, where the lamplighter came with a lighted pole each evening. There were small shops at the street-corner, where one could buy a poke of sweets for a halfpenny, but beyond that corner my world ended. Away down the road were the cluttered streets of dockland, with pubs at the corners, and where barefoot children begged for halfpennies. My father's £2 a week was adequate to screen me from such poverty . . .[19]

In a different, rural setting J. H. Ingram describes his gradual discovery of the physical world, the beginning of an exploration which was to take him, as a young man, to Canada and, ultimately, round the world:

At first I was content to explore the garden. I had been born crippled and could not walk very well, but I discovered that if I sat very still, with my lame leg twisted under me, small animals would appear as if from nowhere and go about their daily affairs just as if I wasn't there . . . The garden became too small, so I learned to squeeze through a gap in the hedge and conduct my explorations in the neighbouring fields. With no brothers or sisters or other children to play with, I was happy enough by myself . . . Next, the roadway outside the garden gate became the focus of my attention, for many exciting happenings took place there. Every evening at sundown the German prisoners-of-war would come marching along the road, followed by an English soldier carrying a rifle with a bayonet. At sunset, also, a deep booming sound came rolling across the Suffolk plain, and I was told it was the roaring of the guns over in Flanders.[20]

Realization of self is clearly distinct from realization of the external world, though the two may be associated. For some it comes as the result of a shock as, in the case of Thomas Cooper, the death of a parent. 'All this pleasant, sunny life of early childhood was soon to pass away. My mother became a widow when I was but four years old . . .' and after a year of serious illness from smallpox, measles and scarlet fever 'I felt – child though I was – the humbling change that had come over me.'[21] Exceptionally a child may be conscious that it inhabits a different world, that it has not yet made the transition to 'reality' as Cooper regretfully did. A strange experience is recorded by Eleanor Hewson in her third year:

In the kitchen was a little, white-painted stool which I had appropriated for my own use. When still a baby I sat on it before the fire, holding my bottle in two fat hands and sucking at it with all the deliberate enjoyment of an old man with a pipe. When past the bottle-sucking stage, I carried the same stool from its corner by the dresser to wherever my mother was working and, while she made cakes or cut up the apples for a tart, I sat gravely at her side 'reading' to her from the newspaper. Sometimes, when moved to protest against my wild inventions, she would exclaim, 'But, my dear child, what a lot of nonsense you're talking!' I would shake my head earnestly and say, 'Oh no, mother, it's not nonsense. I'm not living in your world, you know.'[22]

Some autobiographers can trace their recognition of identity to a specific moment in time rather than a gradual awakening. For Margaret Cunningham it was a blinding revelation which seems to have occurred on her fourth birthday:

Another mental experience I remember vividly happened when I was four years old. Maybe it was on my birthday, for I know I was four years old. I was standing in the window of my father's study looking out at the village street, clad in my navy blue blouse (with sailor collar) and skirt, a dress which disappointed me for it didn't have a whistle . . . But the feeling that came over me was one of vivid identity. 'I am I, and nobody else.' I have no memory of what triggered this off – if anything. Maybe it just came from beyond. But it is an experience that is with me still.[23]

And for Marianne Farningham there were equally sudden awakenings to beauty and her perception of it, in two distinct incidents which she describes as 'the awakening of the soul of a child'. One came from literature, when, on reading a poem by Felicia Hemans, 'The Better Land', 'I was obliged to prevent myself from being overcome by faintness, to put down the book and go to the door for a breath of fresh air . . . I wish I could describe, even if only so far as I am able to live it again, the strange, sweet emotions which overcame me as I read those lines.' The other came, as it has done for many artists and poets, from the contemplation of Nature:

At the bottom of our garden was a wall, just low enough for me to look over . . . I must have spent hours as a child leaning against that wall, and looking out into the world of summer. First there was a meadow, and a gate out of it led into another meadow, in which was a row of magnificent lime-trees, which I loved and almost worshipped . . . At the end of this meadow was the river Darent, which made music day and night . . . Then, far away in the blue distances were gentle hills and shady woods and picturesque little villages . . . The summer sunsets were heavenly; indeed, it often seemed to me that heaven itself was just over there as far as my eye could reach, and I have many a time imagined groups of angels and the 'innumerable company' moving about in the masses of white and golden clouds. Often I have stood with tears in my eyes, and my heart throbbing with love and gladness, and tried to say something to God to let Him know what I was feeling.[24]

Part of the process of discovery of the real world for many children is the ending of certainty and the onset of doubt, particularly about relationships which have never previously been questioned. A good many autobiographers describe the shock resulting from the arrival of a new brother or sister, when they cease to hold the centre of the stage and to be treated as the 'baby'. At the age of four Margaret Cunningham began to doubt whether she loved all her relatives equally, despite her mother's reassurances. '"I do love Aunt Hilda, don't I, Mummy?" "I'm sure you do, dear," she replied. "And Aunt Rosie?" "Of course, dear." I was still puzzled.'[25] In a similar way, others record their first realization that their parents are not perfect and all-knowing but subject to the faults and frailties of ordinary mortals. At the age of seven Ethel Davidson first recognized that her father had shortcomings when he laughed as her kitten leapt into the air in distress on being fed scraps from a dinner-plate which contained mustard.

So my idolized father had faults, like everyone else: and really I had been aware of them all the time but had not considered them as faults. All things emanating from father were evidence of his wisdom. It was very disappointing when I first noticed that he had a little clay on his feet.[26]

From a consciousness of self and of others, many autobiographers record the beginnings of speculation about the nature of life, the origins of the world, space, time, the soul and other eternal mysteries. Such imagining is admirably recalled by Thomas Carter in his *Memoirs of a Working Man*, published in 1845:

My thoughts at this period sometimes turned upon myself, and then I encountered new difficulties. With a natural, although childish, curiosity, I wished to know from whence I came. It seemed strange that I could not remember coming into existence as, in like manner, I often wondered why I could not remember the moment of falling asleep, although I had made many efforts to that effect. I perceived that I was a living and conscious being, surrounded by other beings of the same kind, placed without any effort or consent of mine in a world of whose surface I knew little more than the spot occupied by the town in which I lived. I had, indeed, been taught that this world, with all its productions and its inhabitants, was made by God: and, moreover, could read for myself the Bible history of the creation and of the primitive condition of man, yet I was not hereby fully satisfied. There were many things that I wished to know, upon which both the Bible and my other instructors were silent . . .[27]

4. For many autobiographers childhood was a time of imagination and fantasy not yet inhibited by the formality of education and the reality of external events. A high proportion of children created their secret worlds, though to what extent and for what length of time varied greatly between individuals; generally, it seems to have endured longer among children of wealthier parents, for whom the age of formal schooling was often delayed and the period of domestic protection extended. But the nature of childhood fantasies and fears does not appear to have been a function of social class. The autobiographers who write on this matter, from whatever period of time or income group, concentrate on a narrow range of experiences which suggest a high degree of commonality in the world of imagination.

One aspect of this, of course, is imaginative play in which almost all children engaged in varying measure; dolls, toy animals and soldiers are commonplace examples which receive frequent mention. But more exotic examples turn up readily enough through the pages. One writer, daughter of a rector, recalls how her affection for a newly acquired half-size violin was demonstrated by her imaginary feeding of it with bread and milk from one of her dolls-house basins, pretending that the sound-hole was its mouth.[28] Another clergyman's daughter, under the influence of Biblical miracles, believed that she could walk on water, with all too natural results.[29] For some children, fantasy was clearly an escape from unhappiness in the real world. Ellen Nesbitt, daughter of a coal-miner, felt a sense of shame at her poverty and 'took to hiding myself more and more in the make-belief world':

I would often sit in front of a blazing coal fire and make pictures out of the shapes and patterns of the colourful flames. I would imagine I was in another soft, kind world, dressed in a beautiful flowing gown. A handsome young man would walk towards me, and we would float off into the blue sky . . .

The same author experimented with a pea under her mattress to test whether she was a princess; so strong were her fantasies about her identity that:

> For years I was certain that I was not a real member of our family and had been left with mam and dad for some reason. I was convinced that one day they'd come back for me and I'd be transported to that other world I knew existed where there was always something nice to eat, nice clothes to wear, and people who spoke nicely to each other and didn't shout or swear.[30]

Many children found comfort and protection in a belief in supernatural forces. Here the line between belief in God (to be considered separately) and in other supernatural beings is a thin one, and many seem to have regarded both as fully compatible. During Zeppelin raids in the First World War Eleanor Hutchinson, aged three, put her trust in fairies:

> The Fairy Queen lived and held her Court somewhere in faraway Spain. All the fairies were messengers who went about the whole world doing good. Mostly they worked in towns, and sat on grimy chimney-pots guarding all the people within . . . I cannot say that I really believed in fairies for long, but I lived in their wonderful world far more easily than I did in the world of Red Riding Hood and the Bad Wolf, or Goldilocks and the Three Bears.[31]

Winifred Griffiths writes that she and her friend Louie 'lived in a world of fantasy'. Sometimes this took the form of enacting adventures of Roman times in the old Arrow-Way near their home at Overton, near Basingstoke; at others they played at weddings, 'the only snag being the difficulty of persuading a boy to act as bridegroom'.[32] Speculations about the nature of the universe are clearly at a different level, though they have the same element of fantasy. At the age of five Jack Goring 'tried to think about time and space' and recollects feeling 'awfully overwhelmed when I found it impossible to think a beginning or ending of either'.[33] Here we begin to pass from the happy make-belief of play to sombre and fearful imaginings, which, on the evidence of autobiographers, constituted by far the majority of childhood fantasies. Especially in the earlier half of the nineteenth century – though by no means exclusively then – many writers recall their fears of ghosts, haunted places, 'boggarts' and the like. These seem to be part of a rural tradition, handed down by stories round the fireside of which adults were often the believers as well as the tellers. James Burn recalls how his mother recited incantations and cast spells, which included sticking pins into the hearts of dead animals when she believed that her sick child had been bewitched:

> At the time I am writing of [about the beginning of the century], there was not

a glen, a homestead, a mountain stream or a valley but had its ghost story or some attendant genius in the shape of a good or evil-disposed fairy . . . I have known several instances where females who were suspected of being witches were all but sacrificed to the godly fury of innocent believers; the fact was that to be sceptical upon this subject was tantamount, among the country people, to disbelieving the Bible.[34]

Burn admits that though such beliefs were commoner fifty years ago than at the time of writing (1855), he had not been able entirely to free himself from the power of superstition. But ghosts were not exclusively a rural phenomenon. Charles Shaw remembers that in the unlighted streets and alleys of the Pottery towns in the 1840s 'a ghost was seen almost every night in some dark and lonely spot'.

Many a time, after fourteen and fifteen hours' work, I had to walk a mile and a half home with another weary little wretch, and we have nodded and budged against each other on the road, surprised to find our whereabouts. No wonder ghosts were seen in the dark, gasless 'Hollow', with flashing lights of furnaces in the distance and with noise of water from the flour-mill in the valley. Oh yes, I have seen ghosts and heard their wailings on such nights . . . Boys don't see them now, even in the 'Hollow', because the Factory Act sends them home at six o'clock, and because the road is lit up with gas lamps.[35]

Similarly, John Clare, described by Edmund Blunden as 'pre-eminent among the "uneducated poets"', was burdened as a child with dreams of death and ghosts, and composed some of his first rhymes as a talisman when passing through the haunted places of the village.[36] Clare was born in 1793 into the 'old England' and of poor, illiterate parents, but more than a hundred years later belief in magical remedies survived in parts of the countryside. Reginald Gowshall put down his survival as a child to one such. At the age of two weeks he contracted thrush, which resisted all medical efforts to cure it; at eighteen months he weighed less than at birth and had to be nursed on a cushion for fear of his bones penetrating the skin.

Then one day a gypsy woman came to the door of our house and on seeing me laid in a pram outside told my mother that her people had a cure for the frog. It was rather a gruesome remedy: in fact, it was one that everybody felt too bad to be tried. The cure prescribed by this lady was that a live frog be put in muslin and given to me so that I could suck the very life out of the frog. My mother gave this prescription a trial. It worked – and saved my life.[37]

For many autobiographers fear was one of the overwhelming emotions of childhood. Fear of the dark is very often mentioned, as are dreams and nightmares. Margaret Cunningham had a recurrent dream of swinging out over a precipice on a wire, accompanied by a sickening feeling of falling.[38] Eleanor Hewson's nightmares were directly traceable to her visits to the early cinema, where:

Stories told by the screen eventually penetrated to my consciousness, and made a horrifying effect on my unformed mind . . . The fierce hatchet faces of the Indians imprinted themselves on my brain and became part of my worst nightmares. For some obscure reason they were associated with the green-painted tool shed in our garden. I would see them in my dreams advancing, tomahawk in hand, from behind the green-painted shed, cat-footed and menacing. Of course, I was rooted to the spot with terror, and would awake sobbing and breathless.[39]

And for Harry West:

My early years were trying ones; dreams were strange, the external world rather precarious. I was also a somnambulist, that is I walked in my sleep until I was about ten . . . The world to me was strange, unreal, and the sensation most unpleasant.[40]

Beatrice Stallan, with a strictly religious upbringing, had a deep fear of the end of the world, a subject about which she dreamed many times,[41] while Enid Stuart Scott's childhood was a time of 'rigours and terrors' – of frightening shadows and the weird sound of the wind in the chimney.

Years afterwards I shocked and I believe hurt my mother by declaring that not for all the tea in China would I again endure the rigours and terrors of childhood. The expression on her face betrayed dismay as she said, 'Why, Enid, you had an extremely happy childhood? Unlike mine, for my father died when I was only six years old, and this completely changed our way of life. I also lost dear brothers and sisters.' Poor mother, she was genuinely upset.[42]

Most childhood fears were of this kind, insubstantial and fantastic, and all the more terrifying because unknown to parents and suffered in loneliness. Fairy tales and ghost stories no doubt had much to answer for. But some children's fears were real enough and shared by adults. At three years old, in 1888, Leonard Ellisdon was warned by his parents to be on his guard against Jack the Ripper, and his father's tobacconist's shop in Brixton was equipped with a spy-hole from the living-room so that suspicious-looking customers could be scrutinized.[43] Many children had a terror of certain animals and insects – the 'Cornish Waif' of the caged rats which shared her tenement bedroom,[44] Wilfred Middlebrook of the cockroaches in the oven which he had to clean.[45] But the circumstance which is mentioned most frequently of all by autobiographers as causing fear and terror is death – of animals and, more especially, of relatives or friends. Both the incidence and sight of death were, of course, much more frequent, when brothers and sisters could so easily die in infancy, when grandparents often lived near by, and when it was usual for the corpse to remain in the home until the funeral. Again, children were much more exposed to backyard slaughter-houses, to the visits of the pig-killer and to the sight of dead horses in the street or on their way to the knacker's yard. The reporting of such things is so common as to suggest a major preoccupation with death and the ceremonies associated with it, events which had a dramatic quality which both excited and appealed to a strongly morbid streak in many children. Kathleen Betterton thought the cemetery was 'the nicest of places' and was 'quite overwhelmed by the beauty of the marble angels',[46] but the primitive instincts which the contemplation of death may produce are well embodied in the recollection of Ethel Clark about the death of a local cart-horse:

. . . Jolly Jones was found dead in the Gumstalls field, and when I told my friends we all trooped off to see, and we danced around it, and one girl tried to lift the hoof of the great cart-horse. When I think of the episode now I wonder what made us be so callous, and to act so much out of keeping with our usual behaviour.[47]

Here, play and death are strangely mixed, as when autobiographers record playing at funerals, making toy coffins and telling jokes about death. But many tell with genuine horror of pig-killing, especially in the countryside where it was common for villagers to fatten a pig each year and to have it professionally killed and butchered. The animal had often become, if not a pet, almost part of the family circle; its death was public – in the garden or yard – its screams audible, and its corpse all too visible until the dismembering a few days later. Typical of many accounts – more often by girls than boys – is that by Ethel Clark:

How I hated the mornings when the killing took place. It was so awful to think that the pigs which had been treated almost like humans should on a cold, dark winter morning be rudely taken to the brookside to become meat. Straw was placed in readiness, and the pig-bench placed beside it, with buckets and cloths, pumice stone, and that awful butcher's knife. The poor creature would be manhandled on to the bench, its screams cutting through the air . . . The pigs were not stunned: the poor creatures were held fast while their throats were cut . . . When all was quiet I would peep out, but often at the wrong time – to see one of the men gleefully catching the blood in a bucket . . . While the pig hung in the back kitchen I was terrified. I could not sleep at night in case it moved: it really haunted me. I would not go near it and made detours around the house not to see it.[48]

Others write of watching the killing like ghouls, frightened but fasci-

nated, and of their fear of the pig-killer himself. 'I was usually frightened of grown-ups and their power over me,' writes Ruth Howe,
–'Doctors, Dentists, and a fearful person called Charlie the Pig-
killer, who was a dwarf and travelled the countryside driving a small,
depressed-looking pony and cart, with the knives of his calling
hanging from his belt.'[49]

At least until the First World War the images of human death were
ever-present and inescapable – for the poor, the corpse kept at home,
not uncommonly in the single living-room and laid out on a door taken
from its hinges, for the better-off, elaborate funerals, mourning and
mementos. Few children did not experience the death of a brother,
sister or school-friend, and one autobiographer remembers a Bolton
family at the beginning of the twentieth century which lost four of its five
children from diphtheria within five days.[50] The emotional effect of
such losses on parents and surviving children is not often recorded and
is incalculable, though it is doubtful whether their frequency made them
any easier to bear. Syd Metcalfe, who records the death and funeral of a
baby sister, seems to imply that it did:

As far as I know, that little girl who was interred that day was never mentioned
again. If she had lived long enough to be christened, her name was never spoken
in my presence. But child mortality was so common then, and usually there were
so many children left over at the final count that the loss of the odd one here and
there on the way didn't really matter much. It was as though this elimination
process whereby only the stronger ones survived was accepted as a perfectly
natural state of affairs. Families were built up in this fashion, with so many
defunct and so many living.[51]

No doubt some families developed a protective shield, even a callous-
ness, towards death, though others deliberately kept memories alive by
photographs and other souvenirs; in the parlour of a friend's house
Daisy Cowper saw framed mourning cards of the children who had died
and a photograph of a dead baby in its tiny coffin.[52] Others prepared for
death, and not only by taking out insurance policies to cover the costs of
a respectable funeral; several autobiographers record that, as children,
they accidentally discovered a grandmother's shrouds or 'grave clothes'
carefully put by in a chest of drawers.

Children's greatest fears about death are associated with certain
ceremonies of the corpse in which they were required to participate.
Kathleen Hilton-Foord, who lived with her grandmother in a single
room, remembered the death of a neighbour's baby: 'All the tenants
went in to kiss her and pay their respects. I was very frightened, but
made to go.'[53] Edward Punter recalls the death of his grandfather:

I was told to go in and see him, lying there, for the last time. He did not look like Grandad – more like a wax dummy from a draper's window, and I was made to touch his face to 'ward off the shock'. It was the first dead body I had seen.[54]

Death was a mystifying, as well as a frightening, experience for many children, who could not understand what had happened, what caused it and what became of the body. 'Resentment' is a word used by several to express this mixture of puzzlement, fear and anger. Their doubts were possibly not greatly allayed by the conventional explanations of adults that the deceased had 'gone to Heaven' or 'gone to live with Jesus'. Leonard Ellisdon writes:

I must have been round the age of five, when I learnt that an old lady living at the back of us was dying. I was very intrigued with this, and spent many hours looking at the house from a back window: I wanted to see the poor old lady ascending into heaven. I did not know if she would be in a perpendicular or horizontal position, what clothes she would be wearing, and, particularly, whether she would be able to navigate the railway bridge that stood near the house.[55]

The survival of similar fantasies among adults is recalled by Patrick MacGill from his childhood in Ireland. His young brother Dan had just died within the space of a day:

'Poor Dan is no more,' said my father, the tears coming out of his eyes. 'Twas the first time I ever saw him weeping, and I thought it very strange. My mother went to the window and opened it in order to let the soul of my brother go away to heaven . . . There was silence in the room for a long while. My father and mother wept, and I was afraid of something which was beyond my understanding. 'Will Dan ever come back again?' I asked.[56]

5. Almost all autobiographers as children had some connection with organized religion, and devote varying amounts of space to the part which it played in their young lives. In the period under review some religious connection was, of course, almost inescapable. It was exceptional for a child not to attend Sunday School, and it was usually only on the grounds of lack of suitable clothing or of collection money rather than of religious disbelief that a minority did not. Although church attendance by adults was declining throughout the century, approximately half the population still did so in 1851, the year of the Religious Census, and it was usual for children to accompany their parents as soon as they were thought old enough to sit through the service. Very many autobiographers therefore record two or three church or chapel attendances on Sundays, often occupying the whole day, in addition to Band of Hope and other more recreational meetings on weekday evenings.

Moreover, for the growing proportion of children who attended day-school there was heavy emphasis on religious teaching by the voluntary Church Societies who were the main providers of schooling for the working classes until almost the end of the century; even in the post-1870 public elementary schools daily Bible-reading was obligatory unless parents and children were prepared to accept the stigma of 'contracting out'.

For a high proportion of children, then, the church or chapel was a dominant influence on their childhood. From their accounts, the great majority accepted this domination either unquestioningly or willingly, very few writers indicating any hostility on their part, at least not until reaching an age well after the years of childhood. On the contrary, many write of the love and happiness which their religion brought, and of the anticipation with which they awaited each Sunday as a day of joyous renewal after the trials of the week. Few write, like Arthur Goffin, that 'at a very early age religious views were thrust upon me', a comment which might have been justified after two attendances at church and one at Sunday School, followed by more hymn-singing at home after the evening service.[57] Against this can be set the passionate belief of Richard Dudley that to do any form of work on Sunday was to break God's law; though a small and delicate child he refused his father's orders to turn the grindstone while he sharpened his scythes on Sundays, suffering many beatings for it. 'He was going to Sunday School, and no amount of arguing or even force would deter him from going.'[58]

It is clear that the depth of religious commitment, as opposed to the mere frequency of church attendance, varied greatly between individual children. Particularly in the earlier half of the century religion was for some the total and consuming influence, and several writers, of whom George Mockford is one (pp. 72–7), focus their autobiographies not on external events but on their moral and doctrinal struggles, their consciousness of sin and eventual salvation. Benjamin Taylor, born in Norfolk in 1816, describes how as a child he took no part in the ordinary amusements of his fellows and how, at the age of eight or nine, he had an overwhelming conviction of his sin and persistent dreams of hell which drove him to the brink of suicide:

Being at one time in a very wretched state of mind, through the influence of temptation, I was prompted to jump into a pit and so put an end to my miserable existence. Just as I got to the side of the pit, it occurred to me that I should only leap out of a bad state into a worse; for there was another pit at the bottom of that, namely the pit of hell. I then took to my feet and ran home as fast as I could, believing the devil to be close at my heels . . .[59]

By this time Taylor had not only read Bunyan's *Pilgrim's Progress* – the most frequently mentioned book by autobiographers of this period after the Bible – but had committed most of it to memory; it clearly had a profound influence on both his thought and literary style. Others were more influenced by particular preachers, like James Hopkinson who recalls his first stirrings of religious belief about the year 1825:

Of my early religious impressions I may say I was not more than five or six years old when a Lady Preachess came to a Primitive Methodist chapel near to where I lived. And as a great favour my mother let me go to the service that night, young as I was, the spirit of God was stirring in me. I remember being in tears, but at the same time feeling very happy and different to what I had ever felt before.[60]

It is notable that early and intense emotions of this kind are most often described by those whose parents were not especially religious, and in some cases the extreme religiosity of the child was strongly discouraged by them. By contrast, the children of professional clergy who grew up in homes where religious observance was a normal part of daily life were generally not overwhelmed by emotions of guilt or elevation. Mercy Collisson, daughter of a country rector, enjoyed an affectionate and unrestrained childhood, going to parties and dancing classes and being called 'Baby' by her parents until her eighth birthday; church attendance was, of course, obligatory, but the psalms read each morning before breakfast were always concluded with a family 'huggle'.[61] And Margaret Cunningham remembers that at the Rectory of Cranleigh, Surrey, after enjoyable breakfasts of porridge, bacon and eggs, kippers, haddock or kedgeree, with sausages on Sundays, family prayers were accompanied by the singing of two caged canaries which would often reduce the children to giggles.[62] In such families there was little of the introspective intensity, fervour and strictness which characterized life in nonconformist households, where many forms of play were regarded as sinful, where children's reading was carefully censored, and rigid codes of behaviour and obedience enforced. For Marianne Farningham's parents, both Sunday School teachers at the Baptist chapel at Eynsford, Kent, 'the life of the chapel was their life, and it became mine' from the time she was first taken there as a month-old baby. No fairy tales were allowed nor would her parents let her attend the National School where she would have been taught the Church Catechism as 'it was considered a far greater sin to send children to the National School than to let them remain uneducated'. No canaries interrupted the solemnity of hymns whose verses included:

There is a dreadful hell,
And everlasting pains,
Where sinners must with devils dwell
In darkness, fire and chains.

One incident epitomizes the control which the chapel exercised over its young flock. Marianne's sister, Rebecca, had particularly wanted to go to the great annual Farningham Fair on 15 October. 'We were never allowed to go to the fair. Our part was to watch the people pass by, all dressed in their best attire, and occasionally to hear reports of the shows and dances.' Rebecca was invited to go by a neighbour, who was taking his own girls, and did so without her parents' knowledge. But – 'Mr Reynolds [the minister] had himself given up the afternoon to the fair; that is, he had adjusted his telescope so as to get the field in full view, and he had picked out all the people he knew, especially my sister whom he had watched a long time.' The girls were summoned before their father and the minister, who dilated on their 'great sin' and, worse still, spoke of it in his sermon on Sunday. 'He mentioned no names, but our faces burned with shame, and all the congregation knew that "Rebecca Hearn had been to the fair". I think today that it was very mean of the minister . . .'[63]

A common characteristic of the religious experiences described by autobiographers is that of 'conversion', beginning with a consciousness of their sin and followed by admission into a state of grace, frequently after a series of backslidings. This experience is particularly associated with early adolescence and is more common among male than female writers, though not exclusive to them. It may be that it coincides with a particular stage of physical and emotional development, occurring at the same sort of age as others experience sexual attraction or the delights of nature and literature. In many cases the 'conversion' occurs at a precise moment in time and is ascribed to a particularly eloquent preacher, often at a Revivalist meeting, or to an escape from some accident or disaster which is explained by Divine intervention. Some children evidently felt 'the call' at a much earlier age, as did Beatrice Stallan:

I used to attend every meeting at the Chapel, and we had some Revival Meetings too which I very much enjoyed. Many people at the time were converted, and I was very anxious to join the Church. This my parents did not consent to, as they said I was not old enough to understand the full meaning of it, and I must wait.[64]

At a similar age Winifred Griffiths experienced a Wesleyan Revival in her village of Overton near Basingstoke:

As an impressionable child of nine years I succumbed to the emotional appeal. For quite a long time the effect continued. My inner life had a kind of buoyancy and assurance and a feeling of great satisfaction . . . I had a feeling that I ought to appeal to the known bad characters of the village to be saved while there was yet time! The difficulty was that my parents and relatives, all except my grandfather, were quite silent in private conversation about their religious experiences, so I could not talk about it to them.[65]

And, by a strange coincidence, her future husband, James Griffiths, experienced the great Welsh Revival of 1904 at his home in Ammanford. As a boy who had just started work in the pit he remembered that

everything seemed to be suddenly different. There were services down the mine, in which the 'gaffer' took part, and our home was turned into a chapel. For a year or two it transformed life in the valleys, then it seemed to fade out, leaving behind a void which was later filled by another kind of revival . . .[66]

Frequently, dramatic conversions of this kind did not endure. James Griffiths turned to the 'New Theology' of socialism in his late teens. Thomas Cooper experienced a Primitive Methodist conversion at fourteen after a period of 'great anguish and sorrow for sin'.

My grief continued for many weeks, until I could find no delight in my books or drawing or dulcimer, and could read nothing but the Bible, and was getting into secret places twenty times in a day to pray for the pardon of my sins.

But after some time his 'common sense revolted' at the 'acting of faith' and he rebelled against the censorship of all but 'truly religious books' which the Church Society tried to enforce: 'My mind rebelled completely now and I ceased to frequent the little chapel.'[67] John Bezer underwent a similar 'conversion' and reaction. As a result of hell-fire preaching he developed an extreme consciousness of sin which led him literally to dress himself in sackcloth and ashes; he became head boy of his Sunday School, spending the whole day from 7 a.m. to 10 p.m. in a succession of services and meetings.[68] But, like Cooper, he later reacted against the idea of 'a God of vengeance and, worse still, partiality' and ended his formal connection with the church at the age of twenty.

Most autobiographers did not experience such depths of despair and heights of religious ecstasy, but took religion more or less in their stride, as something mainly reserved for Sundays and solemn occasions but not of great import in everyday life. On the whole, it seems to have aroused sensations of fear and anxiety rather than of joy, a typical comment being that of Adeline Hodges that 'religion in those days was a scarey thing . . . God was never presented as a kindly, fatherly figure, but more of a spy, watching, unseen, any little misdemeanour one committed.'[69] Many children recall the dismal poems and hymns which they learned, and the long sermons they endured, which concentrated on sin and the everlasting torments of hell for those who did not repent. The reality of hell-fire seems to have been deeply believed. 'Many times as a child I prayed that God would let me die before the end of the world,' wrote Lottie Barker, 'for I dreaded being burned up by the fire they told us would burn us all up.'[70] After reading a religious pamphlet, Arthur Goffin 'felt sure there *was* a hell fire. According to this book, even a man who called his brother a fool was doomed to hell fire.'[71] Leonard Ellisdon speculated whether in the Lake of Fire 'you had clothes on, and how they reacted to the flames; whether you stood still or swam about, and if you were allowed to talk, what you had to eat or drink . . . '[72]

If hell was real enough, because it was supposed to consist of a physical quality with which children were familiar, God was a much more mysterious figure whose definition was made even more difficult by the concept of the Trinity. Eleanor Hutchinson writes:

I also knew that God was once a little boy, and that's how I remember Him. The old man with the beard who lived up in the sky was not very attractive, and He only concerned Himself with the weather and thunderstorms . . .[73]

Many children misunderstood the words of prayers and hymns, and received either no explanation or explanations which further confused. 'Our Father Chart in Heaven,' intoned Winifred Relph at her infants' school, where much of the teaching was done by charts thrown over the blackboard.

When we said our prayers in the morning I pictured a long chart something like a plain stair-carpet stretching from the ground up to Heaven: away at the top stood God listening![74]

And for Alice Foley, whose father was a 'rather bigoted, but inconsequential, Roman Catholic', and whose mother's spiritual leanings were 'creedless and pewless', there were equal difficulties:

I thought of God as a majestic, remote being, dwelling in inaccessible regions, with whom I had little contact. On the other hand, the Virgin Mary was passionately adored, and I felt on good terms with a few favourite saints. I had a gross, material conception of Heaven, for it was envisaged as a vast area of red-plush sofas, the space underneath being stacked with boxes of sweets and chocolate creams . . . Vaguely, I pondered on aspects of the individual soul, and pictured it as shaped like a shoulder of lamb neatly tucked under one's ribs. Sinless, it was pure white, but mortal and venial sins showed up like dark and light pencil marks on its virgin surface . . .[75]

Most children's religious experiences were concentrated on Sundays, when, quite apart from Sunday School and church attendance, 'respectable' homes often took on a different appearance – cleaning and polishing completed on Saturday, a clean tablecloth laid for the principal meal of the week, Sunday dinner, when very likely for the only time all members of the family came together. In such households Sunday was pre-eminently a family day, a time for communal worship, for visits to relatives, for family outings in the summer or fireside readings in the winter. The recollections of this type of Victorian family Sunday are happier ones – children in their best clothes, mother bustling about the dinner preparations, father relaxed, with time to talk and even play with his children. In less 'respectable' families where members went more about their separate affairs the images are less cosy and domestic – father late home for dinner from his morning's drinking, children unwillingly packed off to Sunday School to give an hour or two of quiet in small, crowded houses where noisy play and quarrels were inevitable.

A minority of children remember another type of Sunday with equal distaste – the gloomy, puritanical Sunday dominated by religious expectations which they did not share or understand, when conduct was required to be different, the natural inclination to play curbed and a strict censorship of reading and activity imposed. Some strict families never had a hot meal on Sundays, and required their children to put a halfpenny of their weekly penny pocket-money into the missionary box in the hall.[76] Many had their Sunday reading restricted to the Bible, *Pilgrim's Progress*, tracts, sermons and Foxe's *Book of Martyrs* or the carefully edited *Books for Bairns*.[77] Leslie Missen was provided with *Cautionary Tales,* which included the story of Harry who was wicked enough to play cricket on the village green on Sunday afternoon and was deservedly struck by lightning, but was allowed to play 'Missionary Lotto' from which he learned how Bishop Hannington met a lion in Uganda, threw his sunglasses at it and it ran away.[78] George Grundy remembers one of his 'Sunday reading' books entitled *Sunday Echoes in Week-day Hours:*

It was a weary series of pietistic stories for children. Only one tale in it was regarded by us as readable because it contained the account of a missionary who was, I think, named Moron, who fell into a crevasse and was killed. To us the story of his death was an oasis in a literary desert.[79]

No doubt the remarkable resilience and penchant for fun of most children enabled them to survive the Sunday tedium without permanent damage, though, as Grundy points out, 'Attendance at church was a good thing overdone at that time, and in many cases tended in after-life to a certain antipathy to church services.' It is significant that the vast number of over six million children who attended Sunday School just before 1914 did not continue as adult church-goers in the post-war years,[80] nor perpetuate the Victorian Sunday into what was now increasingly regarded as a secular holiday. The poem which Averil Thomas learned and recited at the Wesleyan Chapel around 1898 cannot have survived long into the new century:

> I must not play on Sunday
> Because it is a sin.
> Tomorrow will be Monday
> And then I may begin.[81]

6. By contrast with religion which, in different ways, occupied an important place in children's activities and interests, the modern preoccupation with sex does not feature largely in nineteenth-century autobiographies. This is hardly surprising. Sex was a taboo subject in most Victorian and Edwardian families, and even in later life when most autobiographies were written, authors would not be likely to consider their sexual experiences a proper subject for literary reminiscence. This would apply both to published works, which were frequently written with a view to the moral improvement of the reader, and to unpublished autobiographies set down for the limited readership of future family generations. But reticence alone would hardly seem to account for the remarkable silence of the majority of autobiographers on this subject. Ignorance of sex was, as we will see, widespread, and the means of knowledge very limited. Moreover, many children were seemingly neither very anxious nor interested, perhaps because their energies were engaged in work from a very much earlier age, and partly because the age of sexual maturity occurred considerably later than today – for Edwardian girls the average age at menarche was fifteen, while in the 1960s it was thirteen.[82] It is also relevant that the average age of marriage for women was at an all-time peak of twenty-six years at the end of the century, and that illegitimacy rates had fallen noticeably compared with the first half of the century. If a 'sexual revolution' had occurred in the period 1750–1850, as Edward Shorter argues,[83] it seems that a Victorian reaction had reasserted values of chastity and sexual purity with varying, though significant, degrees of success on all social classes.

Children's ignorance of the 'facts of life', and the conspiracy of silence which parents and teachers maintained on the subject, was clearly a major factor. Nor were all children necessarily very interested

to know. When Margaret Cunningham discovered that she had a baby
brother she was not 'very curious about where he came from . . . John
[her elder brother] knew all about it though. The doctor had brought
him in a black bag, and he had seen the paper in which the baby was
wrapped.'[84] At nine, Mary Denison, a vicar's daughter, was 'in complete
ignorance' of where babies came from; her mother disapproved of one
lady in the parish who told her daughters 'everything', and said that she
preferred not to meet the Connal girls because 'I feel when they look at
me, they know all about me.'[85] In another middle-class household,
Florence Goddard at ten knew nothing of the impending arrival of a
baby brother until the actual event:

> My mother was certainly excessively reserved and prudish upon these mat-
> ters, but not so very different in her outlook from other mothers in those days. I
> have inquired among friends of my own age, and have found no one who had
> received any information of that nature in the home.[86]

And another autobiographer from a similar background, born in 1901,
recalls her mother's rather remarkable ignorance:

> Before she was married she had worked for 'Fallen Girls' and did not know
> what they were. At the age of eighty she asked me what a miscarriage was. She
> travelled far in Europe, and across Canada, but did not know where any of these
> countries were on a map.[87]

These comments are drawn from middle-class families, where there
was an especially high degree of protection of the 'purity' of daughters,
but similar views were apparently shared well down the social scale, and
certainly into the 'respectable' sections of the working class. The comment of Bessie Wallis that in a two-bedroomed miner's cottage which
had to be shared by many children 'there was no mystery about sex'[88] is
not echoed by other working-class autobiographers. It was not the
experience of Ernest Shotton, born in 1878, the eleventh of twelve
children over a span of twenty-five years:

> Talk on sex was very strictly taboo, and so were questionable tales. The girls
> had their sleeping room and the boys theirs, usually in the attic, and mostly with
> two double beds in a room.[89]

Outside the protected home, children often received their first
acquaintance with sex from older boys and girls at school, but many
went through their schooldays in ignorance. Charlotte Meadowcroft
remained 'innocent' until she went into service at thirteen, where the
cook insisted on enlightening her: 'I was shocked, and I remember
thinking how crude and vulgar she was.'[90] Nor did children necessarily

learn from nature. When Winifred Relph was told the facts of life by a school-friend at ten or eleven, she flatly refused to believe such an improbable explanation:

> As a country child I knew that flowers and vegetables grew from seeds, but that was quite a different matter; besides, my mother had a baby, and I remembered the nurse arriving on her bicycle with a little leather bag in which she carried the baby.[91]

For some, knowledge did not come until well after the period of childhood, even up to the eve of marriage. Employed as a nursemaid at fifteen, and with the principal care of a baby whose mother died a few days after giving birth, Mrs Layton knew nothing of the facts of life: 'I had to remain in ignorance, and I really cannot say how I did get my knowledge.'[92]

Many autobiographers, however, do describe the sources of their eventual knowledge, and it is clear that by far the commonest means was verbal communication by older children – brothers, sisters or school-friends. For girls, the onset of menstruation was sometimes the occasion for some sort of explanation by the mother, though many girls were clearly quite unprepared, and record their alarm and embarrassment at its first appearance. What they were actually told on this occasion obviously depended on the degree of education and understanding of the mother, and not all girls were as unlucky as the one described by Eric Powell:

> Once, when I was playing with a group of boys and girls I noticed one of the older girls who remained by herself, so I said, 'Why don't you come and join us?' She looked miserable and replied, 'I can't play with you, as me mum says as me juices are stirrin' and I ain't to get friendly wi' boys.' I wondered what on earth she was talking about.[93]

Strangely, not one of the male autobiographers mentions the traditional talk by his father as his means of knowledge.

Most commonly, the beginnings of sex knowledge for children came at play, and often in the school playground: 'It was a case of "You show me yours and I'll show you mine". It put me off sex for many a long year.'[94] For country children the sexual activities of farm animals sometimes provided the first lesson, while for town children domestic pets like cats, dogs and rabbits sometimes served a similar function. Only a few children seem to have derived their knowledge from books, unsurprisingly, since the available literature was very limited, though some autobiographers report the arousal of curiosity from words encountered in the Bible such as 'womb' and 'circumcision'. Harry Dorrell, raiding his elder brother's collection of books, found *The Mummer's Tale* by Anatole France 'curious and interesting', particularly a passage where a naked lady got into bed with a man, 'because my mother always wore a nightdress in bed'.[95] Betty Sutherland Graeme 'revelled' in a pamphlet entitled 'Why Do We Suffer', which a religious aunt had sent her in mistake for a tract; it turned out to be a treatise on piles and 'in my sheltered life this was pornography indeed'.[96] It seems clear that the extent of sexual knowledge had a class differential and that children from wealthier homes, especially girls, were protected from sources of information such as books and newspapers. For boys of this class, boarding-school often provided the first introduction, but Leslie Missen, at a public day-school (the Perse School, Cambridge) about 1914 found that 'there was no direct instruction by the staff' and 'our knowledge of male and female relationships accumulated slowly through our reading the Bible, Shakespeare, Aristotle, Ovid, Aristophanes and Plautus, and through discussions amongst ourselves'. Though many boys had sisters at the Perse Girls' School there was no contact between the two institutions, and even in the Sixth Form there was generally 'a profound disinclination to become involved with women or girls'.[97]

Autobiographers display a natural reticence in recalling sexual experiences or emotions they may have had as children. As occasional voyeurs of sexual activity or its consequences, the prevailing reaction seems to have been one of shame, bordering on disgust. Elizabeth Harrison thought that the milking of cows was 'rude', and turned away when her mother put the baby to the breast.[98] Several children from poor, already large families who understood only too well the struggle for existence, expressed a pitying contempt when their mothers presented yet another addition to the family which they expected to be admired. When the seventh child was born to Anita Hughes's parents, the eldest daughter would take no notice:

He was three days old before Emmy would look at him. Being the eldest, she had lots to do, and said there were enough to look after without another one. Father was very cross with her.[99]

R. W. Morris, the eldest of nine children born to a Durham miner, reacted similarly by refusing to go into his mother's bedroom to see the new baby:

With my total lack of understanding of sexual behaviour, at least I could see the folly of burdening myself with what I now know to be unnecessary children. As it was, there was little more than eighteen months between each of the nine

children my parents had . . . If the prospects for the boys were dim, those for the
girls who followed were even dimmer.[100]

Only a few writers record direct sexual experiences at an early age.
Two young girls mention molestations by men at the age of four and
five, and their mixture of puzzlement and fright is a similar reaction to
that expressed at cases of male exposure. Edmund Punter successfully
resisted seduction in a cowshed by a member of the 'gentry': ' "Don't be
scared, laddie. You'd like to earn a shilling, wouldn't you?" I hesitated; a
shilling was a lot of money.'[101] Occasionally autobiographies contain a
glimpse of a more pleasurable and exotic sexual experience. Three girls,
older and more sophisticated than Jack McQuoid, then aged about
eight, persuaded him to let them sketch him in the nude (apart from his
boots and woollen stockings), and in return one of them disrobed and
danced for him. It was a beautiful and abiding memory:

> She danced and twisted and turned as the evening sunlight filtered and
> flickered through the trees . . . I could see she was not quite the same way made
> as a boy. She was beautiful, but she did not stir in me what I suppose I then did
> not possess – adult sexual responses, yet in that dancing figure there was for me
> mystery and miracle.[102]

7. All children were subject to some degree of control within the family,
and one of the major themes brought out in the writing is that of discipline –
the code of behaviour which they were required to follow and the
punishments imposed for transgressing it. The subject is, however,
complicated by the fact that the behaviour of children in the broadest
sense was not only a matter for parents, but one which also concerned
teachers, policemen, Sunday Schools and clergy. Although the lines
between these various instruments of control were by no means rigid or
clearly defined, the general consensus seems to have been that what
happened in school, and on the way to and from it, was properly the
responsibility of teachers; that spiritual guidance and precept was,
except in the most religious homes, the concern of the church, chapel
and Sunday School; and that parents governed conduct within the home
and its immediate vicinity where misbehaviour by children could impair
neighbourly relations.

As a further generalization, it seems that within the home the code of
conduct was more often set by the mother and enforced by the father, at
least in respect of the more serious and premeditated punishments.
Since the mother was normally at home and the father usually at work,
she was the one most likely to observe breaches of the family code,
ranging from misbehaviour at table, squabbles, bullying and imper-

tinence to more serious offences like 'bad language', telling lies and stealing. While minor offences could be dealt with on the spot by her, the major ones were usually left for correction by father on his return.

Families naturally varied greatly both over the contents of their codes and the means of enforcing them. Again as a generalization, it seems that the degree of control, and particularly the list of prohibitions, increased with social class, but that the severity of physical punishment increased with descent in the social scale. Much of what autobiographers report about their discipline as children is, in fact, to do with social distinctions, 'keeping up appearances' and 'respectability', rather than with the control of behaviour within the home itself which was to an extent private and unobserved. Much of the 'internal' domestic discipline was concerned with the household duties which children performed, which will be considered separately; after this, behaviour at mealtimes is most frequently mentioned, especially in large families where children might become impatient for their turn or complain at unfairness in helpings. At least three autobiographers mention the cane always being laid on the table at mealtimes; two mention that children always stood at table, only the parents sitting on chairs. At the one communal meal of the week, Sunday dinner, there was often an established priority of service, from eldest to youngest.

Control of play and of playmates was another important aspect of discipline observed in almost all families in varying degree. Although there was often little alternative in working-class districts, really 'respectable' children were often denied playing in the streets for fear of moral or physical contamination, or were restricted to certain streets or the parks. At higher social levels, contacts with 'the poor' were deliberately avoided or carefully controlled. Margaret Cunningham, daughter of the rector of Cranleigh, was forbidden to talk to 'the poor children' who attended the National (i.e. Church) School, though they offered to share a skipping rope which 'I would have liked to have accepted as I was no mean skipper'.[103] Another clergyman's daughter, Ludivina Jackson, was allowed a limited contact with 'the unfortunates' when she became a Sunday School teacher at the age of ten,[104] but here the relationship was clearly one of superior and inferior, not of equals. Jean Nettleton, born of lower middle-class parents in Harrogate in 1916, was 'forbidden to visit houses in the poor quarter for fear of getting these infections' (diphtheria and scarlet fever).[105]

Codes of manners and social etiquette are sharply remembered by many writers, and not only those from the higher social classes: indeed, snobbery appears to have been most pronounced in the middle and lower middle classes. In such families the treatment of parents with obedience and dutiful affection was considered particularly important, and evidenced partly by the way in which parents were addressed in public:

> My mother insisted on my always addressing her as 'Mother dear'. I think she may have come to suspect that my feelings towards her were changing, but it may be that she had read somewhere that this was the way the Royal children addressed the Queen. It was certainly the sort of information that the gossip column of 'Home Chat', which she read eagerly every week, would have regarded as of special interest to its readers.[106]

The normal gradation was from 'Mater' and 'Pater' (upper and upper middle class) to 'Mama' and 'Papa' (middle class) to 'Ma' and 'Pa', with regional variations such as 'Mam' and 'Mammy' (working class); the now universal 'Mum' and 'Dad' are not mentioned until after the First World War. Social conventions and snobberies existed at all levels, and were by no means the prerogative of one class. Gwen Millington was in disgrace with her Victorian grandmother because she unwound a Chelsea bun while eating it[107] and Mercy Collisson's mother had some elderly lady friends who were so shocked when a girl mentioned that she had washed her hair that afternoon that they could not bring themselves to speak to her.[108] Nice class distinctions naturally existed in the matter of school attendance, beyond the major divide between 'state' and 'public'. Elizabeth Harrison at five years old had expected to go to St Mary's in Preston, 'the Infants' and Girls' school within a stone's throw of our backyard', where all her playmates went; instead, her shopkeeper parents sent her to St Wilfrid's:

> We paid a penny a week for the privilege of attending it . . . I did not realize that I had mounted the second step in the social ladder. Nobody there wore clogs. The boys all had jackets and the girls did not need pinafores to hide shabby frocks. They were, in the main, the sons and daughters of tradesmen who ran their own businesses.[109]

In all ranks of society it seems that children were more conscious of social class and of class rivalries than one might suppose. Bessie Wallis, daughter of a Yorkshire miner, had a great friend in Alice, daughter of a railway signalman. But:

> Our friendship was a strange one. In reality it should never have existed, because between the children of the miners and the railwaymen was a deadly rivalry. This antagonism extended to the adults. The railwaymen and their wives looked down on the miners. In turn the miners considered the railwaymen 'cissies'. Perhaps the miners' feeling was envy against those who did a clean job

and could see daylight . . . Scuffles often broke out between the children on the way to and from school. One child would jeer at another's father's job, and there would be a juvenile explosion which never ended until home was reached.[110]

Confirmation of these fine social gradations also comes from a comment from 'the other side'. When Albert Pugh's father was working as foreman on a railway line being built at Pemberton, Wigan, in 1867, he came in contact with the local miners and their wives. 'They called us "gradely folk" because we drank our tea out of cups and saucers while they used basins.'[111]

Codes of behaviour were enforced by sanctions which took many forms according to age, sex, social class and the views of parents about the effectiveness or propriety of different forms of punishment. In general, over the hundred years under review, discipline and punishment of children tended to become more humane and understanding of children's needs, and the nature and extent of physical punishment declined, particularly in the middle classes and the 'respectable' working classes. Exceptions to this could immediately be cited, but the general trend towards recognizing children as sentient beings with rights of their own, rather than as the property of parents to be used as they alone decreed, seems clear. In particular, the maltreatment of children by severe corporal punishment, common in all classes in earlier centuries, gradually sank in public acceptance and, like heavy drinking and brutality towards wives, became increasingly confined to the poorest, least-educated classes. The punishment of James Burn by his step-father about 1815, for example, would be unthinkable a century later. Taking a day's holiday from his life of tramping and begging, he was discovered enjoying himself swimming in the river; his step-father beat him, naked, with a newly cut switch for nearly a mile, through the town of Hexham, where 'it was somewhat amusing to the natives to see me scampering naked along the public street, like a young American Indian, with my back scalped instead of my head . . .' For nine days he could not put on his clothes and was confined to bed. Yet Burn's comment about his drunken parent is equally revealing:

> I know that my step-father never used me with cruelty without regretting it afterwards; in the whole course of my life I never knew any man who was more a creature of impulse; I have known him to kick and caress me in almost the same breath.[112]

The earlier, puritanical view, reinforced by Methodism in the later eighteenth century, that children were naturally sinful until and unless redeemed by discipline and grace, clearly persisted well into the nineteenth century. One manifestation of this view was the belief that they were natural liars, unable to distinguish between truth and falsehood, right and wrong, and that the word of an adult was always to be preferred to that of a child. This is well illustrated by an incident reported in the autobiography of William Esam which happened in the early 1830s and that 'will never be effaced from my memory'. His mother had invited a group of ladies to a 'Dorcas' or working meeting at her house, and William as a small boy had been helping them by threading needles. At the end of the afternoon one lady could not find her stiletto (bodkin) and declared that William must have taken it; the rest agreeing, he was sent off to his room in disgrace 'and threatened with all sorts of punishments if I did not confess'. A week later he found the missing article, which had slipped down the skirting-board:

With delight I called out, 'I have found it!' Alas, alas, they said I had put it there, and I was punished still more because I would not confess. Oh, the misery of that time! My poor mother, with tears in her eyes, begged me not to add to my fault by falsehood. At last, moved by her tears and entreaties, I faltered out (I am ashamed to admit) 'I did do it,' and was forgiven. How many such cases occur with children, I wonder – poor, weak little things![113]

The refusal of parents to believe their children is a theme mentioned by several autobiographers as a deeply felt resentment, both at the time and subsequently. William Wright worked as a 'chimney boy' with his father, a chimney-sweep, for several years till the age of fourteen. One day his sister borrowed his boots, went into the garden, and stripped his father's prize currant bush; William was accused on the evidence of his footprints, though he would not incriminate his sister. He was flogged by his father with a rope and ordered to bed 'where I had a good cry for being so wrongly treated through no fault of my own. I decided to run away to sea . . . '[114]

The severity of corporal punishment undoubtedly diminished later in the century, though it continued to be a normal corrective used by parents and schoolteachers on both girls and boys throughout the whole period. Writing of the decade immediately before the First World War, Ethel Clark reported that:

The usual [punishment] for that age was being sent to bed, and then father came up with the strap. Boys often had the buckle end of the strap, but if anyone accidentally caught a cut from the buckle it was considered just punishment. Luckily, I didn't.[115]

Thomas Yates's six brothers and two sisters were kept under control by father's strap, which he considered 'necessary because we were a healthy lot of lads'.[116] In many working-class kitchens the strap or cane was always on display by the chimney-corner, both as threat and for ready use. Even the otherwise kindly vicar of Wonersh would severely cane his son for wetting his knickers,[117] while Beatrice Stallan's brother was put on bread and water for a week for the grave offence of taking a penny from his money-box.[118]

By the early twentieth century, and particularly among more 'enlightened' sections of the middle classes, greater understanding and permissiveness were developing in child relationships. This was the result of a variety of factors – the decline of the stricter forms of religion which had viewed children as fundamentally evil, the effects of 'the new psychology' on child-rearing practices and of educational theories which regarded children as flowers to be cultivated rather than weeds to be eradicated – but, not least, the fact that family size was declining from the 1870s onwards and that as children became scarcer they became more valued. The growth of affection and of more sensitive, caring relationships between parents and children seems to be borne out by the autobiographies of the period, evidenced, among other things, by greater concern for children's health, education and welfare, and by milder forms of discipline and punishment. Thus, for Mary Denison in the first decade of the new century the worst punishment was to be sent to father's study.

All he did was to talk to you in a quiet voice, but it was far worse than any punishment. In two minutes or less you would be in tears – useless to try to keep them back. You wished so much not to be naughty again, not to give trouble to Mother.[119]

In larger, poorer families the smack or the strap was still the spontaneous reaction to misbehaviour, but in a growing number of cases children were becoming full and valued members of intimate nuclear households, to be 'talked to' not only in anger or sorrow, to be reasoned with, played with and enjoyed. An incident in the life of Sybil Pearce makes an interesting contrast with the treatment of William Esam over the missing stiletto. Sybil Pearce lived in Bedford Park, Turnham Green, at the beginning of the century, the daughter of an assistant director of Public Prosecutions who, despite his dignified dress of frock-coat and silk top-hat, would play 'touch' with her on Acton Green while they walked home from the station. Sybil had, as a child, a passion for jewellery. At kindergarten, at the age of five, she persuaded a friend to exchange her silver and ruby locket for a piece of india-rubber – a somewhat unfair transaction which her parents persuaded her to revoke. More seriously, on a visit to her uncle's house at Kew she stole a turquoise brooch belonging to a maid, keeping it hidden for several days during the hue and cry. 'It all ended with an apology to the maid, and careful explanation to me of why such doings must never occur again.'[120] The significant word is 'explanation'; there is no mention of punishment.

8. Recent historians have argued that the modern family, based on affection and care for children, was born in the later eighteenth century and came into full development in the nineteenth, first among wealthier households but gradually influencing all strata of society. It was evidenced by less harsh treatment of children at home and at work, by greater concern for their health, education and happiness and the gradual acceptance of the separate status of the child with rights independent of its parents and guardians. In particular, it is argued that child-rearing practices changed importantly, and that especially in the middle classes the trend was away from the indifference of earlier centuries towards an affectionate, protective concern. Older traditions of neglect and excessive physical punishment persisted longer among the less enlightened classes – both in the upper classes, and in the lower working class where the need for economic exploitation of children added another dimension of brutality.

The accounts of autobiographers do not on the whole support this class-selective view of child-rearing in the nineteenth century. Poverty and constant anxieties of feeding, clothing and maintaining a large family could, no doubt, blunt the emotions of parents to some degree, but it would be wrong to conclude that affection was necessarily less, that there was less concern for children's welfare or less sorrow at their illness or death. A number of working-class autobiographers state that there was rarely, if ever, any display of affection by their parents – that kissing, embracing or the use of endearments were unknown – but love takes many forms and the way it is displayed is largely a cultural phenomenon. The evidence of autobiographies is that concern for the happiness and well-being of children was present to a varying extent in all classes so far as economic resources permitted, and that as family size began to decline in the later nineteenth century, as fewer wives worked outside the home and fewer husbands drank excessively, gentler, more intimate and loving relationships were able to develop. The closely knit, affectionate family obviously had the best chance of developing where physical conditions were favourable – where the home provided not only shelter, but comfort and privacy, where adequate food, clothes and medical care were available, and where parents themselves were possessed of intelligence and education, and it was therefore particularly in the middle and artisan classes that affective individualism was most evident. Above this level among the upper classes, the interests of parents were less likely to be home-centred and child-dominated, and the care of children was often entrusted to a succession of surrogates – nursemaids, nannies, governesses, tutors and boarding-school teachers. Below it, among the very poor, the catastrophes of too many children, low wages and periodic unemployment gave the struggle for survival primacy of importance, and children as one autobiographer puts it, 'like cats and dogs', had to fend for themselves.

In no case, however poor, do we find deliberate neglect of a sick or weakly child, still less an acceptance of the law of survival of the fittest. Writing of working-class life in Bradford at the turn of the century, Lilian Slater observes:

It has been said that children in those days were not molly-coddled, but looking back makes me realize what care and devotion were lavished on many children – in my case there was no limit![121]

Born into a poor home in the Forest of Dean about 1830, Timothy Mountjoy was a very delicate baby, not expected to live.

I did little else but cry for two years, night and day, my eldest sister nursing me one half the night and another girl the other.

Like many other children he was vaccinated against the dreaded disease of smallpox, though the amateurish methods then used could produce serious effects and even death. 'My sister was literally covered: mother thought she would die. I had a very light burden and soon recovered.' Fevers of all kinds were rife in the Forest, two of his friends dying of 'black fever' in 1840, others of scarlet fever, smallpox and consumption.[122] In remoter parts of the country like this there was much reliance still on folk-medicine, including amateur vaccination and inoculation, and the fact that many poor parents were prepared to take considerable trouble and risk for their children indicates their concern. Roger Langdon, born in 1825, was laid in his cradle close beside a boy who was dying of smallpox so that he might be infected and immunized; this having no effect he was taken to 'Old Nanny Holland, who did duty as midwife, nurse and housekeeper' in the village, who performed the inoculation with a stocking-needle. Although he recovered after a slight attack, his sister was badly marked, and their playmate, a 'chubby, happy cherub of about four years of age', died from Nanny's ministrations.[123]

Although smallpox vaccination in theory became a free and compulsory service in 1853, organized by the Poor Law Medical Officers, it was far from complete or universally accepted. Frank Marling writes of amateur home vaccination about 1870, when his mother vaccinated a neighbour's child with a needle, an epidemic having broken out in the small market town of Berkeley, Gloucestershire.[124]

Lack of means obviously determined access to medical care to a considerable degree, many autobiographers recording that a doctor was rarely called and often only when the patient was dying or dead. The attitude is well described by Abel Jones, writing of the Rhondda Valley in the 1880s:

> My mother's attitude towards doctors was typical of the older inhabitants; fortunately, she did not need them until she was in the late eighties. If she became ill she would suffer for a few days without a doctor, but if her illness refused to submit to hot drinks and Epsom salts she would say, 'If I am not better in a day or two perhaps you had better call a doctor. I don't want an inquest.' For her the chief function of a doctor was to avoid an inquest.[125]

In any case, for poorer patients who could afford to pay very little the ministrations of a doctor were sometimes casual in the extreme. When Kate Taylor's sister was ill with pneumonia the doctor prescribed without seeing her, and when she died ten days later signed the death certificate 'diphtheria'; to her mother's grief, the coffin was not allowed in the church for fear of infection.[126] Even with careful attention, many children were struck down with this and other diseases, and a prosperous shopkeeper's family living literally next door to the doctor was not spared from a fatal attack of diphtheria.[127]

Given the state of medical ignorance about the causes and treatment of many diseases, many parents in all social classes had a considerable suspicion of doctors and a preference for tried and proven home remedies for a wide variety of ailments. Even in a prosperous family like that of Mary Paley Marshall, whose father, a Lincolnshire rector, lived in some style and employed three maids, health was treated in what now seems a rough-and-ready fashion.

> The village possessed one so-called midwife, a Mrs Lancolm, a very tall and stout woman who attended all cases, high and low. She certainly brought my sister into the world very successfully, and probably myself. Large pitch plasters were stuck upon our chests at the beginning of cold weather, and remained there till the spring, when their removal was a painful process. Spring also was the time for brimstone and treacle; and cod-liver oil, castor oil and Gregory powders were used at all seasons. Brass pans with long handles for heating beds were

hung up as ornaments but they were never used, and hot-water bottles were an unheard-of luxury, though we suffered badly from chilblains ... Our teeth and eyes were left to themselves. If a tooth had to be taken out it was done by Mr Higgins, a chemist in Stamford. Spectacles were never used by the young ...[128]

Many autobiographers record their weekly dosings as children, often on a Friday night as an internal accompaniment to the weekly bath. Verbena Brighton, born near Diss, Norfolk, in 1915, remembers Beecham's Pills and rhubarb jam, with Jeyes Fluid added to the bath-water, a precaution when the same water was used by several children.[129] Brimstone and black treacle was a common prescription for 'clearing the blood' in the spring, while sheets of brown paper smeared with tallow or goose-grease were common preventives of winter chest complaints; one writer recalls that 'they smelt horrible, but that was a mere detail', and that they were subsequently useful as fire-lighters.[130]

All this suggests a considerable concern for the health of children, so far as means and knowledge allowed, among almost all classes in Victorian England. The idea that diseases were bred and spread by dirt had clearly taken effect, and many housewives were almost obsessively anxious about cleanliness, partly from prophylactic motives but also, no doubt, because a bright and sparkling home announced the 'respectability' of its occupants. Mothers waged constant war against nits in children's hair, lice in beds, and a variety of insects and vermin in old, dilapidated houses in which the landlord had no interest beyond the payment of rent; one housewife regularly scrubbed all the woodwork in the house, another 'carried her love of cleanliness to the point of absurdity, as for instance when she used her left-over soap-suds on washing days to scrub and wash the pigs'.[131] Children with whooping-cough were held over a barrel of boiling tar or taken to the local gas-works to inhale the fumes; while those who could not afford perambulators would hire them (1d. an hour for one baby, 1½d. for two babies) on washing day, so the older girls could take the babies to the park.[132] In such families, however poor, there was no lack of affection for children though it was often expressed in ways different from our own.

9. Many autobiographers, particularly those from poorer families, make mention of the food which they had as children. In homes where there was a constant struggle for survival its provision was the central concern of the mother who, however great her interest in the welfare of her children, often had to give priority to her husband as the chief bread-winner who was felt to be entitled to the lion's share of food. The autobiographies make clear that in the poorest households children

frequently went hungry and depended on the cheapest filling foods which were far from providing a balanced, nutritious diet. Whenever possible such children supplemented what was provided at home from outside sources – waiting at factory gates at the end of the day for any lunch-food left over by the men,[133] taking a part-time job as a 'step-girl' for 2d. a day plus a breakfast of dripping toast and cocoa,[134] or, if they lived in the country, collecting wild fruits and berries, and even raw turnips, carrots and dock-leaves.[135] There were few things a hungry child would not eat, though the lower limits are recorded in a passage by Mrs Layton. She had knocked at several doors asking for work without success when:

One lady asked me if I was hungry; she said she was sorry she could not have her step cleaned, but if I waited she would give me something to eat. Presently she came to the door with a parcel, telling me not to waste any; what I could not eat I was to take home to my mother. I thanked her and ran off to a sheltered place to open the parcel, expecting to find something I could eat for I was very hungry. But I was doomed to disappointment, for the parcel contained some very dry pieces of bread and some crusts that looked as if they had been nibbled by mice, and a large piece of bacon rind. I could not eat any of it, but had promised not to waste it, so I gave the bacon rind to a hungry-looking dog and carried the crusts to a man who kept a donkey.[136]

At the lowest levels, the food of the poor was monotonous, unpalatable, inadequate both in quantity and quality. In the years of scarcity and high prices in the earlier half of the century, there are harrowing accounts like those by Thomas Carter, who remembered the famine year of 1800 when bread was 1s. 10d. for a quartern loaf (4lb 5½oz) and his father's wage of 10s. 6d. a week had to provide for a family of six; their main food at this time was potatoes with a little melted suet poured over them.[137] In another bad year, 1846, John Castle, a silk weaver of Colchester, was often unemployed for weeks together and his family of three 'made our dinner off a pennyworth of skimmed milk thickened with flour'.[138] Yet for hungry children even a pot of boiled potatoes could make a memorable feast. Mrs Burrows records how, at the age of eight in the 1850s, she began to work with other children in an agricultural gang for up to fourteen hours a day. On one particularly cold day they worked in showers of snow and sleet, and were preparing to eat their cold meal under a hedge when a shepherd's wife invited them into her cottage:

This woman's heart was large, even if her house was small, and so she put her few chairs and table out into the garden and then we all sat down in a ring upon the floor. She then placed in our midst a very large saucepan of hot, boiled potatoes, and bade us help ourselves. Truly, although I have attended scores of grand parties and banquets since that time, not one of them has seemed half as good to me as that meal did.[139]

Ragged clothing, overcrowded, slummy housing and other incidents of poverty were often accepted unquestioningly because the child had never experienced anything else, but hunger was something that touched him immediately and painfully. Several writers record being 'rationed' for food in peace-time (being 'lowanced' as one describes it) – for instance, each child in a family of nine being restricted to two slices of bread, whatever his appetite.[140] Several remember being given only the top of an egg to eat as a treat with their bread at breakfast, the rest going to the father, and in one family the children only had a whole egg once a year, at Easter. Two autobiographers record only ever standing at table, and eating in silence;[141] here, eating was for survival, not for pleasure, and children were expected to regard it seriously, thankfully, almost sacramentally.

Many children came into close acquaintance with food as purchasers, when they were sent on errands to the shops. Here, too, there are pathetic memories – of asking for half a loaf of bread cut with a hammy knife to give it flavour,[142] of long walks to a baker who would sell a pillow-case full of stale bread and cakes for 6d. on Saturdays,[143] of buying cheap 'old' and skimmed milk, and of tiny purchases of a great variety of foods bought literally for the next meal. Kathleen Hilton-Foord, living with her grandmother in Dover about 1910, would be sent to buy five slices of bread for a halfpenny, a farthing's worth of milk in a paper cone sufficient for two cups of tea, a halfpenny-worth of butter or mustard pickle or a screw of tea for the same price. Similarly, Jack Wood remembers that in Oldham a halfpenny would buy jam, treacle, pickles, mustard, onions, red cabbage, vinegar, tea, coffee, cocoa or half a Nelson or Victoria cake; a quarter of a pound of corned beef could be had for a penny, or a quarter pound of steak for 1½d., enough to make a meal for four. On Christmas Day, 1908, when there was literally no food in the house, he and his sister went to Unity Hall for a free Christmas breakfast.[145]

Above this level was the 'respectable' working class, among whom good housekeeping was regarded as a cardinal virtue. Here, housewives were expected to be able to provide good, nutritious meals at low cost and to manage occasional food treats which particularly appealed to children's tastes. In many such families, especially but not exclusively in the north of England, it was considered almost sinful to buy baker's bread, tinned foods, ready-made pies, cakes or other 'convenience' foods, and a regular baking day was fitted into the weekly routine alongside washing, ironing and cleaning. In large families baking was no small task – forty-eight loaves and eight tea-cakes a week as recorded by Adeline Hodges.[146] In such well-ordered homes it was also usual for meals to follow a weekly pattern, not necessarily of identical dishes but at least of similar ones. The starting-point was Sunday, the feast-day of the week when, if possible, a joint of meat was always served – beef for choice, other meats being considered somewhat inferior. In the towns many working-class families bought their joint late on Saturday evening at shops or market-stalls when, in the days before refrigeration, meat which would not keep was sold off cheaply. Children were often involved in this Saturday night family shopping spree, being treated to sweets, fruit or other small luxuries. They were often engaged, too, in the cooking of the Sunday dinner, when either because of the lack of an oven or for economy of fuel, the meal was taken to a local baker's where it would be cooked for a charge of 1d. or 2d.; once very common, this practice seems to have survived longest in tenemented London houses. Monday, traditionally washing-day, was usually a cold meat day, left over from the Sunday joint, with bubble-and-squeak made from the remains of the vegetables. If scraps of meat still remained from the joint, Tuesday's dinner would be a hash. Wednesday was often stew, Thursday sausages or liver, Friday often fish – cod, herring, sprats or fried from the fish-and-chip shop. On Saturday a 'high tea' was common among better-off working-class families, with some cold meat or pork butcher's product as a relish, and home-made cakes and pastries. The pattern obviously varied with locality, individual tastes and resources. Regional dishes adapted to small means survived throughout the period – potato pie in Lancashire, batter puddings in Yorkshire, pasties in the south-west, and so on, while in the towns pease pudding, faggots, saveloys and a wide range of pork products gave variety and palatability to the diet.

Individual autobiographers remember, as children, particular foods with special pleasure, and these were by no means necessarily 'luxuries'. Averil Thomas of Melton Mowbray particularly enjoyed the Friday night supper of 'hot faggots, bought (and eaten immediately) from the pork butcher's shop across the road', but, less conventionally, also liked the home-made ice-cream made from fresh snow ('brought in quickly') mixed with sugar and the top of the milk, and also 'beastlings' – the first milk from a newly calved cow, which was very thick and rich, and made a delicious pudding.[147] For W. G. Elliott, a Plymouth boy at the end of the

century, bread and lard was a favourite food,[148] for Kay Garrett it was
fish and chips (1½d.), boiled beef and carrots or boiled leg of pork and
pease pudding (both dishes ready-cooked, 6d. for three persons).[149]
Jack Wood remembers with special pleasure the hot meat pies sold for
1d. each on an Oldham street-corner: the pie-seller stabbed his finger
into the pie and filled up the hole with gravy ('he even had a bandage on
his finger because it got sore with stabbing the crusts'); he also greatly
enjoyed 'penny dips' – 'they were half a muffin with a bit of "duck"
(liver, pluck and various internal parts of a pig) all stewed together and
seasoned, then minced with some gravy poured on it'.[150]

The frequency of food 'treats' obviously depended on resources, and
for the really poor they were rare indeed. Here, any delicacies or
'relishes' went to the father or other wage-earners, and in some families
they were always served first, the children waiting expectantly for the top
of an egg or morsel of sausage or fish to go with their bread or potatoes.
Even in the 'respectable' working class, children were expected to eat
(not necessarily enjoy) what was put before them, and individual tastes
or 'fads' received little encouragement. In larger families at least, birthdays of children were often not celebrated either by presents or special
meals, and Christmas, funerals, weddings and Sunday School 'treats'
were the main occasions when children might expect food out of the
ordinary. Only once was the plain but wholesome fare of the Griffiths's
household broken when, after his first day in the pit, Jim returned to a
special tea in his honour; it marked the end of his childhood and the
addition of another valuable wage-earner to the family.[151]

10. If autobiographers' experiences of the beginning of childhood are
varied, so too are their perceptions of the end of it, but entrance to work
was clearly regarded as one of the most important factors. When
elementary education became general in the closing decades of the
century, leaving school and starting full-time work often marked an
abrupt transition from childhood to adulthood, uninterrupted by a
period of adolescence which has only been widely recognized in the
twentieth century. The length of childhood was primarily determined
by economic resources. The children of wealthier parents could continue their period of dependence longer through secondary and university education, professional apprenticeship for young men and social
apprenticeship for 'young ladies', but boys and girls of the working
classes were usually pitched without preparation straight from the
classroom into a world where they were expected to work and behave
much like adults, though rewarded very differently.

In the past, this transition had been bridged for many youths by apprenticeship, a period of five or more years when, as both learners and workers, they were under the care and control of a 'master' who exercised many of the rights and responsibilities of a parent. But, with the growth of the factory system from the late eighteenth century, apprenticeship had declined in all but the skilled trades, and children of seven and eight – even, sometimes, of five or six – had become employed in mills, mines and workshops for an adult working day, often in degrading and dangerous conditions. In agriculture child labour had always been general. William Cobbett could 'not remember the time when I did not earn my living', scaring birds as a tiny child scarcely able to climb the gates and stiles, just as, more than half a century later in 1833, Roger Langdon started work at eight as a farmer's boy:

For the princely sum of one shilling a week I had to mind sheep and pull up turnips in all winds and weathers, starting at six o'clock in the morning . . . After this, until I was thirteen years of age, my life was not worth the living . . .[153]

In 1833 employment in textile factories for children under nine was forbidden, and for those between nine and thirteen a maximum of eight hours a day was laid down, but the great majority of child workers lay outside these controls, in agriculture, potteries, workshops and domestic industries. Many of these were not controlled by legislation until late in the century, and a general prohibition of work under the age of ten was only passed in 1876. Charles Shaw began long and arduous labour as a mould-runner on a pot-bank in 1840 when he was only seven years old, working from five and six in the morning until seven or eight o'clock at night.

From education to work. This is the proper order of life . . . I began to work, but I could never see in what way my poor little bit of an education could prepare me for such as came to my hand.[154]

Only a few very skilled potters like the gilders still followed an apprenticeship by Shaw's time; children like him had had a year or two at a dame school, where they learned to read more or less imperfectly and, less commonly, to write, before taking up work which made little if any use of such skills. On the day she was eight (about 1858) the future Mrs Burrows left school in Lincolnshire and started work in an agricultural gang for fourteen hours a day; she was the eldest of forty–fifty child workers, some of whom were only five:

We were followed all day long by an old man carrying a long whip in his hand which he did not forget to use.[155]

After four years of this with not a single holiday the family moved to Leeds, where work in a factory 'felt like Heaven'. At the age of nine in 1867 the future Mrs Wrigley left home in Wales to go as domestic servant to a family in Stockport; she had no wages, but her parents were relieved of the need to board and lodge her. Unable to read or write, she could not let them know how unhappy she was and how she 'fretted very much for my home'.[156] The isolation of such young children in single-servant households, torn from a close, rural environment to work for unknown people in an alien place, is one of the most harrowing examples of Victorian exploitation. Parents were not necessarily inhuman or unthinking, as domestic service could sometimes provide a good home and training for a girl, especially in a large establishment, but all too often she became a slave-of-all-work, with duties and responsibilities far beyond her strength and years. Even at the end of the period in 1912 a girl like Violet Whale could leave home at fourteen for domestic service, and though she 'hated the thought did not dare say a word against it':

It was assumed that we would all [four] go into service as we got old enough, so after three weeks at home to get some print dresses and aprons ready and a black dress for afternoons I was packed off to service.

Allowed home once a month, she was 'totally unprepared for all this work' and 'felt lost and alone'; after a year she was 'a nervous wreck'.[157]

Work of this kind, which involved separation from home and family, clearly marked, and was felt to mark, the end of childhood. Winifred Foley, who also went into service at fourteen, writes of her life in the Forest of Dean in the 1920s:

In families like ours there were only three important birthdays in your youth; the one marking your arrival into the world; the fifth, which meant you could go to school and leave a bit more room under mother's feet; and the fourteenth. This birthday meant, for a daughter, that she was old enough to get her feet under someone else's table; in the case of a son, that he could follow his father down the pit . . . Mam was very concerned that I should be aware of my new status. 'You'll be a young 'oman,' she said, 'now you be goin' into service . . .'[158]

Similarly, Patrick MacGill knew well enough that he had reached man's estate when, at the age of twelve, his parents told him that he must go beyond the mountains of Donegal to 'push his fortune'; like a fledgeling bird, he was literally thrust into independence.[159]

How much before this we can legitimately date the end of childhood is debatable. Those who earlier in the century began to work at seven, eight and nine were still children, and must have felt and behaved as such despite their new role. Sometimes a particular, usually tragic, event precipitated an autobiographer into adulthood, as when Marianne Farningham's mother died and she, at twelve, had to leave school and take over the running of the household: 'My father often said that I never had a girlhood, but grew at once from a child into a woman.'[160] Again, on the death of his father at an early age, Jack Lanigan left school in 1900 at the age of ten, having gained the Labour Certificate, to become an errand boy: 'I wanted to tell the world I was now a man, working and helping my mother.'[161] In both cases childhood was deemed to end with the close of schooling, and as the age of compulsory attendance was gradually lengthened to thirteen by the outbreak of the First World War so, too, was the duration of childhood.

The majority of autobiographers appear not to have welcomed their entrance to work and responsibility; many, indeed, actively resented or feared it and accepted it only because there was no alternative. Occasionally – and this more often among boys than girls – a child would become impatient of schooldays and keen to be out in the real world like his friends or elder brothers, a feeling well described by Jim Griffiths after his former mates had left school to go down the pit:

I felt very lonely at school, and even lonelier of an evening as we gathered for cricket on 'Cae'r Ynys' by the Amman river. My old mates now belonged to a different world to me. They wore long trousers and flashy cravats. They flourished their pink packets of 'Cinderella' fags before my eyes, and blew the smoke curling up to the sky . . . It was worst of all on Saturdays, when we wended our way over the river to the bright lights of Ammanford Square. They would display their silver sixpence which made the penny in my pocket shrink.[162]

Or, occasionally, life at home was so unhappy that escape into work, however unpleasant the thought of that might be, seemed an attractive alternative. Hannah Mitchell, a keenly intelligent girl deprived of all but rudimentary education, found relations with her domineering mother increasingly impossible:

The antagonism between my mother and myself grew worse; she was determined to mould me to her pattern, while I was equally determined to retain my own individuality! She strove to enforce her will by nagging, ravings and beatings. But I was stronger now, and had no mind to allow myself to be thrashed.

She decided to leave home by the only possible route – domestic service. 'I had now given up all hopes of an education . . . Little as I liked housework, even that, I felt, would be preferable to my present life.'[163]

But most children were neither anxious to launch themselves into the world, nor conscious of any choice in the matter. Many autobiographers make the point that they were never consulted about their future and that others – usually parents, sometimes a schoolteacher – solely made the decision. At thirteen, Joseph Armitage in Leeds found that 'the transition from school-desk to work-bench was abrupt, and left no doubt in the lad's mind what was expected of him'; he and another boy were simply told by their headmaster to report immediately at a local engineering firm.[164] In 1898, at the age of twelve, William Belcher left school to work for another engineering firm, fifty-two and a half hours a week for 5s., on top of which he attended evening classes,[165] and, even more precipitately, on leaving school in Plymouth, W. G. Elliott was simply enlisted by his father into the Marines as a boy bugler, without being consulted. 'Father did not exploit my talents in any way . . . I had no say in the matter.'[166] Geography and local work opportunities largely determined employment in these cases, as they did even more inevitably in coal-mining and textile areas. In Dawdon, the mining village for Seaham Colliery, sons went into the pit, daughters into domestic service or the bottle factory – the only other local industry – and the predictability of such decisions did not necessarily make them any more acceptable. Edward Cain, from a mining family, wept at the prospect of going down the pit and leaving home at five o'clock in the morning,[167] and Anita Hughes 'shed many tears' when, at twelve, she started half-time at the mill, leaving home at 4.30 a.m. for a two-mile walk across the fields and returning to school for the afternoon session.[168] Another twelve-year-old half-timer, Doris Hunt, knew well enough that this was the real beginning of working life:

> And then at twelve years of age my childhood really did finish. I had to go half-time to work in the cotton mill . . .[169]

Had her father not died at the age of thirty-five she was to have been a teacher; now she worked a six-and-a-half-hour shift from 6 a.m. to 12.30 p.m., and teachers generally did not trouble the tired half-timers much in the afternoon so long as they kept quiet.

Although for many children school was far from an enjoyable experience, and childhood itself was a mixture of happy and unhappy events, many autobiographers were reluctant to leave them behind, and a good number entered the adult world of work with fear and despair. This was partly fear of the unknown, partly their lack of preparation for work and partly the limited choices which were available. In areas of traditional single-industries like mining and textiles there was often no alternative at all, and the future could be read all too clearly in the faces of overworked fathers and irritable mothers. Yet, on the credit side, there would be a measure of independence and respect for a wage-earner, freedom from the teacher's cane, pocket-money, some new clothes. Once over the initial shock of work, many autobiographers found adolescence a happier, more exciting time than childhood, with opportunities to develop their personalities and pursue their own interests – for some in work, for others in self-education or leisure activities.

Joseph Terry
recollections of my life

Joseph Terry was born in Mirfield, Yorkshire, in 1816. His father came from a relatively prosperous family who owned canal-boats and carried on a profitable inland water trade before the days of railways or improved roads, but, partly through accidents to his boats and partly due to his intemperance, the family fortunes sank to a very low ebb during Joseph's childhood. Much of his early life was spent on canals and he received only a brief and interrupted schooling, supplemented by attendance at Sunday School, where he first 'began to feel a love for religion'. His mother suffered a severe mental breakdown after the barge on which they were living was sunk in a storm, and she, with great difficulty, rescued Joseph's brother; she was subsequently cared for in a poorhouse and at Wakefield Asylum. Joseph's 'childhood' may be said to have ended at the age of seven, when he and a brother, eighteen months older, were often left to navigate the boat through dangerous waters while their father was absent for several days. Somehow, Joseph continued his self-education, reading Swedenborg, Harvey's *Meditations*, and teaching himself to play the violin and flute. In later life he had a varied career as a shopkeeper, manager of Birstall Co-operative Flour Mill, keeper of a Temperance Hotel and a shipping agent; he also became a local preacher and lecturer, superintendent of the Sunday School, founder of the Brighouse Mechanics Institute, and published a collection of his own poetry.

Terry's autobiography, of approximately sixty thousand words, was written in 1865 when he was fifty; he died about 1890. His unpublished manuscript memoir was kindly brought to my notice by his great-granddaughter, Mrs Kathleen Smith.

The first thing I remember distinctly is being a very little boy, some two or three years old, and living at a place called Fold Head, Mirfield, Yorkshire; about a quarter of a mile distant from where the Mirfield Railway Station now stands; and which, at the time I write (1865, near 50 years after my advent into the world) is one of the most busy and important Stations in the country, being a junction which has direct communication with almost every other line in the land; and having completely revolutionized the neighbourhood, destroying all the ancient landmarks which used to divide the few old dwellings and the green pastures and meadows which flourished so richly on each side of the broad, clear river Calder, where, in my boyish days, I used to sit through the long, long summer hours, tending my Fishing tackle, until my pockets, net or basket were well filled with gudgeon, eel, chubb, dare, dace, perch, and, sometimes, such luxuries as the rich silver trout . . . Well, it was here where my Father dwelt, if dwelling it could be called, for being a waterman he was often away from home for weeks, and sometimes months together. I was born, as far as I have been able to ascertain in after life, the 26th of December, 1816 . . . All I remember is having a few companions much like myself, and having a severe attack of sickness, lying in the cradle ill for what seemed to me to be a very long time, where my kind-hearted mother watched over me with the greatest tenderness, often shedding tears on my account when I refused to take the bitter medicines which she so much desired to administer for my relief; at last I recovered, but it was only, as I have since been informed, just an escape from death. After my recovery I did not long enjoy the sweet company of my playmates, and the pleasant walks in the green pastures where we used to go to gather the daisy and the buttercup which grew in profusion; for, as if my parents had been waiting for the event, they immediately commenced to prepare for making their home mainly on board, and only dwelling on the land for short intervals. At this time my father had a boat of his own, and used to trade mostly with Coal, from a place called Hunger Hill Colliery, near Dewsbury, to Knottingly, York, Ripon and Borough Bridge, etc., bringing for back carriage Lime or Limestone . . .

As I stated, my father often made long voyages, and mother when she could, accompanied him. No sooner, therefore, had I recovered from the fever before alluded to than we packed up and prepared for going on board. The Keel called the 'Magpie' was then laid awaiting her turn to load, at Hungerhill Coal Staithe, and my little brother Jim and myself walked there about a distance of two miles from where we lived . . .

Well, we arrived on board and I was much pleased with the sight of the great river as it then appeared to me and wondered how anyone had the courage to venture on and navigate its wide channels, and sometimes turbulent waters. Everything in and on the boat struck me with wonder and delight. The fine cabin with all its drawers, and shelves, and the little snug bed places. The small stove fireplace, fender, etc., and the long dangerous ladder to ascend and descend the same from the deck, and the rich novelty of eating and sleeping on board all combined to fill my young imaginative mind with joy and delight. Well, we got loaded at last and bent our course down the river for York or Ripon I cannot now be sure which. I only remember we went often to Ripon. It was very exciting and delightful as we passed down the river and although I remember it was summer-time on account of what took place in the voyage, and the beautiful and rich appearance of the foliage which skirts the river banks most of the way. I often wondered at the fears of mother as she watched our every movement when on deck, and the plans she tried to keep us in a place of safety, especially when we were passing some of the most awkward and dangerous places, such as Washing Stones lock near Harbury, 'Hell Ford' at Kirkthorp, near Wakefield, Cross channels, Mithley, Harrieshill too, besides great numbers of places too numerous to mention, where in after life I had many a hard tug and many a hairbreadth escape; and where I have often witnessed the death of friends, companions, and relations but most of which places, owing to the cutting of new canals diverting the river, etc., are now disused, and almost forgotten. I must not forget to mention one of our best friends and constant guardians at this time, and one who was our constant companion in all our rambles – Uncle Ben. He was Mother's brother, and had to rough it in childhood and being brought up in poor circumstances owing mainly, as will be further explained in this narrative, to the loose drunken and gambling habits of his Father. He was put to my father to learn the Water business. He was of a wild romantic turn of mind, and our long voyages through the farming district, and along the old broad deep-winding rivers seemed to suit him in all respects. He could run like a hare, leap like a stag, and throw a stone to bring down a rabbit, duck, or bird, with as much precision as 'David's sling', or the arrow of an Indian. My brother Jim and myself were great favourites with him . . . I well remember him taking us in to the fields which were filled with a profusion of all kinds of flowers, taking birds' nests and bringing the young ones to please us, and climbing the crab or wild cherry trees to pluck the fruit with which he would fill our slips . . . At this time we often used to lie for days or sometimes for weeks together at the old towns of York and Ripon, and I can just remember going on shore at those old places with our playmates. But the thing which is of all others impressed deeply on my mind at this age is the joy I felt when brother Jim and myself had our first new suit of what was considered a sailor's dress. It was at Ripon and father and mother went to buy them in the town. Of course we were very young to assume such a dress, but the parents of children who were accustomed to be nearly always on board had pride over their offspring like other parents, and the Tailors who were accustomed to make sailors' clothing helped to foster their pride by making small dresses after the fashion of the larger ones. Those dresses consisted of white woollen trousers and blue short check smock with woollen knitted cap, made to slip on the head, of a kind that would not blow off when on board in strong winds. We did not at this time continue more than some two or three years on board, going home sometimes for a week or two together. My father at this time had the misfortune to lose a valuable horse and a boat, nearly at the same time, which almost ruined him. We were sold up, at our residence at Mirfield, and went to live at Thornhill near Dewsbury in a row of houses not far from the Thornhill Church. Father by some means got another boat and made a fresh start in the world, and for a time my little brother and myself were sent to school . . .

I cannot remember much about Thornhill, only going and returning over some fields to school and stopping to pick the black berries which grew in abundance, the house where we lived, and a few other incidents, especially that mother was often very sorrowful and desponding, which I afterwards learnt was the first dreadful symptom of the malady from which she suffered so much and so long. This was caused mainly by what I have before stated, and augmented and confirmed by another misfortune which befell us not long after by which the vessel and all our worldly wealth was lost and father found himself pennyless.

During this short interval Mother continued to get worse, and when the last misfortune happened she was so bad that it was not safe to leave her alone. A deep melancholy and sadness had taken hold of her, and hope itself seemed to have fled. This could not arise from want of religious belief or consolation, for having attended the Sunday School, and being connected with the Moravian body of Christians, living for a time at Fulneck, the Quarters of the Body, she was deeply impressed with religious truth, and when in her proper state of mind both previous to, and after the shock which caused her suffering, was most tender and regular in her religious principles, and especially in implanting them early in the minds of her children. Well there we were, on the last verge of the forlorn hope of life, and father had no alternative but to commence working as a common man for some ten shillings per week and rations, and mother must be sent somewhere to be taken care of. True he had relations who were well-to-do in the world, and who might have helped him to procure another vessel, but owing partly to father marrying as he did, mother's family being very poor – and partly to family quarrels about money matters, they did not do so, but rather seemed to take against us, as is often the case, in proportion as we became more needy and dependent. In this dilemma father applied to the Overseers of Elland, nr. Halifax, where he had been apprenticed to the trade of a Shoemaker, and served so much of his time before running away on to the water as to enable him to claim it as his parish. Mother was lodged there in the poorhouse, and brother and I who were but still very young were taken to our grandmother's on the father's side – Mrs Jemima Terry's of Eastharp Lane, Mirfield, or as my grandfather lived for a short time after, I might say Mr Richard Terry's. Grandfathers were well to do in the world having a number of vessels going and the business at that time was a very profitable one. But notwithstanding this fact, we did not 'fare sumptuously every day' – but rather the contrary. Grandmother was a clever housewife, but rather too near for us. Besides it was not common then for children either to live or dress as well as they do now. Our food varied very little. Milk porridge morning and night with oat cake sops and oat cake to dinner with very often broth from hung beef and bacon, very salt. For it was very much the custom at this time for those who had got a little at forehand to buy as much beef at once as would fit the remainder of the year, which was all salted and hung like bacon. Often a number of families would join at a beast, and get it killed and divided; but the beasts were very small and lean compared with what are now sent to the slaughter, and butcher shops were few and far between. So people seldom got fresh meat. Wheaten bread was quite uncommon, being very scarce and dear, and I can even now remember enjoying the luxury of a thin slice of wheat bread put on the top of my allowance of oat cake, and a quantity of tea after the rest of the family had done, once or twice a week, but mostly on Sunday.

Here I and my brother Jim were sent to school – first to an 'Old Dame Blackburn's' of Littlemore, near Snakehill, Mirfield, and afterwards to a higher class of school kept by a Miss Lawton of Snakehill. I would like to give a full description of these two schools, and the impression they made on my young mind, but have much to write about and what I think of greater importance. I may just, however, say that Dame Blackburn was a real old-fashioned school mistress . . . dwelling in a house which was part of an old barn at one end, and there was a kind of loft open at one side, or a half-chamber where the dame kept hens, which hens had a free passage through the midst of the seminary, and the ranks of her accomplished scholars, and it was not uncommon for them in their flights up and down in their ascent and descent from the loft to do a kind of business, and drop something amongst our ranks not the most agreeable.

Mistress Lawton's school was a large chamber fronting the High Road, and on a level with it, and much superior in all respects to Dame Blackburn's. Grandmother, who had the sole control over us now, was a real old Methodist, and did not forget our religious training. Grandfather was as far as I can remember much fonder of a good joke than a good sermon – taking much delight in teasing people. I remember him once giving me a little tobacco, as he was a great smoker, which made me very sick and caused me to vomit, and grandmother gave him a good scolding which seemed to take very little effect.

As mother had to some extent recovered by the treatment first at Elland and then with one of her sisters, who was married and had a good house, in about a year and a half or two years as near as I can remember father took a cottage at Battyeford, Mirfield, in a row of houses one storey high, called 'Kalling Alley', and which was no great distance from the Sister in whose care Mother had been; also another sister who was also married and settled. Mother and I were located there while brother Jim remained at grandmothers, being older, stronger, and much stouter than me. He was more of a favourite, being called a 'Terry', while I was more like mother and her family. Jim was soon sent on board one of the Keels, while I had to remain the sole companion of poor mother.

Father at this time was still very poor, and still working as a journeyman, if such a term could be applied to his calling. Sometimes he would be away for weeks together having to make long voyages and all that poor mother and me had to subsist on, and find coals, etc., was five shillings per week.

And now commenced with me a season of intense suffering and privation. I should be about five or six years old when I left grandmother's, or perhaps not quite so old. Our house was but poorly furnished, and there was much poverty around us, and very bare and precarious living. It may easily be imagined that with the above small allowance, even if used in the most economical way could yield us a sufficiency of food, but when it is remembered that poor mother could seldom settle her mind to home, and lay it out to the best advantage, it will be seen that we had to suffer much privation. It is utterly impossible for me were I ever so wishful to do so, to describe what I suffered for want of proper nourishment and clothing for a period of some two or three years, or from about my fifth to my seventh year. I had no shoes or stockings, and but very scanty clothing, which clothing was often the gift of some kind-hearted mother which she contrived to spare from the not too plentiful wardrobe of her son or sons. For be it ever remembered the poor have much warmer sympathies than the rich, and are more ready to help each other. As mother was much from home, and we had often no fire and no food in the house, I had to seek shelter where I could find it, and procure a little food of any kind where I could. Sometimes scarcely would I taste anything for days together, at other times living entirely on turnips taken from the fields or any kind of wild fruit or roots I could procure. In the winter season my feet, and especially my heels and toes, were much frostbitten, swollen and sore – so much so that after we were in a better circumstance, and my parents could afford to clothe me better, it took years of care, scrubbing and washing to bring my feet into a proper and natural state.

My life at this time was wild indeed, ranging about from place to place, except when I was at what was called the 'Setting Shop' where some part of my time was spent Setting Cards, or inserting the Card Teeth into leaves and Garters as they were called to fit on the Scribbling Machines for Scribbling Wool, etc. This was a most wearisome and dreary task, as we had sometimes as many as sixteen hundred teeth to prick in for one half-penny. Great numbers of children and young and grown-up families got their bread by this unhealthy and poor means; the very best hands never exceeding about one shilling per day, and great numbers suffered much in their health from this, worse than slavish employment. But I am very happy to know that for many years now this business has nearly all been done by machinery, and the children of the poor are either at school or much better employed, and that too at much higher wages . . .

It would take up much time and space to describe every house in 'Kalling Alley' where we now lived separately; suffice it to say that they were all much alike, all being poorly furnished and in some cases at least three beds had to be contrived at nights, and as they were in the constant habit of borrowing all kinds of necessary articles from each other from a hair brush, hair or small tooth comb, up to long brush, barrels, dresses, bonnets, soap, candles, tea, sugar, bread, even up to the Sunday, so they were in the constant habit of sleeping at each other's houses – whenever there was room. And it was no uncommon thing to hear the words 'Will George be at home tonight? I wanted our Betty to sleep or lie as her fathers come home, and she does not like to lie at feet.' But with all this poverty and seeming wretchedness, there was coupled much kindliness, and warm friendly feeling, and often much real and earnest sympathy for the suffering ones. I have often looked in vain in the higher walks of life, which I have since trod, for the same self denial and voluntary sacrifice for the good of others, and the same willingness to share the blessings of life with those who are in want, even when those who gave had never a sufficiency, and often did not know from whence the next meal might come, and it has strengthened my conviction that the school of adversity is the best school for educating and maturing a grateful and feeling heart, except where adversity is connected with crime . . .

George Mockford

wilderness journeyings and gracious deliverances:
the autobiography of George Mockford
(for forty years minister of the gospel
at Broad Oak, Heathfield)

George Mockford was born at Southerham, near Lewes, Sussex, in 1826, the son of a poor shepherd. Out at work by the age of eight, he had very little schooling, but like a good many of his generation, he early became deeply concerned about his state of spiritual grace and about doctrinal issues such as election and predestination. His account is not, therefore, a record of the factual events of his life, but a spiritual autobiography in an earlier tradition which reached back to the Puritans of the seventeenth century but was still occasionally employed in the nineteenth. For Mockford, childhood and youth were periods of trial, of wrestling with sin and temptation (about which he is not very specific) and, ultimately, of redemption when he broke from the Anglican church to become a dissenter. Shortly after this extract ends he began preaching, and eventually a devoted congregation provided him with a house and a chapel at Broad Oak, Heathfield, Sussex, where he was pastor for forty years; he also practised as a herbalist, having a dispensary and treating patients for many miles around. He died in 1899, his autobiography being privately published by his widow in 1901. I am grateful to his great-granddaughter, Mrs R. A. Barker, for permission to quote from the earlier pages.

I was brought forth into this world of sin and sorrow at a place called Southerham in the parish of South Malling, Lewes, Sussex, on December 27, 1826. My parents were poor, the occupation of my father being a shepherd. I was the eldest surviving member of a large family of twelve children, the first-born having died in infancy; and this being the case, I had, as soon as I was old enough, to be mother's help, to nurse the baby, clean the house, and do sewing like a girl, so that I was not only prevented from playing with other boys, but also from going to school. I did go for a short time to a dame's school, and thence for a little while to the British School at Lewes. My parents were what is called church people, who did not like dissenters; but they only went to church to have their children christened or to attend a funeral. We were taught the church catechism on a Sunday afternoon, were also instructed to use the Lord's prayer, and for a time I was sent to the church Sunday-school. I was soon noticed as one paying great attention to my instructors, who I remember excited my wonder as to how they knew so much, and I had a great wish to be as wise as they: therefore I drank in very eagerly all they told me; and by their instruction the church and her ministers, ordinances, and ceremonies were soon looked upon by me as having something mysteriously angelic or heavenly about them; and being naturally very credulous, particularly of anything that had some mystery about it, I could easily be made to believe the statements of the mysterious, learned men, the clergy or church ministers.

I can remember, when quite young, having serious thoughts about the great God that made the heavens and the earth, of the judgment-day, and of hell. I remember what an effect some conversation between my father and mother had upon me when very young. I heard father tell mother that some person (mentioning the name) who lived in my mother's native place was dead, and that in his lifetime he had sold himself to the devil for so much money. On the bearers attempting to lift the coffin in which the body lay, they could not do so because of its great weight; this could not be accounted for until they opened the coffin and found the body covered with brimstone, the smell of which was unbearable, and this they said was a proof that the devil was going to take him into hell for ever.

When about eight years of age I was employed, during the summer, to scare the birds from the corn, etc., for which I had a shilling a week, seven days to the week; for though the master went to church, the rooks would go on stealing the corn if they could.

When I was ten years old I was taken entirely from school to help my father in the capacity of shepherd-boy, for which I had two shillings per week, which I thought was a great deal, though I never had the money, as of course my father took it.

I was always rather delicate in health, and had no stamina about me for outdoor exposure; the food for us young ones consisting of little else than potatoes with a little bacon fat on them. Having commenced my new occupation in the winter, I felt it much; my feet and hands became covered with chilblains, which soon broke out into open sores, yet for a time I had to work getting the turnips out of the pie, as we used to call this heap of turnips, covered over with straw and earth. I had some old leather gloves on, but the dry earth used to get into my gloves and fill my sores, and so bad did they become that the doctor was called in, who ordered me to be kept at home for a week at least, and gave directions to my mother how to treat my hands and feet. I got better in a fortnight and went to work again, but caught a severe cold; indeed it must have been a bad attack of bronchitis, as I can remember how I had to labour for breath, and the weazing noise in my chest could be heard all over the house. For this again I had the doctor, but my father who was naturally strong and healthy, had no sympathy with his white-faced son; he said I must be hardened to it, or I should never be any use; so one of the means employed was to send me on frosty mornings to pull up the turnips in the field, laying hold of their frosty tops without gloves on. But as my father was remonstrated with by some of the workmen on the farm about it, I did not go many mornings. The great ambition of my father being to save money, his study was that his children's little strength and time should be all put to such an account as would be conducive to this end. This kind of treatment had no tendency to foster love to him; I began to have a great dread of him, and all I did for him was done under fear of the lash.

I remember about this time, some young gentleman from Lewes often walked in the evening to Southerham, and seeing me in the garden at work would talk to me and give me tracts, etc., that produced sometimes solemn thoughts about death and eternity, and finding I was willing to listen, his visits were more frequent than was agreeable to my father, who said he was most likely some one learning to be a parson, so he busied himself with talking to others; but as for boys who had their living to get, he could not see the good of their reading or being religious.

But as I grew older in years, so I did in sin. I was encouraged to keep rabbits, and any profit I made by them was to be used in buying my own clothes. My father would have been pleased for us to buy all our clothes, though he would not have encouraged me to do what I did to get profit, as I used to steal my master's turnips and hay to feed my rabbits. At first I was much scared in doing it, but soon grew bolder by seeing some of the workmen, who kept rabbits, do the same. In a little while I could go into my master's garden and orchard, and fill my pockets with fruit; but I had at times such guilt on my conscience on account of it, that when I have been out on a dark night, I have felt as if Satan was upon me, and would surely carry me off. I vowed and promised to do so no more, but as soon as the light of day returned, and I got into the company of those who could curse and swear, and take the name of God in vain, my resolution melted away like ice before the fire, and I began to join with those who went to the ale-house, and hear them sing songs. All I heard and saw there was quite congenial to my natural heart; I was delighted while in it, but O the guilt and fear I felt in walking home alone on a dark night after leaving my companions! I kept repeating part of the Lord's prayer or some such language to keep the devil (as I thought) from grasping me; and on reaching my home, I have opened the door, and getting inside, have suddenly closed it to shut out the devil. There was no hatred to sin, no sorrow for it; but the dread of hell and punishment of my sin often made me cry out, 'Do save me; do pardon me, and I will lead a new life.' I do believe that persons from the effects of natural conviction may have great sorrow and long much for mercy, and yet there be nothing in it but the workings of nature. I remember about this time being much alarmed. I attempted to take a jackdaw's nest that was built near the top of a high chalk pit; I tried to reach it from the top by lying down and reaching over, when a portion of the earth underneath me gave way, and but for the presence of mind I had to work myself gradually back to my feet, I must have been dashed in pieces.

At another time I was passing through a field in which was a vicious ox. I did not see him until I heard him close upon me; I cried out, 'Lord help me', and ran towards a fence which I just reached, and leaped over as the ox overtook me, but the fence being on a bank stopped him. I had also a second deliverance with respect to this same ox, when I was trying to detach him and another from a cart; the men would go in front of them to take the locker out that fastens the cart to the yoke, but as I was afraid to do this I went in between them and the neb of the cart, and they started with me in that position, the ox pressing his body tightly against mine. I was so jammed against the neb that I could scarcely breathe; but suddenly the wheel of the cart came in contact with a wall, which stopped the animals, and the pressure being removed, I dropped on the ground, and the master coming along at that instant pulled me out from under the feet of the oxen. It was of course thought that I must be fearfully crushed. I was taken indoors and restoratives given me; but wonder of wonders, no harm had come to me beyond the shock to the system. How plainly we see the truth of the word of God, 'Preserved in Christ Jesus, and called' . . .

When I was between sixteen and seventeen years of age, some unknown person came upon the Downs, and addressing me, said, 'Well, my lad, do you like reading?' I replied, 'Yes.' 'Then,' said he, 'I will leave this tract with you, and when I come again I shall know how you like it.' I put it into my pocket, and thought I am not going to read that religious book; he might keep his book for aught I cared, but this thought came, 'Well, you had better look at it, or you won't know what reply to give him when he comes again.' So I took it from my pocket to look it over, but never did look it over in that sense, as all at once it looked straight into me. It was in this way. As I took the book from my pocket, these two scriptures met my eye, and went to my heart: 'The soul that sinneth, it shall die.' 'He that offendeth in one point is guilty of all.' I was struck as with a flash of lightning; the book dropped from my hand, and I fell to the earth. How long I lay there I cannot tell, but presently I began to crawl into a hedge near; I was afraid to look up, as I felt sure if I did, I should see the eye of God upon me from above; and while lying in the hedge, I cried for the first time in my life, in the language of the publican, 'God be merciful to me a sinner.' O what a solemn sight I had of the majesty, holiness, and justice of God! and I proved his word to be as a sharp sword, piercing my heart. I felt there was no hiding myself from God. I wished that I could find some place to hide myself from the presence of my angry Judge. How I got home that night I cannot tell, but such was the effect upon my body that I could scarcely walk. My parents were terrified at my appearance, and kept wanting to know the cause of my illness, but I could not tell them. Being able to eat but little, and sleep less, I soon became so ill that I was sent to a doctor, who examined me, and shook his head, but said, 'I will try if I can do anything for you.' Every one supposed that I was in a rapid consumption. The church clergyman visited me, to whom I told my trouble; he laboured hard to comfort me, telling me God was very merciful, and only required us to do what we could, and he would do the rest. I puzzled him much because I was so anxious to know what my part was, and how much I was required to do. This he could not satisfy me about; but by reading the books he lent me, and attending to his instructions, I began to feel more quiet in my mind. As I was in real earnest to be right, I gave the greatest attention to my adviser, whom I held in much reverence. I felt sure all his instructions must be right, so I worked hard to do all he told me, and I soon could leave the rest, believing what he said, that God was a merciful God. I soon became quite religious, and was looked upon as such in the parish where I lived.

I began to take tracts to people's houses, and visited the sick, exhorting them to turn to God, repent and believe, and they would soon be as safe as I was. My case excited much interest, as the clergyman set me up as a Christian young man. I was still very weak and feeble in body, and I could not get after the sheep, as I was not able to walk fast enough to keep pace with them as they passed from one part of the Downs to the other.

I remember one of the workmen on the farm saying to me one day, 'Do you know what the doctor thinks of your case?' I said, 'No, what is it?' 'Well,' he said, 'your father and mother do not want you to know, but the doctor says you cannot live long.' 'Oh,' said I, 'I am quite ready to die; my peace is made with God.' It is true I felt as I said, so wrapped up was I in a false peace, and so incased in a false confidence; and had I then died, every one would have said what a good end I had made. I knew not my need of Jesus Christ, nor had I any faith in him or desire after him; my ground of hope of going to heaven was the peace I felt – a peace that I had made with God, as I thought. O what a delusion of the devil! But so he deceives thousands. Of such it is said that they 'have no bands in their death; their strength is firm'. 'Like sheep they are laid in the grave, and death shall feed on them.' But my God had thoughts of peace towards me of a very different nature, blessed be his dear name.

The reader will observe that the sense of guilt that I had felt was on account of actual or outward sins; I knew nothing of heart sins. I was a hearty devotee of my (falsely so-called) spiritual adviser, and at his earnest desire I was confirmed by the bishop. Being honest as far as I knew, I wanted to attend to all things in a way that would not break my peace; but I felt adverse to confirmation, and told my instructor that I shrank from it. And when he asked the reason, I answered that I understood I was to relieve my sponsors of their obligation made at my baptism, and take it upon myself; but I would rather not take it upon myself, as I considered they had promised so much, and now if I failed, all the blame would rest upon me. His reply to this was, that as I had arrived at the age to which these vows extended, even if I were not confirmed, my sponsors would be free of their responsibility, and it must rest with me. So I was confirmed, and then, of course, I was entitled to attend the Lord's supper. This for some time I resisted, as that scripture so stood in my way, 'He that eateth and drinketh unworthily, eateth and drinketh damnation to himself.' This word 'damnation' was very solemn to me, for I often feared I was not quite right; so that church minister and I had several talks on the subject, and I was told that it ought not to read damnation, but condemnation, the difference being explained in this way, that it simply meant that persons who lived in drunkenness, adultery, or open sin, in partaking of the Lord's supper did so unworthily, and thus their sinful acts condemned them. So I was persuaded to attend, and I remember it was a very solemn act in my estimation; but I was greatly put out by seeing some at the table who I knew frequented the public-house, were often intoxicated, and cursed and swore. However, by these means I was engrafted into the church, bound by her hands, and safely folded, and it was suggested to me that I was now safe, and safe I thought myself . . . I began to discover the doctrine of predestination and election as revealed in the scriptures, but O the enmity I felt against it, and against God on account of it! Where was the justice of God in it? I asked, as the doom of all was fixed, and that nothing man could do, would or could turn the mind of God. This was what I absolutely refused to believe. How hard I tried to make the word of God speak a different language! But the more I read it, the more I found the sovereignty of Jehovah set forth in its pages. The passage I particularly disliked was, 'Jacob have I loved, and Esau have I hated'; so I tried to persuade myself that it was wrongly translated.

For months this deep distress continued, and my teacher, the clergyman, and other church people who visited me, pointed out how wrongly I was acting in trying to look, as they said, into those secrets that belonged to God; I was putting a very wrong construction upon these doctrines. They tried hard to persuade me that Jesus Christ died for all mankind, quoting many passages to prove what they said, and I brought forward those parts of God's words I had felt the power of in my heart, which were quite against the doctrine of universal redemption. Sometimes they pitied me, and sometimes spoke very harshly to me. My parents were advised to take any books away that I might have, as they feared my mind was already greatly impaired by much reading. The weakness of my body increasing, I was taken from the sheep, and removed to the farm-house to act as groom, and do anything the servants might require of me. This was supposed to be the only means of prolonging my life, as I should now be sheltered from the weather, and it was hoped that the good farm-house ale, of which I was permitted to take as much as I liked, would strengthen me, and the company of the servants bring me out of my melancholy state . . . I had many talks with the clergyman upon different parts of scripture, and he would sometimes reprove me by saying I ought not to say this portion of the word of God meant so and so; he was my instructor, and I ought to know nothing but what he taught me. I remember on one occasion he said, 'You talk like a dissenter.' I told him I knew not what he meant. 'What is a dissenter?' I enquired. His answer was that dissenters were a people who broke away from the church as sheep sometimes did from the fold. I understood him to mean people who went to chapel, and those I hated, as I had always been taught to look upon them as canting hypocrites, and what he said made me feel more bitter against them. And yet strange to say, there were two of them who walked past our house every Sunday on their way to Lewes, and they both spoke so kindly to me – one of them giving me a shilling on two or three occasions – and their manner seemed so different from that of the people who went to church, that I sometimes did wish I was like them. And when I have seen them pass, I have felt at times such a love to them that I was quite vexed with myself for being so silly as to have any regard to such deluded people, as they were represented to be . . .

William Webb
reminiscences of an ordinary life

The author was born in the village of East Kennet, Wiltshire, in 1830, the son of a tradesman who also acted as the parish clerk. Like many autobiographers seeking to discover their own identity, William was deeply interested in his ancestry, and his access to the parish registers appears to have provided one of the major preoccupations of his childhood. As the child of fairly comfortable parents, his private education continued to the age of twelve or fourteen (he is not sure which), to be followed by apprenticeship to an engineering firm. But, like thousands of his countrymen, he felt that England did not have enough opportunities to offer to an ambitious young man and that he would make a better life for himself in the colonies. One brother had already emigrated to America, and in 1852, at the age of twenty-one, he and another brother set sail for Australia, tempted partly by the recent discoveries of gold. Failing to find a quick fortune, he established his own business as a wheelwright and agricultural implement maker, married another emigrant from the west of England, and settled down to a life of over fifty years in Australia. His short, unpublished autobiography, of which this extract is the greater part, was written about 1880. My thanks are due to his great-niece, Mrs F. B. Ninnes, who brought it to my notice.

In writing the following pages I am actuated, not by any desire to publish my own biography as being of interest to the world generally, but simply to place on record the facts and circumstances of my birth and parentage, together with such incidents of my life as may be of value to my own family in the future, and with the idea that my children, and after them their children also, will feel an interest in knowing from whence they sprung and under what circumstances I left the home of my childhood and became a resident of Australia.

A condensed narrative of my life in this colony and the rise and progress of the community in which my lot has been cast for nearly half a century cannot fail to be of some little interest to those who come after me, enabling them to compare the present with the past. Not that my individual share in the progress of the colony has been at all an important one; not more so than that of thousands of other working men, striving to make a home for themselves in a raw land.

The Parish Registers of the Village of East Kennett, in the County of Wiltshire in England, bear record that I was born in that Parish, on the Fifteenth of October, One Thousand Eight Hundred and Thirty, the child of Robert and Mary Anne Webb, residents and freeholders of that parish.

I quote from the registers because, owing to circumstances which I will proceed to explain, I was enabled to become quite familiar with the Parish Records when I had become sufficiently taught to read and digest their contents, not only as affecting my own family but others as well.

Sixty or seventy years ago, in the small agricultural villages in that part of England, the Parish Clerk was an individual of some importance and had a recognized position in church affairs (of course I allude to the Church of England) and second to that of the Parson himself. He had his small reading desk just below that of the Clergyman and, in the services, repeated all the responses and read the Psalms, verse by verse, with his superior. In small churches he also performed the duties of Sexton and had entire charge of the church building and precincts. This position was, during the years of my boyhood, held by my father and as the clergyman was for a great part an absentee my father had charge of the keys not only of the church but also of the chests containing the registers of Births, Deaths and Marriages. The older records were kept in an ancient oaken chest; but a new one of iron had been provided for the new books some few years before my time. At that time it only contained the Marriage Register.

I was continually in and about the church on some errand for my father. It was a damp old place and whenever there was any sunshine, especially in winter-time, the windows had to be opened for airing the building. As I got strong enough for the job, I also had to toll the bell for the services, or for any deaths that occurred in the parish. As a matter of course my curiosity was immensely excited about the contents of the venerable old oak chest and nothing would do but it had to be unlocked, so that I might satisfy myself as to what it contained. At first I was only allowed to see the precious records when my father was present, but as time went on I was permitted to examine them at my leisure.

As these records went back some two hundred years it may be imagined what engrossing interest they possessed to a child like me. By their means I traced the history of most of the families, both of high and low degree, who had, in that long period, been inhabitants of my native parish.

My own father was the son of Jacob and Anne Webb, both of East Kennett. My great-grandfather was Thomas, son of William Webb, son of George Webb, who carries the record back to the time of Queen Anne, whose name was associated with our village in several ways. For instance, part of the Clergyman's stipend was derived from a fund called Queen Anne's bounty; and I well remember that one bell, in the wooden turret on top of the church, bore all around the circumference of its rim an inscription to the effect that the bell was Queen Anne's gift to the church. I had a great feeling of veneration for the bell.

During the years of my childhood and youth, the state of the agricultural population in that part of England was miserable in the extreme. Wheaten bread was scarce and dear, the farm labourers usually eating barley bread. Epidemic fevers were frequent and half the working population were suffering from ague.

My father's family consisted of the eldest daughter, Anne, who afterwards married James Draper of Easterton, in the same county. The next sister, Jane, afterwards married Alexander Whittick, of the town of Devizes in the same county. There was also an infant daughter Martha. My eldest brother, Maurice, and the next, Henry, were mostly away from home during my childhood, working with friends of my father. The next boys, James, and Robert Barrett, and a sister, Mary Ellen, with myself and the infant daughter, Martha, constituted the domestic circle. As a tradesman with a fair connection and a Freeholder in the parish, my father was enabled, by hard work (which was shared by all who were able), to live in comfort, but there was never anything to spare.

I have already mentioned that epidemic diseases were frequent and fatal. As an instance, as far back as I can remember, I remember being in bed with my brothers James and Robert, when I was hurriedly taken out of bed and carried away to a cottage several miles distant by a friend of my mother's. I did not see my home again for a long time, six months, as I was told afterwards. When I was brought home again my playmates were gone. Black fever had almost emptied the house. I have often heard my mother relate the incident, how the fever had been some time in the village and that my brother James, who, being the eldest at home, had caught the infection, and that my mother's friend had come over to give what help she could. Having no children of her own she declared that Willie, that is me, should not die if she could help it, so her noble instinct prompted her to take me out of bed and away from the infected village to her own home. As I have said before, during the time that I was away my four brothers and sisters had all died and I was the only one that remained of five. As time went on, other children came to replace those who were lost, Robert Barrett, named after his dead brother, George Thomas and Alfred. The last was born in my mother's fiftieth year. Amongst those who might be termed the second family I was the eldest and, after a few years attending school, such as it was, and within reach of fourteen years of age, I had to go into the workshop and begin to do my part.

At the time of which I write, that is between 1830 and 1840, the means of educating the ordinary village children was of the poorest description. I myself went to a Dame's School for some years. I well remember trudging along, morning and evening, along a green lane, in company with a number of others, for a distance of about a mile to one of those venerable village dames, noted more for keeping the pupils out of mischief than for her ability to teach anything beyond the mere rudiments of learning. I distinctly recollect, one gloomy afternoon, my mother coming to the school and vaccinating myself and several others. She performed the operation by means of a darning needle, working three holes in the skin of the arm by the point of a needle and then with the other end of the same instrument, taking some matter from the arm of another child and applying it to the puncture. In my case it took well, as the mark is still visible and it was the only operation of the sort I ever had to undergo. When eight or nine years old I had to attend a school kept by an old man at the village of Avebury, two miles away. The school was kept in the bottom room of the church tower, and it was the privilege of the bigger boys to wind up the weights of the church tower clock. There was also a splendid peal of bells in the tower. Avebury is noted as containing the remains of druidical times, which lie scattered more or less over all that part of the County of Wiltshire.

As I have stated before, when about twelve or fourteen years old, I had to leave school to go into my father's workshop. After a few years, as my younger brother got up, I got a situation in the establishment of Messrs Garden and Perks, Iron Masters and Smiths at the town of Swindon. The Junior Partner of this firm afterwards took orders in the Church of England and died Canon Perks of Richmond, Melbourne, Australia. After being about two years at this place, at my own earnest wish I was bound apprentice for three years to Mr William Cambridge of The Market Lavington Iron Works, a noted manufacturer of all classes of agricultural implements and machinery. Some of the earliest Portable Steam Engines were made at this establishment between 1840 and 1850.

My eldest brother, Maurice, had long been married and in business at Winterbourne Bassett. He, some years later, with his family emigrated to Texas, U.S.A. Both he and his wife died of the yellow fever, shortly after landing at New Orleans. The children found kind friends and grew up and settled at Galveston. One of his daughters has corresponded with me. Her married name is Miluman.

My next eldest brother, Henry, after working in several engine shops in Bristol and elsewhere, obtained the situation of smith at the Great Western Railway repairing workshops at Exeter. While in that situation he had married a widow named Shevill, who had sons, two of whom were telegraph clerks on The South Devon Atmospheric Railway, which was then going through its short-lived existence, on the atmospheric system. This time, 1849–50, was the period of the great gold rushes to California, immediately following the discovery of gold in Australia, causing great excitement in England. My brother Henry, at Exeter, wrote to me suggesting that I should join him in emigrating to Australia. After some more correspondence I agreed and we at once set about the necessary preparations.

In the autumn of 1851, I spent a fortnight in London to view the Great Exhibition and was greatly impressed and somewhat unsettled by the experience of the two weeks spent in the great city. Having completed our preparations, myself, my brother, his wife and her four sons met at Exeter and proceeded to Plymouth and took passage in the ship Prian, for Port Phillip, in May 1852. After undergoing the usual experiences of ship-board life for 96 days, in the month of August 1852 our ship anchored in Portland Bay and, after making some enquiries, we and most of the other passengers elected to land at Portland, instead of proceeding on to Melbourne.

About this time the Government of Australian Colonies devoted a large portion of the funds raised from the sale and leasing of land to the purpose of paying the passage of selected working men and their families to Australia.

The ruling idea in both my own and my brother's minds in emigrating, as there were five young men in the party, or as regards two of them just approaching manhood, [was] a better chance of making something of their lives . . . offering in the Colonies. The gold discoveries in Australia also were attracting much attention at that time in England . . .

When we arrived in Portland and landed we found that most of the men were away at the diggings at Ballarat, or some other of the many places where gold had been found. On getting ashore, we managed to get the use of an empty house, and as we had brought bedding and other necessities for housekeeping with us, we made a start as Citizens of Australia. In endeavouring to hunt up provisions we found the two baker shops open but empty – nothing doing. The same applied to most of the small business places, but the large stores were carried on as usual, so we got some flour and a camp oven and got on very well.

As regards myself, my available money on landing consisted of two sovereigns, but I had brought with me a box containing a collection of farming and digging tools which I had made myself at my father's workshops. These articles found a ready sale at one of the stores, together with several second-hand guns which I had purchased cheap and which sold well . . .

Alfred Ireson
reminiscences

The author was born in 1856 at Whittlesea, near Oundle, the son of a stone-mason whose work on churches and public buildings necessitated frequent moves and absences from home. With a wage of 5s. a day, this was not a poor family, and Alfred could appreciate and describe 'the romance of village life' and the pleasures of a country childhood from the standpoint of one who did not have to suffer the grinding poverty of a farm labourer's household. Although it was a close, loving and religious family, his parents were strict and authoritarian, determined that Alfred should follow his father's trade as a mason; before he was eighteen Alfred had made up his mind to leave home, to 'get free . . . to see and to find a fuller life'. He first went to Cambridge to see a girl he knew in domestic service there, then to London, Portsmouth and Bath, following in the tradition of 'the tramping artisan' who wanted to see the world and widen his work experience. He finally settled in London, continuing to work as a stone-mason and becoming a local Wesleyan preacher and strong supporter of total abstinence. His unpublished autobiography of approximately thirty-five thousand words was written in 1929, and was kindly supplied by his great-grand-daughter, Mrs Anne Hoskins.

My father's name was Alfred. His marriage with Hannah Spencer took place in Oundle in 1853. At this time there was a number of churches under repair. After their marriage they went to Thorney. My brother Charlie was born there.

Next they moved to Whittlesea. Here the only place they could find to live in was a large empty room in a public-house. I was born here on June 23rd, 1856. My first infant breath was drawn in the foul atmosphere of tobacco smoke and drink, no doubt half suffocated. My mother often told us a story of this time. The baby did nothing but cry. It must have been a real howl, and it so annoyed my father one night, that he lost his temper. Taking the crying kid and putting it into a sack, he swung it from the top of the stairs over the bannisters, declaring if my terrified mother interfered he would drop the sack and squalling brat to the bottom of the stairs. Needless to say, my memory is quite a blank on this episode.

Whittlesea was quite unknown to me, for in my early days my parents moved to Warmington. It was here that the first knowledge of my dear mother's love dawned on my childish mind. Among my early recollections of her was her sincere piety. Her children were a God-given trust. The one desire of her heart was to train the infant mind in all good things. Her joy at the close of each day was to take her little ones round her knee, and teach them the simple truths of the Bible, so far as she knew them. Her dear voice rings in my ears now, as I picture her singing and teaching us to sing:

> See Israel's gentle Shepherd stands,
> With all engaging charms.
> Hark! How He calls His tender lambs,
> And folds them in His arms.

How sweet and beautiful is the memory of such a mother! Her kindly thoughts and tender prayers were Heaven's best gift. Oh! that I had appreciated her to the full, and shown her the love I felt for her before her call home.

At this time we had in our home one little earthly treasure, precious to us all. The boys were rough, Annie was sweet and gentle, an exceptionally pretty child. Beautiful eyes, sparkling with love and fun. A little mouth with smiles like the opening of a summer rose. Little Annie had a peculiar lisp in her childish talk. This added to her attractiveness. Though her name was Annie, we always called her Kitt. How she loved to be dressed in smart clothes. In her sweet little way she would say: 'Isn't I smart?'

One day, while at play, she fell and broke her leg. How concerned we all were. With what interest we watched for the doctor who had been fetched from Oundle, to set the broken leg. How sorry we were for our only sister. Dear little Kitt was the angel of our home. A little sunbeam to father and mother. To her brothers a radiance of eternal brightness, a heavenly gift. Always kind, never selfish; her sweet life gave out only love.

Village life during this period was a time of trial and difficulty. The agricultural workers had long hours, the pay barely enough to keep body and soul together. The condition of the children in many cases was pitiable. Rough food and clothes; everything depended on the skill and character of the mother. Nothing ready-made could be purchased, not even a shirt. The struggle for respectability! There were no sewing machines. The tiny needle was the great instrument of industry in the homes. Children were taught early to make good use of it. Children had a Sunday suit, and always looked clean.

Historians have described these poverty-stricken days as the Hungry Sixties. The economic conditions were simply appalling. Commodities of daily life were scarce and dear. Very little sugar and tea came to the children's share. Yet these were the good old times!

Our mother had to adapt herself to the times. She was exceptionally good with her needle, even to the making of my father's clothes. She was a master of arts in pudding-making. Almost every day a good hot pudding provided a healthy meal for her hungry boys. She taught us all to sew and knit, and net. Mother had a hard time. A stonemason's pay was only 5s. per day. Father worked away from home, coming home for week-ends. Often he had to walk 15 miles. There was not even a bike in those days. Journeys had to done on Shank's pony. We lived in Warmington from the time I was two, till about eight years of age.

The village school

The school-master was an old man. One impression he made upon my mind was his free use of an ash stick. I remember while at school trying to write 1860 on my slate. It was a National School – the only one in the place. There was no compulsion to attend, and only the three R's were taught.

On Sundays we were sent to the Wesleyan S.S. Half the time was spent in learning to read and write. I well remember a little dress I wore when I was about four years old. It was blue with white buttons. When we were old enough we were taken to Chapel on Sunday evenings; and in summer, after the service, a walk into the Elton Park. One Sunday during the walk I picked up quite a long snake and ran to show it to my parents. This gave them a fright, thinking it would bite me.

Child life in the village is full of romance. The free open country provides fun and mischief for boys and girls alike. It was here where I learned to swim and fight. These things formed a great part of a boy's life. Youngsters found their fun in a variety of ways. Meetings of the fox-hunters, fires in farmyards and thatched cottages, and the passing through of the soldiers, provided a great time. When troops were moved, they were taken through the country on foot. A horse regiment with its band was enough to bring out all the people from their homes to the village green, which was a resting place. Recruiting was carried on there. The big lads would join the march to Peterborough, swear in, and made part of the British army . . .

When I was about seven years old, my brother Charles and myself were sent here. It was known as the Oundle British School. Quite a number of boys and girls walked the three or four miles every morning. What happy times we had during these walks. Dinner time during the summer was spent bathing in the river Nen. One day a little chap about my age was drowned. The news reached my grandparents that it was little Alf Ireson. How they rejoiced when little Alf turned up.

End of village life

These very happy days came to an end. For some years father had worked at Thrapston, coming home week-ends. Never shall I forget the night when he came home with the news that he had found a house in Thrapston, and that on the Monday morning the wagon would be coming to convey us to our new home. It was an exciting time. We all helped to carry the household goods into the road to be packed in the wagon. Space was left at the back for us all to sit. After a good-bye to everyone, and our little friends, we took our seats for a delightful twelve miles drive.

Arrival at Thrapston

Having left a three-roomed cottage, the first sight of the new house appeared to us a palace beautiful. Three steps up to the front door, on which was a knocker. The front room had a marble mantlepiece. The house was three storeys high. Talk about the Tower of Babel! To our childish minds this was a wonderful house . . .

School days in Thrapston

The school was the Church National School, with a master named Cole. As it was not compulsory to attend, playing truant was common. The stripes administered were soon forgotten. Education was not taken seriously. You could attend when you liked, and go to work when you liked. Child labour was encouraged. Orchards, with their ripe fruit, tempted the boys. I was caught at this more than once, and had to suffer accordingly. Birds' nesting was another temptation to the boys.

One morning, instead of going to school, three of us went off birds' nesting. The master sent a boy to inquire why we were not at school. Mother's reply was: 'They left home this morning in time for school.' We knew we would have the usual stripes on attending in the afternoon. We were all three called out. 'Where were you this morning?' 'Birds' nesting, sir,' we answered. 'I'll give you birds' nesting. Hold out your hand,' the master said.

The two others received their stripes like lambs. When my turn came, I objected, which brought me several stripes across the back. As this was not successful, the master lost his temper. He went into his house, and returned with a stick. Still finding me obstinate, he gave me the punishment of my life. When tea time came, my mother wanted to know what the matter was, for I could not sit down. She quickly examined my body, and found it black and blue with bruises. Without having tea, she took me to the master to show him the result of the punishment. My dear mother was extremely cross. It was only with difficulty she refrained from dealing with the master.

When my father came home and heard the trouble, and saw the bruises, he went off to the parson, taking me with him, in order to show him my bruised body. The parson was sorry and sent me to the doctor. Proceedings in the Police Court appeared likely. Some compensation and an apology from the school- master settled the trouble.

My old tin whistle

I must have been about ten years of age, when Mr C. Freeman started what was to be the town's Drum and Fife Band. I put in an appearance. 'Well, Alf, what do you want?' 'I should like to join the band.' 'Can you play a fife?' 'No,' I said. 'Then clear out. You are no good here.'

With a sad heart I left the room. To be able to play in a band was a great idea to me. Not to be daunted by this refusal, I was determined to make an effort to learn. Having a few coppers – profit from my net making – I purchased a sixpenny tutor and a penny tin whistle. With these I learnt the notes and fingering, without any other help but the book. I set out to master the whistle. To this I gave every moment I could spare. At the end of about a month, I made my second appearance on a practice night. 'What do you want, Alf?' Mr Freeman said. 'I can play now, Sir,' I said. 'Play what?' Mr Freeman asked. 'Play this,' I said, taking from my pocket my tin whistle. 'Let me hear you,' he ordered. At once, I rattled off the old tune of 'The girl I left behind me,' which gave Mr Freeman some surprise. After hearing my story, he said: 'You'll do. Come along.' When I received my fife, there was no boy in the town prouder than Alf.

Rat-catching

The old rat-catcher of the town took a fancy to me. His name was Guest. He had some half-a-dozen little dogs, also ferrets. His work was to catch moles, rats, and rabbits. To have a day with this aged man was my boyish delight. In those days I loved to kill. In fact, everything that came my way had to die. This, I think, was the spirit of the times. All boys delighted in it. It was a hard cruel age. Children are taught now to feed and protect all God's creatures.

Ambition to work

My first job was on a farm. My wages 1s. 6d. per week. My work was to scare crows from the newly growing corn. A pair of clappers were provided. When the crows came I had to send them off on to other fields to feed. I had to be up with the crows, and did not go home until the last had gone to bed – 14 or 15 hours a day. Then my wages were advanced to 2s.6d. per week, but for the additional 1s. about a dozen pigs were put under my care.

A story of the wayside

Our dear mother taught us all to net. This became a financial advantage. I spent my time in making potato nets. Potatoes were then boiled in nets, which I sold for 2d. each. Once a lady who passed by said: 'What are you doing, my boy?' 'Making potato nets,' I said. 'What do you do with them?' 'I sell them for 2d. each.' 'You are a very ingenious lad,' and she gave me 6d., telling me I was a good boy.

I could make two or three of these nets in a day. This provided Alf with pocket money, his keenest interest. I think for a lad my energy for work was above the normal. There was not an employer in the town who did not give me a trial. Very few kept me long . . .

Return to Warmington

The reason why I left work at the furnaces was because my father having charge of building new schools at Warmington decided that I should go with him and learn the stone-mason's trade. Returning to this village at the age of fifteen, I found my old companions, like myself, grown older and bigger. My first little sweetheart was a nice girl named Sarah Baxter. She had a brother about my own age with one eye. The other I poked out with a stick when we were youngsters. I soon discovered that another youth called Ginger was sweet on Sarah. At our first meeting he told me what he would do if I continued to press my company on her. It ended in a stiff fight. He punished me well, so that I became afraid of him. We often met, but there was no particular friendliness between us. A time came when the trouble had to have a final settlement.

It was Warmington's Feast Day. The whole village was out to enjoy the annual event. The dancing booths at the various public-houses were in great demand. The Red Lion's was considered the best. Here Sarah and I met and would have danced but Ginger objected to this. After many words, and the usual pushing of each other, one of us hit out. At once a fight was arranged. The dancing ceased. All eyes were now turned towards the combatants. With coat off for the contest, I fought for all I was worth. More by accident than judgement, I got one in on Ginger's nose. Blood was drawn, and victory came to me. So did Sarah. We danced and loved in peace ever after . . .

At Barnwell I had my first experience as a journeyman mason, with men of the trade. My wages were 18s. per week. I did the work, my father drew the money. He usually handed me 6d. to keep in my pocket, not to spend. My dear mother never failed to come to my assistance. With my clean clothes she continued to put what money she could spare in the toe of my clean socks . . .

Sad memories of the thatched cottage

We had two pretty little baby sisters; one, the eldest, was called Nellie. She was about two and a half years old. She had sweet, beautiful blue eyes and golden hair. Her childish prattle made her very dear to all. After a lovely summer's day of play, she was put to bed about 8 o'clock, to all appearances quite well and happy. Mother and dad came up a little later, as their custom was, to look at us before retiring themselves. They found dear little Nellie quite dead. This terrible shock caused quite a commotion in our home. Mother and dad were broken-hearted. In the morning we were told that Nellie was dead. Nellie dead? We could not understand it. We had all played together until bed-time. For the first time we looked upon death. The sweet angel face, now white and cold, was to us a profound mystery. Our little Nellie had gone to be an Angel. How we all cried. Our hearts were sadly broken. In a few days' time the funeral took place. It was an impressive sight . . .

A few months later, and once more a simple procession was seen going down the same street, to the same spot in the churchyard. Our little baby sister Caroline became suddenly ill, and died. She was 18 months old . . .

Faith Dorothy Osgerby
my memoirs

Faith Osgerby was born in 1890 at Beverley, East Yorkshire, the third of a family of seven children. Her father was a stonemason who also kept a few cows for a milk-round, and gradually moved into cattle-dealing. Faith gives an unusually frank account of her childhood fears and punishments; although her mother was a conscientious housewife and able cook she seems to have had little love for her children and an unhappy relationship with her husband. Despite frequent punishments, Faith loved her school work and found her real identity there. At thirteen, when most girls left to go into domestic service, she was determined to stay on at school, first as a probationer (at £4 a year), then as a pupil-teacher; she ultimately became a fully certificated teacher after part-time attendance at a training college in Hull and a correspondence course. She describes herself as having 'longings and ambitions far above my station', and schoolteaching offered her a route to social mobility, as it did for thousands of other girls of her class. Her unpublished autobiography, of approximately fifty thousand words, was written when she was seventy: it was kindly lent by her granddaughter, Mrs P. Jackson. Faith Osgerby died in 1976.

I have now passed my seventieth birthday, being born in 1890, and I think I will call this 'My Memoirs' as my 'Life Story' would I fear not be pleasant reading all the time. Some of it too would be distressing to me to write. Maybe I should call it the story of my childhood. My life has certainly not been a 'bed of roses', neither could it be called a success story. In fact quite the opposite. I must have been born with longings and ambitions far above my station, and so many of them – in fact most of them – have never been realized. We are all, I suppose, victims of circumstances, and our lives are of necessity bound up with and dependent on others, very much so, and we find it impossible to break away and follow our own inclinations. Consequently I confess I have never achieved very much, but my belief has always been that if we live our lives so that someone is going to miss us, either for the good we have tried to do or help we have tried to give, then our lives are never in vain, and if I thought that might happen to me, I should be happy indeed.

People tell me I have a good memory, so I shall try to remember episodes in my young life which seemed to impress me at the time, and write them down as I remember them . . .

If I am to write my story I shall have to describe my family – each member of it – as they play a very large part in it. I was the third child in a family of seven, and I can just remember 'the house where I was born'. I remember my elder sister Ella who was 5 years older than I, and my brother Albert who was 3 years older. We had a garden with currant bushes where I remember losing a button hook and getting a smacking. There was a wall at the bottom of the garden and over the other side was the Westwood where I could see cows. I dropped my sister's toy mangle over the wall, and again was punished. I remember an old couple next door, Mr & Mrs Marshall, where I once visited and played with a box of buttons which I dropped on the floor and ran home terrified.

My elder sister was a victim of polio and she could only creep around, having lost the use of both legs. Later she had a wheel chair.

But most of all I remember C O W S : my father kept a few cows in a shed there. I must say a few words here about my father. Looking back, I really feel that my father had married beneath him. His family seemed to be slightly 'better class'. My mother was an illegitimate child, and had been brought up by her grand-mother in poor circumstances. My grandmother on my father's side was a very ladylike person and I was rather in awe of her. She made me sit on a hassock and read the Bible to her when she was ill in bed, and she nearly always was . . .

I think I respected and admired my father very much in spite of his narrow ideas. He certainly was strict with us but I can't remember ever seeing him inflict any physical punishment on us. That was always done by my mother, and truly she was very capable at the job . . .

Talking of dress reminds me how differently children were dressed. The dresses were longer than grown-ups wear today. If we showed our knees we were in trouble. We always wore white pinafores and our dresses (made by Granny) always had a pocket at the side. We wore horrors called 'open drawers'. They would be judged quite indecent today. The two legs were made quite separately and only joined at the top with a topband which we fastened round the waist with a button and buttonhole. Thus, little girls' bottoms were so very accessible, and mine was smacked so very often sometimes for such small faults, such as a sulky look when asked to perform some task, or for answering back (we didn't dare do this often) or maybe a childish argument (frequent in a family of 7) when my mother would step in and punish *both* – to make sure she got the right one, she said. And if any of us cried for some reason she was not aware of we got a smacked bottom so that she *would* know what we were crying for. Many times I have gone to school with her finger marks on my poor little seat, and even sometimes on my cheek – and girls would ask what I had done to my face. I used to make up a story (as I went to school trying to hide my tears) about having a fall or running into a door, etc. I must have been a terrible little liar sometimes.

When I was 3 years old we moved into Eastgate, just before my brother George was born. Babies were not welcomed in our family. I have heard my mother say on more than one occasion in her middle age that if she had to live her life again and knew as much as she did then she wouldn't have had one of us. She told me she even took gunpowder to get rid of *me*, mixing it to a paste in a soapdish on her washstand every night. I hope she didn't hold it against me that I refused to budge. When I was born the doctor called me a very strong healthy child, so much so that he used *me* to vaccinate 6 other children from. This seems horrifying nowadays but it was the usual thing then, to take serum from one child to another. Mother even knew the names of some of the 6, who went to school with me.

Well, as I have said none of us had an enthusiastic welcome. I can never remember in all my life being cuddled or kissed or 'loved' as we love our babies today. I think all this gave me an inferiority complex which has lasted all my life. Even today I feel most unwilling to enter a room full of people. I always feel I have no right to be there, and if everyone turns to look at me I wish I could drop through the floor. I always feel even now that I must give place to others. For instance, we were never allowed to sit in either of the two armchairs with cushions which were on each side of the fireplace. One was for Dad and the other for my mother. Of course we *did* sit in them if they were empty, but if Dad or mother came we jumped out very quickly and sat on a hard wooden chair. Well, this must have got into my bones, because *even now* if anyone walks in I immediately vacate my easy chair. I just can't help it. I'm *forced* to do it. Parents were very much above us – people to be obeyed on the instant with no ifs or buts.

All my life has been ruled by fear I think. It must have been the first emotion I ever felt, fear of swift punishment. I seem to be painting an awful picture of my mother. I don't really mean to do that because I do realize she must have had a great deal to put up with all the time. Seven children to clothe and feed and little enough money to do it. Also my elder sister being an invalid from infancy must have been a very great trouble to her. Doctors had to be paid for their services, and I am quite sure my sister had everything done for her that could be done in those days. I remember two doctors coming to the house to operate on her legs and feet. It seems strange to think it had to be done at home. How surgery has progressed since then! My sister had to have no food for 24 hours before the operation but it did no good whatever. Also I remember my mother taking her into Hull every week to be (as she said) 'galvanized', which I imagine was some kind of electric treatment. However, nothing ever did any good, and she lived in a wheel chair for the rest of her life. She was very useful to my mother in the house. She could push her chair around all over the house. She went to a private school for a little while. I believe the fees were 1s. a week. Susannah [my grandmother] took her there each day and she learned to read and also to write a little with her left hand. When the school closed down after about a year my sister's education was finished. She did learn to play the piano and also she had a very good voice, so could amuse herself (and us) quite well. We often had sing-songs.

Well, I believe life must have been pretty tough for my mother, and I excuse her harshness to me although I used to say to myself that if I ever got married and had children, I would love them dearly, and do everything I could to give them a happy childhood.

Nevertheless my mother's hand was very heavy indeed. The most terrible punishment I remember she inflicted on my eldest brother. I never had any great affection for him. He was always a bully and a boor. I remember he hated school, and whenever he could he used to play truant with 2 or 3 other boys. One summer day the gang went into Swinemoor, a large pasture, where there was a big stream. They took off their clothes and had a lovely time. My brother came home with only one stocking!!! These stockings, long black ones, had been hand-knitted by my mother. She also had a fractious baby at the time and used to rock the cradle (a wooden monstrosity on rockers) with her foot. I remember she had a loop of string attached to the rocker so she could rock with her foot while she knitted. Well, when my brother came home without a stocking she saw red. She was in a blazing fury. She made him strip all his clothes off and took him into the cowshed to beat him unmercifully. Ella and I wept and wept . . .

My eldest brother left school at the age of 12. He never did any good there anyhow. He hated lessons. Children in those days were allowed to leave if they passed what was then called a Labour Examination and were given a 'Labour Certificate'. I remember each year a notice would be pinned on the notice board at school about this. I never knew a single case of a child failing this examination. The questions were so easy, fitted to a child of about 9 or 10 years of age, and of course children who applied were almost always the duffers who could never learn anything anyhow, and teachers were glad to be rid of them in any way at all . . .

[My father] always seemed to have an order to make a gravestone every summer, and I loved to see him chipping away at that rough lump of stone until he made it all beautifully smooth. Best of all I liked to watch him do the lettering in Old English Letters. He was so clever at it. When we went with him into country villages selling calves, he would sometimes point to the village church and say which little piece of it he had done or repaired. I can see a bit of his work in Beverley yet. It is the date stone over the door of Minster Moorgate Infants' School.

He was the sort of man who would have a go at anything in the way of repairs or craftsmanship and I should like to think I was like him in a feminine way. Nevertheless there is one taste of his I certainly *haven't* inherited. He certainly liked his drink. Beer was cheap in those days – 2½d. a pint. On cold days when he was delivering he would call at a pub, ask for a glass of rum and fill it up with new milk out of his can to warm him up. Dad in later years bought beer by the barrel from the brewers. It used to cost about 8d. a gallon, sometimes even less, and he would get an 18 gallon cask. In haytime and harvest time it was given as 'lowance' to the men. It was cheaper than tea and certainly less trouble. Any chance caller was always offered a glass of beer.

When we lived in Eastgate he used to frequent the George and Dragon which was only a few yards away from us, and sometimes at midday he didn't arrive for his dinner on time. My mother didn't like this, and I was sent to tell him his dinner was ready. He used to get very cross with me, and told me very firmly never to do it again. Next time I had to do this I protested to my mother and told her he had forbidden me to do it, but as I have said before my mother's word was law and worse still her hand was heavy too, and I had never felt my father's hand at all. So off I had to go, shaking a bit at the knees. When he saw me he was very angry and when I explained that my mother made me come he ordered me 'Repeat the fifth Commandment.' Well, I did know my catechism, word perfect, so I stood there in the pub passage and began 'Honour thy father and thy mother' and broke off and said 'But Dad, how can I honour you both?' He said calmly 'Your father comes *first*, and always remember that.' I am sure I never forgot it . . .

Well, my Dad was a clever man, and he could have done even better if circumstances had been different for him. None of my brothers were like him, except perhaps the third boy Fred, but he was killed in 1918 just before he was 21. My parents were not well matched. They used to have terrible rows sometimes which really distressed me and sometimes it lasted for days and we were all unhappy. I remember one occasion, I must have been about 8 years old, when I woke up in the night to hear my mother crying. I crept out of bed and saw her standing by her mother's bed, and I gathered from what she said that my Dad had gone out to kill himself. Just imagine what it did to *me*. She didn't see me, and I stood and listened. Evidently they had been having a violent row and he had gone out and threatened never to come back. She was sure he had gone because the big gate was unlocked. Anyhow next day there he was doing his work as usual, and he had evidently unlocked the gate to give her a fright and then gone and slept in the hay loft. Well, that is only one episode of many, but I feel that it is terribly, terribly wrong for parents to have quarrels in the presence of their children. It has a dreadful effect on children. Of course I realize I had no right to listen, but I really did envy the happy homes of other people. There were never many consecutive days of peace in our house . . .

As I have said before my life was really ruled by FEAR. Fear of punishments and fear of being found out if I had been naughty, and I know I often *was* naughty. Punishments were very swift and very severe sometimes, often for such trivial faults too which would hardly be noticed today. There was also fear of being bullied by big boys at the Infants' School. This of course ceased when I was old enough to go to the big girls' school where I seemed able to hold my own.

I think I was 3 years old when I first went to school, because that was when we moved to Eastgate and my mother had her fourth baby, my brother George [born] 1893, and she wanted me out of the way . . .

I remember very vividly that school and also the headmistress, a short plump grey-haired woman called Mrs Buttery. She always carried a cane in her hand all the time. Her hair was drawn tightly back and plaited, the plait being wound round and round into a bun at the back of her head. Her very long skirt just showed her feet, and her feet always fascinated me. She wore square-toed buttoned boots and there were bulges on. I had never seen feet with bulges on, and I realize now the poor woman must have had bunions. We were all afraid of her. Her second in command was a similarly built woman called Mrs Watson. I always remember her very large bosom and the edging of white lace round her neck. There were also two or three young pupil-teachers whom we called Teacher Maud, Teacher Edie, etc. We sat on 'galleries', row above row, so that it was easy for the teacher to see us *all* at *all* times. I can hear Mrs Buttery even now shouting in her loud voice 'Faith Campey, come down here!' and I knew I was in for a swish of that cane. I suppose I had been whispering to my neighbour which was a grievous sin. I remember one very heavy swish I had from her was one day when we were marching round the room in twos and I had dared to join hands with my neighbour and walk along with arms swinging. How different school life is today and what a blessing! . . .

Well, Sundays were hateful days. My mother sent us to the Primitive Methodist Sunday School (much to the annoyance of Aunt Lizzie. She said all the family had always been Church). My mother sent us there because school began earlier and we had longer sessions and she wanted rid of us for as long as possible. What I learned there for my good I shall never know. The children behaved very badly (I suppose I did too). Teachers were a queer, mixed crowd who knew very little about what they were supposed to teach. They gave us to understand that we were all in danger of hell fire if we were not good. I knew there was no hope whatever for me. Children were spiteful and jealous. Girls flaunted their new clothes, poking fun at others not so fortunate. Altogether a horrid lot. Teachers had favourites. I hated Sunday School. I didn't grow very fast and my Sunday clothes fitted me for 3 or 4 years. How I hated that red coat and that beastly horrible green felt hat I could have stamped on! I couldn't compete with most of them. We sang (or yelled at the top of our voices) 'Rescue the Perishing' or 'Hold the Fort' (boys used to sing very rude words to that one) and 'Shall we gather at the River?' We nearly raised the roof.

Every morning after Sunday School we were marched into Chapel, and a more boring service I can never imagine. Most of us didn't understand a word. The preacher would compose prayers as he went along, being carried away by his emotions as were some of the congregation. At first it used to frighten me. During these impromptu prayers there would be dead silence in the congregation, and all at once someone would loudly interrupt with 'Pra–a–a–ise the Lord' or 'A–a–a–a–men' or 'Halleluia'. It really did scare me at first but I gradually got used to it and even waited for it, wondering who would be the next. The hymns were always sung with great gusto, the congregation giving it all they had got. I got dreadfully bored during the service. I could see the clock from my seat. I thought if I count 60 slowly, that's one minute gone, and I amused myself by

doing this until at last it was time to go. Of course sometimes there were bright
spots – a baby to be christened or a visit from Filey Fishermen who came in their
jerseys as though they had just left their boats. They could be quite interesting
too if they didn't pray too long and too loudly. Once a year there was a Camp
Meeting in the open air on the Westwood. My mother didn't let us go because
we should have been late home for dinner, so we had a holiday that day. I used to
pray for a fine day, because if it was wet the meeting was cancelled.

Most of all I hated the time when an Evangelist came, because then I knew I
should have to be 'saved' again. I shall never believe that it was right to teach little
children religion in this frightening way. It made me unhappy for several days.

All those who wanted to be saved had to go forward near the pulpit and kneel
on a cushion in front of everyone else. We went in groups. Some children
absolutely refused to go and would have made a scene. If only I had dared!! I
remember on one occasion I made up my mind I *wouldn't* go, but unfortunately I
happened to be sitting at the end of a row and the teacher (I remember her name
was Miss Sissons) pushed me out into the gangway, so I was lost again. I
remember we used to have to sing:

> I'm H-A-P-P-Y
> I'm H-A-P-P-Y
> I know I am. I'm sure I am.
> I'm H-A-P-P-Y
>
> Because I'm S-A-V-E-D, etc.
> Through F-A-I-T-H, etc.

(Oh! Dear! That was my name and all the other children stared at me and giggled.)
And so on – with various 5 letter words G-L-O-R-Y, etc.

Well, after I had gone through this ordeal and had long prayers said over me, I
felt dreadful. Now I really must never be naughty again. How could I live up to it?
What if I ever forgot? If I did I knew I should go to Hell. My mother and father
were sinners. My Dad even said swear words. He said 'Blast' and 'Devil' and
'Damn' and he liked drinking beer sometimes. I had heard my mother say
someone was a 'Bitch'. It was awful to think we had all to go to hell fire. Well,
after a few days this awful burden seemed to grow lighter and I felt better again.
Then I realized I was being punished because I had been naughty again. I was
indeed a lost soul. My heart was black! There was no hope for me. Oh! Well!
What's the use? If I am to go to hell, I might as well give up trying . . .

Jack Lanigan
incidents in the life of a citizen

Jack Lanigan's account is one of a good many which describe a childhood of poverty in the industrial north of England, though his is more moving than most. He was born in Salford in 1890, the son of a skilled engraver who died at the early age of thirty-seven; he, his elder brother Matthew and their mother then had a bitter struggle to survive at a time when there was no social insurance. Having gained the Labour Certificate at ten, Jack left school to become an errand boy like his brother, and this event he clearly regarded as the end of his childhood: 'I wanted to tell the world I was now a man, working and helping my mother.' For a time, family circumstances improved, but his mother, too, died shortly afterwards at the age of forty-eight and the boys went to live with a married step-sister. Adolescence was a happier period for Jack, now working as a grocer's assistant and able to pursue his hobbies of boxing and athletics at a Lads' Club in Collyhurst, and singing in a concert-party in the style of G. H. Elliott. After working as a labourer for the Health Department of Manchester Corporation, he qualified as a sanitary inspector in 1914 and had a long and happy life, dying in 1976 at the age of eighty-six. His unpublished autobiography, of approximately forty-three thousand words, was lent by his daughter, Mrs Lillian E. Milner.

'Ave yer any bread left, master?'

That was the theme song of hundreds of youngsters of whom my brother Matt and I could be counted. We had our pitches for begging. I along with two other hungry kids, stood outside the gates of Mather & Platt, Ltd, then situated off Bury Street, Salford, waiting for the gates to open at 6 p.m. When they did, the workers would file out into the street carrying their wicker lunch baskets and when they heard our voices, 'Ave yer any bread left master?' they would hand anything they had left out to us. When I had got sufficient for my mother and brother, I made tracks for home and these left-overs would be shared with a cup of tea; if no tea then with a cup of water. We drank more water than tea even if the latter was only one shilling a pound.

The days of 1890–1910 were tough, they were days that were not easily cast aside. One cannot go to bed hungry and get up in the morning with that same feeling without leaving a scar on the memory . . .

Besides the heartbreaking cry, 'Ave yer any bread left master?' there was another common cry at all the 'Fish and Chip' shops, 'Can you spare any scrapings, Sir?' Believe me this was no joke. The kids, myself included, travelled from shop to shop to ensure we had collected sufficient for the family; we became regular customers as one would say. These scrapings with some bread made a meal.

The facts of the story, if ever printed, are not the story of a dream, but of cold, stark staring truths; even Dickens' characters did not come into contact with the realisms of everyday life of the thousands who resided in Manchester and Salford and if those two cities were taken as a specimen, then the whole of the country was in a sorry shape.

The streets were cobbled, some with large paving stones, others with a smaller granite sort. They were dirty, dismal, unkempt. The majority of the dwelling-houses were more like hovels, small, dark and overshadowed, and in thousands of them the sun never entered; lighting of streets was by gas lamps. The sanitary conditions were appalling. Stinking privy middens and pail closets were the fashion. There would be one midden to every two, three or four houses, the larger the family, well you can guess the rest. These horrifying conveniences were the rendezvous for flies and bluebottles.

We lived at No. 1 Thomas Street, off Brewery Street, Salford (since demolished), two up and one down, no back yard, because it was back-to-back with a large six-seated privy midden – it was known as a communal midden. The back bedroom, where Matt and I slept, was immediately over this privy midden, the bedroom floor also acted as ceiling of this obnoxious structure. The smell in our bedroom was vile, we had to keep the bedroom window open summer and winter. There was very little sleep at weekends on account of the drunks and free-for-all scraps. I cannot remember having any bedding on our bed. The coverings to cover our little bodies where old coats and sacks, the mattress was a hard straw one, which was kept in position by long iron laths. If ever I was invited to the house of a playmate, their beds were similar. The scene was so common we kids never gave it another thought. That was our bed, so we laid on it.

However I reached my present age is a miracle. The thoughts of those days still make a shiver run down my spine, and a handkerchief must be handy to wipe away the tears. My pen cannot describe the heartbreaks, the poverty and suffering.

Father, before he died, was an engraver at Locketts Ltd, Strangeways. I think he was one of the best engravers. He engraved the Lord's Prayer on one side of a sixpence, but could he drink beer.

He must have his pint every morning before going to work, so my brother and I took it in turn to bring that beer. Opening time was 6 a.m. and we had to be on time. There were no restrictions in those days against young children being served with beer. I can see so vividly the morning which was the last for us kids to go that familiar errand. Mother must have been given the power to say, 'Those children are not going for any beer this morning.' His answer to such a challenge was to take a swipe with one hand to everything on the mantlepiece. Clock, vases, one or two ornaments, crashed to the floor. What a clatter. Then father crashed also to the floor, he had fainted. Matt, although so early in the morning, ran for a doctor, and in a very short time he was placed on a stretcher, into a horse-drawn ambulance and taken to Hope Hospital, Eccles.

After a few days he pulled round sufficiently to have a few words with mother, but his brain became affected and poor father died thinking he was Billy Gladstone. Mother told us after visiting one day, he said to her, 'Don't look round now but that silly bugger over there thinks he is Billy Gladstone, he doesn't know I'm Billy.' What a tragedy in more senses than one.

Mother having no money, father was laid to rest at Mode Wheel Cemetery, Weaste, Salford, in what was known in those days as a Public Subscription Grave, better known as a pauper's grave. Brother and I did have a new suit for father's funeral (purchased on tick), blue serge, short trousers, and a stiff peak cap.

The Sunday following the funeral, feeling like King of the Kids, we took our usual Sunday afternoon stroll, a favourite spot on the banks of the River Irwell, Irwell Street, Salford, where a portion of the river bank had fallen into the river. When one of the pleasure steamers passed this spot the water was carried with the steamer and exposed the boulder stones. We kids ran on to the stones as far as we dare and then ran like hell back to the bank, or else we would get wet. During that afternoon one poor kid was not sharp enough and fell into the on-rushing water. My brother with his brand new suit on, dived into the river and saved that boy from drowning. Did he get a medal? He got the biggest tanning from mother for spoiling his suit. We never saw those suits again. Mother washed and pressed that suit, and into the pawnshop they both went.

We became very hungry kids after father died. I was seven years old. After a while Matt became a lather boy and could no longer go out begging for bread. He worked from 5 p.m. until 9 p.m. Monday to Friday, 8 a.m. until 11 p.m. Saturday, 8 a.m. until 12 noon Sunday, for one shilling per week.

Mother did not enjoy good health, but she tried to do washing for others, who could afford to pay her sixpence for their weekly washing. In those days it was hard work, no boilers, no hot water, no detergents, everything had to be boiled in a large pan on the open fire.

Everywhere you visited you would find the kettle on the hob of a large old-fashioned firegrate. I do not remember seeing a gas fire or stove in my younger days.

Coal was sixpence a hundredweight and you brought your coal from a coal yard, the owners providing two-wheel coal carts. Mother would send me for a half hundredweight of coal for threepence, you then borrowed the wagon (without your leave), to go to the Corporation Gas Works for a half hundredweight of coke.

If mother could work hard enough for the rent, three shillings and sixpence a week, I begged the bread and knocked on neighbours' doors enquiring if they wanted any errands. If they should need a loaf of bread I would go to the baker and ask for a two pound loaf. On weighing it was always short in weight; so as to make it weigh two pounds, a slice was cut from a loaf to balance, and this was known as make-weight. That make-weight was my reward. I believe that is how the term make-weight came about. If you did not ask for a two pound loaf, you got no make-weight.

To obtain food in winter was grim. We kids every school day at lunch time paid a visit to the Police Station, Berley Square, Salford, for a bowl of soup and a chunk of bread, which was issued free. Some days mother would want soup. I would go to the nearest pork shop where they sold soup, twopence for a jugful. We lived on soup and other people's left-overs . . .

Matt and I never went to Sunday School because we never had any decent clothes to go in. You were considered posh if you could attend Sunday School, but we went to Gravel Lane Ragged School on a Sunday evening. You never saw such a bunch of scruffy kids in all your life. If we had been bunched together you could not have made a suit from the lot.

Shoes on your feet were the last thing you could expect. It was so common to see boys and girls playing in the street without shoes and stockings. Many were the days during winter we went to school with sacking round our feet.

I well remember the winter of 1897 (I think). There were thirteen weeks of frost. The death rate seemed incalculable, fires burning night and day in the cemeteries so that grave diggers could get along digging graves. I never saw so many kids with sacking round their feet. Practically all outdoor work ceased.

The adult population (I would estimate 90%) wore clogs, and you could hear them half a mile away. The people employed in the cotton mills, building industry, railway workers, municipal employees such as dustmen, highways and gas departments, wore clogs. Nowadays we are concerned with noise. Can you imagine nearly all the people walking up and down Market Street, Piccadilly, Oldham Street, wearing clogs, all the horse-drawn vehicles with their wheels of steel or cast iron rims, rumbling along the granite paved streets? You could not have an ordinary conversation without shouting. Oh! those good old days? And we kids even found time to be patriotic, why and what for God alone knows.

When the Boer War broke out in 1899 I was getting a big boy, in standard six and ten years old. Our school was a Church school and went under the name 'National School'. The Church was St Philips, and the vicar dare put a Boer Flag out of one of his windows at the vicarage. We kids at the school were told of this, so we armed ourselves with stones of all shapes and sizes, marched to the vicarage, broke nearly every pane of glass, marched back to the school, but marvel of marvels, we never heard a word about the incident, not even from the headmaster, and if ever there was a disciplinarian it was the man with a red beard, the teacher who always displayed his cane on his desk in the centre of the classroom. If ever fear was in us kids it was when we saw that cane. Once bitten, twice shy . . .

I must admit I did not know of any children in my district who could not read or write, do arithmetic and know something about history and geography . . .

Public houses in those days were commonly known as beerhouses; each beerhouse, in summer, had their annual picnic for their customers – half a day somewhere in the country. They could not go very far, their transport was a coach and two horses. Those were great days; it meant getting in some practice doing the cart wheel. The men and women would throw coppers for which we scrambled. When we became exhausted we shouted cheerio to the coach and walked back home, God knows how many miles, but not before we shared our loot. This would be taken home to our mothers, because we knew the money would be spent to the best advantage.

I became a lather boy at a barber's shop in Bury Street, Salford, closely situated to Mather & Platts Engineering Works and quite a few customers recognized me as one of the kids who used to say, 'Ave yer got any bread left, master?' They gave me their left-overs, so as well as earning one shilling a week and perhaps a few pence in tips, there was something to eat for mother and my brother Matt . . .

I was now (1900) turned ten years of age and under the then Education Act, a child ten years and over could sit for a School Leaving Examination, if that child had no father. The summer holidays had commenced and I sat for the Examination. Shall I ever forget visiting the Education Offices in Chapel Street, Salford, to enquire the result, and to my sheer delight I had passed. If I ever saw delight in anyone's face, it was my mother's, because it meant so much to her from the economic viewpoint.

That same afternoon I went accompanied by mother to a very well known second-hand clothes shop in Salford, Hertzog by name. I was fitted out with coat, trousers, shirt, stockings and shoes, for the sum of four shillings and sixpence, which was a lot of money in those days.

I completed my week at the barber's shop, and the boss was a very understanding man, he even went to the trouble of providing a box for customers to drop a coin in, also telling them I was leaving. By Sunday closing time, 12 noon, there were two shillings and sixpence in that box. The boss handed those coins to me and wished me all the best. This was the golden handshake if you like, it seemed even better, it was as though I had a share in a Klondyke gold mine.

Why the fuss of some second-hand toggs? Well you see, the following Monday morning my mother accompanied me 'looking for work', and we were not long in finding it. Two shops in Victoria Street, Manchester, next door to one another, were advertising for errand boys, the first John Williams and Sons (grocers), the second John Allen & Co. (provision merchants). The former was advertising at six shillings per week, the latter five shillings per week. Needless to say we applied for the six shillings and I was successful and commenced the next day . . .

I now wanted to tell the world I was now a man, working and helping my mother. She was receiving my brother's wages, now ten shillings a week, and my six shillings. After paying the rent, she had no need to go out washing every day, only when she felt like it. How happy she seemed to be. I had not seen her smile for years. If Matt or myself received any tips they went to her; she could spend the money much better than we, but we received our reward for when we returned home each day there would be some kind of food and soup and now and again a little meat . . .

Alice Foley
a Bolton childhood

The industrial north is rich in working-class autobiography, partly because the harsh environment had an exciting, dramatic quality, and partly because it helped to produce many men and women who overcame their disadvantages to make successful and fulfilling lives. Few can have had a more inauspicious start than Alice Foley, who was born, unexpectedly, after a 'moonlight flit' from Dukinfield to Bolton, Lancashire, the child of an illiterate mother and an intelligent but aimless Irish father. She provides an extremely perceptive account of her home, her own development and her relation with her parents. Educated only at the local Catholic elementary school, Alice's real education came from her intelligent elder sister, Cissy, who was an official in the textile trade union, a suffragette and a member of the Labour Church. Leaving school at thirteen, she became a 'little tenter' in a cotton mill, and although having to rise at 5 a.m. continued her education through evening classes and the cultural opportunities which Manchester offered. She became a trade unionist, a social-ist, and, after the passing of the National Insurance Act in 1911, a 'sick visitor' for the Weavers' Association. For the next half-century she worked as a trade union official, rising to become President of the Bolton United Trades Council in 1956–7, a Justice of the Peace, and a leading figure in the Workers' Educational Association. Her autobiography, of which this extract is the first chapter, was published by Manchester University Extra-Mural Department and the North-Western District of the W.E.A. in 1973. I would like to thank Mr & Mrs H. Bellis; the Bolton and Manchester branches of the Workers' Educational Association; the Bank Street Chapel Trust, Bolton; and the Manchester Area Health Authority who represent the Charities and Residuary Legatees of the late Miss Alice Foley and Miss G. Bellis.

I was born on a scurvy, inhospitable day, in late November, 1891, a premature victim of nature and the hazards of a 'moonlight flit'. Or so it was told to me many years later by my eldest sister. It seems that the family I was destined shortly to join, consisting of father, mother, three boys and two girls, had recently uprooted themselves from their native town due to poverty and chronic un-employment, and had followed the bread-winner to Dukinfield where he had found a job in a factory. But, as the story was told to me, this open-mouthed braggart of an Irishman had celebrated too soon, or too boisterously, and was promptly chucked out by his boss. This stroke of bad luck left the family in dire distress, poor relief being denied them and cautious shop-keepers reluctant to extend credit to strangers. The mother's plea was to get back to the home town,

Bolton, where they might find temporary aid from friends or neighbours, so on a dark evening the beds and few sticks of furniture were piled on to a cart; father and the three boys, perched precariously on upturned chairs covered with sackings, jolted off on the midnight flight from Dukinfield, leaving the rent and paltry debts unpaid.

Mother and the two girls, the younger one aged two and the elder twelve, caught a late train only to find that its final destination was Manchester. The forlorn little trio somehow managed to trudge through the bitter night, mother and the older girl carrying the younger child in turns, eventually reaching Bolton in a state of utter exhaustion. I was to learn years later that mother collapsed on a neighbour's sofa and, in no time at all, another unwanted addition to an already harassed household yelled its way into existence.

As the new, puny arrival was not expected to live, it was wrapped in a shawl and carried down to St Patrick's, the local Catholic Church, for baptism. The priest, Canon Burke, was celebrating Benediction at the time, but at close of service he came down the altar-steps to speak to the small girl near the communion-rail holding a tiny bundle in her arms. On hearing the story, and as there were neither parents nor God parents present, the priest called to an altar-boy, now busy snuffing out the candles, to be sponsor at the ceremony. In the fading light of a darkening church, the solemn words of baptism were pronounced and a frail mite of humanity was received into the mystical membership of the Body of Christ. Deeper significance was added to this odd ceremonial when, on coming out of the vestry, the good Father stuffed some food tickets into the girl's hands to help tide the family over a cruel Christmas.

'Rejoice, rejoice greatly,' so sang the ancient prophet, 'for unto you a child is born.' But no jubilation sounded on this occasion; only the dull acceptance of another hungry mouth to feed; yet strange to record, the unwanted babe survived, and thrived, after a fashion.

The growth of infantile consciousness and the awakening of awareness arouses misty visions of a crowded room with many figures moving around, the family being herded in that one small compass. There was a wooden cradle, rocked by a string attached to a person near the window; I suppose the baby must have cuddled against a warm bosom at odd moments, yet no memories remain, only a sense of rebellion against the weaning period. Poor mothers daubed their breasts with soot to discourage suckling, and dim memories remain of spasmodic howls of rage produced by the offer of those coal-black nipples. There were other fits of screaming when mother wore a poke-bonnet in lieu of the familiar shawl, and peace could only be restored with the removal of the offending headgear.

As a crawling infant I recall exploring a long dirt yard lined with rows of stables which housed huge horses and there I learned to anticipate the comings and goings of noisy carters bedding down the animals.

At about the age of three the family circumstances improved, for we moved from Milk Street to a better house in an open street. This social uplift was probably due to the added earnings of our eldest sister who had left school and was working as a 'setter-on' in a spinning mill. The second house must have seemed roomy after our former cramped abode, yet it was only a two up, two down dwelling in the middle of a row, with a cobbled yard, privy midden, and earth closet. The front door opened directly on to Rankin Street; I remember it boasted a brass latch which caught my childish vision because it was kept brightly polished.

The living-room floor was flagged and sanded, the hearthstone eidelbacked and surrounded by gleaming fire-irons. Over the fireplace was a false cornice, a wooden shelf with a faded brocade pelmet. This served to hide a string stretched across the range from which hung damp stockings and handkerchiefs. On top of the mantelpiece stood a pair of china dogs with golden neck-chains, an old clock, and the family tea-caddy. Above father's armchair hung a pink-backed copy of the 'Racing Handicap' which was daily consulted by him in his search for possible winners. On the same hook also dangled a stout leather strap with five thongs which provided an occasional clout for the noisy or gigglesome ones.

The walls were adorned with several shabby pictures which attracted my infant curiosity and wonder. One of these revealed two black-rimmed fretwork cards behind the glass with slender angel forms blowing trumpets and small printed verses underneath them. On dark evenings when the lamp-light threw ghostly shadows round the room, this picture was a source of fascination. Climbing on to a rush-bottomed chair and peering at the small words I struggled to spell out the story:

> Have pity on me, have pity on me,
> at least you my friends,
> For the hand of the Lord hath touched me.

So read the inscription to Michael Foley, who I learned, had departed this life December 18th, 1866, aged 83 years. Below was the epitaph to his wife, Catherine:

> We have loved her in life,
> let us not tire until we have introduced her,
> by our tears and prayers,
> into the house of the Lord.

In the shadowy emotion evoked by this sad news I, somehow or other, always found Catherine's plea more healthy and comforting than Michael's forlorn note of anguish.

In more knowledgeable years I heard that my paternal grandparents had emigrated from Ireland during the terrible potato famine and had settled, or at least tried to do so, in a poverty-stricken quarter of a Lancashire cotton town.

The other picture that captured my infant gaze was much more colourful; on the canvas were a group of figures, an old man with flowing beard, with outstretched arms bending over a kneeling form; behind stood a scowling man and in the foreground a smiling person holding aloft a golden object. For quite a time I felt that God was the patriarchal one, the kneeling figure a penitent, the smiling countenance that of a friendly angel, but the scowling visage quite eluded these childish probings. Then one day I heard the story of the Prodigal Son, and lo, my picture was made plain and forever unforgettable. 'I will arise and go to my Father, and will say unto Him . . .' the words ring down the century with their ineffably lovely and human message, recreating a moment of ecstatic joy and comprehension in the mind of a questing child, brooding in the dusk and absorbing queer images from fading, yellow pictures.

In comparison with our living room the back-kitchen was dull and bleak with its whitewashed walls, rows of shelves, and a dark slopstone in a state of perpetual wetness. A cracked mirror hung on the small windowframe, and nearby dangled the family comb. Below this toilet requisite appeared a note in father's fine writing to his progeny which I later deciphered – 'Please clean the comb after using and replace on this nail'. We may have been lacking in wordly goods, but certainly we had our points of nicety, if not of fastidiousness!

Mother kept the home beautifully clean; each morning the 'ash-hole' and grate were thoroughly raked, the hearthstone re-eidelbacked, and the floor freshly sanded. Friday morning was given over to the ritual of scouring and polishing the numerous fire-irons; they were then placed on the sofa, carefully covered up, and only replaced on Saturday afternoon when the house was really spic and span.

Our furniture comprised a cheap but much prized red dresser adorned with three globes with hanging glass jingles; a sewing machine, the property of our eldest sister, stood by the window, bearing the family's cherished aspidistra; but more treasured still was an old dilapidated horse-hair sofa which we younger ones claimed as our particular property. Its numerous prickly rents scratched small bottoms, but its hairy arms unrebukingly received our confidences in infantile griefs and joys.

On autumn afternoons whilst mother starched and ironed piles of shirts and collars (for she took in other people's washing) I played by the window, breathing on the glass and watching eagerly for the approach of the lamplighter. He carried a long pole and as the minute points of light began to twinkle in the street opposite, they looked so pretty and friendly that I was loath to drop the curtain and let mother pull down the blind. A little later the heavy bell of the newspaper man could be heard, clang, clang, down the row; doors opened in welcome as the 'Evening News' was thrown in; the oil lamp was trimmed and lit. This charm of home lingers in the memory and will not let me go.

About this time there emerged the consciousness of accompanying mother on her weekly visits to the near-by pawnbroker's. Each Monday morning, after brushing and sorting out the Sunday clothes, such as they were, a big parcel was made up; mother carried this whilst I, clutching her skirt, trotted along quite joyfully. Walking quickly down the back street we nipped smartly in at the side door of the 'Golden Balls' at the corner of Punch Street. The pawnshop was owned by a big, jovial man who I later knew as 'Bill'. He was invariably perched on a high stool behind a long wire-netted counter. As mother was a regular customer he never opened her parcel, but placed it in one of the cubicles just above his head, and then slipped some silver coins to her under the grill. The pawnbroker endeared himself to me because he made mother laugh at his jokes and ready gossip, and I laughed also to see her become so young and gay. Whilst they chatted, I stood by the counter gazing upwards at a framed notice and trying ever so hard to spell out two big words in the middle of rows of small print. Eventually, they fashioned themselves into 'Pledge and Redeem'. Years afterwards I often pondered and wondered how two such lovely and gripping words had found their way into the money-lender's vocabulary!

In these early days we lived frugally and austerely. I recall that we had no cups and saucers; just blue and white ringed basins. Our diet was mainly milk, porridge, potatoes, and 'butties' of bread and treacle with a little meat at weekends. At tea-time our parents shared a savoury tit-bit from one plate, father getting the lion's share, for mother doled out tiny morsels from her portion to the younger children. We usually stood at the table and were forbidden to chatter or giggle if father was in a bad mood. At suppertime father drank beer, mother relished a piece of bread spread with slices of raw onion, and we youngsters went to bed on a 'butty' and a drink of cold water.

Cissy, our eldest sister, but known as 'Katie' to her workmates and friends, often acted as 'little mother' in the home. On Friday evenings, after the departure of parents and brothers, a big pancheon (a huge cream and brown mug in which the family dough was kneaded) was carried on to the hearth and filled with hot water. Then taking turns to stand in the mug we received our weekly scrub-down; later, our hair was fine-tooth combed and neatly braided. Cissy scarcely spoke to us during these ministrations, but her luminous brown eyes (more tragic than mother's) invariably wore a far-away look as if exploring worlds other than our humble kitchen with its presence of two damp, lithe bodies curling on the rug before a glowing fire.

Mother was a kindly, undemonstrative woman, wholly unlettered, but with a rich vein of Lancashire 'gradeliness' in her make-up. She had a comely face, trim body, dark braided hair, bright, velvety brown eyes. I loved her passionately.

Father was an odd contrast. He was a big, intelligent, but unruly Irishman, with a genius for aggravation. He worked in fits and starts, punctuated by bouts of heavy drinking and gambling. Occasionally, he disappeared for weeks, leaving his whereabouts unknown, then just as suddenly he turned up penniless, unkempt, and minus his voice, which he had lost stumping the country on behalf of Home Rule agitation. Oddly enough the family took him in and nursed him back to health even if the ministrations were a little ungracious. Mother had grown resigned to these domestic flights, but the older end of the family were becoming more critical and rebellious against the paternal exits and entrances, invariably accompanied by feigned gestures of repentance.

During these years mother plodded gamely on, battling with a feckless husband whom she neither loved nor understood, and succouring her six children whom she never really wanted.

We were brought up mainly out of her wash-tub earnings. Frequently I accompanied her to various better-off houses, and sitting on the floor amongst a pile of dirty clothes played games and prattled aloud whilst she silently scrubbed shirts or mangled heavy sheets. During one of these infant rummagings, I remember purloining a knitted doll's frock and hiding it under my pinafore. On reaching home, I slipped it over a battered dolly and gazed in wonder and admiration at her transformation. But, alas, all too soon the misdemeanour was discovered; there was no rebuke, but the little pink treasure was immediately returned to its rightful owner.

Poignant memories remain of a particular afternoon with mother bent wearily over the dolly-tub with her small child at her feet in fidgety and peevish mood. Suddenly, she said quite sternly – 'Now if you're not a good girl, I shall run away with a blackman.' Stunned and bewildered, I looked up, but found her face grim and unbending. 'She must mean it,' I thought, and immediately crept away to sound the full depth of childish misery caused by this terrible threat. For days and weeks I moved around in terror and heaviness at the threat of desertion. If a coloured person came in sight I wondered dumbly if that was The Man mother had in mind. In a panic I dashed off home; if mother was there, fears were temporarily allayed, but if not, I hung around miserable and disconsolate, fearing the worst had happened. Pathetically, I tried to find ways of pleasing mother in the hope that she would not leave us, and on quiet evenings by the fire when we played Ludo or Snakes and Ladders, I cheerfully manoeuvered to send my counter down a long snake so that mother's could reach 'home' safely. Then clapping my hands in glee there would be a shout, 'Oh, mam, you've won again.' If there was an answering twinkle in those dear brown eyes, a foolish, childish heart pulsed freely again with joy and relief.

Mother's rare, unintentional dagger thrusts had, I felt, a teasing quality, but father's were more enduring and purposive. In maudlin moods he tormented my small soul with the anguish of choice. Taking me on his knee, and enveloping me in rough arms and beery breath, he had a habit of posing painful propositions. 'Now,' he said, 'suppose we three, you and I and your mother, were together in a small boat on a lake; it suddenly capsizes and you can only save one of us; which shall it be?' Deep in my infant consciousness I knew that if ever such a trial arose, the rescued parent would be mother. But I pitied father, for I sensed a secret yearning, so I hugged him closely, crying, 'Both, both; I would save both.' Yet he was never satisfied and continued to press and pester, and on going to bed the conflict turned into nightmarish struggles in the water by an upturned boat. Vainly, I would strive to reach mother but was forever frustrated by father's frantic arms closing round me. I would awaken in a sweat of anguish, desperately relieved to find myself safe in bed, but always dumbly aware of a tragic dilemma that lay beyond my youthful comprehension of solution.

When father was recovering from a boozing bout, his temper was most vicious and unpredictable. I recall his following mother persistently round the kitchen whining monotonously, 'Lend us a penny, Meg; lend us a penny; I'm choking.' At length, in a fit of desperation, a penny was flung on to the table, whilst mother snatched up her shawl and vanished into the street to find temporary refuge in a neighbour's home.

It was then my job to fetch a gill of beer from the nearby 'White Hart'. I conjured up the odd idea that if I dawdled there and back, the one jug of ale might last father until he staggered off to bed. Round the pub corner was a quaint jeweller's shop kept by a Unitarian who was also, I think, a town councillor. Invariably, I lingered long, peering through the glass door, fascinated by the array of clocks round the walls, all ticking away for dear life, the grandfather's solemn and dignified 'tick-tock' competing with the giddy oscillations of the younger breed.

On arriving home with a jug of flat beer, I was greeted with 'Where the hell have you been?' and a volley of oaths. Sometimes I dodged out of the back door, but more frequently mooned around sacrificially in the hope of coaxing father to go to bed and so leave the family in peace. The following morning was no improvement on the evening and, on one memorable occasion, on getting up late and finding nothing to his liking for breakfast, I was sent to buy a pennyworth of liver from the butcher's shop. I ran there and back, but on delivering it, was sent spinning round the kitchen by a heavy blow. Father was not usually unkind to me, and I was stunned and bewildered. Curtly, he ordered me to take the liver back as 'it was all kernel', and to demand the penny in return. Slowly I obeyed, but this time feeling wholly rejected and dejected, yet on reaching the shop, I felt more sorry for the butcher than for myself, for we were, in a sense, both rejected. Waiting until the shop was empty, I timidly approached and asked for the penny back as father said the liver was 'all kernel'. In silence the offending bit of offal was taken back and the penny pushed across the counter. Hurrying home, I sneaked into the back kitchen, laid the coin on the table and fled to avoid further wrath.

Yet in happier moods, father could quickly capture my imagination by his store of Irish folk-lore. He told me that on mid-summer nights the wee folk came to play about the house, and encouraged me to place a basin of water on the table for refreshment during their gambols. This excited me tremendously, and early the following morning I crept downstairs, avoiding the creakers, and rushed to see if the fairies had been; then calling aloud to my sister, 'Oh, Emmie, they've bin,' a voice from the back bedroom, where father and the boys slept, growled, 'Who's bin?' 'Oh, the fairies,' I replied, 'they've drunk some water.' 'Hell, she's at it again,' came the retort. Mother then came on to the landing, saying in a coaxing voice, 'Come to bed, child, you're waking all the house and it is only four o'clock'. Sadly I mounted the stairs, discomforted by my family's lack of courtesy for our fairy visitors.

During his boyhood, father had worked as a scene-shifter at the local theatre, had heard many of the great tragedians of the day, and had learned by rote most of the Shakespearean soliloquies. Often, with unexpected dignity, he stalked round the house declaiming magnificent passages from the plays. On occasions, when quoting the Moor's noble lines, I was used as the unfortunate Desdemona, flung on to the old horse-hair sofa, and half suffocated by a sweaty cushion; then falling back into his arm-chair, he murmured in dull stupor, 'The pity of it, Iago, the pity of it'. And this might have been father's own epitaph.

But life with father was not all sordid, for somehow he had managed to scrape the twopence per week required for his basic schooling. This he put to use during long winter evenings when, in sober mood, he read aloud to the family the novels of Dickens and George Eliot. Mother was not so fortunate for she received no schooling and never learned to read or write. She was one of a big family, the Morts, her father being a poor Bolton hand-loom weaver plying his craft in the cellar of their home. Mother loved to recall how my grandfather wove 'worsteds' and then the finished cloth was peddled by his wife round the outlying villages. With the money so received, fresh yarn was purchased and the craft resumed; the younger children all assisted by labouring or winding weft on a small spinning wheel for use in the shuttles. During the American Civil War the cotton famine, aided by sacrificial loyalty to Abraham Lincoln's Cause, reduced most of Lancashire's hand-loom weavers to near starvation. Mother's family was no exception, and she retained vivid memories of standing in queues at the soup kitchens. On the early death of her father she was put out to work on a farm, at the age of seven, for one shilling per week and her keep.

One of my most cherished memories is of mother sitting by the fireside near a gleaming steel-topped fender, and the lamplight falling on the bent head as she firmly held an old, cracked bobbin inside the heel of a stocking, zigzagging the needle of coarse black wool across a gaping hole. Now and again, in the course of its removal from the stocking, the bobbin slipped from her lap and, with an odd chuckling sound, rolled wickedly away on its one remaining flange until it came to rest under the furniture. We children, who had to sit almost immobile on small stools during father's readings, hailed the fugitive bobbin with glee, for it gave us the opportunity, and excuse, to crash round the room in pursuit. When retrieved it was patiently accepted, tucked again into another stocking, and the ritual resumed.

I never knew the age of our bobbin or where it came from; possibly from a near-by factory, for occasionally father deigned to take a job there, mainly spending his time in whistling, spouting poetry, or cursing the English, until he found himself outside the gates, workless but free. Mother called it a 'throstle bobbin', but that only added to its charm and curiosity, for I thought of singing birds, yet there was no manner of music in our maimed treasure. Years later I learned that there were throstle-frames in the big spinning mills and I liked to imagine that our bobbin had once danced merrily on its spindle, proudly winding the satiny yarn round its slender trunk.

And so, my little cracked treasure, worn and polished by time and usage, remains a cherished symbol of those fragmentary, yet imperishable moments, crystallized by the passing years, of a mother's cheerful acceptance and benign endurance of the sum of human frailties and fecklessness – a strange blossoming of spirit in an odd corner of strife and poverty.

Stella Entwistle
web of sunny air: a tapestry of childhood

By contrast with the poverty and wretchedness of some of the childhoods previously quoted, Stella Entwistle's early years were happy, contented and, above all, secure, a period of innocence and gradual discovery by experience, not over-burdened by formal education. Born in 1909 at Marshchapel, between Louth and Grimsby, Lincolnshire, she was the younger of two daughters of the vicar – an unusually small family for this time and occupation; these circumstances gave her the advantage of loving parents who had time and opportunity to devote to their children, and of an upbringing in a countryside where daily life was still simple, ordered and, in her eyes, beautiful. Her unpublished, fifty-thousand word account is an evocative re-creation of that Edwardian village life and a perceptive study of her own development within it. Because it was an overwhelmingly happy time, she has 'collected the bright objects of childhood's experience', but it is not a sentimental account and not nostalgic. 'Web of Sunny Air' was written in later life when she herself, as the mother of two sons, lived in a north country vicarage.

Marshchapel is nearly midway between Louth and Grimsby, and was once a hamlet of Fulstow, four miles to the west, on the road to Ludborough. My father was inducted to the living in 1906. I was born some time after and christened with Jordan water brought back by my grandfather from a Palestinian tour – not that that had any very tranquillizing effect, because I am told that I howled my way right through the service. The Old Wives of the village said that this was a good omen – the Devil departing under protest! – which I understand is the origin of the 'Passing Bell' at funerals, rung, according to legend, to drive evil spirits away. (In later years it was tolled when someone was dying so that everyone might pray for the departing soul.) Be that as it may, I certainly had a happy childhood for the most part, if my education was somewhat limited. I learned little from books for the first nine years of my life, not being considered physically robust enough to stand up to the rigours of boarding-school, (which was the educational requirement for parsons' daughters of even moderate means in those days) but I learnt much in the way of living, and it has left a legacy of joy which I feel is denied to the educationally over-burdened child of today. Without conscious morbidity, the tombstones provided my first reader, and I received a little daily instruction in the three R's in my father's study, working on a slate with a wet sponge for cleaning purposes, and with a saucerful of haricot beans as an abacus! I learnt that King Alfred burnt the cakes and that 'big booted Italy kicked little Sicily into the Mediterranean Sea', but the fact that we were living on a spinning ball would have been thought quite unnecessary information!

With the coming of the first World War, and the influx of many soldiers to camp in the village, life became too busy for anything but infrequent instruction, so the difficult art of 'pot hooks' and 'hangers' was postponed, and 'The Cat sat on the Mat' a long time whilst I explored the topography of my surroundings. The village was my world, and I loved it and its people, and my life was bounded by its intimacy and kindness. If I was bored by idleness at this time I do not now remember – it must have been a happy, active kind of boredom – because I bowled a wooden hoop through the village lanes, skipped endlessly to the quickening pace of 'pitch, patch, pepper', whipped a top to kaleidoscopic beauty, and, when the children came out to play, joined them at Hop-Scotch, Rounders, Statues, Follow m'leader, Tickie Touchwood, or marched up and down a grassy mound to the tune of 'The Good Old Duke of York' . . .

I was introduced to 'the facts of life' in the green and growing years of childhood by biblical extracts, secretly read and only faintly understood, as well as by rhymes which we all helped to compose. My sanctimonious offering:

> Little girl,
> Pair of skates,
> Brown ice –
> Heaven's gates

did not cut nearly so much 'Ice' as the somewhat bawdy verses of my companions! The word 'Sex' was unknown to me, but I had no need to be told where babies came from – had we not all got a small hole in the middle of our tummies – where else could they possible come from? I loftily dismissed our gardener's Gooseberry Bush theory, and startled a rather elderly maiden lady by asking her when she was going to have a baby? Her reply, that perhaps if she had been married it might have 'come to pass', did nothing to enlighten and much to puzzle me.

After fifty years only two of my childhood companions stand out with any clarity in my memory, and these two because of certain physical defects, I regret to say. A squint-eyed child was welcomed gladly into a group because this characteristic signified a Bringer of Good Luck to his associates (I wonder why?) – but not so the child who suffered frequently from 'Nose Bleeds'. I played often with a little girl so afflicted, and in the middle of the most exciting game someone always had to dash off to fetch the big, heavy iron back-door key to drop down her back – an old trick, but surprisingly effective.

I am amazed, looking back, that the other children accepted me so readily. Perhaps they enjoyed watching the incredulous expression on my face as they painted their highly coloured word pictures of what went on behind the closed doors of the village school, although I must add that one at least of these stories had circumstantial evidence to back it up. It was rumoured in the village that the local schoolmaster was a spy, and had been seen sketching near the foreshore, and also working late at night at his desk at school – 'When all good people should be a-bed!' One villager, having climbed up on to the back of another to peer through the school window, 'had seen him pouring over a map in dim candlelight', and so the stories went on. The village buzzed with excitement. Then suddenly the climax came, and unfortunately sealed the mystery, because the schoolmaster disappeared, and as far as I know nothing more was ever heard of him. Whether the antagonism created by suspicion caused him to decamp, or whether he was indeed an enemy agent we shall never know. This event shook the village badly, because its schoolmaster was a person of great importance to the whole community. Most children attended only one school for the whole of their school life, and as he was guide, philosopher and friend to pupil and parent alike, his influence extended far beyond the school walls, moulding the minds of a whole generation.

The size of the average Parson's family used to be proverbial in the early years of this century. Certainly the neighbouring Clergy should have been happy men because their 'quivers' were full, but I was a solitary child. My sister, nearly eight years my senior, was away at boarding-school most of the time we were in Lincolnshire. I only remember her as a vision of pinafores and pigtails which appeared and disappeared from time to time. So I spent much time alone in the garden, keeping a close watch beneath the gooseberry bushes for the baby companion that I was told would appear there one day; and sharing the gardener's wonder when, under those same bushes, he unearthed two Roman coins . . .

Fifty years ago winter in the country was something to be faced with courage. I remember the weather being so cold that I was allowed to smuggle a hot potato into my little fur muff to keep my fingers warm during Sunday services. It was a time of hard-won warmth and patient endurance for grown-ups, but for children, though it was cold and long, on the East coast especially, it could bring magic. The beauty of fern and feather frost pictures crystallized on window panes must surely instill an awareness of design into a child's mind, and to awake to the absolute silence of a cotton-wool world spattered with silver spangles glinting in the sunshine, where hedges had become waves with high curving crests, and all other familiar objects were transformed into grotesquely satisfying shapes, was joy indeed to me. I loved to run out in the early morning across the wide white expanse of lawn, writing my name with a stick in large capitals on its dazzling surface, trailing like a hound the delicate scurrying imprints of birds and small creatures patterning the 'fair linen cloth' of the pristine snow. Surely it must be one of the few remembered sensations of childhood not blunted by maturity. Never, indeed, did the old vicarage look more lovely than after a heavy snowfall, or the house seem more snug than when feathery flakes started piling up against the window-panes, gleaming white in the mellow light of the paraffin lamp making a golden circle on the table where my sister and I sat to read or sew, or play games of dominoes, snakes and ladders or tiddlywinks.

There were occasions when it seemed as if the feathered rain would never cease and we were confined to the house until it was possible to dig our way out. On these days my mother took full advantage of the reflected white light from the long windows to catch up with family and household repairs, using the old treadle sewing machine her mother had used before her. Sometimes she would say 'The Old Lady must be plucking all her geese today,' and we would smile, joining in the fantasy of the winter wonderland outside.

Sunday night always stood out for me because of its peculiar feeling of security and peace, especially in winter time, when, Evensong finished, mufflers, leggings, gloves, coats and hats discarded, and the supper over, the thick plush curtains were drawn across the shuttered windows and the world of wind and storm was bolted out – bolted out literally because the internal shutters folded out from panels on either side of the window and were kept in place by iron bars. Then, with the fire brightly burning, and the light from the candles on the piano throwing flickering shadows across the clematis tracery of the Bluthner's front panel, it was time for my father to lovingly take out his violin from its green-lined case and endeavour to render Handel's Largo on the inexpensive instrument on which he had taught himself to play.

After that the red and lilac cover of the gay waltz tune 'Nights of Gladness' took its place on the music stand, or my mother played a party piece. 'The Maiden's Prayer' was one of these, but she could upon occasion struggle with the more difficult running notes of 'The Robin's Return'. The Vicarage was a damp house and the piano rarely tuned, so I doubt if these family concerts were particularly musical, but willingness counted more than ability in those days and everyone sang. It would have been thought extraordinary not to do so – or not to wish to do so. A natural shyness was understood and accepted, but tone deafness seems to have been almost unrecognized – 'everyone must be musical at heart' it was asserted – so my father sang 'Daddy' and brought tears to our eyes, my mother sang negro spirituals, especially 'O dem Golden Slippers', which was her favourite, and I piped up with 'Oh, Mr Teddy Bear, I do love you!' and went off to bed warmly comforted. My sister was the soloist of the family. Her repertoire consisted mostly of the sentimental ballads of those days – 'My Ain Folk', 'Little Grey Home in the West', 'The Indian Love Lyrics', and 'Down in the Forest', and these she sang with the unabashed fervour of that vocally uninhibited period. If the words of the songs that were sung at that time could have been read the result would have been quite startling to respectable ears, and the choice indicates some deep psychological problem I expect; however, Freud and Jung were but clouds on the horizon, and there was no need as yet to explain ourselves to ourselves! In retrospect, the evenings of my childhood stand out as happy and peaceful times, without any of the frustration and boredom felt nowadays when the television breaks down! I suppose the worst that could happen to us was the habit that the gramophone had of running down or the needle sticking in the middle of a favourite piece, but these were faults soon remedied, and it gave us hours of pleasurable entertainment. I can see it yet with its enormous fluted horn and big base taking up a lot of space on the chenille-tasselled tablecloth, against a background of aspidistras and bric-a-brac which was the fashionable decor in those days. The thick records with the fox-terrier labels bearing such names as Clara Butt, Sir Henry Wood, John Coates,

W. H. Squire, Albert Sammons, etc., were heavy as ironstone dinner plates to handle; stacked up, these records made an impossible weight for a child to carry, and the vibrant crackling which accompanied the 'Holy City' and 'Ave Maria' would be considered blasphemous to modern ears, but it was all very wonderful to use . . .

Life at the Vicarage was lived on quite an earthly plane, though Sunday certainly had an atmosphere all its own, created partly, I think, by the feeling that it was a day of restricted pleasures. We never had a hot meal for one thing, because, in those days of lack of domestic facilities, someone would have had to stay away from church to cook the lunch. Again, although my parents were not Puritanical, one was given to understand that religious books made the best reading for what was known by the older people of the parish as 'The Sabbath' – though the unholy glee and satisfaction obtained from the crude, and sometimes gory illustrations, as well as from the sound of words that as yet I failed to understand, in the Sunday books of my acquaintance, rather defeated the object of the exercise. Daniel's expression of bland indifference in the Lions' Den did not surprise me, nor did the apparent unconcern on the faces of Shadrach, Meshack and Abed-Nego in the burning fiery furnace, but the picture of St Paul falling down before the great light struck terror into my soul because of an inherent fear of lightning. Such I think must be the usual child's reactions to situations strange to its experience. Later, when on holiday in Lytham St Annes I visited the Blackpool Zoo and heard a lion roar, Daniel became for me one of the most satisfactory of biblical heroes.

We accepted pictorially so much in my childhood, but I do remember a print hanging on a bedroom wall that stirred my curiosity, perhaps because it stretched a little too far the credulity of a pre-Space age child! It was called 'Hope' and depicted a woman, with bandaged eyes, sitting on top of the world, plucking at a lyre with only one unbroken string. I had seen illustrations of angels sitting on clouds playing harps in picture books and thought little of that – at least they could see what they were doing – whilst nothing could prevent this lady from slipping off an object round as the ball with which I played every day. A certain quizzical mood overcame me whenever I looked at this picture I recall, but, in the main, everything was black or white and there was no need to question. Heaven was a city of golden gates and pearly streets above the bright blue sky, just as hell was unquenchable fire and dreadful and endless torment beneath one's feet, but I never quite knew what the 'Tinimies' were until I was old enough to read and found in the fourth commandment the words 'and all that in them is'! . . .

From the perspective of childhood everything had a certainty completely lacking today, not least in the seasons of the year. Spring started on Palm Sunday, just as winter was heralded by the Sunday next before Advent – 'Stir-up' Sunday as it was known in my young days, and a signal to the housewife to begin preparation for her pudding mixture, not, as in these days, just 'so many shopping days to Christmas'. The Church festivals made a yearly pattern for the peaceful background of our lives . . .

It was whilst lying under a beech tree, on one of those summer days that seem to vanish with childhood, that I had an extraordinary experience. Looking back it now seems rather like the act of falling in love, when everything takes on a new significance. I was lying with the sun warm as a friendly arm about my shoulders, the air soft and heavy with the scent of summer flowers, when suddenly the swinging pendulum of Time seemed arrested, the living silence of deep sleep hung over the garden, and I felt quite alone. Then (without the aid of mescalin!) I had a sudden awakening to the miracle of detail in nature. I remember – and I must have been small for the thought lies deep in the well of memory – gazing up along the smooth, clean pillar of the tree to the fan-vaulting of dark branches above, its foliage moving as though it were gently breathing, and to the stained-glass green of summer leaves shot through with dazzling shafts of light as the great tree drew its shadow into itself in the midday heat, and feeling myself not separate and distinct from the life and beauty about me, but a pulsating part of it, caught up by a wave joining earth and sky in a crescendo of praise. It must certainly have been an experience born of the mood and the moment – perhaps one could call it a child's first intimation of God – if so, the keyword must certainly be innocence, when every sight, scent, sound or touch is new as in the beginning. With this feeling came worship in its earliest form, the wonder and awe as felt by a small child listening to heartbeats through a doctor's stethoscope, but this experience then was beyond the scope of childish senses to comprehend or put into words – 'a heart beating through Time and Space' – bringing a peace from which all the songs of childhood are distilled . . .

Edna Bold
the long and short of it

Edna Bold was born into a 'respectable' working-class family in Beswick, Manchester, in 1904, neither rich nor poor, but hardworking, somewhat narrow and puritanical. Her father was a baker and confectioner who triumphed over a business crisis though at the cost of his own and his wife's health, and for some years the family was cared for by a stern, unbending aunt. Despite the unpromising physical landscape, Edna found Manchester 'at once a terrible, beautiful, exciting place', and she describes her development and discovery of self there as a happy period. A sensitive and intelligent child, she went on to secondary schooling and training for teaching, involving, as she says, 'a transition from working class to lower middle class, the kind of thing that occurred to a great many families in my younger years'. Her unpublished autobiography, of approximately forty thousand words, was written in 1978.

Childhood

Happy and glorious

> I remember I remember
> The house where I was born,
> The windows where the sun
> Came peeping in at dawn.

If Thomas Hood's sun ever shone, it certainly never peeped, nor his roses, violets and lily cups grew near the smoke-blackened walls of our house. Not a blade of grass, not a tree grew anywhere in the district. Rows of terraced houses, factories, cotton mills, engineering works, belching chimneys made a Lowryesque townscape for our beginning over a baker's shop not far from the centre of Manchester.

When we were very young it was at once a terrible, beautiful, exciting place. My twin brother and I had no sense of deprivation as we roamed and played in the labyrinth of mean, intricate streets.

The sounds of trams rattling and clanging into the town, the clog-irons striking hard pavements as shawled figures raced headlong and unheeding to the mills, the ear-shattering bellow of hooters urging the hurrying figures to a final burst of speed, were our earliest recollections.

Every morning we heard these sounds as we lay in the warm, dark security of our beds. They were as evocative as Thomas Hood's sun, roses, lilies, for they touched our tiny hearts and minds to life.

The road

We lived on the main road that ran like an artery through the district of Beswick and wound one way to the centre of Manchester and the other way to the residential quarter of Clayton and the small industrial town of Ashton-under-Lyne beyond.

It was a safe road where vans, lorries, cabs drawn by horses of every size, colour and description rolled incessantly over the sets. It was possible to cross between this steady stream of traffic with ease and comfort. There was never any report or tell of accidents in the whole of the district.

The 'Road' was a social centre where everyone met, shopped, talked, walked. The butcher, the baker, the grocer, the milliner, the draper, the barber, the greengrocer, the pawnbroker, the undertaker were friends, confidants and mines of information. All needs from birth to death could be supplied from these little shops. As soon as arms and legs were strong enough, every child joined the 'club' that supported these small businesses, for every child was obliged to run errands for mothers, relations, neighbours.

Of all the many resentments that every child harboured in its exuberant heart, this running of errands was the chief. It interfered with and subtracted from the play-way of the beautiful, long intoxicating excitement of the day.

Every morning, a little before nine, doors were unbarred, latches lifted, blinds raised and the shops 'opened'. Every morning a small hand-van pulled by a thin pale-faced boy would stop before our own front door, and tray after tray would be off-loaded from the van and carried on the head of the boy into the shop. This done, and his van empty, he would close and latch the doors, stand between the shafts and set off rick-shaw fashion, back to the bakehouse to pick up his next load.

In the meantime the white loaves, brown loaves, tin loaves, box loaves, cottage loaves, banjos and brunswicks would be stacked on to shelves by the pert, diminutive Florrie who worked in the shop. She cleaned, she polished, she arranged, she served, she gossiped to the shawled customers. Everyone wore shawls. They were warm, convenient, comforting, secretive.

Intermittently, throughout the morning, the straw-haired youth appeared. As the day advanced, his pace slowed, his tread became cat-like, his arms and shoulders sensitized to the delicate pastries he carried in the van. To his great credit the heady aroma escaping from the van neither induced him to an unseemly trot nor a poaching raid on the delicacies inside. The custard tarts, the fruit pies, the vanilla slices, the macaroons, the eccles cakes, the chelsea buns arrived with a bloom of freshness second to none.

He was never complimented on his skill, never recognized as a balancing artist of promise. He was a 'casual', likely to be sacked at the drop of a hat. There were plenty of other boys ready to take his place. What became of him, where he went, what he did I never knew nor thought to enquire. I never even knew his name . . .

Haddon Street

The bakehouse was in Haddon Street. We could walk there if we didn't dawdle, within five minutes, that is if Hannah accompanied us.

We sensed rather than knew there was something wrong with Haddon Street, for here we saw children with unwashed clothes, lank uncombed hair and red, bare feet. We were not encouraged to ask questions, to pass remarks or intrude on our betters and elders, so we never knew why this state of affairs disturbed and frightened us. We were hurried to and from the street and were never sorry to be out of it.

As we grew older my father would speak of the brawls and fights that occurred, of screaming women running from the savagery of drunken husbands and of infants scalded and burnt by lazy sluts.

My father rendered first aid to every hurt and needy child, fed the hungry families and subsidized penniless widows and orphans. My father never came to any harm in this terrible slum street. His premises were never robbed nor his small working staff molested. He was as safe in his mean, cramped property as if he had been in Haddon Hall itself with its spreading green acres.

Peas and beans

To dig up the dirt betwen the nicks of pavement flags was every town child's impulse and the next to grow something. Peas and beans were always forthcoming from kitchen cupboards, being part of the staple diet in every household. They were planted with such loving care, watched over hourly and willed to life and being.

That they grew with startling rapidity and as rapidly wilted and died was no discouragement. Nothing in all nature could ever transcend the miraculous appearance of tender, green shoots sprouting between grey flagstones in one's own backyard. Trembling we would crouch, trembling we would lie on the cold flags peering through the translucent green of the tiny leaflets. Nothing in the streets, nothing in the house seemed to match these tiny plants. They were different, suggesting a different order of things to which we were not accustomed. Revelation creates hunger and nature in her own way has a mysterious and inexhaustible supply for every need. It was not long before we discovered the incredible and different order of things we had begun to sense as the peas and beans struggled to grow in their inadequate, unlikely seed beds.

Buttercup meadow

When we were four or five and my younger brother Harold, a babe in arms, we went to stay at a farm in the countryside behind Bispham.

One sunny afternoon my father sat in the middle of the buttercup meadow that stretched in front of the house. In his arms he held the child. Monstrous animals with lowering heads and menacing horns and disgusting, dribbling muzzles streamed through the field on their way to the farm.

I could not cry out. I could not move. The sickening creatures were going to kill my father and the sleeping child. I was never surer of anything in my life. My father continued to sit, smiling and unconcerned as I agonized, transfixed and paralysed. I passed into oblivion, and the next thing I knew we were walking in a lane that skirted the meadow. How we got there I do not remember. We were 'just there' as we are 'just there' in dreams. My father and the baby were going ahead. My mother and my brother, Stanley, were following behind.

The thick, white branches of hawthorn, the overpowering scent of blossom, the hum of insects and the unfamiliar softness of earth beneath our feet were too much for my excitable nature. Another fainting fit threatened. But walking precludes any sudden rush of blood away from either extremity. The moment passed unremarked. In some secret recess, hidden deeper than deep, lay the knowledge of some celestial state of affairs that was reflected in the beautiful lane and the buttercup meadow . . .

Free play

As soon as we could walk and talk and be trusted out alone, we played on the main road or in the streets adjacent where our Grandfather, Grandmother, Uncles, Aunts, Cousins, friends lived. We loved the short terraces of black, brick houses, whose doorsteps and window sills were yellow-stoned, buttercup bright, whose lace curtains hung like white or cream veils to hide the small, trim parlours inside. We loved the smooth, grey flags where we walked, ran, skipped or danced to a barrel organ. We played with 'bobbers and kibs', whips and tops, shuttlecocks and paddles, hoops and sticks, balls, ropes, dolls and prams, tricycles and scooters. We played a variety of racing, catching games, ring games, singing games. The older children taught the younger the art and skill of tent making that occurred in the summer. Hessian, old blankets, old rugs, clothes horses, poles, ropes were begged, borrowed or stolen. The crude, bedouin-like tents were hitched against the wall of a house, the 'wigwams' were built with great difficulty on the hard, dirt floor of the croft.

There was little in all life that ever rivalled the moment of ecstasy as we crawled into the confined, stuffy, smelly interior of these tents. There each one would sit like a diminutive grand turk, cross-legged and inscrutable, munching stale buns and biscuits. The sun would pour down. The heat became insufferable, but no child would leave his beautiful shelter till shrill voices called the little sultans home to bed where the day's play would be recreated again in dreams.

Nightmare

I loved my dreaming life. I loved my waking life. The one was undoubtedly a reflection of the other. With one exception. In sleeping, dreaming, came the nightmare and the discovery of a fear unknown in our happy, protected lifestyle. There was no 'feed in' from any source apparently.

If the horror film had been invented, it was not yet our 'scene'. The pantomime was the thing. Each year we had the choice of Red Riding Hood, Cinderella, Jack and the Bean Stalk, The Three Bears, Goody Two Shoes, Puss in Boots, Mother Goose, Robinson Crusoe, etc., etc. We were allowed one pantomime, sometimes two. With the exception of Robinson Crusoe, the magic and splendour of these spectaculars brought glamorous dreams, but in the case of Robinson the very epitome of horror filtered through into my first nightmare.

At the back of our house was a small bedroom with a small casement window. It was through this window that the cannibals with frightful yells and spears and knobkerries came bursting in to slaughter the whole household. They were more real, more terrifying than any of the blacked-up stage versions I had seen in the footlight's glare of an afternoon performance.

It was never possible to sleep for many years in an unlighted room or sleep alone in any house. From this time, when I was no more than five or six, fear permeated the tangible and the intangible. The fear was driven deep. Communication with our elders was not encouraged. Psychology had not been invented.

Mercifully the old cliché that 'Time cures most ills' seems to work for me. Age with its 'change and decay' killed the phantoms of the night, stone dead.

Back-bencher

Not all the hours of the day and night were directed to entertainment and play and dreaming. There were the hours of school, state school. A timid, 'good' child could qualify as a 'back-bencher'. The truculent, ebullient, strong children were mustered on the front rows of the very hard, long benches under the watchful eye and within close reach of the strong right arm of the teacher.

I remember little of the school room with its high bare walls, its high small windows and grey light. The sun never shone on the greens, greys and browns of that featureless, colourless room in which we were 'incarcerated' morning and afternoon.

The backless rows of benches ran the length of the room. Little boys and girls sat close together, side by side with their arms folded across their chests or clasped behind their backs. They never moved or turned their heads or spoke except to chant in unison or write on squares of slate with thin slate pencils.

The teacher in a black, shiny apron, yellowing, celluloid cuffs, a high-necked blouse and long sweeping skirt, stood beside a large blackboard, a stick in one hand, a piece of chalk in the other. Both these instruments of her trade were used to such good effect that by the time I left this room I could read, write and spell. Everyone could read, write and spell.

How this miracle came about, or where I had been during these lesson times, I have no idea. Not a sound echoes, not an image flashes on that 'inward eye', all is blank save the memory of a goldfish that swam in a bowl of crystal clear water. But not for long could the creature withstand such confinement and the dust-laden atmosphere of the place. The goldfish disappeared with the suddenness of a snuffed-out candle flame. No other distraction ever impinged on the margin of our eyes. Visually, aurally, mentally stultified, the days passed, featureless and painless.

The superintendent

By contrast the time we spent in Sunday School was distressing and miserable.

Each Sunday afternoon we would go through the unnaturally quiet streets to a large, barn-like hall with a platform at one end and rows of benches immediately below. The 'Superintendent' stood on the platform behind a wooden table. A decanter of water and a tiny, shiny bell were its sole furnishing.

The Superintendent towered on high. His thin figure, his pale, narrow face, his thin, drooping moustache, his small, narrow eyes surveyed his flock with severity and distaste.

The children would sit mute, their eyes glazed, their fat legs dangling listlessly and flabbily, expressing a paralysing boredom.

There was singing, praying, reading from THE BOOK, lessons, more singing, more praying and a sudden release from restraint into the street outside.

There the little boys teased the little girls. The girls attacked the boys, beating and thwacking with their Sunday best umbrellas. This was the only likeable, telling thing of the afternoon. The Superintendent had done his best, the teachers had done their best and in my case had succeeded in producing an agnostic. I was fourteen.

I left the establishment, never to return, ready to obliterate the unpleasant incidence of 'Sunday School' from my mind for ever. But the memory of the boring little man who stood on a platform nearer to God than anyone I knew in our narrow little circle remained indelibly imprinted. To this day I cannot pass any non-conformist chapel without a sense of great unease and gloom . . .

'Seks'

We were as innocent as Adam and Eve walking in the garden. My twin brother and I knew we were different. The ritual Friday bath night in front of the kitchen fire brought the matter to mind. We had no interest, no curiosity and paid little attention to the phenomenon. Neither did we pay any attention to the marked difference in our appearance. My tall, blue-eyed, fair-haired brother established his Saxon blood. My short stature, dark brown hair, brown eyes, advertised some far off Celtic origin.

As we grew and developed, the difference in temperament was obvious. It went unnoticed and unremarked. Self consciousness was not encouraged. We were never allowed to put ourselves forward, to attract notice or speak out of turn. I had to stand with my feet together, sit with my knees together and never, under any circumstances, lift my skirts. I wore a serge top skirt, a cotton petticoat and a flannelette petticoat. Beneath these I wore an unmentionable garment that never went on display on the washing line, but was hung on a rack near the ceiling amongst other articles of washing.

Vaguely, slowly, haphazardly I sensed the layers of petticoats that hung down like drawn blinds had a significance I did not yet comprehend. Revelation came one summer afternoon as we walked to school. We had to go part of the way along a high wall that divided the street from the railway. It was along this length of black, brick wall that a child overtook us and said, without introduction or preamble, 'Do you know where babies come from?' 'No,' we said, neither knowing or caring. Whereupon streamed out from the lips of the soft young mouth such a torrent of obscenity that we stood transfixed, unable to proceed. We were late for school.

The fear and revulsion of 'Seks' crippled and stunted our natural appetite till affairs of the heart shed a more credible and acceptable meaning to a dark and terrible business.

In the meantime, my cousin Dorothy, who had shared this traumatic experience, unearthed a large medical book from the highest shelf of a kitchen bookcase. Whenever we were left alone in the house she would climb up and secure the book, and together we would continue our education. At the same time, she would extract a volume of the Foxe's Book of Martyrs. Childbirth and martyrdom were synonomous. We suffered the torments of the damned. Neither my cousin Dorothy nor myself ever underwent such physical torture as we discovered in those two hideous books. We never 'reproduced'. On this score she went unrepentant to the grave as I shall go to mine . . .

Edith Hall
canary girls and stockpots

Born in 1908 near Hayes, Middlesex, a formative period of Edith Hall's childhood was spent during the First World War while her father was away from home for nearly four years. During this time she was much influenced by the 'canary girls' who lodged with them, and who had come from the East End to work in a local munitions factory; this mingling of cultures and the struggle to acquire food at a time of shortages seem to have largely dominated Edith's childhood experiences. Unable to sit for the scholarship examination to the grammar school as her mother thought it would be 'a waste of time as girls got married', she left school at fourteen to go into a number of dead-end jobs in factories and domestic service before training as a nurse; later she obtained work with an insurance company investigating sickness benefit claims. Her autobiography originated from a Luton Workers' Educational Association class in 1975, and part was published by the Branch in 1977. This extract is approximately one-third of the whole, and was kindly brought to my notice by her daughter-in-law, Margaret Hall; a longer manuscript version remains unpublished.

My poor jolly uncle

Just prior to the Great War of 1914 when I was about six years old, postcards with the then half-penny postage were sent between my relations each day. My grandmother would send us a card *each evening* which we received by first delivery the next morning. She would then receive our reply card *the same evening*. If one lived in the same town as one's correspondent, an early morning posted card would be delivered at twelve mid-day the same day and a reply card, if sent immediately, would be received the same afternoon.

I still have many of these postcards proving what a wonderful service it was; *all in one day* – and that families like our own could keep in daily touch if they so wished. With such efficiency, who would need telephones, which working-class people did not have anyway?

My greatest and most remembered pleasure was being present at the frequent family reunions; my cousins and myself being put to sleep in a long row in a bed made up on the floor. Guest rooms were unheard of in our extended family. Trains must have stayed in stations quite a long time in those days because my aunts and other relations living en route to my grandmother would be notified that we would be passing through their town, and an aunt and cousin would be on the platform at Grantham and another aunt at Peterborough. We would chat and exchange gifts through the lowered window of the carriage door, then continue on our journey.

Annual holidays were not general but many day trips by coach and horses were arranged; the phrase 'going out for the day' has a pleasant reflection for me, as does the sound of feet on a cobbled street because my grandmother's house was flush on such a street.

I lay in bed at seven a.m. listening to the men going to work at the foundry at the end of the street. My grandfather had worked and been killed there by machinery in 1903, five years before I was born. I think some of my jolly uncles and cousins had also worked there. Grandmother and my parents were devout Christians and I was early made to realize what a fortunate little girl I was, and in my prayers each night I thanked God and named many of my relations whom I asked Him to bless. I was so happy to have so many loving people around me that I did not know that we were poor, but I was no more deprived materially than most other children then.

Then, suddenly, it wasn't like that anymore, 'War had broken out!' Uncle Stanley, for whom I had asked of God a special blessing because he used to give me 'flying angels' on his shoulders, was killed on his 21st birthday. My father joined up in the Royal Army Medical Corps and I did not see my dark-haired upright daddy again for three and a half years after that, and when I did, I called him 'mister'. He was so grey, bent and ill-looking and suffering from dysentery; I simply didn't recognize him after his experiences in a prisoner-of-war camp. He went to war a confirmed Imperialist and returned an ardent pacifist and remained so for the rest of his long life.

We lived in a small town on the Uxbridge Road, eight miles from Oxford Circus; well, that's what it said on the signpost. There were a few factories on the periphery of the town and very soon munitions were being made there and at Hayes, which was the next town.

Grandma was still the placid comforting type of a few years before although her two sons were 'in it', one fighting at the front and the other, my father, who later became a prisoner, although a non-combatant in the R.A.M.C. Then I was secretly glad that he had been taken prisoner because my friend had been told by her father that R.A.M.C. men weren't really in the war and didn't face the dangers of the fighting men.

'Now, all the wars,' said Grandma, 'kill off the men; then they make a fuss of the leaders, like they did of General Smuts.' But this war will be a 'different war'. It won't be like that after this one. Her brother had been killed in the Boer War but as the news had taken such a long time to reach the family, it didn't seem so bad then.

At about this time we used to wear 'footed' stockings and most uncomfortable they were, too. They were made from the legs of one pair and the feet of another. The black wool of the seams worked into my chilblains and it was very painful.

Also, my mother just could not repair our shoes properly; I walked on little leather-patch platforms during the whole of the war.

She managed to build a rabbit hutch for our bunnies which we acquired to augment our food but after watching them for months running round the garden, we just couldn't fancy eating them, and even when we sometimes had one given to us, or bought one cheaply, to me, they always looked like baked babies.

Stockpots

I think it was about two years after the war began that food became scarce. This was due, I was told later, to the sinking of our food ships by enemy submarines; the shipping losses being published in the national press every week.

There was so much talk about food shortages but very little of the actual substances and variety, that food value and nutrition took second place; at least as far as my immediate neighbours were concerned; quantity, rather than quality appeared to be more important.

There were few factory canteens and no school meals for the children as is the case today. Housewives tried to give their families a good cooked meal on the one day the father would be at home which was the Sunday. My own father, before he was a soldier, did not get paid until he finished work on his so-called half-day on Saturday, usually at four p.m., when we all used to meet him to relieve him of his hard-earned pay packet to enable us to get the week-end shopping. By the time we got to the shops, the shoppers would be gathered round outside the butcher's window where he would already be auctioning off what meat he had left, there being no general refrigeration then, sixty years ago.

If we managed to get a joint, it set the pattern for the following three days' dinners. Sunday would be the hot roast; Monday was always cold meat and pickles day, eaten to the smell of clothes boiling in the copper; on Tuesday, what was left of Sunday's joint became rissoles with the added content of bread and potatoes. Come Wednesday, the bones were simmered wtih the contents of the stockpot, including any celery left from Sunday's tea, which clung, sodden and stringy, to the bare bones of my plate.

Nearly every housewife along our row kept a stockpot which formed the basis for many meals and, no doubt, a medium for many germs. The stockpot was kept day and night at the back of the large solid fuel stoves with ovens known as kitcheners. Into the pot went meat bones and the parings of vegetables. Sometimes this stock was given to needy families along our row.

As practical as my mother was, she seemed more concerned with getting us filled up than with the nutritional value of the food. It took a long time to prepare; for instance porridge was mixed overnight and left on the kitchener to be cooked in the morning. With what satisfaction did mother send me to school with a stodgy oatmeal blanket lining my stomach. Some children had only porridge for breakfast, and as it is only carbohydrate and digested early in the alimentary tract, they were hungry again by playtime, so out came the 'hunks' of bread and jam or margarine, never both. If it was jam only, it would have seeped through the bread into the newspaper in which it was wrapped. My mother gave us fried bread as well as porridge, the fat being served from the lodgers' bacon breakfast. The fat kept me from feeling hungry but I often felt sick. Bilious attacks were common and so was diarrhoea in infants, particularly in summer; my own baby sister had died from it. Even in clean houses there were swarms of flies in the hot weather.

We used to send parcels of food, including ready-shelled nuts, to my father when he was a prisoner-of-war, but he received few of them.

For one project we kept chickens and I found it distressing when brown Betty, who all the year had kept us supplied with eggs, had her neck wrung for us by a next door neighbour so that we could have a good Christmas dinner. When mother started to clean and pluck the bird, she felt too sentimental to carry on. The neighbours decided with us, to change the birds round and this became the practice every Christmas. As Mrs Hardman from next door said, 'After you have fed and talked to them for so long, it would be like eating one of your own children.'

Such a lot of energy had to be expended on housework; stair-rods to be polished, knives cleaned with brickdust, great slabs of hearthstone to whiten the front step, window sills and copings scrubbed and as we were never allowed to walk on freshly whitened steps, we found it ever so difficult to stretch our small legs over. Women even cleaned a portion of the street past their own steps to prove how clean they were.

My mother was asked, or applied, to board girls who worked in the munition factories at Hayes; it must have been difficult for her to get sufficient food to satisfy hungry hard-working adolescents.

The munition girls' clothes added greatly to the family wash, which was an all-day job. Early on Monday morning the copper would be lit with wood and coke for the long day's boil and toil. First, the clothes were scrubbed by brush or kneaded with knuckles on a corrugated wooden scrubbing-board because of the commonly held belief that otherwise the 'dirt would get boiled in'. Any suds after use, would be handed round to the neighbours to wash their floors. Should washday be postponed until Tuesday, it would be to enable us to 'dirty out' our Sunday dresses because we kept a special dress for that day. This procedure must have been uneconomical; wearing repaired clothes for weekdays, and outgrowing the Sunday best before it was outworn.

As I considered the neighbours' suds to be dirtier than ours, I tried to avoid washing our floors with their kindly proffered mucky water. With much effort, the soaking wet clothes were lifted on to the wooden shelf of the large mangle and fed into the rollers; the handle would then be turned and the clothes came out on the other side past the dripping stage . . .

Canary girls

Some of the young munition girls' skins were yellow through working with explosive chemicals and because of this they were called 'Canary Girls'.

Excepting Olive, all the Canary Girls came from the East End of London; all were 'common' and all were a comfort to my mother whilst her husband was missing and then found to be a prisoner-of-war.

In the absence of my father, I shared the family bed with mother, my sister sleeping on a smaller bed in the same room; Olive, a shy girl, had the small middle room and Annie, Doris and Rosie shared the long back room. We had a small front room downstairs and a through room from the passage to the scullery. We all ate and had our being in the through room in which was the large kitchen stove.

When it was very cold mother would suggest that the girls dress in front of the kitchener; she would hang their clothes over the open oven door so that they would be warm when they came down.

There was an intriguing garment called a 'four-three' which two of the girls wore. It was supposed to help fill out women who considered themselves flat-chested but hardly succeeded as it was not shaped; just a thick pad of calico material and apparently costing fourpence three-farthings.

They wore camisoles with ribbon through the top and shoulders and when they bought new narrow pastel ribbons they would give me the discarded ones to tie the end of my long plaits.

The Canaries must have been with us for about three or four years and were no doubt a great influence on my formative years and it pleased me that I received pretty French post-cards from my Daddy as they also did from their soldier boys. Those were pinned onto a dangerous monstrosity known as a mantle-board; a kind of red velvet material edged with dangling chenille tassels. This was either tacked on to the edge of the board or laid on top and held in position with ornaments. One such ornament we had was a seven-pound empty marmalade jar. Enormous vases were also in use and were repositories for such sundries as screws, pins and odd pills, etc.

Old chocolate boxes held the family insurance policies known as 'me papers' and at the end of the mantle-board was a fretwork letter rack, the first and last effort which the head of the house made many years before in his so-called carpentry class at the Board School.

I do not remember going into a working-class home of that period without seeing one of these chenille tasselled mantleboards, many of which caught fire, taking with them the boxes of fire insurance policies to destruction.

Out of the chipped vases came the Friday night purging pills, whether or not needed. A twopenny tin of yellow basilcon ointment which had great drawing power both for septic spots and boils; the finger which gave one application to such infection was applied to the surface of the ointment tin again and again and rubbed over the infected area. The next time the tin was used may well have been for an exposed cut or grazed knee.

Right through the war mother still tried to take us on small outings when she was able. One Sunday when the girls came with us, little sister riding in her push-chair, we walked along the canal tow-path passing several locks to Brentford where the canal ended. Along the Brentford High Street on our right we came to an almost-concealed path leading to narrow steps which took us right down to the River Thames. There, a ferryman would row us over the river to the Kew bank. It was a penny each to cross the water and another penny per person to go into Kew Gardens, which I had always loved from the time my parents had first taken me, before the war.

The girls thought it was Paradise. They had never seen so many flowers and trees before in their young lives. 'You hardly ever see a tree at all where I live,' Annie told us.

Another walk, after we got off the ferry, would be along the Thames to Richmond, eventually going on to the common where I once said, 'There aren't many lavatories for ladies, are there?' 'Well, we are more lucky now,' mother told my hopping figure, 'there didn't seem to be any at all when we were young.' And she said that either ladies didn't go out or ladies didn't 'go'; either was puzzling to me. Once, when I was out with Rosie I said I wanted to 'go'. 'Well, behind the bushes,' she said, 'but you mustn't let any boys see your bottom.' I didn't, but it left me curious as to what would happen if one should have. The next time we children were taking shelter under our desks during an air-raid warning I pulled down my navy bloomers and presented my bum to the small boy who shared my desk in the infant class. No reaction.

I used to take him broken biscuits and even bread because, as he told me, he was 'lownced out' at home, an expression used by children who were allowanced out with bread. He did appear to be a frail child suffering from the then chronic and common and not endearing discharge from ears and nose. He wore a large handkerchief or rag always pinned to his front to enable him to wipe away these offensive emissions.

On a cold day in the playground he, with four or five other seven-year-olds, were keeping warm chasing the infant girls around and when they caught them lifting their dresses. Although there appeared to be no sexual significance in all this, it just being one more game, they were all sent to the elderly headmaster of the 'big boy's' school to be beaten, apparently being considered too depraved to be punished by a female infant teacher.

The Canaries did long hours at work, six days a week, and had to walk to and from our house a couple of miles each way, either along the canal or through North Hyde Lane and across the little bridge and over the Water Splash, then home at night; but they were always willing to help mother as much as they could. They would spit on the flat-irons and when they 'sizzled' they would be the right temperature for ironing. The irons, of course, were heated on top of the kitchener. After the ironing was finished and the irons still hot, they were wrapped in flannel and put in my and my sister's beds and if they then still retained any heat by the time the girls went to bed they were popped into their beds as well; their long back room was icy.

Time was truly wasted by the use of gophering irons which crimped the frills on our pillow-cases and pinafores. This was no doubt the result of 'good service' on my mother and other women; she liked to keep up her standards against great odds.

Rosie, who may have never seen a flat-iron in her East End home, let alone a gophering-iron, put ours to good use when she popped them into the fire and curled up her 'side-bits' as the girls called them. She always managed to singe them slightly which they seemed to think was 'good for it'. 'Rosie, you look pretty with your side bits all frizzy.' 'Yes, I meant to,' she would answer and my sister would say to her 'You smell nice and warm when you're a bit "burny".'

The Canaries could not get home very often due to their long hours but they sent money home out of their very high wages. They came from 'part-houses' which meant that two families would share a house, one family occupying the ground floor and the other the upper part. They thought our little terraced house a mansion with its small front and back gardens.

Then Annie got the news that the tenement block in which her mother and brothers lived in Cornfield Street, Bethnal Green in East London had been badly damaged by a Zeppelin bomb. Every woman I knew seemed to have her troubles and they all relied upon each other for help.

Annie immediately said she must go and see if they were all right and Mother said that if they were, to bring them back with her. Sure enough the same night she returned with her mother and four dirty little boys; I cannot think why I should have expected to see bombed-out children other than dirty. The mother was badly shocked and could not go upstairs so they all slept underneath our big table in the living room until after a few weeks they all returned to Bethnal Green . . .

Bim Andrews
making do

The author was an illegitimate child, born in 1909, and brought up in poverty in Cambridge. Her autobiography has perceptive comments on her adolescent life in the 1920s when, as a scholarship girl at the Higher Grade School, she was 'looking in' on the very different life-style of the fee-paying pupils. In a similar way she observed the lives and amusements of the Cambridge undergraduates, without envy, even with a certain pride of propinquity. Her emancipation began as a teenager, with employment as a Co-operative Society clerk, evening classes, a bicycle and shorts ('It seems as though I was getting free from the need to conform'); after this came socialism and work for the Workers' Educational Association where 'I began my real education'. Her short, unpublished autobiography, of which the extract is approximately half, concludes with a quotation from Kierkegaard: 'Life can only be understood backwards, but it must be lived forwards.'

I suppose as we tumbled into the third decade of the twentieth century there were sighs of relief and a quickening of hope. And a feeling that something needed celebrating. So marquees went up on Parker's Piece, and mothers and children milled around waving paper flags and clutching oranges. We were on the outside, looking in at the long trestle tables, the loaded plates and buckets of beer, which were Cambridge town's thank-you to the 'boys back from the Front'. I think it must have been the first time I saw the Mayor wearing his chain of office. It wasn't the first time I heard a row between my mother and my father; mother tired, and, I expect, jealous of the food, and father too well-oiled. I think it was the only time she took the carving knife out and waved it about. Nothing came of it. Nothing ever did – only release of tension.

This memory says quite a lot about lives of wives and children. We were well-practised in making do and going without. It didn't necessarily make for unhappiness. As an experience I am sure it had some validity all its own; everyone we knew was living like this. We led meagre lives; our expectations were unformed. We never questioned our circumstances. We endured, and sought enrichment in fantasies, fed by the pile of old papers in the WC at the bottom of the garden, the occasional library book doled out to children with clean hands, and the Saturday afternoon 3d. of cinema (sitting two on a seat for the next instalment of Pearl White's adventures).

My father left his leg at Ypres. He was a sociable man, and most at home in the pub on the corner. A hero, with tales to tell, and a pension from the War Office to spend. Not 100% pension for half a leg because he wasn't completely disabled. As I remember, something like one guinea a week. Sometimes this was all we had, unless my mother was earning. But, with hindsight, I know there were others with no pension at all, reduced to singing in the streets with caps held out for pennies. As well as the money problem, my father had to learn to walk with his artificial leg. Straps, buckles and metal – it haunted us all. Much of our home life was over-shadowed by the need to bathe a sore stump, try a new piece of padding, or find the crutches again, so that he could hop down to the pub in something like comfort. He managed his leg at last, helped no doubt by technical improvements as the years went by. He learned to ride his bike again. After several abortive training sessions – carpentry, tapestry making, shoe-mending – all a far cry from his pre-war job as whistling fish-monger's delivery man on a tricycle with a big box carrier, he settled down on an instrument maker's assembly line. The Ministry of Pensions kept an eye on him. There were regular medicals which he hated. 'Do they think the bloody leg will grow again?' Perhaps he misjudged them. They may not have wanted to cut his pension, but to make sure his disability had not increased. If so, they did not give him that impression when he went for those medicals, but misunderstandings seem to arise easily between individuals and authority where hand-outs are involved.

We were good companions during his period of unemployment and re-adjustment. We played cribbage, did water-colour paintings and sang songs, while my mother was out cleaning the houses of people who lived along Park Side. I recollect her as sharp-tongued, and later in life I understood why. Her

real talents were never used as a housewife. The social deference expected of
her in those tall houses where the Vicar, the Sunday-school Superintendent and
some university teachers lived, did infuriate her. But she had to accept it, and so
she passed it on to us. I remember going with a message to one of the houses
where she worked. By some oversight, I was shown into the drawing room – I
suppose I went up the front steps and not down to the basement, and I stood
there beside a piano in a carpeted room, unable to move and rather afraid to
breathe. This petty-bourgeois grandeur was certainly a come-down for my
mother, who had been a trusted house-servant with Sir James Frazer, author of
The Golden Bough. The saucy fellow from the fish-mongers had brought her
trouble. One child could be fostered, but when my brother was born and the war
came changes had to be made.

I was eleven years old in 1920, and due to change schools. I won a scholarship
to Cambridge County School, but my mother knew we could not cope with
uniform, books, satchel and hockey-stick. She was realistic and right. It would
have been painful. There were no grants in aid, even for the children of 'heroes'.
So I was inserted into the Higher Grade School which, like my father's pub, was
at the bottom of the street. It was a step up from the all-purpose school at the
shabbier end of the town.

I began life at that school with several problems; one large and many small.
The large one arose because I was born before my parents decided to get
married. My birth certificate said 'Strange', and so did the elementary school
register. My mother wanted the records straight, and I was told to speak up and
get myself listed as Ball. Such a lot of lists, and so many teachers to speak up to. I
did not have the sense to say that my mother had married a second time, so I
could only face the avid ring of playground questioners with hot humiliation.
The smaller problem related to clothing. Home-made gym slip and white blouse
were not standard pattern, and my bloomers had to be pulled down rather than
tucked up because my black stockings were too short. For a long time I even had
to make do without a school hat, which ensured my absence from formal school
functions, when by rights, as a 'clever' girl, I should have been well to the fore.

I also had an embarrassing habit of fainting at morning assembly or in singing
class, which we took standing up. Something to do with my mother's lumpy
porridge, no doubt. It nauseated me. I used to hold it in my mouth, to spit out
somewhere, and because I took so long to eat it I didn't get any bread and marg.
My packed lunch wasn't exactly an appetizer, either. Our house was run on the
dregs of my mother's energy and my father's bumbling erratic help. We couldn't
afford to waste anything, so often the rice cake or rock buns which went wrong
were my lunch portion. In the end, the school authorities, who had no school
dinners to offer, made me do with a daily spoonful of codliver oil and malt. More
nausea.

Later in the decade, my mother would spread her wings and speed on her bike
to Newmarket Racecourse. When she had a winner she would overwhelm us
with rich cooking, like jugged hare, which we could hardly digest, but which
must have reminded her of days when she lived with the gentry. When she was

really happy, she would make steak-and-kidney pudding. Which is still one of my favourite meals.

The school had fee-paying pupils – in the majority, I think. They were mostly tradesmen's daughters. I envied them. Their lives, as I glimpsed them, seemed so right. Long fine stockings, dainty lunches, bicycles, tennis racquets, parties, summer holidays by the sea. I wanted to play tennis, but I had no access to the gear. So the teachers, in their wisdom, gave me extra arithmetic and needlework. I do not think they developed my skills, only my inferiority complex. And they gave me, working unsupervised, more time for day-dreaming.

I dearly wanted to be one of the ordinary girls, with frizzed hair (mine was dead straight) and a splendid disregard of class work. They knew quite clearly what their role in life was, embryo wives and mothers all. I endured the acute embarrassment of always being top of the class, and the attention of one teacher who pulled me out front to show how my straight short hair shone unadorned, when she wanted to rage against untidy frizz.

I had no idea at all where my 'cleverness' would lead me. My mother had a firm intention to keep me out of domestic service, which was still an option for working-class girls, and which had started for her when she left home at 12 years old and came to work in Cambridge with a wooden box of clothes and one shilling. I think some of the teachers thought I might join their sisterhood, but they were all un-married and were therefore clothed in the kind of oddity I wanted to shed. It took another social upheaval consequent on a world war to allow women the right to be married and teach. I suppose there was a faint whiff of women's lib about a school which included sharp-tongued Miss Ferguson, but I think it was too faint to linger on us when we left school, and in any case it was odd. We were partisan at elections, and wore our colours, and we were keen on 'the vote' for our elders, but other ideas about freedoms were successfully blocked by the influence, vestigial though it was, of our Church. I seemed to remember that I thought it more practical to aim at being good rather than to imagine riches or fame. The substance of my day-dreams was powerfully influenced by such runes and rhymes as 'Two men looked through the self-same bars, One saw mud and the other saw stars' and 'Be good, sweet maid, and let who will be clever, Do noble things, not dream them all day long.' But not wishy-washy good. Maggie Tulliver and Jo in *Little Women* were characters I identified with very strongly. Like these characters, I experienced internal pressures towards self-expression, which broke through my desire to conform. I argued with my Sunday School teachers, and wrote letters to the Cambridge Daily News, one of which provoked the vicar into a sermon of condemnation, though he never cracked my nom-de-plume, and I, not having the courage of my convictions (if that's what they were), never let on.

I had no ambitions which were set in reality, and nobody to help me formulate any. I suppose the three other scholarship girls at the Higher Grade School had the same problems, but I hated being grouped with them. It would have been easy to say that we were being educated out of our station in life. In my desire to be ordinary, I expect I was not very sympathetic to Bessie who was anaemic and had to eat raw liver, or to Dolly whose parents were socialists, and who gave her the annual torture of bringing a note demanding her withdrawal from Empire Day ceremonies.

Of course, there are some pleasant school memories, too. Winning essay competitions, and so acquiring books. Taking part in plays, even French ones; happy singing sessions with inspired Miss Orchard; and History with witty Miss Morley. May Day, when the school was full of flowers and we had a May Queen.

> All is bright and cheerful round us
> All above is soft and blue
> Spring at last has come and found us
> Spring and all its treasures too.
> Every flower is full of gladness
> Dew is bright and buds are gay
> Earth with all its sin and sadness
> Seems a happy place today.

My father was fond of fishing, and he cycled to meadows and woods by the river for his days of escape. So he knew where cowslips grew. I can remember filling a small tin bath with these fragrant flowers, to make chains and balls for the decorations. I had one moment of significance each year which gave me satisfaction. The fact that I lived just outside the school gate involved me in much running home to borrow baths and buckets and other utensils for flower containers. I became the recognized helper for the May Days I shared, and I hoped secretly to be a Maid of Honour in my final year. But in 1924, I was 14½ years old when my mother told me to apply for a job in the office of the Co-operative Society; a good job, she said, with steady rises and a superannuation fund. I had to take a written examination, and of course I got the job at 8s. a week. As I said, Prospect Row and the Higher Grade School are in Cambridge. So when, many years later, my daughter won an Open Scholarship to Newnham College (and one to Somerville, Oxford, but she chose Newnham) 'it was (you may say) satisfactory'.

In the mid-twenties, I learned how to become a clerk at the Co-op, and after evening classes in shorthand and typing, a higher grade office worker. A dutiful, heads-down-all-day, worker, with no ideas at all about my rights. Not even my basic rights as a human being, never mind my rights as part of a deal involving my work and their money. True, there was some talk of a Trades Union, but no girl or woman ever thought it applied to her. Some of my work kept me standing up all day, and when I had bad menstrual cramps, as I often did, I would slink off to the lavatory to sit down for as long as I dared. No rest room, not even a chair in our crowded cloakroom.

Some new ideas did take root – the Co-op was quite an evangelical movement then, and it was their evening classes which I joined. But my emotions and understanding were still at sixes and sevens. Which was the right way to live? Like Nellie, with her placid face and her engagement ring, and her pieces of linen and underclothes in tissue paper, brought for display to the girls before settling in her bottom drawer. Or like Jessie, coy and nudging – what we would now call sexy – surrounded by men, single and married? Or like Miss Marshall, the General Manager's secretary and our immediate boss. Composed, and sharp with us, the owner of a little car, involved in a sly relationship with the Manager of the Grocery Dept?

When my wages reached 17s. a week I bought a new bike for £5, to be paid for on the never-never at 2s. a week. It had down-swept racing handles, and we wore trousers for riding (we called them shorts, but they covered our knees). It seems as though I was getting free from the need to conform, for these ugly garments did cause a commotion at home and in villages where we stopped to rest and look. They made sense to us, however, as cycling kit, and so we took over where Mrs Bloomer left off. We covered a good many roads in East Anglia on our Sunday trips. My friend's half day was Thursday, and mine was Saturday. No five-day week, and only one week's annual holiday. We took books and sand-wiches in our saddle bags, and read to each other and together, on river banks, on top of hay stacks, and even on Newmarket Race Course. We went to public dances, too – 6d. or 1s. hops, but the boys we met all backed away – we *talked* at them. About the films we saw and the books we read. These were all sorts. Weepies like Florence Barclay's 'The Rosary', W. J. Locke, Warwick Deeping, Dornford Yates, James Barrie, Galsworthy. We even struggled through Bernard Shaw's novels, now forgotten and mostly un-read.

As Town Girls we were titillated by the young men in Gowns who surrounded us, and who gave us much interest, though we never 'went with undergrads'. Whether this was in deference to the widely held belief that nothing good came of such behaviour or whether it was lack of close encounters, I cannot now tell. The antics of the young men on November 5th and 11th should have been recognized as hooliganism, but in the early years after the war they were tolerated. Townspeople turned out in hundreds to watch, and once we were menaced by a crowd of lads driving a burning taxi-cab down a narrow street to the bonfire in the market square. Shops were boarded up, University Proctors and their Bulldogs (large men in frock coats and top hats) scuttled about to nab obvious offenders, who would be subject to internal college discipline only. We were thrilled really, and only half censorious. And we thrilled again when it was May Week and the Boat Races and the College Balls. From Garrett Hostel Bridge we could see dancers in evening dress, hear bands playing and watch the lucky ones taking to punts for the night ride up the river to breakfast at Grantchester. Although we were on the outside, looking in again, we did have a vicarious share of this glamour. My only recollections of the General Strike and its impact involve a trip to the railway station to watch the undergraduates driving trains. I'm afraid we did not see them as black-legs, but as heroes . . .

PART TWO

Education

INTRODUCTION

1. Almost all writers of autobiography received some schooling, however brief and rudimentary, and almost all included some account of it in their memoirs. The acquisition of learning was evidently regarded by all classes except the poorest as having important social, economic and cultural attributes, and as the century advanced an increasing proportion of space was devoted to the period of education and to its significance in people's lives: in not a few accounts it came to occupy the centre of the stage, replacing religion and work as the dominant life experiences. It is with the reactions of autobiographers to their education – and, sometimes, to the lack of it – that this chapter is concerned.

The growth of a schooled society, accompanying at some remove the rapid industrialization and urbanization of Britain, has been fully described elsewhere[1] and requires only brief mention. Before 1870 elementary education was provided either by individuals engaging for profit or by voluntary, philanthropic bodies which saw religiously based education as the means of moral improvement of the masses: of these, the Sunday Schools (established from 1785 onwards), the National Society for Promoting the Education of the Poor in the Principles of the Established Church (1811) and the British and Foreign School Society (1814) were the most influential. Initially offering free day-schooling, the two Societies were quickly obliged to charge 'school pence', and from 1833 onwards they began to receive a small, but increasing, annual government grant. Despite such encouragement, however, the efforts of organized philanthropy could never provide sufficient school places for the rapidly expanding child population, and in 1870 the state hesitantly became a provider of elementary education. Under Forster's Act local School Boards were to be established to 'fill in gaps' left by the Church Societies, and charged with providing sufficient places for all children. By 1876 it was possible to make attendance compulsory to the age of ten years, to eleven in 1893 and to twelve in 1899, by which time schooling had also become free. By the end of the century the School Boards had added approximately three million new school places, and the position of the churches as principal providers of schooling for the masses had ended.

*

2. Until late in the nineteenth century, therefore, access to formal education depended partly on local school provision, partly on the resources of parents to pay fees, and partly on the opportunities for child employment on which the frail budgets of the poor often had to depend.[2] Autobiographers make it clear that schooling often had to take second place to the needs of the family economy, that it was often extremely brief, interrupted and prematurely ended, and not a few comment with sorrow or resentment at this denial of educational opportunity. 'My school life came to an end when I was about eight years old,' wrote Thomas Wood, referring to the year 1830. 'I now went to work at John Sharpe's mill at the bottom of the town, and quite close to the school I had left.'[3] More poignantly still, Charles Shaw, working as a mould-runner, also at the age of eight, described his reactions on seeing a young man who had the time and means to be 'reading of his own free will':

> I felt a sudden, strange sense of wretchedness. There was a blighting consciousness that my lot was harsher than his and that of others . . . I went back to my mould-running and hot stove with my first anguish in my heart.[4]

Yet, despite all the obstacles, the great majority of working people who wrote their life histories had at least some schooling. In his study of forty-nine published autobiographies of the first half of the nineteenth century, Dr David Vincent discovered only two written by men who had had no formal instruction either in day-school or Sunday School, a fact which led him to the conclusion that 'the sum of elementary provision was greater than appears from an analysis of its parts'.[5] In some cases the experience was very brief indeed – for John Clare, it was often only three months in the year that could be spared from farm work[6] – and although it has been estimated that the proportion of children attending day-schools doubled between 1818 and 1851[7] there still remained at the later date about one-third of all children who escaped any daily instruction.

Particularly during the earlier part of the century, therefore, substantial numbers of working men were left to acquire their education without benefit of formal teaching, and the fact that so many of them did is a striking testimony to the force of the spirit of self-improvement which was a leading characteristic of nineteenth century social development. A group of autobiographers have described their struggles for self-education – sometimes solitary, in the woods and fields on Sundays or in attic bedrooms by candlelight, sometimes collectively in mutual improvement societies, Mechanics' Institutes, or informal groups of friends. Almost always, these activities seem to have been motivated by a genuine desire to pursue knowledge for its own sake rather than for material gain, and it is with some surprise that we find working men devoting themselves to literature and poetry (not uncommonly leading to poetic writing of their own), to theology, philosophy, history and the classics, but only rarely to mathematics or the sciences. For a minority whose interests lay in radical politics there was a long-term, practical objective in the transformation of society, however utopian that may seem, but, ironically, most self-taught autobiographers pursued what was, in effect, a 'polite' education which had little or no relevance to their occupations or daily affairs.

Precisely what impulses drove such men to study after long and arduous labour remains mysterious. Thomas Carter, a tailor of Colchester, describes how as a small child he had 'even then a taste for reading', how from the first 'childish trifles' he progressed to the Bible, *Pilgrim's Progress* and Harvey's *Meditations,* reading while knitting under his mother's eye and occasionally escaping with his books into an 'arbour' of runner beans. Reading 'enabled me to discover new sources of mental pleasure and, moreover, to express my emotions in an intelligent and appropriate manner', and from books and from 'the beauty and grandeur of nature' he drew the inspiration himself to write poetry, ultimately publishing a volume of verse and a collection of *Lectures on Taste* as well as his own autobiography.[8] Carter was certainly no testimony to the material values of self-help, for he lived and died a poor man, his health prematurely ruined by over-work and his enthusiasm blunted by the world's indifference.

One great obstacle to self-improvement in the early nineteenth century was the lack of suitable literature on which children could learn to read. 'At that time,' wrote James Watson, born in 1799, 'there were no cheap books, no cheap newspapers or periodicals, no Mechanics' Institutions to facilitate the acquisiton of knowledge';[9] in later life Watson himself became a printer, publisher, and founder-member of the London Working Men's Association. Similarly, William Linton records that he was reared on a diet of sensational chap-books which included the *Newgate Calendar* and *Legends of Horror,* 'affording much amusement, if not very valuable instruction, to the young'.[10] Until at least the 1830s, when penny periodicals began to appear, there was little literature specifically for children beyond a few fairy tales; children were expected to read the Bible and, if they had educational ambitions, to pass immediately to the world of adult literature. Even then, the problem was likely to be access to books, which were expensive and not available in public libraries until the later half of the century;[11] many working men joined local societies of a philanthropic character or the Mechanics' Institutes after their foundation in 1823, mainly to have the use of a library rather than to improve their technical skill or knowledge.

Self-education clearly brought deep satisfaction and sense of achievement into the lives of many working men and even, to a few, national acclaim. John Clare, the son of an illiterate shepherd, became pre-eminent among the 'uneducated poets'. After brief and interrupted schooling, he was at work in the fields by the age of ten, already separating himself from his companions in order to read and write in his little spare time, and spending his first shilling savings not on sweets but on a copy of Thomson's *Poems*. Unable to afford paper, his own early works were written on his mother's used tea-packets, yet by the age of twenty-five, while working as a lime-burner at 1s. 2d. a day, he published his first collection of poems and was on the way to recognition.

A similar route brought Roger Langdon to a different, though not less remarkable, destination. A ploughboy at eight, he later joined the Great Western Railway, achieving a position of responsibility as station master at Silverton, Devon. Though he had only had a Sunday School education, he taught himself Latin and Greek and became a widely recognized astronomer; on a wage which never exceeded 30s. a week and with eight children to support, he constructed four telescopes of increasing magnification, built an iron observatory at the station, read a learned paper to the Royal Astronomical Society, and corresponded with leading scientists of the day including Dr Blacklock and James Nasmyth.[12]

Langdon was unusual among his kind in pursuing scientific interests, for these often required both more outlay and more training than were available to poorer working men. George Jacob Holyoake, born in Birmingham in 1818, the son of a mechanic, at least had the advantage of his father's instruction and membership of a flourishing Mechanics' Institute, but although his name was put forward to George Stephenson, nothing came of it and he abandoned the idea of an engineering career because of the lack of higher educational opportunities:

Had there been in my time means of higher education in evening classes, when degrees could be won without University attendance – impossible to me – I should have remained in the workshop. There is more independence in pursuit of handicraft, and more time for original thought, than in clerkship or business.[13]

What engineering lost in Holyoake, it gained in Nasmyth, and the differences in the two careers are instructive. James Nasmyth was born into a cultured, middle-class Edinburgh family in 1808: his ancestors had been architects and builders, his father was a successful professional portrait-painter, and all seven daughters and four sons were talented artists. James's great passion lay in model-making and scientific experimentation, and after an inescapably classical education at Edinburgh High School ('My mind was never opened up by what was taught me there. It was a mere matter of rote and cram . . .') he took private lessons in mathematics, attended lectures at the University on mechanics and dynamics, and performed practical experiments at a friend's iron foundry. At twenty-one, with his models as evidence of his skill, he obtained the post of private assistant to Henry Maudsley, probably the foremost engineer of the day, accepting a nominal wage of 10s. a week. After two years with Maudsley in Lambeth, he launched his own highly successful firm, where he invented and manufactured the Nasmyth steam-hammer, the pile-driver, and numerous self-acting tools, becoming one of the group of highly influential men who had a decisive effect on the course of the Industrial Revolution.[14]

Self-education was particularly characteristic of the earlier half of the century, but not restricted to it, and throughout the whole period working people continued to build a successful education on the most slender foundations. The titles of some later autobiographies – 'Workman's Cottage to Windsor Castle', 'Thomas Burt, M.P., D.C.L., Pitman to Privy Councillor', 'From Workshop to War Cabinet','From Chimney-Boy to Councillor'[15] – indicate the pride of the authors in their achievement as well as the greater opportunities of mobility which came with changes in the social and political structure. Evening classes, correspondence courses, the Workers' Educational Association and the Women's Co-operative Guild afforded important opportunities of study and intellectual stimulus to people who had no access to university education. Thus, James Griffiths, who was born near Llanelli in 1890, left school at thirteen to go down the pit like his brothers, but his interest and involvement in trade unionism and labour politics led him to study first at the local W.E.A. branch and later at the Labour College in London. His remarkable career included Minister of National Insurance (1945–50), deputy to Hugh Gaitskell in 1956 and Secretary of State for Wales under Harold Wilson.[16] But also remarkable is the career of Doris Hunt, born in Manchester in 1900, a half-timer in a cotton mill at twelve and a full-timer by thirteen. After a ten-hour day she went on four nights a week to evening classes in English, mathematics and commercial subjects, 'For I was ashamed of the fact that I was a mill-girl – had my father lived I was going to be a teacher.' At seventeen she gave up her £2 a week job for half that wage with a firm of chartered accountants, becoming the first woman auditor in Rochdale;

thirty years and the raising of a family later, she embarked on an
eleven-year study of the History of the English Novel and of European
Drama.[17]

Throughout the century, but especially in the earlier part of it,
self-help autobiographies were largely confined to male authors. This is
easily explained by the fact that until after 1870 girls had less access to
schooling than boys, and that where parents had to make choices about
their children's education the preference was almost always determined
by sex rather than by intellectual capacity. These facts reflect the male
domination of Victorian social life and the view, prevalent to a greater or
lesser extent among all classes, that the serious education of girls was
unnecessary, if not positively harmful – a view which survived until
recently in the preference given by parents to boys in respect of opportunities for secondary and university education. Although such discrimination was no doubt accepted more or less willingly by many girls,
it could result in a bitter sense of deprivation, as illustrated in the
autobiography of Hannah Mitchell. Born on a remote Derbyshire farm
in 1871, she was required as a child to help with heavy household tasks
while her brothers were allowed to read and play in the evenings: 'My
mother honestly thought me lazy because I didn't like housework, and
held that reading was only a recreation, meant for Sundays.' 'Education'
was not spoken of at home, only 'a bit o' schoolin', and as the nearest
school was five miles away daily travel was impossible: the six children
went into lodgings by turn as they grew old enough and as family means
allowed. Hannah, in fact, enjoyed only two weeks of school before she
fell ill and had to return home, but by chance the seed of culture was
sown when a hiker, Hans Renold, called at the farm for shelter and left
behind a copy of Wordsworth's poems. Determined to escape the
nagging and punishments of her mother, Hannah had no alternative but
to go into domestic service, but in later life, self-taught and determined,
she became a suffragette, a socialist, a Justice of the Peace and a
councillor.[18]

3. For the many children who had no access to day-schooling until late in
the century, the expansion of the Sunday School movement was of great
importance, bringing educational opportunities of a kind to millions
who had to work on six days of the week. The Sunday Schools introduced into England the idea of universal, free education on which
ultimately the system of day-schooling was built, and through their close
association with the churches and with the 'respectable' elements in
society helped to break down the resistance to the education of 'the

masses' which tended to associate the spread of literacy with the spread of social discontent. Furthermore, it has recently been argued that at a time when church attendance among the working classes was on the decline, they formed an important part of a distinct religious sub-culture that was 'deeply rooted in the ethic of education, religion and respectability which was embodied in the Sunday School'.[19]

From the foundation of the Sunday School Society by Robert Raikes, a newspaper proprietor of Gloucester, in 1785, the movement made rapid progress, claiming three-quarters of a million pupils within the first ten years. Poor parents were encouraged to send their children with offers of free meals, clothing clubs and similar material benefits, while the 'respectable' classes were involved as teachers, patrons and visitors. The motives behind the movement were at least as strongly religious and social as they were intellectual. The great aim was to teach children to read and understand the Bible so that they could grow up in the hope of divine salvation; secular subjects were specifically excluded from the curriculum, the Rules of the Society including the injunction: 'Be diligent in teaching the children to read well . . . Neither writing nor arithmetic is to be taught on Sundays.' In fact, many of the larger schools developed weekday night classes in these subjects, originally intended for the better education of the teachers, which became valuable instruments of adult education.

In terms of recruitment, the Sunday Schools were outstandingly successful, claiming 1,550,000 pupils attending 16,828 schools in 1833;[20] by the time of the Religious Census of 1851 2,400,000 were on the registers and 1,800,000 in attendance, suggesting considerable popular-ity. How much was learned in two or three hours a week of what must in any case often have been irregular attendance is much more difficult to know. David Wardle has judged that a child who attended regularly would learn to read 'but only the exceptional pupil would learn anything more'[21] – though this, of course, was not a principal objective. There was certainly a good deal of contemporary criticism of the efforts of the volunteer teachers as 'altogether unsystematic and feeble', though equally certain is abundant evidence that those children who persevered with attendance, graduated to the Bible classes for older students, and, not uncommonly, became Sunday School teachers themselves, had often laid the basis of a sound elementary education.

The popularity of Sunday Schools continued unabated in the years up to 1914, even increasing after the general introduction of day-schools in 1870, the number of pupils on register reaching a peak of 6,179,000 in 1906.[22] They were remarkably successful in adapting to changing social needs, abandoning secular education after 1870 except for special sessions for adults, but concentrating on religious instruction, social activities and para-religious institutions like the Band of Hope (founded in 1839 but incorporated into the Sunday School organization in 1874) and the Boys' Brigade (1883). A wide variety of social events, ranging from the famous Whitsun Walks and massed choral concerts at the Crystal Palace to the humble magic lantern show and annual outing, continued to keep children, young people and parents strongly attached to the Sunday Schools at a time when recreational opportunities were still limited.

From the frequency with which they are mentioned in autobiographical writings it is clear that they occupied a highly important and, generally, highly honoured place in the lives of the working classes. Only rarely is there a critical note. John James Bezer, 'One of the Chartist Rebels', wrote in 1851 that 'I learnt more in Newgate than at my Sunday School', though explaining almost in the same breath that during the fifteen years he attended, he eventually became head teacher. 'I can truly say I loved my school – no crying when Sunday came round.'[23] His main complaint – that there was 'plenty of cant, and what my teachers used to call *explaining* difficult texts in the Bible' – was echoed by Marianne Farningham, both of whose parents were Sunday School teachers:

The knowledge received at the Sunday School was very definite and dogmatic . . . I was made to learn by heart long passages of Scripture . . . Naturally, I did not understand them, or even try to do so . . . As to the hymns which I learned, and repeated to my teachers, I am amazed that books containing them were ever put into the hands of children. Of course, like everybody in the school, I learned:

> There is a dreadful hell,
> And everlasting pains,
> Where sinners must with devils dwell
> In darkness, fire and chains.

Hell was a very real thing to me . . .[24]

Many teachers themselves, especially in the remoter areas, were barely literate, and Ben Brierley remembers that his teacher at Failsworth, near Rochdale, in the 1830s, could not manage 'hard words' of more than two syllables.[25] And, at the end of the century, Faith Osgerby thought that:

Sundays were hateful days. My mother sent us to the Primitive Methodist Sunday School . . . because school began earlier and we had longer sessions and she wanted rid of us for as long as possible. What I learned there for my good I shall never know. The children behaved very badly (I suppose I did too). Teachers were a queer, mixed crowd who knew very little about what they were supposed to teach. They gave us to understand that we were in danger of hell fire if we were not good. I knew there was no hope whatever for me. Children were spiteful and jealous: girls flaunted their new clothes, poking fun at others not so fortunate.[26]

Social distinctions and snobbery were not absent in Sunday School, any more than in the House of God. With a middle-class upbringing, Gwen Millington attended the Young People's Service on Sunday afternoon, commenting:

Here was the inkling of the social divide. Those attending the Church Elementary School for the most part went to Sunday School and an annual Sunday School Treat. The Young People's Service was in the Church – most went to private schools, and went to an annual Garden Party in the Rectory garden.[27]

At the other end of the divide, very poor children could sometimes not attend for lack of suitable clothes, shoes or the 'collection' penny. 'In those days,' wrote J. Smetham of Romsey, Hampshire, in 1912, 'all the children that I knew in our lane went to Sunday School with the exception of one or two families who didn't have any Sunday clothes. They were not allowed out on Sundays, and had to stay at home and play in the back garden.'[28]

But criticism of their Sunday School experiences by autobiographers is untypical. In general, they write enthusiastically, often glowingly, even when attendance at Sunday School and church or chapel services meant two, three and even four visits, and occupied virtually the whole of the day. Alice Moody, who attended Elm Grove Sunday School, Portsmouth, for twelve happy years in the eighties and nineties, echoes the feelings of many when she writes of the school having

an atmosphere of love, peace and joy, with teachers of good education and children like ourselves – well-behaved without being smug, and lively without being unruly. Lovely, lovely Elm Grove Sunday School. Every hour I spent in its walls was a foretaste of Heaven.[29]

Similarly, for the anonymous 'Cornish Waif', Sunday School was 'the brightest thing in my life'.[30] Whether religious or social factors account for this enthusiasm is impossible to know. The Sunday Schools were adept at combining the two, maintaining the interest of children and young adults by carefully graded classes as well as by organizing choirs, competitions and a wide range of social events: not a few pupils met their future husbands and wives at Sunday School. In isolated and rural areas, where considerable journeys were sometimes involved, it was not uncommon for families of parents and children to spend the day at school and chapel, bringing food with them and filling in the gaps happily with friends and neighbours.[31] Few can have devoted so much time as Christopher Thomson, who, as a Sunday School teacher around 1820, used to rise at 5 a.m. and was then involved in a continuous round of classes, services and choirs until 10 p.m.,[32] but Edward Brown in the 1880s 'usually put in four attendances a day at the Congregational Church and Sunday School, going to school at ten o'clock, church at eleven, school again at half-past two and church again at half-past six'.[33]

For many people Sunday School was clearly much more than a step on the educational ladder, important though that was. Though initially established from 'outside' and with strong undertones of social control, it came to be absorbed and, ultimately, largely taken over by the working classes themselves as an institution well suited to their intellectual and spiritual needs. It fitted neatly into the enforced routine of work and leisure; it had strong local and community associations; by informality and neighbourliness it helped to keep alive a sense of 'belonging' at a time when the old bonds of society were loosening; above all, perhaps, by involving different generations in its activities, it reinforced the importance and integrity of the family when this, too, was threatened by the disruptive forces of industrialization. The portrait of the little Welsh Sunday School drawn by Robert Roberts (pp. 182–6) is an extreme, but probably not idealized, one: even in the large, more regimented city schools the same affectionate relationships and the same spirit of dedication to the cause of Christian education seem generally to have prevailed.

4. For those parents who could afford to pay for any day-schooling for their children, the dame school often provided the only real opportunity – particularly during the earlier part of the century and in areas not well served by the Church Societies. Dame schools were 'adventure' or private schools, generally kept by a single mistress in her own house or cottage where the living-room might be used to accommodate a dozen or twenty little children. Unqualified, and even uneducated in a formal sense, she undertook to teach the alphabet, reading, and sometimes the simpler rules of summing, in return for a few pence a week; in some areas, where there were well-established local crafts at which children worked from an early age, 'academic' study was combined with instruction in lace-making, straw-plaiting, glove-stitching or knitting. The

'typical' dame school therefore defies definition. At its worst, in some of the so-called 'lace schools', it was no more than a means of exploiting tiny children on the pretext that they were learning a useful trade; most were in the nature of nursery-schools where busy mothers could leave their children out of harm's way in the reasonable expectation that they would be taught to read; at the top, some merged into the private schools and 'academies' where children of the better-off classes were introduced to penmanship, mathematics, the use of globes and other polite studies.

Judged solely on their educational achievements, many dame schools must have been less than successful, and official opinion, forcibly expressed in the Newcastle Commission of 1861, considered that they were 'generally very inefficient'.[34] Yet they evidently performed what was regarded as a useful function, and were often accorded an affectionate place in popular literature.[35] In an article 'The Dame School Forty Years Ago' written by a 'Working Man' in 1872, the author compared his experiences there very favourably with the education he later received at a National School.[36] The writings of autobiographers who attended such schools indicate a wide variety of experience, with the majority more favourable than critical. Their attendance usually began at a very early age – often at three or four – and almost always ended by seven or eight, sometimes followed by schooling elsewhere, and since dame school was the first experience of separation from home and mother, recollections of it may be clouded by the fear and trauma which this sometimes involved. The anxieties of Christopher Thomson on starting school can hardly have been assuaged by the drilling of letters and the recounting of ghost stories by his teacher, and James Hopkinson spoke for many when he wrote:

> I did not like going to school. I can remember my Mother having to carry me across the street to an old woman's school while I squeeled all the way we went. Arrived at school, I was so naughty that the school mistress had to pin me to her apron. But I was so determined to be a free agent that I tore a great hole in her apron in my efforts to be free. She then put me behind the door, which I liked very well, as I pulled out my marbles and began to play . . .[37]

His early antipathy to school continued, and he later ran away from another establishment while the master was punishing him.

But, more typically, autobiographers recall their days at dame school with gratitude, affection, and admiration for the skill of their untrained teachers. That attended by Joseph Gutteridge in Coventry about 1820 was kept by a Quaker 'of gentle, placid face and motherly kindness'; no physical force was ever used in her school, for she had 'a facile and winning mode of attracting attention'. By the age of seven he could easily read the local newspaper.[38] And one of the warmest tributes was paid by Thomas Cooper, who later himself established a school:

> As soon as I was strong enough I was sent to a dame's school near at hand, kept by aged Gertrude Aram, 'Old Gatty' as she was usually called. Her schoolroom – that is to say the larger, lower room of her two-storied cottage – was always full; and she was an expert and laborious teacher of the art of reading and spelling. Her knitting, too – for she taught girls as well as boys – was the wonder of the town. I soon became her favourite scholar, and could read the tenth chapter of Nehemiah with all its hard names 'like the parson in the church' as she used to say, and could spell wondrously.[39]

With children of various ages and abilities crowded into one small room, with little or no equipment and a shortage even of books, some of these schools evidently achieved remarkable results. Like Cooper, William Esam who began his education at a dame school ('or, as it was called, a "Ma'am School"') later became a teacher and school proprietor; although he was at first afraid of the teacher's huge mob cap and the cane she always carried, 'she taught me well, for I could read the New Testament at four years old and knew something of ciphering and writing'.[40] He had started at three, while Frederick Hobley had begun attending a dame school at Thame, Oxfordshire, 'kept for very young children' when only two years old.[41]

Dame schools survived in name into the early twentieth century, Leslie Missen attending one so-called in Cambridge from 1902–5. By then, however, their role had changed into something more like preparatory schools, and the syllabus had widened to include such things as nature study and piano; by the age of eight Missen was sufficiently well grounded to pass directly into a Higher Grade School and, later, to win a scholarship to the Perse School.[42] The humble dame school, which had started life by offering a rudimentary educational service, mainly for the poorer classes, at a time when the state did not do so, ended its days by teaching a more ambitious curriculum than the elementary school to children of more prosperous parents and as a preparation for a much longer period of formal education.

5. Progress towards a national system of day-schools for the working classes lay with the two great voluntary organizations, the National Society and the British and Foreign School Society. The National Society aimed to establish a Church of England school in every parish in the country, its pupils being required to learn the catechism and the

Liturgy and to 'constantly attend Divine worship in their Parish Church'; the British Society with a broader sectarian base representing the main nonconformist churches, contented itself with the declared object of 'instructing youth in useful learning [and] in the leading and incontroverted principles of Christianity'.

These voluntary efforts to spread a form of Christian education to the masses, aided from 1833 onwards by small but increasing government contributions, achieved impressive results in terms of numbers of school places. In 1851 it was estimated that between them (but with the National Society a clear leader) the two Societies were providing approximately 1,400,000 of the 2,100,000 day-school places in the country, and that it was mainly due to their efforts that the proportion of the population attending school had doubled from one in seventeen to one in eight during the past thirty years. The strongest criticism that has been levelled at the Societies, however, is that this remarkable expansion was achieved at the expense of low standards, large classes and mechanical methods suited to the 'monitorial system' on which the Societies based their teaching methods and curricula. Both Andrew Bell of the National Society and Joseph Lancaster of the British Society claimed to have 'invented' the system whereby the actual instruction was given by older pupils recruited at the age of ten or eleven as monitors, the main functions of the teacher then being to punish, reward and keep order over the whole school, and to teach the monitors the lessons they would later relay to their groups.[43] A contemporary commented on the role of the schoolteacher under this system that 'little else is required of him than an aptitude for enforcing discipline, an acquaintance with mechanical details for the preservation of order, and that sort of ascendancy in his school which a sergeant-major is required to exercise over a batch of raw recruits'.[44]

Such men – and at this period, when a school of up to a thousand children might only employ one teacher, this was invariably a man – were drawn mainly from those who had failed in other trades where they had acquired just enough learning to satisfy the low academic standards of the Church Societies. Both Lancaster and Bell established training departments in their schools so that promising monitors might 'qualify' as teachers, but both complained of the poor quality of the adult entrants, in many cases 'unable to write and, in some, even to read'. Much of their training was basic, remedial work in elementary education; for the rest, they 'learned the system' for a few weeks by walking round the school and observing the monitors at work.

The beauty of the monitorial system, to contemporaries at least, was that it exhibited 'the division of labour applied to educational purposes'. The material to be taught was subdivided in such a way that each section was completely simple: the monitors taught from cards on which each lesson was reduced to components which could be learned by heart, and were not allowed to go beyond what was on the card. Indeed, it was claimed as one of the merits of the system that as monitors themselves knew no more, they could not digress or waste time. As children learned the work of one 'draft', they were promoted to the next, and the principle of dividing pupils into groups or Standards according to ability was an important innovation in English education. Joseph Lancaster's original school in the Borough Road, London, took a thousand children and used sixty–seventy monitors; as the sole teacher, his task required constant vigilance and organization, the preparation of some fifteen lessons for each class (no lesson took more than fifteen minutes), the training of the monitors, the testing of the work, the recording and promotion of the children and 'animating and directing the whole'.

Few autobiographies by monitors or by those they taught have survived on which to base a judgement of the system. The criticism that monitors themselves were among its victims, since they had very little opportunity to learn beyond the limited lessons they were required to teach, seems to be borne out by the reminiscences of Thomas Dunning, who in 1820 at the age of seven attended the National School at Newport Pagnall 'to learn but very little'. This was evidently a much less highly organized school than Lancaster's, and probably more typical of those outside the large cities:

> The boys who could read moderately well were appointed to teach the younger or lower classes. I was one of these, and I had very little time allowed me for either writing or arithmetic, and none for grammar or geography. Our schoolmaster, Mr Johnson, was the parish clerk, and he had to see to the bells being chimed for prayers on Wednesdays and Fridays; he sent the biggest boys to perform the chiming business, I being amongst them. All the scholars had to attend church on Wednesdays, Fridays and Sundays, and gabble over the responses.[45]

The success of the system doubtless varied greatly according to the skill and training of the teacher and his monitors, the size of the school and the social and educational background of the pupils. James Bonwick, who was a monitor and, eventually, head monitor at the Borough Road School in the 1820s, probably saw the system at its best. His account (pp. 171–6) indicates that even at this early period of curriculum extended well beyond 'the three Rs' to include geography (mainly, it appears, of the Holy Land), grammar, geometry, science and singing. At fifteen he was sent out as a 'qualified' teacher in charge of a school, which he apparently managed with success; he subsequently had a remarkable and remunerative career in Australia as explorer, gold-miner, school inspector and proprietor of boarding-schools.[46] Natural ability like his was clearly not destroyed by exposure to the monitorial system, and, for all its obvious defects, it was the means by which many thousands of children achieved a degree of literacy at a time when considerations of economy were paramount.

6. Improvements in the quality of teaching in the elementary school began in the 1830s, when James Kay-Shuttleworth, the Secretary of the Committee of Council on Education, promoted the 'pupil-teacher' system as an alternative to monitorial methods. Under this, promising older pupils were apprenticed to a schoolteacher for a period usually of five years, during which time they both taught and received further education which was completed by a period of full-time study and training in a Normal School. The scheme was officially adopted by Minutes of Council in 1846, under which the government agreed to pay small salaries to pupil-teachers who, if successful in an examination (the Queen's Scholarship) at the end of five years, would then receive full-time education in a training college; if again successful in this, they would qualify as 'certificated teachers', eligible for an addition to their salary (an 'augmentation grant') and also entitled to extra fees if they themselves undertook the training of other pupil-teachers.

The new system brought the state importantly into the recruitment and training of teachers and therefore, indirectly, into the control of educational standards. It also provided a route by which clever boys and girls from the working class – usually drawn from artisan rather than labouring backgrounds – could acquire higher education, a nationally recognized qualification, and a social status approaching that of a professional person. Pupil-teaching supplied the majority of recruits to elementary schoolteaching in the years up to 1914, gradually replacing monitorial methods first in the larger towns and only later in small village schools. Many teachers did not complete all the arduous stages to full certification, and, in particular, a high proportion of women did not proceed to college after their apprenticeship, remaining as 'uncertificated mistresses' at a lower salary, but all had at least the benefit of a long period of training under a qualified teacher.

Although schools receiving government grant were subject to inspection by Her Majesty's Inspectors, it seems that at first these examinations were generally carried out in a relaxed, informal way which got the best out of teachers and pupils. The autobiography of John Kerr, an H.M.I. of this period, records that

... both teacher and inspector had more elbow-room and more free play ... A teacher whose heart was in his work gave instruction under healthier conditions and with greater efficiency from feeling that he was free to do what he thought best for those under his charge, free to take account of and adapt his teaching to varying degrees and kinds of ability ...[47]

These happy relationships were abruptly broken in 1862 with the introduction of the Revised Code, following the Report of the New-castle Commission which criticized both the cost and the inefficiency of elementary education. The Code introduced the principle of 'Payment by Results' whereby the government grant to a school would in future depend on the success of pupils in annual examinations conducted by H.M.I.s. 'If it is not cheap, it shall be efficient: if it is not efficient, it shall be cheap,' said Robert Lowe, the Vice-President of the Board charged with the implementation of the new system. The main intention of the Code – to improve standards of attainment of pupils in the basic tools of knowledge, the three Rs – was, regrettably, to be achieved by turning the teacher into a grant-earning instructor rather than an educator. For each child in regular attendance the school would earn 8s., subject to a deduction of 2s. 8d. for every failure in one of the three 'grant-earning subjects'; schools were to be organized into six Standards above the Infants, with detailed curricula laid down for each on which the annual examinations would be based.[48] The effects on children were to empha-size mechanical drilling of the three Rs, to restrict the curriculum, and, often, to vitiate relationships between teachers and pupils since teachers had little choice but to try to earn the maximum grant – by threat, by punishment, even by bringing sick children into school on examination day if they were likely to win points.[49]

Many H.M.I.s were themselves unwilling agents of the new system and spoke out boldly against it. Among autobiographers, one of the sharpest critics was the Rev. R. H. Quick, who stressed the distinction between real education and mere instruction, and the deadening effect which excessive rote-learning was having on understanding:

I maintain that it is the greatest mistake possible to have grind, grind, grind and nothing else. But according to our present system the three Rs are the sole object of our school course, and while they are pursued as the be-all and end-all of school, instruction can be nothing but grind.[50]

Fortunately, the full, grinding rigours of the Code did not endure for long. In 1871 grants were awarded for passes in 'specific' subjects available in higher Standards which included history, geography, grammar, algebra, geometry and natural sciences, and in 1875 were extended to 'class' subjects (history, geography, grammar and needlework for girls) which could be taken throughout the school. The effect of these changes was to reduce the dominance of the three Rs in the curriculum, though full advantage could only be taken in the larger town schools which had more highly trained, specialist staffs. The village schoolmaster or mistress typically offered a couple of 'class' subjects for H.M.I.'s approval but rarely any 'specific' subjects, since by doing so he ran the risk of losing grant on the three Rs which still remained the primary source of school revenue. 'Payment by Results' was finally abolished in 1897, the annual examinations of each child being replaced by periodic general inspections of efficiency.[51]

By the end of the century, major improvements had occurred in the elementary school. Gone were the days when the early Reports of H.M.I.s had revealed some appallingly low standards of teaching by brutal and ignorant staff, and had spoken of teachers 'wholly unfitted for their office' and 'utterly incompetent and unfit'. Classes were still very large – often of eighty or ninety children, though in this case there would usually be a pupil-teacher to assist, but the hundreds of new Board Schools which were built in the 1870s and 1880s were at least designed for educational purposes, with assembly halls, tiered classrooms and others whose size could be altered by movable partitions. The curriculum, too, expanded under the influence of better-trained teachers and more enlightened counsels at the Education Department. Some School Boards, like that of Birmingham, instituted a seventh Standard for more advanced work; others grouped these activities into Central Schools or Higher Grade Schools which in effect offered a form of secondary education and provided a valuable opportunity for some working-class children to gain qualifications in scientific, technical and commercial subjects. At the Leeds Higher Grade School, for example, under the headship of Dr Forsyth, 'the masters are all men who have been trained as elementary schoolmasters and who have obtained, or are on the way to obtain, university degrees'; even Latin and modern languages were taught here, but the school's chief reputation lay in its mathematics and science, and many former pupils went on to advanced studies at the Yorkshire College or elsewhere.

Such innovations, important as they were as signposts for future developments, initially touched only a few children. Most left the elementary school as early as the school-leaving age allowed – at ten when compulsory attendance was first introduced in 1876 but gradually raised to thirteen by 1914. By then, and under the vigilant eye of the School Attendance Officer, most children went regularly to school for a minimum of five years and, usually, for seven or eight, though in rural areas attendance long continued to be interrupted by the employment of children in fieldwork, even by farmer-magistrates in contravention of their own by-laws.[52] For all its obvious defects and limitations the achievements of elementary education were immense – 6,000,000 children at school taught by 150,000 teachers, basic literacy and numeracy brought to the mass of the child population and, on the evidence of autobiographical writings, not always at the expense of low standards and stifled imagination. Emotional and physical development were not, at the time, seen as the school's primary purpose; on the other hand, great importance was placed on the inculcation of discipline, order and obedience in the classroom, through which these virtues would later be transmitted to working-class life generally. It was the evident success of this disciplinary aspect of schooling which most struck observers, including not a few H.M.I.s, towards the end of the century, one of whom commented:

Anyone who can compare the demeanour of our young people at the present day with what it was five and twenty years ago must notice how roughness of manner has been smoothed away, how readily and intelligently they can answer a question, how the half-hostile suspicion with which they regarded a stranger has disappeared; in fact, how they have become civilized.[53]

The reactions of autobiographers to their elementary schooling naturally varied according to their differing experiences and a wide range of variables, but nevertheless certain common themes stand out clearly. The most frequently expressed is the dislike of school, the punishments and the constant fear of teachers. These feelings of mixed respect and antipathy are well summed up by one writer, J. C. Tait:

Chillingham Road [Elementary School] had a fine standard . . . The main idea was to get us out to earn money . . . The schooling was based on discipline. Reading, writing and arithmetic were essential, and children were clobbered until they mastered them. We were severely caned, unless too bad an offence had been committed – then the Head had a special session on our behinds with the thonged leather. At least, we knew where we stood – we certainly couldn't sit![54]

So, too, in Harry Dorrell's autobiography:

I started school at five years of age. The event was preceded by days, if not weeks, of anxious apprehension. Being sent to school was a threat for a naughty child. The day of starting was a day of reckoning . . . The huge, empty hall, the strange, pale headmistress, clinched my apprehensions . . . Some time later, a year or so I suppose, I became a reformed character and rambled to school unwillingly, but urgently, in fear most of the time. I learnt to hate school, and retained that hate until I left. For me it was nine years of deadly torment that only a shy child can know.[55]

The use of school as a threat by parents is frequently mentioned, and is often reinforced by experiences on the first day of unkind treatment by teachers or other pupils. On his first day Arthur Allwood was given such a 'terrible lecture' by the headmistress that he ran away and was eventually found by his father, in the dark, three miles from home.[56] In the village school she attended as a five-year-old in 1912 Mrs Palmer remembers that the infants were caned if they were late,[57] while the anonymous 'Cornish Waif' recalled her terror on her first day at school when the teacher threatened to cut out her tongue if she spoke.[58]

Corporal punishment was, of course, normal for older children at least and was expected for disobedience and all more serious offences, almost equally for girls as for boys. But many teachers caned for mistakes in arithmetic or writing, for blots or allegedly careless work, even for slowness in learning which was put down to 'not trying' rather than to lack of ability. The impression emerges from the autobiographies that most teachers caned almost automatically, without special vindictiveness; the cane was a symbol of office, and even young pupil-teachers, who were not supposed to cane, would carry a short stick concealed in their jacket sleeve. 'Every single teacher of every rank had his cane, and we used these canes, not often brutally, but commonly, without much discrimination and without scruple, indeed, without thought.'[59]

The reaction of many children to such treatment seems to have been initial resentment followed by gradual acceptance and even of respect. Edward Brown typifies this half-affectionate attitude:

The Headmaster, James Churchill – 'Jimmy' to us boys – a very fine specimen of the nineteenth-century type of pedagogue. He had a forbidding appearance with his square, black beard, clean-shaven upper lip and severe expression. But all this was more or less superficial, and behind it he was a just and capable man, with a sense of humour . . . He could be very stern and determined when roused or opposed, and was a firm believer in the use of the cane, as I found out to my cost on many occasions.[60]

But some of those who write of women teachers speak of a conscious cruelty, even of sadism. Daisy Cowper remembers her headmistress in Liverpool in the 1890s:

She was ugly: she couldn't help her ancient, sallow, wrinkled skin, which hung under her neck and chin in disgusting folds, or the yellow-tinted whites of her eyes, but she could help being cruel and unloving. The only words I ever heard her speak were harsh, bad-tempered ones . . . It was the big girls of the school she vented her sadistic instincts on, and she would bring down her beastly cane on the palms, one on each hand, with such a full-arm action and sickening thwack that I was terrified that the hand would drop off at the wrist . . .[61]

Similarly, Emily Lea writes:

I was always scared of the teachers. Only one during my three years in the Infant Department seemed really fond of children to me. The rest seemed to spend their time in devising various forms of torture to my small mind.[62]

Other autobiographers' comments include 'I was so terrified of her that nothing she said would sink in' and 'She never smiled or laughed – teachers never did laugh *with* the children.'

Sometimes the environment of the school seems to have been one of only partially suppressed violence which could erupt into something approaching open rebellion. A number of writers speak of the rough bullying behaviour of children, especially towards newcomers, several of whom had to fight to defend themselves on their first day. It was all too easy to offend against 'the unwritten laws', and to be accordingly punished by other children, and some schools had initiation ceremonies, one of the more unpleasant being that experienced by Eric Powell:

At school the boys held a sort of initiation ceremony when one became 'one of us'. The victim was taken to the grass playground, his trousers pulled down, and he was spat upon by several of the boys who chewed up grass for the purpose, and the filthy mixture of grass and saliva was deposited accordingly.[63]

At the village school of Sutton Courtney about 1880, where one master with the assistance of a young pupil-teacher had charge of a hundred unruly country children, Henry Lock recorded that 'I have seen boys kick the master's legs and throw slates at him after having the cane,'[64] and Reginald Gowshall remembers the boys locking out the master because he did not give them a half-holiday on Shrove Tuesday – the consequence being that when he did gain access he set about the class with an ash-plant.[65] But one of the most bizarre rebellions was 'the strike against the cane and strap' at St Anne's Roman Catholic School, Oldham, about 1910, when two or three dozen boys broke out of school and tried to bring out the scholars of neighbouring Smith Street School in sympathy; again, retribution followed next day by the instrument they had tried to abolish.[66]

One of the many causes of unhappiness at school was the cast-off clothes, boots and shoes which poor children often had to wear, and which made them the target for bullying by other children and, occasionally, for sarcasm by teachers. In an East End school cast-off clothes and boots were publicly handed out to the worst-dressed children by the headmaster, including, on one occasion, a complete Eton suit, the incongruity of which was deeply felt by a sensitive child.[67] George Rowles writes:

Today, at the age of eighty-four, the sound of a school bell fills me with dread . . . Even in a Board School there were social grades. My feeling of inferiority was probably caused by the fact that my boots were of the cheapest kind – hob-nailed to make them last longer – and that my clothes were made by my mother . . . [68]

And for Edward Brown, the shadow on his schooldays was the second-hand clothes which his mother's employers passed on for him:

They caused me a good deal of mortification. One suit in particular I remember to this day. It was of corded velvet, gold in colour and beautifully made, but it stood out against the drab cloth suits of my associates in quite a startling way . . . [69]

Another theme which emerges clearly from the autobiographies is the lack of contact between home and school, and the little interest which many working-class parents took in the education of their offspring. Children were consigned to the care of teachers at the age of four or five – frequently, in the later nineteenth century at three – and thenceforward it was assumed that the school had sole responsibility during school hours and that no interference was warranted.

There was very little or no connection with parents. The girls were in entire charge of teachers, and discipline was very strict . . . There was no familiarity between teacher and pupil . . . Teachers never took children on outings, and there were no open days for parents.[70]

Behind this apparent indifference often lay the ignorance of parents who had had little or no schooling themselves and hesitated to grapple with figures of authority who they seem to have held in a curious mixture of respect and contempt. Very occasionally an irate father would threaten a teacher who had over-punished his child, but more often a pupil punished at school would receive a supporting beating at home.

A common view of school, and of education generally, was that expressed by George Gregory's parents, both of whom were illiterate, that 'books were not intended for us' – the single exception being the

Bible, for the learning of which he would be tied to the bed-post.[71] It was
for this kind of reason that Minnie Frisby was made to leave school at
twelve, though she had been a monitress and wanted to become a
teacher; her parents, who were nail-makers in Worm's Ash, near Birmingham, 'said thay wanted me to do some work – school wasn't work'.[72]
This attitude compares with that expressed by Alfred Ireson, who
attended the National School at Thrapston in the 1860s:

> As it was not compulsory to attend, playing truant was common. The stripes
> administered were soon forgotten. Education was not taken seriously. You could
> attend when you liked, and go to work when you liked. Child labour was
> encouraged.[73]

Parental zeal for education was generally greater in towns than in
villages, greater in the north than in the south of England, and in
better-off rather than poorer families. In Todmorden, on the borders
of Lancashire and Yorkshire, among the 'respectable' working-class
families 'there was always a great desire to better oneself, and the road to
this seemed to be education'.[74] But perhaps the greatest enthusiasm came from parts of Wales, like Tonypandy in the Rhondda, where
Abel Jones went to elementary school, taught, and later worked as an
H.M.I.:

> The full story of efforts made by parents of small means to give the best
> education to their children would read like a romance if it were ever told. One
> example that comes to mind is that of a family of nine children, where the
> father's income was probably no more than £100 a year. Two of the boys became
> mining officials and later succeeded in business, another did well in business
> and a fourth entered Parliament. All five girls went to College, gained their
> Teacher's Certificate, and became headmistresses.[75]

Happiness at school is recorded less frequently by autobiographers
than unhappiness. When it occurs, it is usually associated with a kind
and able teacher who develops a child's imagination as well as affection,
with being interested in the lessons and performing well at them, and
with achieving some success in the school such as winning prizes, being
appointed a monitor or being promoted rapidly through the Standards.
Thus, for William Belcher in the 1890s:

> Life at Dunscombe Road Higher Grade School was an unceasing panorama
> of knowledge . . . School life to me, at least, was a harvest of kindly instruction,
> coming little short of a college education. At ten we were doing what secondary
> children do at fourteen.[76]

Such appreciation usually only came later in life, and one of the rare instances of immediate recognition must be that of Edward Punter on leaving his elementary school in 1909:

When I rose from my seat for the last time and joined in the queue for the door, Gaffer [the headmaster] drew me aside and waited until the last boy had left the room. Then he looked at me sourly, 'If you want a reference for a job, I'll give you one, Punter.' 'Thank you, Sir, that will be useful.' Then, in a sudden impulse, I added, 'And thank you for teaching me.' I think I must have been the first boy ever to have said that to him, for his face lit up, and he almost smiled.[77]

One of the happier memories was that of Jessie Sharman, who attended a school owned and run by the Colman family of Norwich (the Carrow School) for children of their employees; here, a large mattress was provided for any of the babies who fell asleep, and there were exciting 'demonstration lessons' like one on volcanoes.

Although the cane was always in use in other schools (so I heard) there was never a cane used in Carrow School.[78]

There are, too, among the autobiographies numerous examples of individual acts of kindness by teachers, especially in villages where the teacher often assumed a position in the community akin to that of a clergyman or social worker. Fred Boughton remembers children in the Forest of Dean coming to school with dirty boots and being sent to the headmaster:

I have heard the master ask, 'Why did you not black your boots this morning?' 'Because we had no blacking, and no money to buy any, Sir. Mother spends all the money on food.' Many times I have seen the master give him a penny and say, 'Go and buy a tin.'[79]

One pupil at a village school in Cheshire would sometimes help the schoolmistress at home by going on errands for her: often she was sent to cottages with mysterious parcels, told to take them to the back door, and never to say who had sent them. Only later she found that they contained such things as a pair of clogs for a boy who had come to school barefoot, a blanket, a bag of oatmeal or potatoes, or a shilling to buy a bag of coal. At last it was discovered that Miss Gilchrist had used up her savings over the years in this way and had to continue teaching though her health was failing. The villagers, most of whom were former pupils, opened a subscription list out of which they were able to pay her a pension of £2 a week 'some return for all the love and care she had cast upon waters'.[80]

The reactions of autobiographers to their lessons and to the school curriculum illustrate the surprising variety of practice which existed under a supposedly common system of instruction. Many writers naturally stress the narrowness of the curriculum, the concentration on the three Rs and the mechanical methods of teaching.

Teachers had to work to a definite syllabus drawn up for each class, and carried out under the strict supervision of the Headmaster. Pupils had to pass an oral and written examination each year before passing to a higher class, and these examinations were carried out by the Board Inspector. There was none of the self-expression nonsense in those days . . . [81]

Probably the typical syllabus of the later nineteenth century was that experienced by Edward Brown – a half-hour scripture lesson to begin each day, followed by long sessions of arithmetic, writing (to a common pattern, practised by drawing pot-hooks), reading and grammar, which included much parsing and analysis of sentence structure in the senior Standards. 'Reading, writing and arithmetic were the foundation, with history, geography, music and art as embellishments.'[82] Sometimes the 'embellishments' were totally omitted. At Maud Clarke's school at Tipton, about 1900, the girls were taught nothing of history or geography, though cookery, dressmaking and domestic science were included as relevant, practical subjects: 'We were groomed as future housewives and mothers.' Here, as in nearly all the larger town schools, boys and girls were separated at seven, after the Infant stage, to follow different curricula considered appropriate for their sex and life expectations.

Two extracts, one by Charles Cooper (pp. 192–8) and one by Daisy Cowper (pp. 198–204), provide good details of the elementary curriculum, the first in a village school during the period of the Revised Code in the 1870s and 1880s, the second in a large town school during the last decade of the century. The latter clearly indicates the widening of the curriculum after the end of 'Payment by Results', the efficiency and dedication of the qualified teachers and their ambition for their clever pupils to pursue further studies. But the autobiographies make it clear that there were many variations in practice, both before and after 'Payment by Results', depending on the particular interests of the headmaster, the size of the school, qualifications of the staff and local employment opportunities. At the Great Western Railway elementary school at Swindon in the early eighties, boys in Standard V took mechanics and algebra as 'specific' subjects, and in Standard VII physiography and agriculture; though they never performed or even saw an experiment, most of the boys passed and earned grants. But another thing 'of great moment in the school' was music, for it was a passion of the Welsh headmaster, 'Shonnie', whose voluntary singing class tackled difficult oratorios. And surprisingly, for it carried no 'grant', 'Shonnie' introduced 'drill' on Friday afternoons under an ex-Indian army sergeant: 'There was no nonsense about physical education: it was just straightforward army drill.'[83]

The school experience of children depended not only on what was laid down for their instruction in the Codes but, often more importantly, how individual teachers interpreted or transgressed them. Arthur Allwood traced his interest in geography to the large, clay relief model of Shropshire which his enthusiastic teacher made.[84] Ethel Clark writes of her elementary school during the First World War:

> Thinking back, I am amazed at the amount of English Literature we absorbed in those four years, and I pay tribute to the man who made it possible . . . Scott, Thackeray, Shakespeare, Longfellow, Dickens, Matthew Arnold, Harriett Beacher Stowe and Rudyard Kipling were but a few authors we had at our finger-tips. How he made the people live again for us![85]

In a little Derbyshire village school about 1900 the children received 'a very good education in subjects outside the three Rs', including botany, geology and music; here the schoolmaster, who was the leader of village life, had formed an orchestra and choral society and produced concerts, pantomimes and operettas.[86] Sometimes a teacher's enthusiasm led to rather inappropriate results, as at Harting Coombe, Sussex, where eight-year-olds in Standard II began to read Shakespeare, and had to learn by heart the scene from 'King John' where Arthur pleads with Hubert not to put out his eyes; the top Standard here learned French, etymology and domestic economy.[87] Such accounts at least suggest that the later elementary school was often a livelier, more original and imaginative institution than has sometimes been supposed and that not a few children emerged from it with a genuine love of learning and a considerable ability to write.

7. Beyond this, the main opportunity for an elementary school child to progress to more advanced education lay in acceptance for a teaching career, through the stages of pupil-teacherdom and completed by full-time study at a training college. As evidenced by Frederick Hobley's auto-biography (pp. 177–82), a very informal system operated in the 1840s before the Minutes of 1846 were generally adopted, Hobley being 'employed' as a monitor at a halfpenny a day until going to training college at the early age of sixteen. By the 1880s, when F. H. Spencer was engaged as a pupil-teacher at Swindon, a regular 'apprenticeship' for

five years had been instituted, with early morning lessons for the
pupil-teachers before school assembled; once school began, however,
he taught a full day, usually the brightest set of forty–fifty children.
Later, as an H.M.I., he was very critical of the form of instruction, and of
the low standards demanded of pupil-teachers. Maud Clarke's autobiography provides details of the more fully developed system in operation at the end of the century in West Bromwich. She was first appointed
as a monitress at thirteen, earning 3s. a week until she took Candidates'
Examinations two years later; successful students then attended a day
pupil-teacher centre for three years of full-time secondary education,
taught by specialists who were usually graduates. At eighteen she sat for
the government 'scholarship', which meant that those successful were
qualified to teach a class of fifty children (at 15s. a week) or to go on to
further study at a training college for two years at the student's own
expense:

> There were no grants given for further study, and very few girls went to
> college . . . Some male teachers borrowed the cost of study at college and repaid
> it by instalments on obtaining their first post. This kept them very poor for a
> considerable time.

Like many others, Maud Clarke began full-time teaching at eighteen
and took a correspondence course, paying for her own fees and books;
she was successful in the five-day examinations, and on receiving her
'parchment' became a certificated teacher on a salary scale rising to £90
a year.

Certification was normally the highest qualification for an elementary
school teacher, and many never achieved this, continuing their careers
as 'uncertificated ex-Pupil-Teachers'. By the end of the century, a
handful of students in pupil-teacher centres entered for the Matricula-
tion, the prerequisite for admission to a university course, though in the
absence of grants the actual possibility of going to university was extremely small. Faith Osgerby, who had been the top student at Driffield
Pupil-Teacher Centre, sat for it in 1908, but 'It was just a crazy notion,
doomed to failure, because the dreaded Latin would fail me.' With great
difficulty she extracted the £2 entry fee from her farmer-father ('It's
price of a good calf'), but the result was as she feared – a pass in all
subjects except Latin and, therefore, an overall failure.[88]

By extraordinary effort and great natural ability a very few elementary
schoolteachers succeeded in using their training as a basis for graduate
study, usually by working part-time for the external London University
B.A. degree. This considerable feat was accomplished by Michael

Llewellyn, a blacksmith's son from Glamorganshire, who after attending Tretowyn Training College from 1906–8, took his degree while holding a full-time teaching post; he later became an H.M.I. and, ultimately, a Director of Education. His autobiographical account of life at Tretowyn, which was apparently modelled more on a debased public school than on a university pattern, suggests that a training college course was not the best foundation for graduate study. Here, the timetable of the two-year course was extremely heavy, beginning with a lecture on Divinity at 7 a.m., and ending with supervised private study at 9.30 p.m.

The subjects we were supposed to study were numerous. Mathematics, English Language and Literature, Welsh Language and Literature, Divinity, Teaching Method, Psychology, General Science, Music, Physiology and Hygiene, Botany, History and Geography I can remember as figuring in our very general education. There were practical subjects like Art, Handicraft, Physical Education and Practical Teaching. They were too many except for a superficial education.

The senior students tyrannized the juniors in rituals presided over by the 'Smoke Hole Chairman', and all students were compelled to wear a school-type College cap: 'How symbolic was that cap of the inferior position in the educational scheme which the training college student then held.'[89]

The other possibility of a secondary education for working-class children lay in admission to a grammar school. Many of these ancient foundations gave a small number of free places, often filled by nomination or recommendation rather than by competition, the rest being taken by the sons of local tradesmen, farmers and professional people as fee-paying pupils. In 1867 there were 830 of these schools, providing about 75,000 places.[90] Many were small and decayed, some even decrepit, with a handful of scholars and a single master who treated his post as a sinecure; 'grammar' still meant Latin, and, sometimes, Greek grammar, and until late in the century most did not attempt to teach mathematics, the sciences or modern languages. The narrow and irrelevant curriculum had little to offer to a working-class child until reform began in the 1870s and was hastened by the establishment of local authority secondary schools after 1902, but even in 1914 the odds against a child from an elementary school obtaining a free secondary education at eleven were still forty to one.[91]

The reactions of relatively poor children to what was considered an elite type of education varied widely and appear to have been determined mainly by the degree of adaptability of their own personalities and the extent of parental support and encouragement. Some autobiographers valued and enjoyed the experience, making an outstanding success of their secondary schooling and proceeding to university or to professional careers: others never made the difficult transition to a different social environment, feeling themselves disadvantaged and inferior to the fee-paying majority. Many of these left school early, either because they were unhappy or because parents needed them to contribute to family income. Thomas Wood, a handloom weaver's son, surprisingly gained admission to Bingley Grammar School in 1822 at the age of six after 'some influence with the Vicar' had been brought to bear. Here the practice was to teach Latin free, but all other subjects, including writing, had to be paid for. After only two years he was taken away to go into the mill:

> Working folk derided the idea of their children learning Latin, or, indeed, anything at all if it cost anything or entailed any inconvenience.[92]

It was, of course, quite exceptional for a boy from such a background ever to have entered a grammar school. Typically, free places were secured by the sons of skilled craftsmen and small tradesmen, who could contemplate a long period of schooling and often had professional ambitions for their offspring. The autobiography of William Esam, who was born in Norwich in 1826, illustrates the opposite extreme of extended schooling from that of Thomas Wood – from three to five at a dame school, from five to twelve at a private 'gentleman's school' until his father received a presentation for him to Norwich Grammar School. Here he continued until the unusually late age of nineteen, under splendid teachers.

> In those days nothing was taught in the school but Latin and Greek, with a lesson in English History on Saturday, but we had four half-holidays a week which we devoted to writing and mathematics under the writing master in a gallery over the end of the School.[93]

Esam had first left the school at sixteen to work in the counting-house of a wholesale ironmonger, but finding it not to his liking returned to prepare for an academic career; after various teaching posts he became a school proprietor and headmaster.

Several autobiographical accounts of these small, old grammar schools of the later nineteenth century stress the camaraderie among the boys and the virtual absence of class consciousness. At Risley Grammar School, Derbyshire, in the 1870s, the senior (or 'Latin') school consisted of fourteen boarders, mostly the sons of well-to-do people from the Manchester area, and about forty day-boys who were socially 'a very mixed lot'.

Neither at Risley nor at Lichfield [where the author attended later] do I remember anything like a social distinction or division between the sons of gentlemen (to use the wonted term) and the sons of farmers, tradesmen and even of agricultural labourers so far as the intercourse in work and play was concerned . . . There was a complete absence of class-consciousness in the schoolroom and playground.[94]

The fellowship apparently extended beyond the playground, for on the half-holiday which followed Founders' Day the tradition was to play kiss-in-the ring with the village girls, of whom the reigning beauty was the innkeeper's daughter.

In less well-endowed families the attitude of the parents towards the educational ambitions of their children was all-important. Reginald Farndon, the son of a decorator who was often unemployed in the winter months, was constantly reminded while at grammar school that he was being educated above the family's station in life; his elder sisters had had to leave school at thirteen for domestic service, though they later took evening classes in shorthand and typing at 1d. a lesson and obtained office jobs.[95] Here, as in many cases, the boy took educational precedence over girls. Nora Lumb, daughter of a railway clerk, had to win one of the ten scholarships awarded by Sunderland to get to grammar school in 1923: her parents would have paid for a boy, but not for a girl.[96] Even by this time, when the scholarship system from elementary school was in operation, many autobiographers record having to reject the offer because of the cost of books, uniform, sports equipment and other 'extras'. Bim Andrews remembers sacrificing a Cambridge County scholarship in 1920:

. . . my mother knew we could not cope with uniform, books, satchel and hockey-stick. She was realistic and right . . . So I was inserted into the Higher Grade School which, like my father's pub, was at the bottom of the street. It was a step up from the all-purpose school at the shabbier end of the town.[97]

The experience of Edith Williams, who had won a scholarship to Cyfarthfa Castle Secondary School in 1910, is particularly poignant. Though doing well there, she had to be withdrawn when the cost of text-books became too great in a family of eight children, and after the local education authority had written to inform parents that if they withdrew children for this reason they would be exempt from the usual fine for early withdrawal. 'I was heartbroken and bitter, and my sense of deprivation was so great that I nursed this grievance for many years afterwards.'[98]

Many scholarship-holders were conscious of the difficulties they faced in the struggle for higher education – the walk of seven miles each way to Cinderford High School[99] or the obligation laid down by a father that his son must milk three cows daily before and after school[100] – though they rarely wrote complainingly. Perhaps most sharply felt and expressed was the sense of social inferiority and isolation in the large, post-1902 secondary schools, where the scholarship-holders were often more intelligent than the fee-payers, and not infrequently at the top of the class, but could find themselves socially ostracized by a mixture of envy and contempt. A particular problem for poor children was dress, as school uniform was not universal and even where it was laid down could still allow for petty social distinctions – a home-made gym slip and blouse not quite of the standard pattern, or the lack of a school hat for which Bim Andrews was excluded from formal school functions.

They [the fee-paying pupils] were mostly tradesmen's daughters who had long black stockings, dainty lunches, tennis racquets (I made do with extra needlework when these were in use), bicycles, summer holidays and parties.

Averil Thomas had always worn a pinafore at her elementary school, like all the other girls, but quickly found that this was not done at the High School.[101] And Doris Frances, who won a scholarship to grammar school from a poor home in 1919 (her father was an illiterate bus-cleaner) was gradually transformed from a happy girl into a shy, nervous one, completely lacking in self-confidence: on many occasions she suffered acute embarrassment, such as the time when the headmistress required (unnecessarily) that her hair be washed with green soft soap and combed with a fine-tooth comb.

The insinuation behind the message was all too clear. It is doubtful whether such an offensive message would have been sent to the parent of a fee-paying girl, especially without positive justification.[102]

Against these must be set the larger number of autobiographers for whom secondary education was successful in the sense that they were absorbed into the system, accepting its values and manners, making friends from among their own 'set' and achieving recognition in the accepted ways – in the examination room or on the playing fields. Successful integration often involved the rejection of former values and former friends, even a distancing from parents and kin who were not capable of sharing the experience. Thus, Mary Hollinrake writes that life at Todmorden Grammar School was a closed circle, extremely interested in itself but not at all in the outside world. Children who had not passed the scholarship now regarded the successful with distaste, but at the grammar school, as well as the interest of the work, there was plenty of fun and enjoyable social occasions like lunch at the King's Café in the town and formal dances in the winter term.[103] The reactions of Leslie Missen, who won a scholarship to the distinguished Perse School, Cambridge, in 1908, were similar. Here he encountered a public school regime, but a 'mixed bag' of boys who included the sons of a college tutor, a vicar, a fishmonger and brewer's assistant in his class of twenty-three – at his previous school the class had numbered seventy-three.

I gazed at the great Honours Board with the names of all old boys who had become Fellows of their Colleges, and counted an array of oak shields extending over three walls, each one recording the winner of an Open Scholarship and his subsequent academic distinctions.

At the Perse there was hard work and hard play – fortnightly marks in the junior forms and intense competition between the boys, sometimes leading to over-strain, compulsory games on three afternoons a week and membership of the Officers' Training Corps, besides plenty of homework. Much of the school's organization and discipline was in the hands of the prefects, and relationships with the teaching staff were generally happy and relaxed. In this atmosphere Leslie Missen flourished, entering the Sixth Form to read classics and prepare for an open scholarship to Cambridge when the First World War interrupted his studies. But his parents' strong support of his academic ambitions almost cost his father his job as a corn-buyer, his employer telling him that 'I cannot employ a man with a son at University.'[104]

8. The ability of a school to effect change in a child, not only in the extent of his knowledge but also in the nature of his character and personality, was greatest of all in boarding institutions which could control the total environment of a child, at least in term-time. Boarding-schools were, of course, normally the privilege of the wealthy, and hardly within the experience of the working class except as penal institutions such as Borstals, but two distinct kinds of encounter with residential schools have received some attention from autobiographers. One was the interesting experiment embarked upon by some local education authorities in the early twentieth century of making available to elementary schoolchildren a handful of scholarships at public boarding-schools.

One of these, at Christ's Hospital School, Hertford, fell to Kathleen Betterton in 1924. The daughter of a liftman in the London Underground, she had been picked out at her elementary school as a potential scholarship girl at the age of eight, when 'the race for survival' began; promoted through the Standards every six months, she and other bright girls were given special attention and at eleven passed for both Godolphin and Latimer (a day grammar school) and for Christ's Hospital, choosing the latter because she wanted a 'wider life' than her restricted home could offer. Her autobiography (pp. 204–11) shows that the school absorbed her completely, 'tolerating no other loyalties'; the school was always right, daily life was totally organized, and in term-time parents lost their authority. For several months she was extremely lonely and unhappy, though perhaps not more so than some other new girls: her problem derived from the total uprooting from home life rather than from a sense of social inferiority. Gradually, the regime with its insistence on academic success was accepted, and Kathleen ultimately won an Exhibition in Classics to Somerville College, Oxford; in that respect, at least, the selective system which had picked her out at eight had succeeded.

Life at a workhouse or poor law District School, totally different though it was in social composition, had many of the same characteristics as life at boarding-school, heightened by the fact that for these pauper children there was no compensating home environment. Some of these institutions, which dated from 1844, were extremely harsh in their treatment of the innocent victims of poverty, following the contemporary belief that pauperism was a social disease which could only be rooted out by deterrence, but as these attitudes softened towards the end of the century District Schools were either modified or replaced by more domestic treatment in Cottage Homes or boarding-out. A late survivor was the Central London District School of Hanwell in Middlesex (known as the 'Cuckoo School') where E. Balne attended from the age of two-and-a-half (in 1897) to fourteen. He was evidently proud of his achievements at this 'academy' as he describes it, deriving many of the same values and loyalties as from a public boarding-school: many of the amenities were similar – the large school buildings, the dormitories, chapel, hospital, swimming pool and extensive playing fields, and the seniors took a large share in the discipline, not as prefects, but as boy sergeants and corporals in a military hierarchy under the 'Yard Master'. As in a public school, the day was fully organized from 5.30 a.m. onwards, with a normal elementary school curriculum morning and afternoon, strong sporting activities, a military band and so on. To

Balne, life at the 'Cuckoo School' was generally a full and happy experience on which he looked back with affection and gratitude. It was marred by only two things – the cruel punishments, which included the public birching of the boys by the 'Yard Master' which others were obliged to attend ('Sometimes we spectators would have to listen to the screams of the victim, and I have known boys to faint watching these ghastly scenes'), and the fact that the totally protected and isolated environment of the school in no way prepared him for the prejudice he encountered in the outside world:

... when I was fourteen, it was while scoring for the Hanwell team one Saturday afternoon at an away game that I first became conscious of my lowly status in society. And being a highly sensitive lad, I was never to forget the incident (which I will not describe here) which occurred that afternoon. The shock of the realization that I was considered to be a member of the lowest form of human creation was an experience from which I have never fully recovered.[105]

Balne had never known any other but institutional life, and his adaptation to it was complete and total. Nora Adnams, who lived in a Dr Barnardo's Cottage Home at Barkingside, Essex, from 1904 to 1911, never accepted it, and throughout her years there continued to have feelings of fear, hate and rejection. One of seven surviving children of very poor parents, they were deliberately abandoned by their unemployed father so that they could be taken into care, and although, unusually, the four sisters were allowed to stay together in the Home 'we were as isolated from the world as if we were on a desert island'. Her autobiography is dominated by accounts of the punishments which she and others suffered, mainly for disobedience: these included having to sit absolutely still for two hours, an extra half-hour being added for the slightest movement, denial of food, being forced to eat the food provided (all meals were cooked by the older girls, without adequate supervision, and were often nauseous) even when this meant vomiting up every spoonful of cabbage, soup or burned porridge, being locked in a cupboard, and, for more serious offences, ritualized 'whippings'.

These whippings were really a nightmare. We were made to go up to a bedroom, undo our knickers, pull up our dress and petticoats, and lie across a bed and await 'Mother', who usually arrived with two girls to hold our hands and legs, then smacked us with the hairbrush. One could not struggle, one was held too tightly. Oh! the indignity of those whippings: I still blush with shame when I think of it.

Although she insisted on her nightly kiss, this 'Mother' was not loved.[106]

9. No simple conclusions can be drawn from these autobiographical accounts of varied educational experiences in which the reactions of individuals depended on a complex inter-play of personality and environmental factors. Nevertheless, some general features, to which there are always exceptions, appear to stand out. The writings demonstrate a contrast between the struggles and sacrifices of highly motivated individuals for education and self-improvement in the earlier part of the century and the more passive acceptance of the majority when schooling became compulsory after 1876. Similarly, there is noticeable contrast between the essentially religious basis of Sunday School and Church School education, which often had profound influence on its recipients, and the more secular context in which mass education was spread by the post-1870 Board Schools. The early age at which schooling often began – commonly at four and sometimes at three years – was surprising, and to some extent compensated for the early ending of school life and the onset of employment; the very restricted possibilities of secondary education until the twentieth century are also clearly documented.

The limited assumptions about the purposes of elementary education, both by teachers and parents, are also evident from the autobiographies. Education was seen as being for work rather than for life, for producing efficient, manageable workers and law-abiding citizens rather than for developing individual personality, intellectual or emotional independence. The great majority of working-class parents, too, accepted the role of the school as the arbiter of values, rarely intervening in an area in which they felt incompetent and excluded. Only in the higher strata of the working classes was pride in a child's achievement and positive encouragement to further progress usually found; elsewhere, schooling tended to be regarded more negatively, as a necessary interlude between babyhood and the world of work which relieved an over-burdened mother from some of her domestic responsibility and, at best, inculcated skills and values which would help a child to become an early breadwinner.

The narrow definition of the objectives of education had direct effects on the school curriculum, and many autobiographies record the concentration on the three Rs, the neglect of other subjects and of other aspects of child development such as physical education. They also emphasize the large classes, the mechanical methods of instruction and the rigid assessment of academic progress by means of Standards, each with a defined syllabus. The system of teacher-training, based on a long period of pupil-teacherdom followed by a brief spell of further education in a training college, was itself unacademic and essentially practical, emphasizing the importance of pedagogic skills to the virtual exclusion of intellectual development.

It was not, of course, supposed or intended that children should enjoy their schooling, and the autobiographical evidence suggests that very many, probably the majority, did not. Beginning school was almost always an anxious, sometimes traumatic, experience. Many children settled down after the initial shock to a stolid toleration of an irksome duty, finding companionship outside the classroom, eagerly awaiting the holidays and the final release from bondage, but significant numbers continued to dislike school to the point of hatred, never adjusting to the demands of obedience and concentration. A recurrent theme in many accounts is the fear of unkind teachers, of harsh corporal punishment and humiliating verbal reproof. Until more enlightened views about child psychology and learning methods began slowly to penetrate the elementary school in the twentieth century, 'education' for many children meant little more than discipline, the enforced acquisition of some elementary skills and the memorizing of a mass of largely irrelevant facts. Only the remarkable adaptability and acquiescence of the majority of children enabled such a system to survive.

Some of these characteristics are brought into sharper focus by contrast with the educational experiences of middle- and upper-class children. While working-class children usually started school early, sometimes even as 'babies', with little or no previous knowledge, wealthier children usually began school life much later, often after considerable grounding at home by parents, an older sister or a governess. By the time such children went to their day- or boarding-school, usually not earlier than eight, most had already acquired the basic skills of reading and writing on which the elementary school concentrated so much of its efforts. For girls of this class, informal education at home often lasted much longer, sometimes even up to the age of fifteen or sixteen, to be followed by only a brief experience at a 'finishing' school, while for boys it was expected that education in some form would continue through the teens, either in school or university, or by professional training or apprenticeship.

In most middle- and upper-class homes, therefore, parents recognized an important responsibility for the education of their children, involving themselves as amateur teachers or, more often, as patrons of private schools. The higher the social class, the greater the delegation, so that in wealthy families the care and education of children became entrusted to a succession of surrogates – nannies, governesses, tutors and boarding-schools – which could virtually isolate a child from the outside world. Such children experienced a protected and protracted childhood and adolescence, in sharp contrast to the working-class child who was rarely in school after twelve, and was often working part-time before that. The view long persisted that elementary and secondary education were quite distinct systems, appropriate for different social classes, not successive stages in a single process to which all children had a right. Robert Lowe, the Vice-President of the Department of Education in 1860, had argued that it was perfectly possible to teach a working-class child all that it needed to know by the age of ten: the evidence of autobiographies suggests, regrettably, that many parents and children believed it too.

James Bonwick
an octogenarian's reminiscences

Bonwick was educated at the Borough Road School, Southwark, where he went in 1823 at the age of six, ultimately becoming head monitor and a 'qualified' teacher at fifteen. After working as a British School teacher, he emigrated to Australia in 1840, where he taught, wrote text-books and inspected schools, interrupted by spells on the gold diggings. On his marriage in 1840 he had been earning £80 p.a., but in Australia he made a considerable fortune from gold discoveries, land speculation and private boarding-schools. He retired to England and wrote his autobiography at the age of eighty. It was published by James Nichols in London in 1902.

The following extracts describe his early life as a pupil, monitor and young teacher.

The Old Boro' Road Boys' School

The New Building – the one I first knew – was raised on a leasehold from the City of London, and consisted of a central Home for the training of Teachers, with two wings, one for boys and the other for girls. This really fine edifice was opened June 4th 1817 . . .

The room for the boys could accommodate 500 scholars. The windows were six feet from the floor. The central part was occupied with desks and forms, fixed by iron supports. Spaces left around were for semi-circular 'drafts' for some eight or ten lads, engaged under Monitors in reading, spelling or arithmetic. Curtains of baize, suspended from the ceiling, were stretched across the upper space to prevent an echo.

At the entrance end of the room was the long, raised platform for the Master's desk, etc. At the other end was placed the portrait of George III, with the motto 'The Patron of Education and Friend of the Poor'. Underneath, in gold letters, were the words uttered by our late Queen's grandfather to Lancaster at the interview of 1805 – 'It is my wish that every poor child in my dominions be taught to read the Holy Scriptures.'

The first desk, lower than the rest, was for little ones learning the alphabet, and imitating the letters hung in front by drawing with a stick or finger in sand provided for the purpose in front of each child. The sand desk was nine inches broad, having a hole, with a tin slide for the sand, and a smoother of wood or stiff leather, as well as a stick for marking.

Other desks were three inches higher. Though sloping for writing convenience, there was a narrow, flat top for the reception of a pewter inkstand. A sort of slit, at the back of the desk, was for the reception of a slate, when not in use. The form had no back, and the boy sat thereon, with his hat or cap tied behind him with a string.

A clock was fixed over the platform, and a large bell stood on the Master's desk. Yet that was seldom used, as the sharp call 'Halt!' for order was distinctly heard over the room.

Each of the eight classes in the School was indicated by a board on an iron rod, fixed in a standard at the end of a desk. The first class was at the sand desk. The second included boys in two-lettered words; the third, in three letters; the fourth, in four or five; the fifth, in two syllables; the sixth, in three; the seventh, in four; the eighth being the highest.

The 'drafts' were marked out by semi-circular lines cut in the floor, or by chalk when necessary. The board, from which we read or spelt, was fixed on a brass-headed nail in view of the pupils, who stood with their hands behind them, the Monitor having his station at the end of the curve . . . The 'drafts' were two feet apart, and left a passage-way between them and the desks . . .

Monitors

The Monitorial System was the distinctive feature in the methods of both Bell and Lancaster. The first had larger classes than the last, but the teaching was almost wholly in the hands of boys or girls. Neither man was the inventor of the plan. The Chevalier Paulet used it in Paris before the Revolution, having devoted his fortune to the instruction of very poor French boys in mathematics, history, geography, music and English . . . Long before, however, the plan was in exercise among Hindoo schools, and Dr Bell brought it to England from Madras . . .

Without doubt, this system revolutionized Public Instruction in England. The great difficulty had been the expense of educating poor little ones. The Monitorial System let in the sunshine of hope by relieving the expenditure.

While some derided its efficacy and predicted its early collapse, not a few enthusiastic persons spoke of it as a sort of Divine illumination. Its very weakness proved a source of strength . . . Monitors, however, received not their due attention in their own studies, and suffered thereby . . .

Other teachers at the Boro' Road were young men and women who were sent, or had come at their own charge, 'to learn the System' as it was then styled. They were recommended by subscribers to the British and Foreign School Society, were supposed to have had some previous schooling, adding thereunto some extra while under the training, and all were of approved pious character. After three months' stay, they were reckoned fit to go forth as masters and mistresses of British Schools.

My alphabet in sand

I began my ascent of the ladder of learning after the very primitive Oriental style of sand marking. I was placed at the 'Sand Desk', which, with its form, was suited to little fellows . . . In front of the row the Monitor held a board on which were plainly printed the capitals and small letters of the alphabet. My little teacher pointed to a letter and shouted its name, which we repeated aloud. He then told us to smooth the sand in front of us, and try and make the letter by marking the sand. After this was done, we again shouted the letter. When the mark was removed by the smoothing flat stick, we took up another letter for copying . . .

When able to go into a 'draft' at the side of the School, I stood before a printed card stuck upon a wooden board, and learned my A, B, ab, etc. My promotion from monosyllables to longer words came in slow process of time, after judgment, upon examination, had been pronounced by a superior Monitor. I know not now how long it took me to ascend from class 1 through 2, 3, 4, 5, 6, 7 and 8, carrying me round the sides of 'drafts'. In the same way I had to pass the classes and 'drafts' for arithmetic.

Spelling

Mr Lancaster is reported to have utilized sheets torn out from old spelling books, such as appeared about a century ago, and stuck them up before a 'draft'. He afterwards used Spelling Lesson Sheets, mounted on boards, like the Reading Extracts. The sixty folio sheets contained some 6,000 words. The boys would repeat the syllables in varied tones, and always sufficiently loud to stun the visitor . . .

[Details then follow of similar lessons in Writing.]

Reading

Our only reading was from the Scripture lessons, that is, selections from the Bible, not the Bible itself. One issue of this work was in book form, the other, printed in large type, was in sheets, fitted for posting upon boards, and suspended in front of a 'draft' to be superintended by a Monitor . . .

Messrs Dunn and Crossley [the Head Masters of Borough Road School in Bonwick's time] ultimately broke down the traditional confinement of learning to the 'One Book' by the publication of their Secular Reading Books. But, during the whole of my School life at the Boro' Road, the reading was rigorously confined to the Scripture Extracts.

At noon each day took place the Monitors' Reading Lesson before Mr Crossley, himself a famous reader. About fifty of us assembled in the space below the platform . . .

In my long life, I have heard famous readers, and some good actors, but none, as I fancy, equal to some in that class. Nothing, at our Annual Examinations, excited so much attention and enthusiasm as our upper class when reading a chapter of Bible History. At times, at our noon gathering, a sudden and wild burst of applause would rise from the class at some extra fine rendering.

Schoolboys are not generally sentimental, but I have seen tears shed at the reading of a passage. Some boys' voices were simply perfect in expression . . . [Details follow of lessons in Arithmetic.]

Geography

It may be taken for granted that, in a School where biblical instruction had the first place of importance, the Scripture Maps would receive prominent regard. Even Lord Brougham, when at our Annual Examination, was struck with this feature, and afterwards narrated his experience before the House of Lords, saying, 'I saw a boy take a slate, without having any copy, and, solely from memory, trace upon it the outline of Palestine and Syria, marking out all the variations of the coast, the bays, harbours and creeks, inserting the towns and rivers, and adding their ancient as well as their modern names' . . . [Lessons on Grammar, Geometry]

Singing

As may be suspected, music was unknown to us at the Boro' Road . . . We boys thought our Master, who liked music, kept back the singing out of regard to the Quakers on the Committee.

At length, Mr W. E. Hickson, seconded by some of our Young Men, ventured to give us some fine songs, of moral tone, and which came out in the 'Singing Master' about, I fancy, 1831 or 1832 . . . At our next Annual Examination we sang some of these, in parts, with electrical effect. But when, inspired with confidence, we ventured upon a proper Hymn, there was a small agitation among broad brims and silken bonnets. As, however, the soft, delicious notes of 'Hear My Prayer' rose, in excellent time and tone, numbers of those present fairly broke down in sobs and tears. Music had triumphed . . .

Science lessons

In my schooldays, instruction in Science was limited enough anywhere, even to us whose reading was absolutely confined to Bible Extracts. I learned nothing of Science but on the Twelfth-Night Magic Lantern Show. Then some rude astronomical slides were exhibited, along with lions, elephants and 'funny bits', with the aid of bad oil. The description of the heavens was not brilliant, nor heard to advantage in the buzz of 500 boys.

After all, the primitive-looking orrery did illustrate the globe's daily and annual revolutions, though our Biblical impressions were not after Copernicus. We gathered from Genesis and the commentary of our Teachers, that 4,000 B.C. the creation began, upon the sudden call of a mysterious Light; that the sun and earth were formed out of nothing; that man appeared in God's image, after the creation of plants and animals; but that no creative work was done on the seventh day or Sabbath.

We naturally thought more of the sun than of Jupiter or the Fixed Stars, and were quite convinced that the formation of the Heavenly Bodies was only in the interest of our earth, and service thereto. The first chapter of Genesis satisfied scientific inquiry. We pictured the heated state of Mercury and cold of Saturn. It was not the age of criticism, but it did seem odd to us that Light should come before the Sun was made.

We boys had a much more hazy notion of Geology. I could have little doubt, from sunset and sunrise – in spite of being told that the earth was round – that it was really flat; that the hills were everlasting, and that the sea had its fixed boundary. The first geological news or heresy came before us in the daring supposition that the six days were, possibly, uncertain periods of time, during which great changes might be effected. No Boro' Road boy could reasonably accept so doubtful an interpretation of a Biblical declaration.

The Deluge was to us, as to Voltaire and some other philosophers, a way out of the difficulty of accounting for fossil shells in the Alps, as they simply got stuck in the long-soaked rocks. The ungainly fossilized bones of monsters could be no other than remains of the giants that lived before the Flood.

Training as a teacher

Lancaster had such implicit faith in his Monitors that he thought little of adult service. He instituted, therefore, House Lads, from whom he selected his future Masters of Schools. They were boarded, lodged and prepared to be sent forth for work . . . One of my early friends was sent out at fourteen to open a School, and I was but fifteen when sent to organize one . . .

Before the age of competition by examinations, the training required for an Elementary School was trifling, as children were not expecting much instruction. No one dreamed then of a man or woman trying for a B.A. or M.A. in order to become a British School Master or Mistress. What was sought for in candidates was rather character and enthusiasm for service than any great extent of knowledge.

The 'House Lad' plan led to the 'Young Men', so called, who entered the Boro' Road for training, or, as it was termed, 'to learn the System' . . . While in the House as students, a few had free board and lodging, but the majority were expected to pay from six to twelve shillings a week . . .

To Leicester and Ipswich

My earliest venture in teaching out of the Boro' Road was to aid Mr Soar, in April 1833, in the introduction of the British System at Leicester. The School was mainly supported by the Society of Friends, and the Secretary, Mr Alfred Burgess, a manufacturer, was a gentleman and Christian philanthropist . . .

After helping Mr Soar for three months I returned to the Boro' Road. Then I was ordered to Ipswich, to take charge of the British School while the Master of it came to London for three months, in which to acquire some knowledge of the improvements in 'the System'.

I was taken by a Committee-man to the School, and formally introduced to about a hundred of rough-looking Suffolk boys, to whom my London pale face and delicate appearance presented a decided contrast. I was suddenly exposed to a nerve trial.

No sooner had my introducer gone, leaving me upon the platform, than I detected a coming storm of rebellion. All at once, there was a rush towards the door, with loud cries. Being pretty active, I leapt over the platform rail, locked the door, sprang back with the key in hand, and calmly called out, 'No, no, boys: it is not 12 o'clock. Go on with your work.'

They were cowed in a moment. I then came down good-temperedly among the classes. Not the slightest insubordination ever afterwards appeared, and we were good friends till the Master returned to the School . . .

To Hemel Hempstead British School

The first independent situation to which I was appointed by the Committee, as British Schoolmaster, was at Hemel Hempstead, in Hertfordshire. This was in June 1834, when I was not quite seventeen, and still wore a short jacket . . .

My first duty at this new School was to examine the newcomers for classification. But I could not introduce the British System without Monitors, and how was I to get these among boys I never saw before?

Tact and former experience overcame this difficulty. I selected a few sharp lads, and showed them how to lead scholars at a lesson board. That natural love of authority in some was balanced by an equal love of submission to authority in others. Upon this simple basis rested the Monitorial System.

A selection as Monitors brought the boys some distinction, and they all received from me special lessons after school hours; and these I sought to make as attractive as possible.

The main difficulty with these country lads was discipline. How was I to maintain order and enforce work when unable, from age and inferior strength, to attempt corporal punishment? But I had been, as Head Monitor at Boro' Road, the recognized ruler of 500 boys. Besides, as a London youth, I felt my superiority to the rougher and stronger field lads.

By tact, alertness and good humour, I did without the stick. I could narrate pleasing cases of moral conquest and gratifying reconciliation when, after School hours, I tackled some obstinate, surly fellow . . . It was in this School that I had considerable success as a Teacher, though now satisfied that the sending of such juvenile Masters had disadvantages for themselves, and not unmixed good for Society . . .

Frederick Hobley
the autobiography of Frederick Hobley, written at the special request of his children, October 1905

Frederick Hobley was born at Thame, Oxfordshire, in 1833. The extract describes his education at dame school, and at the National School, where he was later 'employed' as a monitor at a halfpenny a day. At sixteen he went to the Oxford Diocesan Training School at Summertown (later removed to Culham) and after a three-year course was appointed to take charge of the school at Narberth, Pembrokeshire, with three pupil-teachers to assist him. He continued teaching until 1871 when he resigned to become a commercial traveller and, later, a book-keeper, finally retiring in 1899.

His unpublished autobiography was privately communicated by Miss C.Hobley; sections of the original autobiography of ninety-five pages were published in *Alta*, the University of Birmingham Review, No. 6, Summer 1968.

I, Frederick Hobley, eldest son of Edward and Harriet Hobley, was born on April 26th in the year 1833, at the small market town of Thame, in the County of Oxfordshire; and though I was present on this, to me, all important occasion, I do not know at what time in the day, or on which day in the week, I came into this world.

There were in all, in our family, ten children, that is six boys, named Frederick, George, Harry, Edwin, Sydney and Herbert Charles, and four girls, namely, Mary Ann, Jane, Emma and Fanny.

My earliest recollection carries me back to the time when I was not quite three years of age. Then I was sent to a Dame's School, kept for very young children by a person named Whitehead, situated on the left hand side, and near the top, of Friday Street, a brewery finishing up this side of the street, but I do not remember the name of the brewer. I have a distinct remembrance of the teacher giving me a needle and thread and a piece of rag to pass away my time during one of the afternoons.

I did not remain here long, only a few months, then I was sent to another Dame's School, kept by Ma'am Lund. This was situated in High Street, two doors above the 'White Swan Inn' and next door below the house of Mr Joseph Seymour, the Chief Constable of the town, whose youngest son John was one of my special companions and schoolfellows afterwards for many years . . .

There are two or three items that I distinctly remember in connection with Ma'am Lund's school. One was if a boy was naughty he was shut in her dark pantry as a punishment, and on one such occasion the little culprit ate up some cold plum pudding that was in the pantry. I do not recollect what further punishment he had for this offence, but the pantry was *not* used for this purpose for some time after.

Ma'am Lund eked out her living by selling Bulls'-eyes and Brandy-balls. These were at that time the chief sweets for children to buy. Every Tuesday, she replenished her stock. On that day, each week, an old man, named Jackson, called on her, he had a good sized oblong tin box, which was strapped on his back, and this was filled with Bulls'-eyes, etc. He used to give one to the child who sat near the door as he went out. I remember I sat there more than once.

Occasionally at this time, I was taken out for a walk on a Sunday, and if we went near this school, I remember, I used to run by as fast as possible lest I should be taken into it. So it seems I did not cherish much affection for my second school.

When I was about four years of age I began to attend the National School, and continued to do so for a number of years. I distinctly remember the first day I went to this school and could go now and sit down in the very class in which I was then put. It was the fourth class in position and was at the bottom end of the school.

Very shortly after, Victoria was publicly proclaimed Queen, and a great stir was made in our little town. Large numbers of people paraded the street, and as I was somewhat frightened thereat, my mother took me in her arms and carried me to school. I can remember seeing three men riding on horses and followed by a lot of people . . .

There was an Annual Treat given to all the scholars attending the National Schools. We attended a service in the Parish Church, and then paraded the town, returning to the schools where we were feasted with a good substantial *Dinner* of Roast Beef and Vegetables, and Plum Pudding. I remember on one occasion feeling very proud as I walked in the procession, for I had on a new pelisse, it was of a dark green colour, had a fitting body, and a full pleated skirt, this was before I wore trousers. I also recollect that at one of the Feasts the Boys' Schoolroom was beautifully decorated with flowers, a special feature being a large balloon of flowers – this was suspended from the high ceiling and at the bottom of it was a nice little car, containing two pretty dolls.

The name of the Schoolmaster was Thomas Bonner – he was lame, one leg being shorter than the other. He always carried a stick in his right hand, and frequently and unexpectedly, this stick, generally a supple ash plant, would come down smartly on the backs of any of the boys who were not busy at their proper schoolwork. I remember once seeing him give a bad boy a thorough whipping. The boy was put on the back of a much bigger lad who walked all round the inside of the schoolroom, the master walking behind, repeatedly and regularly striking the back and hind part of the bad boy who was greatly relieved when his novel ride came to an end.

There were many incidents that occurred during my school days – these I will now attempt to relate as near as I can remember, but they may not be told in chronological order.

Thus I well remember when I was first 'breeched', that is wore trousers for the first time – these were long enough to reach to the ankle – still they looked rather short. But there were no nice-looking knickers in those days. My first suit consisted of the above style of trousers buttoned round the waist to a close fitting jacket, so no braces were required – these came later when we began to wear both waistcoat and jacket . . .

When I was about 10 or 11 years of age I was appointed one of the Choristers of Thame Park. The Park was a very large one reaching miles each way and belonged to the Baroness Wenman, and there was a very fine and very large old mansion in the midst of the Park. About 200 yards from the house was a small Chapel-of-Ease, wherein the Church of England services were conducted. It was nicely fitted up with good oak pews and seats, and contained some stained glass windows. Her Ladyship bore all the expenses of this place of worship, providing a stipend for the clergyman, and paying the salaries of the organist and a choir of eight singers. The boys of the Choir received one shilling for each Sunday, and were paid quarterly. Occasionally we were also invited to have dinner in the Servants' Hall. There was quite a procession of servants as they walked into the Hall, 'according to their grades', then stood around the table, while 'grace' was said – then we all sat down to dinner. There was always a good spread of good things in season. The Head Butler brought in the home-brewed ale in large and bright copper vessels, jug-shaped, and poured the ale into drinking horns – I think a few of the higher order of the servants drank theirs out of glasses . . . Now and then we were sent for by the Baroness and had to see her in one of her large private rooms, and at such times we generally came out with a piece of gold in the hand. There was only one service in the Chapel on the Sunday when the worshippers consisted of her Ladyship and any visitors that might be staying with her – also the large retinue of house servants, besides the gamekeepers and workpeople of the Park . . .

Attached to the National Schools there was a very large garden. The Master had an extra large portion of it. The Schoolmistress had a nice piece, and some 12 or 14 of the older and best-behaved schoolboys had a small piece each – about 2 square poles. I had one of these plots – it was 5½ yards wide and 11 yards long, and in it I grew quite a number of useful vegetables for use at my own home. We used to see who could grow the best, and keep his garden the neatest and cleanest . . .

I think I must have made very fair progress at school, for I do not remember that the Master ever flogged me and I was also allowed several privileges. I sat at a desk, in winter, to do my lessons, which was very near the fire. I was frequently allowed to do some drawing from copies, having pencil and paper supplied to me. These drawings were shown to visitors and friends – and small presents were given me for my successful work. I remember also being sent for by Robert Barnes, butcher, who was going to kill a very fat pig for the Christmas Show, and he wished me to take a sketch of the pig, while alive, to hang up in his shop at this Show. So I took a pen and ink sketch for him.

Then a Mr Hewland, a baker and flour merchant, killed a very fine tame rabbit and he wished me to print a card for him; the words were 'Eyes on – hands off'. This was put up over the fat rabbit, when hung up for show in front of his shop, so persons could look as long as they liked, but must not touch!

After a time too, I was promoted to be a monitor – that is to teach the younger children in the lower classes. For this we were paid a halfpenny a day, that is 2½d. per week, and this gave us some pocket money. I remember also receiving coppers from neighbours and friends for going errands for them, and I have very pleasant recollections of thus being able to purchase some extra nice things for my suppers at home, such as penny crusty little cottage loaves, squares of baked plum pudding, bits of pickled fish, etc. . . .

I must, after this, have returned again to School, for during the early part of the year, I think 1849, I was asked if I would like to go to Oxford and learn to be a schoolmaster. I said I should. I do not remember who made the request. But in the month of March, I went to Oxford to sit for Examination. I must have walked there, 13 miles, passed thro' the Examination, and then walked home again. The Examination took place in Merton College, and at its close I was told that I had passed, and was instructed to get some sheets and towels and take up my residence in the Oxford Diocesan Training School, which was at the village of Summertown, about 1½ or 2 miles out of Oxford. This I did, and remained here nearly three years. By passing the above-mentioned Examination, I became entitled to an Exhibition Fee, given by the Bishop of Oxford, of Ten Pounds a year, for three years, that is thirty pounds towards my maintenance and instruction at the Training School. This covered about half of my expenses for the three years. The Rev. Amos Hayton, Chaplain at Thame Park, undertook the responsibility of collecting the other half required – this he successfully carried out, besides a small amount for my pocket money. Before going to live at Summertown I went over to see Baroness Wenman to thank her for all she had done for me, and when I left she gave me a sovereign. Thus I started on my new career, training for a Schoolmaster. Altogether I had an enjoyable and happy time at this School, but amid my varied experiences there, not many events stand out very prominently. However, I remember a few and these I will now relate.

We rose each morning about six, having been called up by the ringing of a bell. Then we had private study in the Schoolroom, under the superintendence of a Monitor who was generally one of the older residents in the College. Then at 8 o'clock breakfast was served in the same room. The bread and butter was always good and wholesome and consisted of fairly *thick* slices, piled up on pewter dishes! Each student also was supplied with a good sized mug of tea. If any more were required, the Monitors for the week would send to the kitchen for it. There was always plenty.

At 9 o'clock, lessons in classes, and lectures on special subjects, were begun and lasted until 12 o'clock. Then we were expected to be outside in the grounds and field for fresh air. Dinner was served at one o'clock. Good plain joints were always provided, soup occasionally, and puddings every day, sometimes one sort and sometimes another. The Principal, the Rev. John Thorp, always did the carving, and he was always anxious we should have a good dinner, asking us to

have more meat or vegetables (generally two sorts) or pudding. In my mind, I can
see him now, standing where all could see him, holding up the sugar basin, and
saying out loud, 'Now then, who says any more sugar!' At 2 o'clock classes began
again for about 2 hours, except Wednesdays and Saturdays. On these afternoons
we were allowed to go where we liked in the district, or into the City of Oxford,
provided we returned at the appointed time. Tea was served at 5 o'clock – this
was limited to *two* pieces of bread and butter and *one* mug of tea for each – no
more was allowed at this meal. Then at 8 o'clock we had a little bread and cheese
and beer. After a time, at the special request of the students, these two limited
meals were changed into a full tea at 7 o'clock. There was private study all
through the evening, and at ½ past 9 prayers were read, and we had all to be in bed
and lights out at 10 o'clock. So days and weeks quickly and pleasantly passed
away. There were generally from 15 to 20 students. Every six months, there was
an examination that lasted a fortnight and consisted generally of one, two or
three subjects each day when we had to answer the questions, etc. on paper,
except on the last day, when the process was entirely 'viva voce'! And as all the
questions, problems, etc., were prepared by university men, and all the examinations conducted by them, this searching of our attainments was very thorough
and good. Our examination, that is, my first one, was in the end of June. I had
only been in residence 3 months, and all the work and system were new to me.
Now, I well remember sitting next to another student, named Tom Warner, who
entered the College when I did. Each one was expected to answer all the
questions by his own unaided efforts, but we two, in our blissful ignorance and
innocence, thought we knew a better plan, so looking at each question we
conferred together and made up the answer from our combined knowledge. Of
course the result was that our papers were quite alike, all our answers in the same
words, and this was quickly noticed by the various examiners. We were sent for,
and had to go into the Principal's private room, when our offence was pointed
out, and we were solemnly warned not to do the same thing again! But as we had
done it all, as it were, innocently, we had no further punishment. I also
remember on the last day, when the 'viva voce' examination took place, that I was
very much astonished and surprised at the amount of learning shewn in many of
the replies given by the older students, and I wondered if I should ever be as
clever and as well informed. I inwardly resolved, at that time, that I would do my
very utmost to become so, and my ambition was realized in two years and a half
after, at my last examination just before Christmas 1851, when I was referred to as
one of the best students that had ever been to the College, being first in eight
different histories, first in mathematics, and so on. At this examination also,
there was a very severe contest in Euclid between me and a man named Smith,
the Senior Monitor of our schoolroom. He was a married man, had had a school
in London, and came to Summertown just for self-improvement and to become
a more efficient teacher. The questions were set us by a double first-class
university man, and consisted of ordinary propositions and also of problems and
theorems founded on them. To solve all these we were allowed about 8 hours,
that is 9 to 12, 2 to 5 and 7 to 9. I completed my paper in about 7 hours. Smith kept

on the full time. On the last day of the examination, the result was announced. I had obtained the full number of marks given, namely 28, and my opponent was accorded 21. So I was carried shoulder-high by my friends . . .

There was a large field, near the school, and here in summer time we had many enjoyable games at cricket. Occasionally we had special matches, always among ourselves, when the losers had to pay a certain number of eggs – these were cooked at tea time, and I well remember helping to cook quite a lot in a large boiler which was above half-filled with eggs . . .

Near Christmas time, at the end of the year 1851, I was appointed by the Committee to go to Narberth, Pembrokeshire, South Wales, and take charge of the School there!

Robert Roberts
the life and opinions of Robert Roberts,
a wandering scholar, as told by himself

Robert Roberts was born in 1834 at Havod Bach, Llanddewi, North Wales, one of eleven children of a reasonably comfortable tenant farmer. The autobiography was written about 1870, when Roberts had emigrated to Australia, but not published until long after his early death in 1885. It was edited by J. H. Davies in Cardiff in 1923. Typical of his place and time, Roberts became a considerable (though unrecognized) scholar on the basis of little formal education, studying extensively in the classics, French and German; he devoted many years to research in the Celtic language, and prepared a detailed Welsh-English dictionary. His autobiography gives a valuable picture of the social and religious life of Wales in the mid-nineteenth century of which only two short excerpts are included here – the descriptions of the Sunday School and of the extended family, characteristic of what was still a pre-industrial society. This rare work was brought to my notice by Huw Williams of The University College of North Wales, Bangor.

My earliest recollections reach back to one of the farmhouses at Cwmcammas. I was born there about the middle of the fourth decade in the present nineteenth century. My father was tenant of the farm of Havod at the upper and most barren end of the *cwm*. Havod was a wide extent of bad land, wet and cold, of which my father's family had been tenants for more generations than were recorded in our family annals. He had married, while young, the daughter of a neighbouring farmer and had by her a family of eleven children, of whom I was the fourth. His father, who had resigned the farm to him on his marriage, continued to live with him at Havod for many years, till he was carried to Llangammas Churchyard a patriarch of ninety. But we had a member of a still earlier generation among us in my mother's grandmother, a brisk stout old woman of about ninety, a good proof of the salubrity of our climate, whatever might be said of its pleasantness.

One of the first things I remember is the tall figure of my grandfather in his 'spencer' and homespun suit, as he sat in the carved oak arm-chair by the wide fireside with the large family Bible on the table at his side, and myself as his pupil, a little urchin about three years old, sprawling on the table close by and commencing to learn the letters from the large capitals at the beginning of the chapters. Then comes a recollection of being found one day in the same position and in unlawful possession of the big book which had been left there by the old man in an unguarded moment, of my mother's scolding me for meddling with grandfather's books, of my pertly replying, 'I can read it mother,' – of the astonishment of the family when I read out without hesitation the first chapter of St John, and of the prodigy I was accounted in consequence. How the story spread abroad that I had learnt to read without any previous teaching, how our ignorant neighbours thought it miraculous that a child of three should be able to read at all, how crowds flocked to our house to see the prodigy, how I was carried about by my proud mother to display my wonderful talent, how every childish saying was taken up and treasured as marvellous wisdom, how my infantile arguments were magnified till they seemed miraculous: how, in that period, I became a 'genius'. These are some of the great events of my early childhood, events indeed not worthy of even this brief chronicle, except in their bearing upon the course of my future life . . .

[Inside the farmhouse] From a literary point of view there was not much to be seen. Two or three broadsides, adorned with woodcuts, hideous no doubt, but in our estimation, creditable specimens of the pictorial art, were pasted on various parts of the white-washed walls. One is a doleful ditty about the great storm of 1839, detailing in unmelodious numbers the damage done to ships and buildings by that calamity; over the letterpress is a woodcut of Menai Bridge, coloured green, surprinted by a bright yellow ship in full sail. Another is a song of 'meditations' on a clock striking, aptly embellished by a picture of an eight-day clock, surrounded by various nondescript figures. A third is a ballad about the Chartist riots at Newport adorned with a wonderful picture of a skirmish in a wood apparently and not in the streets; but this slight departure from fact was of no moment and the illustration was thought to be a great success. Two or three small engravings of wonderfully ill-favoured Nonconformist divines make up the list of pictorial illustrations.

In one or two short shelves near the great pewter-adorned dresser rests the humble stock of books which, scanty as it is, is larger than is usually found in Welsh farmhouses in the days of my youth, whatever may be the case now. Conspicuous among them is a large folio Bible, with Peter Williams's Commentary. This is the family Bible, where the births, deaths, and marriages are entered. This is the great Hall Bible, always used at family prayers, and it was out of this that I learned my first letter.

The taste of the readers is easily seen from the fact of most of the books being theological. Among the older sort are *The Whole Duty of Man*, the *History of the Faith*, *The Pilgrim's Progress*, and the *Welshman's Candle*, or the *Vicar's Book*, a great favourite with old-fashioned Welshmen to this day. This book, next to the Bible, was my earliest reading book. I read and re-read its homely rugged rhymes till I could repeat the greater part off by heart. It was my great-grandmother's constant companion. In spite of her great age she could read large print without glasses, and the *Vicar's Book* was seldom out of her hands, except when she was knitting. My first quarrel with the old lady was about taking possession of her book. Among the newer are two commentaries, half a dozen volumes of polemical tracts, and the works of Gurnal, a work very popular in Wales. Of profane literature there is very little: the *Mirror of the Primitive Age* and *Afternoon of Wales* furnish all the history, and *Roberts's Geography* a good book, written on the plan of Guthrie's *Geographical Grammar*, supplies all the geography; a few poems, those of Goronwy Owen, Lewis Morris, Hugh Morris, and some of Twm o'r Nant's *Interludes*, or religious plays as he calls them, served for *belles lettres*. There were no English books, all were Welsh, save an old battered Adam Lyttleton's Latin dictionary, a relic of the more varied taste, or education of some member of the family in remote times. There were no newspapers, for there was none published in that part of Wales at that time, but there were two monthly periodicals, *Y Drysorfa* (a Methodist magazine), and *Y Gwladgarwr*, a secular paper something like the old *Penny Magazine*.

It is a bright Sunday afternoon – the weather is fine for our part of the country, that is, it is dry and the sun is cheerful though there is not much heat in its rays. The mid-day dinner is over and the house is set in order for the Sunday School. The people living in the upper part of Cwmcammas lived far from any place of worship. The church was three miles lower down the valley, and the nearest chapel was about two miles off, over the hills in a *cwm* which ran parallel to ours. To remedy, in some measure, this want of spiritual accommodation, a Sunday School had been held at Havod for some years. Our house was the largest of the farmhouses about, and had therefore been fixed upon as the most convenient to hold the school, though there were other houses more centrally situated. Shortly after dinner the neighbouring farmers and their families began to drop in, each with his Welsh Bible under his arm. They liked to come early that they might enjoy a little gossip before school commenced. Here they discussed the preachers at the chapel, the news of the week, and sometimes a little politics. When the kitchen got pretty full, my father would ask some 'religious' man to commence by singing a hymn and offering a prayer. They would then disperse through the house to their several classes, for the large kitchen would not hold them all. We had one class of women in the parlour, presided over by my grandfather; another occupied one of the bedrooms. Young and old were there, from my great-grandmother in my grandfather's class down to the young children of five or six who sat on the hob by my mother's side. My father, who was reputed to be a better-educated man than any of the others, had a 'teachers' class' at the large kitchen table. In this class I was permitted to sit as a genius who was fitter for the company of grown-up men than that of the boys of my age who were puzzling over their horn books away by the dresser. I was privileged further to read out to the class such portions of the commentary as were wanted to elucidate difficult passages, and great was my state of glory as I sat on the window seat with the large folio spread on the table before me. Most of the adults can read pretty fairly, for the reading of Welsh is an easy matter and does not take long to learn. But to some of our older scholars, reading was a great mystery. There is old Robert Hughes, of Moelogan, for instance, a man of seventy and upwards, who sits on a form at my right hand with two of his middle-aged sons by his side. They have been attending school regularly from its first commencement and they have not passed the 'a, b, ab' yet.

'Morris Hughes,' says the teacher to one of Robert's sons, 'you don't hold your book right – you've got it upside down.'

'Why, Morris, you fool,' said his father, shaking a long sheep crook, which he always carried, at his hopeful son, 'you'll never learn – how many times have I told you to put a mark on your book so that you may see which is the right side. Look at mine – I've got a mark on the top of mine. Why don't you do like me?'

Poor Robert, I am afraid that he died without acquiring further knowledge of letters than what sufficed to distinguish the R.H. on his sheep; and as to Morris I doubt if he ever attained to any certainty as to the up or the down side of letters, for I saw him many years afterwards branding his sheep with the same letters upside down. That class of incorrigibles is the crux of the school. Many teachers have tried it and given it up in despair. Now it is in the hands of Robert Wynne, the leader or *blaenor*, a good easy man who presides over their dullness with a respectable and Christian laziness which suits his pupils well. It is strange to watch those strong men puzzling Sunday after Sunday over characters that are as undecipherable to their poor faculties as Etruscan. Look at David Jones, the giant, whom I used to think the very counterpart of the picture of Goliath in the big 'Josephus'; he is strong as a bull and can lift the anvil in the village smithy with one hand and twist a new horseshoe with the greatest of ease, but the youngest brat can beat him hollow at his books. How his heavy, goodnatured face is twisted with mental pain and perplexity, in his endeavours to distinguish between those vexatious u's and n's! And Tom Evans, the best ploughman in the district, who has gained prizes for the straightest and evennest furrows; how is it that he cannot plough his way through that column of monosyllables? As to Robert Hughes and his sons, they are known to be good and thriving sheep farmers, cunning in footrot, and deft shearers; but here they are floundering through difficulties insuperable to them.

In our class we have the most intelligent of the farmers and farm labourers around, men of a quiet, uniform temperament, with great reverence for the Bible, and almost, if not quite, as great for James Hughes's Commentary. We had one rather eccentric character, to be sure, Robert Griffith, the little withered old man who always sits at the end of the bench next the fire. He is the only one among us who attempts to dispute the dicta of James Hughes. Robert has notions of his own on Scripture, and talks of promulgating them in a sort of new Institute of Theology to be called 'The Truth for all the World'. Unfortunately he cannot write, and being already smitten in years the world has lost the advantage of this new revelation. He is very fond of the last chapters of Ezekiel and frequently interrupts the class with some allusion to that favourite portion of Scripture, which I think he likes because it is so unintelligible that James Hughes despaired of trying to interpret it.

We like the Old Testament best, and read it right through, genealogical portions and all. We relish the list of names quite as much as the other parts, though we stumble a good deal over the pronunciation of Hebrew proper names. Indeed it is quite a promotion to be in the Bible (i.e., Old T.) Class.

The New Testament Class is an inferior one altogether. When we come to certain details of Hebrew crime, or details of Hebrew ceremonial which contain pretty plain speaking, we read it all through utterly unconscious of there being anything like indecorum. We repeat a good deal of Scripture by heart, but as the chapters are mostly the same Sunday after Sunday, the amount so learnt is not so great as one might expect. We also say certain chapters of the *Hyfforddwr (Instructor)*, a sort of expanded Church Catechism; but as most of us hold the books open before us without any disguise during the examination, it can hardly be called a satisfactory proof that we have really learnt it. The children are regularly examined every Sunday in a little book called 'A Mother's Gift'; and as the questions are of the simplest and the answers to most of them, Yes, No, or some other monosyllable, it is soon picked up and the youngsters get through it with great success.

There was no day school in the *cwm*, nor ever had been; therefore all the learning ever acquired by most of its people was in the Sunday School. Hence it was an important institution among us. It was also the only church for many of us, especially for the old and infirm.

John Shinn
a sketch of my life and times

The author was born in 1837 in St John Street, Clerkenwell, London, the son of a cabinet-maker and furniture-remover. His is the classical account of self-advancement through hard work, thrift and self-education – in his case, in music. After fifteen years he gave up the cabinet trade, at which he worked with his father, to become a professional organist, choir-master and music teacher; he also composed and published a number of works, the most popular of which was his 'Services of Song' used in Sunday Schools, and opened a shop for the sale of music and instruments. He continued to teach until 1923, when at the age of eighty-six he wrote his short, unpublished autobiography of forty-six pages.

In spite of lack of schooling and his obvious sense of deprivation, he achieved considerable success in the musical world, passing the Cambridge Mus.B. by examination, and being urged to take his Doctorate, an honour which his economic circumstances did not allow. John Shinn's manuscript was supplied by Mrs M. Benge.

I have made a brief and rough sketch of my childhood and life to show some of the hardships and trials that I went through in my early days, and also to give some idea of the condition of things, generally, 80 years back. The reader may think that my statements are overdrawn – not so. The worst I have not told. When I consider the hard struggles of my early life, I often wonder that I have been able to attain my present position, but it has only been by self-denial, perseverance and constant hard work and careful saving which has never ceased.

The condition of things generally 75 or 80 years back were very much worse in every way than one can have any idea of at the present time, or have ever been since. At that time little or no help was given to the struggling poor or the working classes. Labour was very badly paid for, and the hours of labour were very long, generally from 7 a.m. until 8 p.m. and in many cases much longer and it was frequently done under very trying circumstances in unhealthy workshops which was most painful to the workers. The comforts of the workers were never thought of in any way. I have been through it all, so that I can speak from experience. The life of the workers in those days was indeed very hard, and one cannot be surprised that the workers at the present time are both troublesome and dissatisfied and try to claim and gain what they think is their just rights . . .

About this time trade became very bad, and my father's business fell away almost to nothing, and from that time we gradually drifted into distress and trouble, and during the next fifteen years we suffered very great privations and hardships in every way. I remember the brokers taking possession of our home three times during that period and were paid out by friends at the last hour to save our home being sold up. From 1840 to 1850 was the most distressing time of the 19th century. During that period a very large number of people were in the greatest distress. Riots and Chartist meetings were constantly taking place. The great meeting place was on Clerkenwell Green. These I well remember. We children seldom got sight of any money. At that time there was an old lady who lived on the top floor who suffered very much from rheumatism, and could do but little for herself, so I used to carry up all the water she required, which I had to carry from the basement to the third floor up, for which she occasionally gave me a penny, which I always spent to purchase paints or pencils to draw and paint with as I was always very fond of drawing and painting from my earliest days. About this period (1843–4) we children were frequently kept in the house for weeks together, for want of boots and clothing, and Sundays were very long dreary days, and the shop being closed, and we children found little to occupy the time. We only had two or three children's books, and they had been read through many times.

About this time (1845) my father had a very serious illness (a nervous break-down) which lasted about three years, and was quite unable to do any work. This greatly added to our distress and trouble . . . We were terribly short of both food and clothing. Our food was of the plainest kind and at times very short. We seldom tasted meat more than twice or three times a week, frequently only a piece of bread and butter between breakfast and tea, and often bread without butter, only a little sugar sprinkled on the bread, and in the winter we were very short of fuel, and frequently had to do without a fire . . .

The greatest and most serious misfortune of my life has been the loss of schooling or education. At the time of my school age my parents were very poor and in great distress. There was no free education and private schools were few and very expensive, therefore my education was entirely lost, which has been to me the greatest trouble, but that was no fault of mine. The want of education has been a most serious drawback all through my life. As a child I was passionately fond of drawing and painting and spent much of my time in that way, when I could get paper and paints to work with, but our distress at that time made this a great difficulty. The few halfpence I did get were all for that purpose which afforded me very great pleasure and satisfaction and occupied my time and mind. Sundays were long and weary days when we were kept in for want of decent clothes. My mother who was a good pious woman did her best to keep us occupied during the long dull winter Sundays. During the evening she would read to us from the Bible and other suitable books and when we were tired would lead us in singing some favourite hymns for a change and thus we got through the time. She would sometimes (after dark) when our clothing was shabby she would take us to some chapel a distance from home, where we were not known, which made a little change for us children.

About this time (1845) my father came into possession of a violin, which he gave to me as I was fond of music, and for a small sum I purchased a cheap tutor and set to work to teach myself. I used to practise in the workshop by the light of a candle at the end of the day after work was done . . .

At this time my brother and I joined the Sunday School at Trinity Chapel, Leather Lane, and there I received my first musical instruction in a singing class under the organist of the Chapel (Mr C. Dury). This was my first start and which was very useful. Some years after Mr Dury gave me an introduction into the London Sacred Harmonic Society at Exeter Hall where I remained for many years . . .

My first touch of a piano. About 1847

The first chance I had of touching a piano came about in the following way. A customer of my father's named Lasny (?) (a Swiss gentleman) wanted to warehouse an old cabinet piano and asked my father to take it in, which he did, and it was placed in the kitchen, that being the driest room, and he gave us permission to use it, so I bought a second-hand piano tutor and set to work at once to teach myself. With much hard work and perseverance I made fair progress. This I kept up for some years, and thus my musical knowledge increased.

During the first half of the 19th century many people were unable to read or write, and in chapels all over the country it was the custom for the clerk who gave out the number of the hymns, first, to read it all through, and then to give it out again, two lines at a time for the people to sing. After singing the two lines, they waited for the next two lines to be given out, and started the singing again. In churches at that time, all the canticles and psalms were read (not sung), the minister and the congregation taking a verse each consecutively.

1847. Being sent into workshop about 10 or 11 years of age

As my parents were unable to send me to school, I was sent into the workshop to occupy my time and give me something to do. In a little time I became useful in assisting my father in many ways, and gradually drifted into the cabinet trade (which I never liked) but there was nothing else to be done but to remain and do my best, and wait and see what the future brought forth. The life in a workshop in those days was very rough. The working hours were very long, from 7 a.m. to 8 p.m. Saturday was the same, no half holidays at that time. The only holidays allowed during the year were Christmas and Boxing days, Easter and Whit Monday (not Good Friday), which left very little time for study or self-improvement. About this period we were in very straightened circumstances, and my brother Edwin and I were sent one day to try and sell two ottoman footstools to raise a little money. We could only sell them at furniture dealers. We carried them from Clerkenwell to Walworth then on to Camberwell Green, then across to Kennington Green, from there to Westminster through St Giles's to Tottenham Court Road, and Euston Road and back to Clerkenwell, a distance of about 12 or 13 miles, and brought them back unsold . . .

First step on the organ, 1847–8

When I joined Trinity Chapel and Sunday School and the singing class under Mr Dury the organist, I offered to blow the organ at the Sunday Services (it was only a small organ with four stops). After some time I was allowed to practise on the organ once a week. I had been working hard on the piano which was a great help to me. When I had advanced sufficiently to play hymn tunes I was sometimes asked to play at the week evening services which was a great step in advance, and thus I gradually moved on step by step.

Exeter Hall concerts and singers

The practice and experience I gained at Exeter Hall was most useful to me. The Society performed all the greatest work and engaged the best solo singers of the day . . .

About 1853 or 4 I became a performing member of the Polyhymnian Choir (as

190 *Education*

alto) under Dr William Rea who was an excellent conductor and choir trainer (a choir for male voices only). It was the best of its kind in London. The concerts were given in Crosby Hall, Bishopsgate Street, in the City, and at the Hanover Square Concert Room. The Choir numbered about 70 voices and the concerts were of a very high class. On these occasions a large orchestra was engaged to take part and perform some of the best concertos and symphonies. I was present at Hanover Square Rooms at the performance of the G Minor Concerto for Piano and Orchestra by W. Sterndale Bennett when Dr Rea was at the piano and Sterndale Bennett conducted.

In this choir I gained much experience and knowledge in voice training and I remained a member for some years until Dr Rea left London, when the choir ceased to exist.

My first organ appointment

I first played the organ at Trinity Chapel, Leather Lane (occasionally), when about 13 years old, on a small organ of four stops and one octave of pedals, in 1850.

My first real appointment was on 19 December 1858 at St Peter's Church, Peter Street, Hackney Road, Bethnal Green (I became voluntary afternoon organist at St Helen's Church, Bishopsgate Street, very soon after). This church was frequently called the Abbey of the City. A beautiful and ancient abbey church.

At St Peter's I was organist and choir master. I received no salary the first year. At this church I worked very hard at the organ. On two evenings a week after 8 o'clock I walked from Clerkenwell to St Peter's a distance of over two miles to practise on the organ. I remained at this church five years. After the first year I received a salary of six pounds a year, for which I was very grateful, as I found the money most useful at that time.

While at St Peter's I took a course of twelve organ lessons of William Carter who was a very good teacher, but before the course had finished he went to Toronto Cathedral to do duty for his brother Henry while he came to England for a year's holiday, and my lessons were transferred to George Carter (another brother) who was then organist of Trinity Church, Sloane Street, Chelsea, who was also an excellent teacher. Some years after I took a short course of organ lessons from Dr E. J. Hopkins at the Temple Church, later on I also took lessons on the pianoforte and counterpoint from Mr Carter (who was a pupil of Her Paner, the eminent pianist of that time). The above were the only music lessons I ever received. All the rest I did by hard work.

1863, St Jude's Church, Whitechapel

My next appointment was to St Jude's, Whitechapel, 24 June 1863 (by competition) at a salary of £25 per annum. This was a great advance at St Jude's I obtained a few pupils. I then first contemplated the idea of giving up the cabinet business and devote my whole time entirely to music as I considered combining the two could not be carried on well together. At the same time I thought that teaching alone would not keep me, so I then thought of a music business to increase my income as many other musical men had done in times past with success. After well thinking the matter over I took a small house and shop in the Holloway Road, Islington, which I opened for the sale of music and musical instruments.

I started in a small way at first as my capital was very limited. For some time it was very slow and hard uphill work, but in time it gradually (but very slowly) improved. It was a great struggle to live and make ends meet expenses (my sister Maria was my housekeeper at that time). After a time things looked up as business increased, and I felt that I had established a somewhat regular income though not very large. I then thought it would be an advantage to marry, as I found many inconveniences in living and working single handed and as I had been engaged to Miss Ward for some time we seriously talked the matter over together and came to the conclusion that such a step would be for the best in many ways, so after a little time we acted upon our decision and married, a step which I have never had cause to regret (quite otherwise) . . .

At this time I thought that a university degree would greatly help me and from the time I went to St Matthews I began to prepare for it which also greatly added to my work and labour. This work continued for some years, and in 1889 I sent in my exercises to the University of Cambridge for Mus. Bac. degree which was accepted. After this I went to Cambridge for the examinations and was very fortunate in passing satisfactorily without a failure. There were only two or three out of 60 who went through all the exams without having some of their work returned or had to go up again. After I had finished the final Professor MacLarren before I left Cambridge came to shake hands with me and said Now come up as soon as you like for your Mus. Doc., but I had made a great sacrifice for my Mus. Bac. and with the family I had at that time I could not afford the money so had to give up the idea of taking the Mus. Doc., although it appeared so near . . .

Concluding remarks

In taking a survey of my life, I don't think I ought to be dissatisfied with the social position I have attained and the progress I have made considering the many hardships and difficulties I had to contend with through my whole life. What I have done has been done only by hard work and persistent perseverance. Considering the circumstances of my early life it is surprising that I have been able to do so much. My earnings have always been very modest, I may say small, but I could see from the first that unless I could put by something, however little, no progress could be made, and no provision made for sickness, misfortune or old age, therefore from my early life I resolved to save something out of my small income for future help, which I have done the whole of my life. I have had many difficulties and trials to bear, the greatest trial has been the want of education, but this was no fault of mine. All the education I got I had to get for myself. It is a most unfortunate thing to be born of poor parents, and lose all the advantage of schooling which is so essential in the present age. Seventy years back there were no Board Schools and private schools were very expensive, quite out of the reach of the poor working classes in those days. The want of a better education has always been a great drawback all through my life, it has always made me feel nervous and timid and gave me a great lack of confidence in myself, but I have done the best I could under the circumstances and must rest contented with what I have attained. Had I had the opportunities which I have seen many have, I could have done much more. One thing I shall always regret, that when my parents were getting old and were in need that my own circumstances prevented me from giving them more assistance. But I did what I could.

Charles Cooper
reminiscences of school life in the latter part of the nineteenth century

Charles Cooper was born in 1872 at Walton, a mining village two miles from Wakefield in the West Riding of Yorkshire. His short, unpublished autobiography describes his life at Walton National School where he was successively infant, scholar and pupil-teacher from 1876–89; later, he trained for teaching at St John's College, York, and took a London B.A. degree externally. Most of his teaching career was spent in Bristol, where he was headmaster of Sefton Park Senior School for twenty-seven years. His memoirs were written in 1964 at the age of ninety-two.

The school building was a large single-roomed, church-style buttressed stone building, oblong in shape. The corner of the narrow playground stood at the corner of the road, and a lamp post was placed at this corner in the playground. I never saw a lamp or light there. The iron post was used by the boys for one of their original games – Chevvy Lennett.

The north side of the school faced towards Leeds, and the south side towards Sheffield and Derby. The Midland Railway ran about three hundred yards away from the west end of the school; the station was quite near and the people on the platforms easily and clearly seen.

The Canal lay across the road at the east end, quite near. The Canal Garth and locks and paths were forbidden ground. Below the bridge over the Canal were some low-lying fields, part of a farm called The Low Lanes – also a spot forbidden to us but where we often wandered birds'-nesting.

Opposite the school, across the road, was a laundry used for training poor and needy girls. Behind the laundry was the drying ground and the Head Master had his rose garden and a small greenhouse. A part of the laundry was used by the Infants. Here the Infants and Standard 1 were taught by a Mistress, assisted by a girl from the Orphanage.

The big school consisted of one large room, with no partition or classrooms, in which upwards of a hundred boys and girls were taught in Standards 2, 3, 4, 5, 6 and 7 by the Head Master and two Pupil Teachers, in mixed classes.

The girls were taken in needlework in the afternoons by the lady who was really responsible for the school, and the older girls were taken in cookery and housework in a house near the school under her supervision. This lady devoted herself to good works. She ran the school, laundry, orphanage and an annual blanket club, and had other activities to help the poor.

On Sundays, a morning Sunday School was held, after which the scholars proceeded to Sandal Church with the lady and the Head Master in frock coat and silk hat. The lady always wore a crinoline and I never saw her dressed otherwise.

Sunday School was held again in the afternoon and was followed by a service in the school, with sermon by the Vicar or an address by the Scripture Reader. The lady of good works was the sister of the local baronet, with whom she lived at Chevet Hall about two miles from Walton . . .

The Head Master of this school, Mr W. G. Bott, was a Shropshire man. He had been trained at Cheltenham College. He had achieved a high reputation as a successful teacher, and his school was highly regarded.

Many children came to Walton School from neighbouring villages, and there was not a little grumbling at this neglect of their own village schools – but as long as they could pay the fee – 2d. per week – they were allowed to come. Some came from as far as five or six miles, and it all had to be walked – there being no means of conveyance.

Mr Bott was a widower. He lived in a house well in sight of the school with his old mother and four surviving children, two boys and two girls. There were no fads or fancy frills in his teaching, which consisted of the three Rs, with spelling and a bit of geography, botany and singing thrown in. The old lady used to get boys who stayed for dinner to get the coal in for her and she used to tell us to do it 'this-a-way' or 'that-a-way'. The girls were named Polly and Rosie and the boys Frank and George . . .

I attended Walton School first in 1876, four years old and dressed in petticoats. I had to walk two miles there and two miles back and could not go home for dinner. I attended this school until I left in 1889 to go to College. I passed through all the Standards 1 to 7 and became a Pupil Teacher at about twelve years old, then I passed the Queen's Scholarship Examination and gained the 14th place on the list of all Pupil Teachers in England, Scotland and Wales. I entered St John's College as top student and was Senior Monitor in my second year.

In those days the amount of the Government Grant paid to a school depended on the status gained by the school in an examination of all its scholars in the three Rs by H.M. Inspectors. Of course the Head Master's ideal was to get 100 % passes. His school was then marked 'Excellent' and was paid the highest grant. Less success meant a lower status and a lower grant. The record of each child was marked 'X' or 'O' on a schedule prepared by the Head. Hence every effort was made to get every child passed in all three subjects.

It was a cruel system. The cane was used freely for both boys and girls. Children were not regarded as mentally deficient. The idea was that every child could do the work if he tried hard enough. And he was made to try by threat of punishment.

For reading, the same books were used year after year until they were ready to fall to pieces. Usually then they were sent up to the Hall to be patched up and made usable again by the indefatigable lady.

For writing, Copy Books were used and the correct holding of the pen was insisted upon – 'Thumb on left side of pen, first finger on top, second finger on right side, little finger resting on the paper, wrist flat and end of pen pointing towards the right ear'. Blots and finger marks were punishable by cane; and the correct size, shape, height and length of each letter had to be as shown in the copy.

Pens in those days had steel split nibs; the nibs often got crossed and they dripped ink readily. There were no fountain pens or ballpoint pens. All these disadvantages tended to make us very careful and nervous, with the fear of the cane ever before us ...

And now we come to the case of spelling. Here again there are faddists and work avoiders who say there is no need to bother to teach spelling to a child. He will pick it up automatically as he gets older. In the old days we had to learn to spell correctly, usually with the fear of the cane haunting us. Each mistake had to be written out correctly a given number of times. Simple rules were taught, and correct spelling was insisted upon and was regarded as being very important.

In arithmetic the addition and subtraction of simple figures came first and more difficult examples were gradually introduced. Then the rules were applied to £.s.d., and in Standard 4 and upwards to sums including weights and measures. Some sums were taught which could be of no future use to the children. It was a good thing to drop some of these unlikely types and to introduce others of more likely use.

The two Pupil Teachers would be responsible for the arithmetic of Standards 2 and 3 and the Head Master would take the remaining four Standards and keep them all going full out at the same time. It was a clever performance and required intense and concentrated work, and he kept each child working at full pressure. This was his method. All work was done on slates. The children were stationed alternately all round the large hall – no two children of the same class being next each other. A sum would be given to each class one after another. After an appropriate period the first class would be called to the bottom end of the school where a blackboard rested on the mantelpiece over the fireplace. Here he would mark each child's sum right or wrong, would point out any error in an incorrect attempt, would work out the sum on the blackboard with full explanations, and inevitably would punish any child guilty of carelessness with the cane. Each child received individual attention. Then he would give this class another sum to work out and would send it back to its place and call up the next class, with which the same procedure would be performed. He would get through four or five sums per session for each child. It must have been exhausting work for him, for he kept everybody busy and every bit of work was fully dealt with. This type of work included boys and girls, but in the afternoons when the girls were sewing, the boys would work from cards. There were many packs of cards in the cupboard for each class, and sometimes when the master had a large batch of essays to mark, or other urgent work to do, all classes would work from cards at early periods. Then the marking of sums would fall to the monitors and the Head always came round with his cane to inspect and punish.

Multiplication tables from two to twelve times were memorized and were regarded as very important, followed by money tables, weights and measures and the aliquot parts of £...

The furthest I got in arithmetic before I became a Pupil Teacher was to acquire the ability to solve square and cube roots. A kindly senior Pupil Teacher showed me how to work them out and I was proud when I could do a cube root. Until I became a Pupil Teacher, Algebra, Geometry, Mensuration or Trigonometry were quite unknown and were looked upon as being quite beyond reach.

We were not taught any history at school, but some smatterings of geography; not geography as it is known today but lists of Capes, Bays, Seas, Oceans, Countries, Towns, Rivers, Lakes, Mountains and so on; we were called upon to point out any of these on a map of the British Isles or the World.

Also we tried to understand the mysteries of fog, ice, rain, cloud, snow, wind etc.

We were told much about the Solar System and we had to memorize useless facts about the sun, moon and planets. We had a machine which showed the phases of the moon and the seasons. We had to learn to draw (on slates) diagrams illustrating the Solar System, the Tides, the Phases of the moon and the Seasons. This was all to the good and I have found this knowledge and ability of much use to me in my long teaching career. We found the drawing of elliptical orbits very difficult and instead of smoothly curved orbits we usually got them very pointed and angular.

Mr Bott was a lover of nature and a well-known rose grower. He belonged to a Nature Society in Wakefield called The Paxton Society. He used to give them a paper on gardening – usually roses – each year and the local paper always eulogized his address and his clever use of words – word painting – was greatly praised and much admired.

This Paxton Society held yearly an exhibition of interest to gardeners and flower and nature lovers. It introduced classes for school children, evidently at Mr Bott's instigation ... Well, we received a fair elementary knowledge of botany under Mr Bott, and this is the earliest introduction of science into the curriculum of an Elementary School I know of.

We received absolutely no vestige of Physical Instruction or Physical Drill – we were not even taught to keep step in marching or to form fours or to do the turnings.

Our drawing was confined to map drawing, diagrams of the Solar System, Tides, Phases of the Moon and Planetary System – all on slates.

Nothing like Freehand, Geometry, Sketching, Perspective or Model Drawing was ever mentioned.

It seemed that the main reason for a child's attendance at school was to gain sufficient ability in the three Rs to enable him to pass the examination by the Government Inspectors, and thus help him to earn the highest grant for the school. Little or no notice was taken of a child's health, comfort or well-being; that was someone else's business, certainly not the schoolmaster's.

At Walton School the heating was done by a stove set in the middle of the school. A long pipe reached up to the centre of the roof. Fireplaces were at each end of the large room, but these were never used for school times; they might be used for the Sunday service in extreme weather. It was the duty of a Pupil Teacher to light the stove fire and to keep it going.

In winter, at dinnertime, those children who came from a distance were allowed to sit round the stove to eat their food, but afterwards had to go out-of-doors for the rest of the hour. No milk was provided free or for purchase – similarly no food was available – everything had to be brought from home and nobody cared whether you brought anything or had sufficient. No drinking or washing water was available on the premises. A swill or a drink could be got from a well on the other side of the railway, at least three hundred yards away. This well had been restored and made available by the same lady of good works.

After dinner the children had to amuse themselves as best they could in their own way. The playground was small, and the pupils were forced out on the roads for most of their games, although there were plenty of suitable fields quite near the school. No one thought it worth while to provide a proper playing field for the children. No games at all were taught at school and no articles for games were supplied – not even a bat or cricket ball or football or hockey stick . . .

I have not mentioned the music we were taught. We received very elementary instruction in the music signs and were taught a few simple songs. The master had a tenor voice, and he could play chants and hymns on the harmonium, but I should not say he was a very good musician.

Songs were taken last lesson on Friday afternoon. The harmonium was at the east end of the school and at the opposite end was a crude pulpit used for the Sunday afternoon service. The girls and boys were arranged in standing lines on each side of the instrument and the master walked up and down between the rows, cane in hand; he would sing the tune or play it and would then exhort the children to sing likewise. The result was lifeless and lacked pleasure or enthusiasm . . .

The master lived in a small house across a small field near the school. The bell was rung at 9 o'clock and 2 p.m., but he never appeared until fifteen or twenty minutes later. In the meantime the children straggled into school as they arrived and awaited his advent under the charge of Pupil Teachers. In the morning a short service, and in the afternoon a brief grace opened the proceedings. Scripture was always the first lesson up to 10 o'clock.

We noted with anxiety each morning which trousers he was wearing. If he had a tight fitting pair of a check pattern we knew that he was certain to be in a bad temper.

The reading lesson invariably developed into a bald, boring sort of grammar lesson. We were taught to analyse sentences, sometimes very involved, principal and dependent, and to parse words, number, person, gender, case, transitive, regular, irregular, mood, tense etc., – all very boring and seemingly of little use to us, but which some have found very useful in after life.

School was never closed at twelve and four punctually. Every class had to quite finish its work before it was allowed to go and then the master would think nothing of stopping thirty, sixty or more minutes longer, struggling with backward children. Then he would depart for his own dinner or tea – and would return in due course ready to resume the fray.

The Pupil Teachers often lived too far away for them to go home for tea before their lessons after school. If the master was late in going for his tea he was also late in coming back to instruct his Pupil Teachers. Often they did not get away until 8 o'clock or later, having had no meal since dinnertime. I had then a walk of two miles home and was lucky to get there by 9 o'clock. Then after my first and last good meal of the day, I had to get on with my homework, study and lessons for tomorrow. Bedtime came at last with much too short a time left for sleep as I had to be up and off for school by 8.15 next day.

As a closing aspect, reference must be made to the lack of interest and guidance taken in a child when leaving school – in those days at twelve years of age. Nobody seemed to bother about what happened to him. He just had to take up any job that happened to be going at the time. Perhaps I was fortunate that a Pupil Teacher was wanted at Walton School just when I was available, and that I had a reputation of being a pretty good scholar. I just dropped into teaching – I had no special wish or desire for teaching and might just as easily have dropped into farming, gardening, mining or some sort of engineering. Of course, the teaching facilities and pay of today are tremendously improved, but then it was hard labour with little pay. But there was nothing better in those days and we had to endure it.

A Higher Grade or Grammar School such as are available to all today was quite out of the question. How I should have valued the chance that children of today have – a possible straight course to the University! . . .

Before I conclude I should like to say that the school stood in a district abounding with religious, historic and commercial associations. Yet we were told little or nothing about such interesting things. The teaching of the three Rs seemed to dominate everything – but possibly the cash element was really at the bottom of it. How much interest would have been aroused, and how much boredom would have been avoided, if we had been told about these things, and shown and had them explained!

Daisy Cowper
'de nobis'

The author was born in a poor area of Liverpool in 1890, the youngest of nine children. Her mother was then aged forty; she was widowed five years later when her husband was drowned at sea. The extract describes Daisy Cowper's education up to the age of eleven in a large, progressive town school now freed from the constraints of 'Payment by Results'. Failing to win one of the very few scholarships to the High School, she stayed on in her elementary school preparing to be a pupil-teacher through a long series of examinations – at fourteen to attend a pupil-teacher centre for two years full-time study, at sixteen to be accepted as a probationer for half-time pupil-teaching, then at eighteen for admission as a two-year residential student at Edge Hill Training College, Liverpool, where the fees of £25 had to be borrowed. She finally qualified in 1910, achieving an 'A' Grade Certificate, and was appointed to her old school at a salary of £71.4s.0d. p.a. rising by £5 p.a. Her unpublished, 109-page autobiography was written in 1964. It was kindly supplied by her son Alan C. Fraser.

I commenced school life at St Silas's C. of E. school for mixed infants! Miss Sawyer, the headmistress, was a gentle-looking lady who dressed in a violet dress with a purple topaz brooch, and looked (to me) about ninety. For the first few days Mother took me: we called for Albert Johnson, en route, a kind little five-year-old who helped me to hang up my coat and bonnet . . .

My feeling to life at this infant school can best be described as neutral, with brief, unnecessary flashes of apprehension of which I'll tell as I go on. We, in the babies' class, sat on long forms facing the teacher and the black-board, over which hung at lesson time the stiff, glazed linen charts – sheets of coloured letters, appropriate pictures and simple sentences . . .

We learned numbers by twiddling coloured glass beads on a wire contraption, something like a miniature gridiron, held in the left hand. It never conveyed much to me, but I seemed to get along with the rest. Handiwork, as we grew to be six-ish, was another boredom to me. One queer task was to join four longish, black pins, pointed at both ends, into pre-soaked split peas, so to form a square, with a pea at each corner. It sounds easy, and it was, as far as handling peas 3 and 4, with a couple of moving pins dangling in space, and the darned peas all continuing to split – (their sides laughing at our infantile efforts?). I was no good at all, at it. Another daft-seeming lesson was up-turning a box of small bricks, cubes, triangles, etc., itself forming a cube, and withdrawing the lid of the inverted box, at the word of command: 'Now lift the box', and hi, presto, there was the cube (of bits). So far, so good: I could do that, but I hated the end proceedings. The cube was re-formed, the box placed over it – all to the word of command – and now for prestidigitation! The upturned box and contents had to be drawn off the desk, to rest exactly on its lid which the hapless child held jammed between chest and desk, and it was sure to collapse!

But paper weaving was a pleasure indeed. You threaded strips of coloured, shiny paper held in a special clip-holder through a coloured paper frame of vertical strips, thus forming a pretty pattern. One horrid thing about those days was the use of slates, not that I object to slates, having found them most useful in teaching my own children – but it was disgusting to see them being cleaned by spitting and rubbing with a slate-rag: if no slate-rag was at hand, the bare wrist would serve! On rare occasions, a monitress might be sent round the rows with a small ink-well filler full of water, to bestow a few drops, but usually a small cataract would descend on a few slates, wetting one's clean pinny – and the supply was exhausted.

One last memory I have of this dull patch in my school life is of our classroom for six or seven year olds, and hanging on the wall in front, a linen-faced picture of a lush Autumn hayfield: but like everything else in that school, it was old and shabby, and one bit of glazed-linen sky had dried and curled back, revealing the dirty, plain cotton backing. Our teacher was called away, and left the room saying no one was to speak in her absence. All was silence, until I found myself, to my own surprise, telling my equally surprised audience, in a clear voice, 'That's God, peeping out of Heaven.' I awaited the teacher's return, scared stiff, expecting her usual, 'Who spoke while I was out?', when I'd be for it on two counts, disobedience and blasphemy, and I knew which was the greater of these. 'Thus conscience doth make cowards of us all.' Nothing happened! . . .

Now came a big change, for I was old enough to be promoted to the big girls' school, a very small one, I'm sure, tho' numbers didn't mean much to me then. I suppose I would be in Standard I or II, but it's all rather vague, because nothing nice seemed to happen there to give incidents or definition. I have few happy memories of the place, although my life apart from school was so pleasant that no one at home ever thought of my being anything but well content with my lot. Of course, I'd nothing to compare it with! The one really pleasant memory is of the Curate, a Mr Stanley, who used to come to talk to us about something called 'the catechism': he had a charming way of talking to children, and smiled readily with his kind, brown eyes, and I fell in love with him. But, alas, some one else did, too, and he disappeared. I learned later that he'd eloped with a lady, leaving his own wife and child. But the terrible ogress of my life was the Headmistress, a Miss McLaren: I never feared and disliked anyone in all my life as I did her. She was ugly: she couldn't help her ancient, sallow, wrinkled skin which hung under her neck and chin in disgusting folds, or the yellow-tinted whites of her eyes, but she could help being cruel and unloving. The only words I ever heard her speak were harsh, bad-tempered ones. I never saw her actually teaching, but she would look in to terrorize a young teacher or to hand out punishment, tho' I must admit, not to my young group. It was the big girls of the school she vented her sadistic instincts on, and she would bring down her beastly cane on the palms, one on each hand, with such a full-arm action and sickening thwack that I was terrified that the hand would drop off at the wrist, and lie there, cut off, on the floor! I could easily have been sick!

We had no lessons on such subjects as Flowers, or Fruits, or Pet Animals – oh, no, but we had 'Science'! We learned about sand, and glass, and water. One day our young teacher was struggling along, all flustered and pink patches on her neck, with Madam seated on a high chair alongside: Miss Bessie was teaching us all about sandstone. (Ugh!) Madam was taking notes, for the young teacher's later castigation, I suppose, when she interrupted, to ask us, in a voice that sounded as if she hated the very sight of us, what was the power that held the particles of sandstone together. I wanted to opine God, but feared I might be wrong, and my hand might litter the floor, so we were given until the following week's lesson to find out, and 'lightly bring me word'. So here, clever big brother Bert came to my aid, and told me the queer phrase 'power of cohesion'. Lest I forgot it before the Day of Judgement, he wrote it on a scrap of paper, I placed it in a matchbox, and carried that around in the leg of my knickers. At the appointed time I had the phrase off pat, and was the only one to have delved deeply enough to find the treasure. But although no cane came my way, neither did any hoped-for verbal bouquets – but Bert had risen vastly in my estimation. No wonder he was called Solomon at school!

The depression that predominated in my attitude to St Silas's was deepened by the general atmosphere of the place – dinginess and severity – as well as by its horrible Head.

Our poem for recitation that year was:

> Tell me not in mournful numbers
> Life is but an empty dream,
> For the soul is dead that slumbers,
> And things are not what they seem.

What utter abyssmal dreariness for seven-year-olds . . .

[After an absence due to scarlet fever] But all things come to an end, and with my hair shorn off like a boy's I returned to school and a higher class. Almost the first morning, Miss McLaren had a group of us round her high chair, being tested on tables, seven times, I remember. Of course, I'd missed school and tables, and felt scared as I awaited my question. It came, and I made a ridiculous guess, just to show willing. My reward was a slap in the face with the back of her hand. I expect it was more of a flip than a backhander, but to a gently-handled child it was humiliating and frightening, and I wept. But next morning I shed tears to better effect, for when mother's urging me to be a lot quicker in dressing only produced a flood of tears, very unusual for me at rising, she wanted to know why. 'I don't want to go to school: I'm afraid of Miss McLaren – she hit me in the face' – my good sister was full of indignant wrath. On hearing my story – doubtless, my flipping backhander was now a heavy blow – she made an announcement. 'She's not going back there! I'll see Miss Roberts tonight, and ask if Daisy can be taken in at her school.' I was, the following Monday morning, and that decision of Agnes's probably did a great deal to alter my future life, and for the better.

Miss Roberts was the Headmistress of Upper Park St Board School, Girls' Department, and also Head of the Evening Classes. It was Agnes's attendance at the night-school that had led to her knowing Miss Roberts. So to Miss Roberts I was taken, to fall completely under her charms. She must have been about twenty-seven then, lovely to look at, and sweet and gracious to everyone. I can't recall time exactly, but it seems about a week later that I was one of a string of half a dozen or so, who were out on the floor in disgrace, and Miss Roberts was sent for to see the shocking state of our blotted and scrawled messes. She decided we deserved to be slapped, and we were – two little slaps each that 'wouldn't have hurt a skeeter', as Topsy said, and a reproachful glance from the kindest eyes imaginable, that seemed to smile because they couldn't help it. Oh, it was much nicer to be slapped by Miss Roberts than to be overlooked in the mass. But – desolation was at hand, and in what seems to have been another week, word went round that Miss Roberts was leaving to be married – and it was only too true. She married a Mr Moore, brother to Miss Florence Moore, another splendid teacher at the school whom I grew to know and esteem over a long period . . . So, to celebrate, a teaparty was given to all us scholars: we sat at the long desks and had tea in cups we had carried from home, and a piece of seed cake and half a sour orange: nothing, indeed, to call a special occasion, but how wrong would be such a conclusion: a really momentous event took place that day – I first set eyes on Miss Amy Jones, an odd little black sailor-hatted figure who came to the party as the prospective headmistress. She was a unique personality, who proved an increasingly strong influence in my life for the next twenty years. Assuredly, she, mother, and the vice-principal of my training college, between them, nurtured any subsequent traits in my character that may be deemed worthy ones. I owe so much to them . . .

Miss Jones was a plain-looking, plainly-dressed tiny person who was, in fact, an overpowering personality in a small frame. Her appearance seemed never to vary: to me she looked about sixty when I first saw her, and much the same at her retirement, thirty years later. There was nothing to redeem the plainness of her facial appearance: it, and her dress, were alike, neutral, if you get my meaning. Her hair was thin, and drawn tight back from her face, twisted into a little bun on top – just like a Spanish onion was my husband's remark after she had partaken of a post-marriage tea with us – and it was apt. She was sparse of eyebrows and eyelashes, and the eyes themselves were small. One rarely saw them fully open, so I suspect a muscular weakness, though not a weakness of sight – oh, no! They were almost always screwed up, so that it was almost impossible to tell whether her expression indicated merriment or displeasure. After long experience you found the clue, in the corners of the mouth, whether up or down. But many a hapless child had a sharp dressing down for reciprocating an apparently crinkley-eyed friendliness which in reality was a screwed-up frown of disapproval. But she was a Napoleon among women! There never was a harder worker anywhere, and she feared no one! She never spared herself, and she spared no one else, adult or child. She was due in school by 8.45 a.m., but was unfailingly at her desk, ready for work at 8.10, and every single minute of the school-day was filled with conscientious work . . .

School began now to be a daily delight, with a kind teacher ready to praise, and interesting lessons: life began to be more or less what the poet called 'a grand, sweet song' – very different from St Silas's . . . We had no painting, or drawing, or physical exercises, but what you've never had, you never miss, and there was certainly never a dull moment . . .

So now, up I went to Standard IV: another big class of a hundred or more for Miss Tucker and her pupil teacher. I, at once, noticed that my new teacher wore a brooch just like my last teacher's, and also, that Miss Moore for whom I intended to be especially diligent at Scripture, wore one the same. So, in case any of them hadn't noticed, and would be interested in their remarkably similar choice, I went to each in turn, before school, and politely told them my observation. They pleasantly agreed, and that was all! Had I known it, Miss Jones, too, might have been so decorated, but she only wore one dreary little antique brooch throughout my school days. I little thought that I, myself, would be entitled to wear one, with great pride, eleven years later, for it was the silver lily badge of the Edge Hill Training College Guild, and it bore the silver initials, L.H.P. (for Love, Hope and Patience); the badge was founded on a poem by Southey, I think – if not, Coleridge, in which he speaks of the immensely important part played in child-education by these virtues, and ending, I remember (for I only saw the whole poem once), with the fancy that when Hope and Patience are well-nigh exhausted in the task, 'then, Love, supporting, does the work of both' . . .

But to return to St. IV. I was growing to enjoy school more and more. Every minute of the day was occupied, and there was someone, either Miss Tucker or Miss Mary willing to explain things; but the teaching was so clear that one didn't seem to need further help. Memory training played a big part in our education, and it is my firm opinion that this cannot be over-estimated, and I base my judgement on my own personal knowledge of its value, and my experience as a teacher. Children's minds are so receptive, so unconcerned with matters that call for much thought that oft repetition seems to make impressions that are altogether indelible . . . So to help our arithmetic, we chanted tables aloud – all sorts – before the lesson. (Often, five minutes before afternoon closing were also popped in: modern authorities would be scandalized), and we memorized texts at Monday morning's Scripture period, a suitable time as the coming-in of children who'd been at the Penny Bank was slightly distracting. Such lots we learned, and all, once learned, were rehearsed each Monday, beginning with John v, 39: 'Search the Scriptures, for in them etc.' (I *do* hope I'm right this time!) Spellings were learned every single day, morning and afternoon, without fail, in

Sts. III, IV and V – in this way. Our history or geography books were on the ledge under the desk-top. As soon as we sat down for the first lesson, and while our teacher marked the attendance register, we learned all the hard words in certain specified paragraphs. *But*, and herein lay the value of the whole exercise, our books were then closed and we were tested on what we'd just done. This was a rule never broken under any circumstance, and any teacher failing to test (or mark) any work set, however short or simple, would have incurred Miss J.'s severest censure, not at all pleasant! But it was excellent training for teacher and taught. Nothing suggesting the slipshod was ever tolerated at Upper Park Street Girls' . . .

Grammar, even in St. IV, was a very pleasant lesson, so easy, like a game. Anyone, however dull, could learn that nouns were names, with lots of examples. (Of course, we had real, live teachers, and didn't do our exercises from an individual, printed booklet), that adjectives describe (a fine game, making up examples), that the predicate – a bit harder – is the telling word: it came easy with practice: and so on to subjects and objects and a simple sentence . . .

Meanwhile, what had become of my old bogey, the cane? Well, Miss Jones had one: it lived in a drawer in a little black cabinet next to her big desk in the main room. She reminded us of it from time to time: 'It was there for any girl who – gave – her – teacher – trouble: she didn't want to use it, but . . . !' Nor did she, except rarely: a girl was only sent to her after several warnings, and never for inability to do the lessons. Any new teacher sending a child to Miss J. for the cane for bad work was given to understand that in her school a child that couldn't do its work was a reflection on the teacher, not the child. That teacher sent no more. Occasionally a girl, an older one, would be sent, after warnings, for impudence. Then the cane *was* produced, and one good hard smack delivered, but from the elbow, not the vicious, full-arm swipe of the McLaren . . .

So now, at ten and a half, I find myself going up into St. V, a large class, the usual hundred or so, presided over by a trained teacher, helped by a pupil-teacher. They taught and supervised some fifty pupils each, the P.T. taking the brighter ones, the A section, and the trained teacher tackling the tougher group. For needlework and recitation all the class was taught as one; on Wednesdays two P.T.s were there all day, instead of the usual half-day, the other half day being spent at the P.T. centre, Clarence Street. When not actually teaching, they helped with supervising needlework, marked exercise books, heard spelling corrections, or helped a small backward group at reading or sums. They didn't waste a moment! . . . Miss J. took the senior Scripture group on two mornings a week, and I wish, most sincerely, that I could make it possible for you to experience what her lessons were like. Perfect silence to commence: she insisted on that, and would not have uttered a word until she had it. From then on, she kept it, with no effort! Her clear voice carried well, there was no faltering in her delivery, she had such skill as a narrator, and those screwed-up eyes took in every one of that large company. The moral that followed the narrative was simple and clear. 'Influence' was a favourite theme, but whatever it was she held her audience spellbound, and as her closed book on her knee indicated the closing of the lesson, a soft sigh would be heard, and then the scuffle of feet. What a tribute to a tremendous gift and a tremendous personality! She had a brother, a Vicar: I wonder if he did as well for his parishioners! . . .

In Miss Stephenson I had another wonderful teacher: she was short and quick-moving, with kind, dark, bespectacled eyes, and she wore pretty blouses. But she had no time to waste: we had to get on with our work all the time, but she always praised when praise was due. She had been trained at Stockwell, London, which shared Edge Hill's position as the two leading training colleges of their day. She must have been quite young, although she seemed so staid and capable, for at her wedding, some six years later, she was apparently 29 or 30 . . .

But Miss Jones was, I think, at this time weighing me up, and remembering my unpredictability over 'upon', yet hearing Miss S. praise me fairly frequently for compositions and word-meanings, she wasn't sure, and she wanted to be. Actually, she was scouting for talent, I think the modern phrase is, ready for the scholarship exam. of next year. This chosen group of smarties had to be cleansed of dross, tried in the fire, or what you will, before she expended extra trouble on them . . .

There were very few scholarships in those days for such a big city, but the number was considerably increased in the next few years. If my memory of seeing the printed list of successes is right, I should say there were about eight awards to boys, and certainly not more than six to the girls. Such a scholarship gave the winner free education at the Liverpool Collegiate School for Boys, Shaw Street, or Liverpool Institute, Mount Street, and for the girls, Grove St High School or Blackburne House High School . . .

Kathleen Betterton
white pinnies, black aprons

Kathleen Betterton was born in 1913 in a small flat in Fulham, London, for which the rent was 12s. a week; her father was a liftman on the London Underground earning £3 a week, while her mother, the youngest of thirteen children from a remote Essex village, took in dressmaking at 5s. a dress. This was a highly respectable working-class family which struggled to 'keep up appearances' even when her father was unemployed. Kathleen's elder brother attended a Central School and went into a successful career in journalism; she herself was one of very few children from elementary school to win a scholarship to a public boarding-school, Christ's Hospital, Hertford, in 1924, from which at eighteen she won an award to Oxford.

The extracts from her unpublished, 143-page autobiography describe life at a large London elementary school where, by the 1920s, easier relationships had

developed between teachers and pupils and great importance was attached to
the winning of scholarships. They also tell of her first experience of a very
different life at public school.

Of all the groups in our family album there is one that is a favourite. Taken on a
summer's day in 1917, it shows the Infants' class of Queensmill Road School
carefully posed for the camera. There we are in three submissive rows, neatly
graded according to shape and size, the smallest on the ground cross-legged, the
next biggest on chairs, the biggest of all standing up behind, with only their
heads, frizzed or curled or sleek and smooth, just showing above the shoulders
of those in front. We are all in our party best, scrubbed, brushed and shining. A
few of the girls wear white frilled pinafores but these, as we know already with
precocious snobbery, are the poorest ones since white pinafores, like white
button-up knickers, are already out of date, even among working-class children
like ourselves. Almost all the little girls have long hair (bobbing came in some
years later) and most of them, myself included, have ringlets – and I know by
painful overnight experience just how they came by them. Collectively we look
prim, almost priggish . . .

I can pick out the children from my street: fat Georgie with a grin that
stretches from ear to ear; Hilda who lived in the flat below us, handsome and a
little haughty, with dark eyes and dark curls; Alice Rose, as pretty as her name,
who died of diphtheria at ten years old; and here in the corner myself, round-
faced, flaxen curled, holding my head on one side in an attitude of embarrassed
coyness, and wearing a smirk of self-conscious enjoyment.

Our background is a brick wall and a drainpipe, our foreground asphalt. Had
the photograph been larger it might have included the three storeys of red brick
and yellow tile and the surrounding expanse of asphalt that combined to make
up the architectural pattern of most London council schools of that period. The
district was Fulham, the part that lies close by the Thames, so close that we
could hear at night the sirens of passing boats and in damp weather smell the
dank unforgettable smell of the river . . .

But school in those days seemed almost uniformly pleasant. Discipline was
strict. We stood up and sat down, opened desks and shut them at the teacher's
order, and even on occasion blew our noses in unison. Yet classes must have
been in spite of their size fairly informal, and we were most of us on quite
intimate terms with Teacher. We would bring her bunches of flowers from the
back garden and we would burble about our family affairs, doubtless disclosing
domestic secrets and scandals with innocent candour. We brought along our
choicest treasures to show her – dolls, foreign coins, picture postcards, seaweed
from the seaside. Someone once brought a cat – a fine tabby cat but unfortunately a 'lady'. Her mother didn't want it. Could Teacher please find a home for
it?

Miss Wood encouraged acting and makebelieve. Once when I came to school
in a scarlet cloak and hood that my mother had made me from a 'remnant', she

decided that we must act Red Riding Hood. I was to be the heroine and make my way to my grandmother's cottage (under her desk) through a deep forest (an assembly of aspidistras in pots). It was too exciting and I was much too shy so Hilda had to play the part and afterwards perform it in other classrooms as well. My red cloak was ever afterwards my pride and my embarrassment . . .

Until the age of eight we were graded as Infants. Thereafter we passed into the 'Big Girls' and life became more serious. We had entered upon the race for survival. Ahead lay the scholarship stakes: for the winners, free schooling till sixteen or over with the hope of a good job at the end of it; for the 'also rans', a makeshift education ending at fourteen, and unskilled work that might end in unemployment and the dole.

We thus confronted destiny in the form of the Junior Scholarship at the age of eleven, and our future was decided by our ability to multiply awkward decimals and to write a 'composition' in tolerably accurate spelling and grammar. The chanciness of the system was clearly shown in my own family where my much cleverer brother, later a journalist and writer, was awarded only a place at a Central school, while I, with far less brilliance, climbed steadily up the scholarship ladder till I reached Oxford.

The 'Big Girls' were divided into seven classes or 'standards', and we changed classes, if we were good enough, every six months. Standard Six was the 'scholarship class', the apex of our careers; Standard Seven the limbo of the 'also rans'. From the first the sheep were divided from the goats. The brighter of us were picked out on arrival and placed in Standard Two. If we fulfilled the promise of our infancy we were hustled through the school, missing Standard Five, and settling in Standard Six for intensive brushing and grooming in preparation for the fateful scholarship day.

On the dubious evidence of papers in arithmetic and composition, scholarships were awarded to the local secondary schools and to certain independent schools. Half a dozen scholarships usually fell to Queensmill each year. Apart from these, places were awarded to the local Central school (roughly the equivalent of the post-war Secondary Modern); children with practical ability sat for Technical Scholarships, enabling them to learn a craft or trade at a Technical School. The residue who failed to gain a place anywhere languished in Standard Seven and were thence ejected, with a smattering of knowledge and a sad sense of inferiority, into an indifferent and unwelcoming world.

We, of course, were only dimly aware of the cut-throat struggle in which we were engaged, but it had a profound effect, not only on the syllabus and the organization of the school, but on the attitude of teachers towards their pupils, and most of all upon the pupils themselves.

By the time we were half-way up the school the likely scholarship winners had been marked down, and from then on they received a quite special degree of attention. I was always a teacher's pet so I know by experience just what it means in a class of sixty. What I hardly like to speculate about are the feelings of the other fifty-nine. The system, not the staff, was responsible for this favouritism. They would not have been human if they had not liked teaching the odd few who showed ability better than they liked ramming knowledge into the heads of the unimpressionable remainder. The only method with a class of such size was regimentation. Accordingly, they set a small group of us work to do on our own, while they drilled their unwieldy classes in arithmetic and spelling, and basic knowledge; any time left over they gave to a responsive half-dozen who rewarded them with ardent interest and sometimes personal devotion . . .

Looking back I marvel at their patience and general good humour. They spent six hours a day and ten months a year teaching classes of sixty. They had to teach a variety of subjects from Old Testament History to quite difficult arithmetic, and they had to present their lessons in a way that was clear to the slow ones, yet interesting enough to hold the attention of the brighter children. As it was, some lessons were amusing, some painfully dull.

It is less surprising that they were most of them good teachers than that they remained nice human beings. They so rarely lost their temper that, if one of them did, the occasion seemed dramatic and memorable. In all my time there I can remember (and then with solemn horror) only one instance of a girl being caned. Yet discipline was good without being made unduly important, and there was a generally cheerful atmosphere . . .

Perhaps the greatest obstacle which confronted our teachers was the narrowness of our background. I was unusual in having parents who liked reading and actually had books of their own; the evening paper was the only reading matter in most homes that I knew, and the football results were much more important than the political situation. Wireless sets were rare: you listened with difficulty through earphones, and what you heard was less exciting than the fact that you could hear anything at all. In the drabness of our environment there was nothing to awaken any latent sense of beauty; the school itself merely reinforced the dreariness outside. Its paint was a dull institutional green; the tiled walls of the staircases and cloakrooms resembled those of public lavatories; the pictures were sentimental or dull and on all the window-sills there were aspidistras . . .

The Junior County Scholarships mainly provided a means of entrance to London secondary schools and to a few independent schools in the area, but a few scholarships were awarded to a boarding-school in Hertfordshire. If we wished we might put down our names as candidates; if we were lucky, if we were very lucky, we might win a free place with 'all found'. Edith's parents demurred; she was an only child and they did not wish to be parted from her. My own were reluctant, but gave way to my enthusiasm. For I was transported at the mere suggestion. The word 'boarding-school' had for me all the glamour of romance. My imagination had battened on Angela Brazil, lent to me by Flora; the very word conjured up muddled visions of midnight picnics, sweet girl prefects, hockey, house-matches, and exploits that saved the honour of the school. It never occurred to me that Mother and Father might be hurt by my anxiety to leave home, or feel that in letting me go they were losing a part of me. With the heartless self-absorption of childhood I was longing for a different world, less circumscribed than the one I knew. The prospect of going away to school seemed the merging of make-believe and reality. Such is the stuff of our delusions.

I had been carefree before. Now I became prey to torturing doubts. I prayed in bed each night, 'Please, God, let me win that scholarship,' and woke in the morning quite unable to trust in the Lord. I suffered alone since Edith thought it unfriendly of me to want to go away without her. We took the examination and were both awarded county scholarships. We both chose to go to the Godolphin and Latimer School at Hammersmith, and were accepted after an entrance test and interviews. In the excitement I almost forgot my nightly prayer. Then one morning I heard that the scholarship to Christ's Hospital, Hertford, was mine. My daydream had turned into reality.

My new life began on a misty September day in 1924. School had assembled the day before; we, the new girls, were to follow after, and punctually at two o'clock we assembled at Liverpool Street under the eye of the headmistress and the head-matron, as cheerful a company as the ghosts waiting for Charon to ferry them across the black waters of Styx. We clutched attaché cases containing our statutory personal requirements – brush and comb, house shoes, sponge-bag, prayer-book and bible . . . Some had recourse to toffees, some to pocket-hankies. I merely blew my nose. It was a relief when the train steamed out and mother's face, puckered and anxious, could no longer be seen.

We sat silent in our compartment, gazing suspiciously at each other, afraid to open our mouths lest anything we said might be used in evidence against us. I was luckier than most for I had Constance. She was a plump phlegmatic girl from the class below me at Queensmill who had won a scholarship six months later than I. She was not nearly as amusing as Edith, not half so impressive as Flora, but she was someone I knew. I was determined never for an instant to let her out of my sight.

All my bright illusions about the fun of boarding-school had by now quite vanished. I did not feel at all like Paula on her first day at St Hilary's. Anything indeed less like St Hilary's than the school for which we were bound could hardly be imagined . . .

Socially, we were an odd mixture. Of the four girls in my ward who were my form-mates, Florence was the daughter of a vicar, Margery of a salesman, Laura of an army officer killed in the war, and Sybil of a bank cashier; my father's job placed me well down the social scale, as I was soon aware. Outwardly, there was nothing to distinguish us. We wore the same clothes, plaited our hair in the same tight pigtails, blew our noses on the same outsize handkerchiefs. But there *was* a difference, and we all knew it. One of the first questions put to new girls by the rest was always – 'Are you a scholarship girl?'

This mingling of social groups made it an unusual school. In other respects it followed tradition; it depended for patronage on the wealthy upper-middle-class, and it aimed at fashioning us in a correct middle-class pattern. Since we were dependent upon the school for everything, its authority was absolute, unhampered by any parental criticism. When parents came to see us, they were put firmly in their place and stayed there. If they had been tempted to complain or protest, we ourselves should have shut them up in a fierce whisper before they started. The school absorbed us completely into itself, tolerating no other loyalties. Dimly we discerned a divergence between home and school standards but we could hardly help believing that the School was always right. Parents lost their authority: if it was never precisely stated, yet it was often plainly implied, that they were foolish or misguided in their outlook. Headmistress, matron and monitresses by degrees loomed more important in our minds. The weekly letter home, written under supervision on Sunday evenings, the three half-holiday visits from parents – these during term-time were our only family links. Home, though nostalgically remembered, became remote and foreign. Of this gradual process we were at the time unconscious, yet it exercised a strong psychological influence. It produced division, doubt, a sense of divided allegiance. In my own case, though school counter-acted the ill effect of being the baby of the family, the emotional shock of being uprooted was like being dropped into a wintry pond.

My first impressions of school are confused and distorted by panic. Everything appeared oversize; people multiplied or melted into one another as in a feverish dream. The day-room opened in a vast perspective; its walls were painted an institutional green; its new-scrubbed floor had the unfriendly smell of carbolic. The dormitories, each with sixteen iron beds and sixteen iron washstands, seemed larger and bleaker still. We were taken first to the wardrobe mistress to be fitted with school clothes. These were handed down as children outgrew them, so we rarely started with anything brand-new – not that we minded. When I had changed from my own clothes into a box-pleated navy tunic and blue-striped blouse, I felt as much of my identity as Alice when she drank from a magic bottle and shot up to nine feet high. From the start there was a bewildering amount to absorb; rules to be explained, names to be learned; then tea, and unpacking, and prayers, and bed . . .

Tea was an ordeal. We ate at the long day-room table, sitting in order according to age and form. At each place was a crusty hunk of bread; on each plate a portion of butter and jam. Tea was served, already sugared, in thick blue and white bowls, six inches across. It was considered good manners to use only one hand to lift them; cautiously, I used both and still felt I should drop mine. Eight o'clock bed promised peace from so many faces, so many voices, yet even going to bed had its ritual. We undressed behind drawn cubicle curtains; we folded our clothes and placed them in long wicker baskets and stowed them under the bed; we shrouded ourselves in stiff nightgowns of unbleached calico. Then, when the curtains were drawn back and we were all in bed, permission was given to talk, and it seemed the evening had just begun. It was the tradition for new girls to sing a song on their first night at school. I could never sing in tune, and had already formed the habit when in church of soundlessly opening and shutting my mouth. 'The Red Flag' was the only tune I was sure of, and I sensed somehow that this would be out of place. Constance had already rendered 'Felix keeps on walking' with verve and expression; I cleared my throat and in wobbly and untuneful alto sang 'God save the King'.

The clanging of the seven o'clock bell roused me next morning to a new and troubled existence. Time, which at home had ambled by without anyone greatly caring, was at school our taskmaster. Life became an obstacle race in which I started with a hopeless handicap and finished last dead beat. First we queued for the single loo at the end of the dormitory passage; then at the sink where we filled our tall enamelled jugs with warm water for washing. My troubles began with putting on my clothes, and there were so many of them: tickly woollen combinations with sleeves and buttons at the neck; liberty bodices with buttons all over; white calico under-knickers, always discreetly known as 'garments'; navy blue bloomers; a button-up blouse; a tie; a blue calico 'pocket' that tied (eighteenth century fashion) round the waist; a navy blue box-pleated tunic; ribbed black woollen stockings. My tie and my suspenders caused me most anguish. Even later when I had hit on the notion of tying my tie in the comparative leisure of Sunday and wriggling in and out of it during the rest of the week, its appearance was apt to invite bitter comment. As for my suspenders, not being mechanically minded, I never discovered the right method of adjusting them until the end of my first term, with the result that my stockings concertina'd round my ankles and were voted 'a disgrace to the ward'. Dressed at last, bedclothes neatly folded, the mattress propped up in a hoop to air, washing water emptied – I had still to do my hair, and I had so much of it. It fell stiffly round my shoulders like Alice-in-Wonderland's, but unlike Alice's had to be confined in a plait. Two plaits, which I could have managed more easily, were forbidden; presumably they were felt to be a temptation to vanity. My thick single plait was my daily problem, and always made me late in my place for seven-thirty prayers. How gladly I would have shorn it off to be free of this tyranny, but short hair was not permitted in 1924, though outside the school bobbing and shingling were universal. New girls with short hair had to grow it; consequently half the children in the lower school had long wispy locks that made them look like Yorkshire terriers . . .

But gradually, as the days passed, I fell into a familiar routine. This was made easy because, from the moment of waking, our movements were governed by a strict time-table, designed so that those in charge of us might know what we were doing at any moment of the day. Lessons occupied three hours each morning and two each afternoon, and we younger ones spent an hour each evening on prep. From two o'clock to three we played organized games or went for organized walks or took other approved forms of exercise under strict supervision. Then there were meals, ward duties, ward prayers (twice daily) as well as school chapel; any time left over was mainly given up to music practice or mending. Half-holidays allowed us a little more leisure; Sundays a little less . . .

As a day of rest, Sunday was a delusion. True, we got up a little later, but once up, every moment was organized. As well as ward prayers, we went to both matins and evensong; we had an hour's scripture lesson and half an hour's scripture prep; and we wrote letters for an hour in the morning and an hour in the evening. By way of exercise, we went for a very prim walk after lunch, and walked up and down the square demurely, with hats and gloves on, for half an hour after each morning and afternoon chapel. Happily, it was the day we had cake for tea – a thought that tantalized and sustained us through the vast hungry spaces of the afternoon. Our leisure (the time when we might read a book or do what we liked 'within reason', as the grown-ups say) hardly amounted to four hours a week. It was a mercy that we were sent early to bed for only between the cold but friendly sheets was it possible to think without interruption.

Life was complicated by the multiplicity and apparent irrationality of the rules. Ritual was all important; everything must be done according to a prescribed pattern; to deviate from the pattern was a punishable offence. In the daily ritual the crocodile played an important part. We were arranged two by two according to age and form, the younger ones in front, their elders behind. In this order we marched up to hall for breakfast and midday dinner; in this order we walked to morning chapel; in this order we trotted solemnly on a prescribed circuit as part of our pre-prandial exercise. We sat in this order for meals and, however little we liked our pre-ordained partners, in this order we went for walks on Sundays. 'The animals went in two by two . . .' It was no use blaming authority since the system had originated in the careful mind of Noah.

A great body of rules was concerned with keeping silence. 'I must not talk at wrong times', to be written out fifty times – this was a favourite punishment. And the wrong times were so many and so seemingly unreasonable. It was wrong to talk while dressing and undressing; it was wrong to talk while meals were being served or dishes cleared; it was wrong to talk in the bathroom or the passages; it was wrong to talk after we had passed the corner of the field on the way to chapel; it was wrong to talk while marching up and down to meals . . . Other rules were concerned with places. It was wrong to play in the playground in the mornings; it was wrong to play in the square in the afternoons. It was always wrong to play on the field in winter, except to play hockey; it was wrong to play *anywhere* on Sundays . . .

Though I did not cry like some new girls, I wearied for my family, for the crowded comfortableness of home, the fire glowing in the kitchen range, the friendly cat I could smuggle to bed with me. School was so large, so bleak, so full of noisy people who asked very personal questions and never stopped to hear the answers. The matron was so elderly and forbidding, and never used my Christian name without adding my surname as well. Worse still was her habit of using no name at all but my ward-number (which was intended only for convenience in marking). 'Twenty-five!' she would cry, pouncing on a hymnbook lucklessly left behind after prayers, 'Where *is* Twenty-five?' Scolding and stocking-running were nothing beside the desolation of losing even one's name . . .

PART THREE

Home and Family

INTRODUCTION

1. Autobiographers' accounts of childhood are inseparable from descriptions of home and parents. Almost always they record in greater or lesser detail the physical environment of the home – the kind of house, the number and furnishing of rooms, the presence or lack of amenities and the character of the street or area in which the home is set. Judged by the clarity with which such details are remembered the material aspects of the home were of great interest and importance to children: they constituted the immediate physical world which, together with parents, represented order, familiarity and, usually, affection. Rich or poor, squalid or luxurious, the physical home is nearly always described lovingly: everyday objects are often invested with an importance akin to reverence and the details of domestic organization given ritualistic significance.

The first striking fact which emerges from the writings is the great variation in the numbers of people which the home contained and, particularly, the extent of what we now would regard as severe overcrowding. Occupational density was, of course, to a large extent determined by income – the wealthier, the more space, the poorer, the more crowded. Family size also went roughly in line with income, though not so precisely, the largest numbers of children being found in the poorest families, the number falling in the middle classes but, inconsistently, often rising again in very wealthy landed and aristocratic families. Particularly by the later nineteenth century, when birth control was coming to be adopted in sections of the middle and upper working classes, the gap between the three- or four-child family and the seven- to ten-child family of the lower working classes is especially marked, and heightened by the fact that more infants and children were now surviving to adult life. All this meant that compared with the present day many parents and children had much less space in their homes, either for themselves or for possessions, and almost no privacy or quiet, and in such conditions 'home' necessarily meant very different things to different social classes. The pattern of middle-class family life, based on a comfortable home, a high degree of privacy for the members, abundant food and services provided by the labour of domestic servants, was impossible of attainment in a farm labourer's cottage, a back-to-back or a two-roomed tenement. Equally, the intimacy of family life and the strong sense of community which came from the shared experiences of close neighbours were often less strong in the spacious but more private lives of the wealthier classes.

From the many instances of crowding which autobiographers record only a few need be quoted. Amy Gomm, born in the Oxfordshire village of Charlbury in 1899, remembers that the family of ten lived in a small cottage consisting of living-room, scullery and three bedrooms; despite this, and her father's small wage of 17s. a week, there was an open invitation to friends and relatives to stay since extra visitors could always be accommodated either in the boys' or girls' bedroom. As many as fourteen would sit down to Sunday tea, and in summer there might be up to six resident visitors. In addition, relatives lived on both sides of their cottage.[1] In the great cities, and especially in London, overcrowding had always been normal for the poorer sections of the population, whether they occupied rooms in tenemented houses which had once known better days, or purpose-built accommodation in a block of working men's dwellings. The Austin family of eight lived in two rooms in Paddington, one a bedroom, the other the living-room which also had to contain a bed.[2] But the difficulties of rearing a large family were even greater in a miner's 'one-up and one-down' back-to-back cottage such as that occupied by the Morris family in Durham in the 1890s:

> In most cases, and especially in mixed families, every room was a bedroom including the living-room, and this was the room around which the whole of the life revolved . . . Could there be any wonder that in a lot of households, including our own, there was from time to time an angry bitterness that sometimes exploded into real violence?[3]

Here conditions were especially difficult for the housewife, who, in addition to the normal tasks of cooking and washing, had to contend with the pit-dirt of a family of miners in a room which was living-room, kitchen, scullery and, at night, bedroom. Mrs F. H. Smith, who had been brought up in Cardiff but married a Rhondda miner, found the life of a pitman's wife particularly trying.

> I was very shocked that we had no convenience for our husbands to bath in. We had to bring a tub or tin bath, whichever we had, into the same room that we lived in, and heat the water over our living-room fire in a bucket or iron boiler, whichever we possessed . . . We had also to do our weekly wash in the same room, so our one room was not much to look at . . . You want the duster in your hand continually.[4]

Perhaps the overcrowding record goes to Mrs Layton, born in Bethnal

Green in 1855, who was one of fourteen children who lived with their
parents in three rooms, one of which was so dark that it could rarely be
used.[5]

Although writers have clear recollections of apparently unacceptable
housing conditions they generally record them without resentment and
even with feelings of nostalgia. The eight Austins 'did not feel overcrowded' in their two-roomed flat, and ten Gomms always welcomed
visitors because boys and girls could be accommodated separately, and
Jack Wood living in an Oldham cellar-dwelling where the walls ran with
water (rent 2s. a week), could write, 'I honestly think, when I look back at
my childhood days, they were happy, though at times sad.'[6] There is, of
course, a sense in which people do not miss what they have never had,
and only in later life, when some autobiographers had achieved a much
better standard of life, do they remember their early material conditions
as disadvantaged. Equally, the accounts of children from wealthy
homes, where there was ample living-space and every comfort, are not
markedly different in tone or consciousness of their privileged position:
rooms, contents and comforts are reported as dispassionately as the
absence of them, presumably for the same reason that the writer had no
experience of any other way of living. A typical example is from Audrey
Prior, born in 1905 the daughter of a prosperous Devonshire doctor,
commenting on the alterations which her father had made to the house:

> After the house had been added to, there were nine bedrooms, a drawing-
> room, study, smoking-room and servants' hall, besides fairly commodious back
> premises. The kitchen with its Eagle range, large scrubbed table and dresser
> had a comfortable atmosphere . . . Above one of the doors was a bell indicator,
> and when a bell was rung in the house a numbered disc would quiver, showing
> from which room the summons had come. Coal at that time was £1 per ton and
> 20 tons were delivered at a time . . . It was just as well that we had three or four
> staff then as there was so much work to be done and none of the modern aids that
> we have today . . .[7]

Sometimes the sharpest impressions come from 'outside', through
the eyes of an observer from a very different background. Joan Rhodes,
daughter of a bank manager, had the unusual experience of living in a
large house in the centre of a Lancashire mill-town, and thus being able
to observe the habits of the 'other nation' about whom so many of her
friends and contemporaries were ignorant.

> The cottage doors were often open as I passed and I had many a glimpse of a
> life sadly different from my own. The open doors were usually to enable the
> mother or babyminder to keep an eye on the children as they played in the street

... Although the cotton trade was nearly always bad in my childhood [the 1920s] and there was a lot of hardship, that does not mean that the cottages were slums. As I peeped in the open doorways I saw tidy, clean little rooms with bright fires and shining grates, and not a sign of the squalor usually associated with poverty ... The people may have been poor, but they were proud, especially of the outsides of their houses ... I hardly ever remember seeing dirty windows or curtains, and yet the trees in our garden were black with soot.[8]

This concern with cleanliness and polish, order and tidiness, both inside and outside the house, is constantly mentioned by autobiographers except those from the poorest homes. This preoccupation, amounting almost to an obsession in some housewives, was a distinguishing feature of the 'respectable' working class, marking them off from what were often regarded as feckless, dirty, uncaring and undeserving poor. The house-proud mother and wife who 'kept up appearances' showed that she cared for her home and family and struggled unceasingly against the smoke and grime of industrial towns or the mud and excrement of country lanes. But the preoccupation with the conquest of dirt seems to have been principally an urban, and especially a northern, phenomenon. It was almost as if the world outside was, indeed, dark and satanic but, by contrast, the home could be spotless and shining, the fire burning brightly, the fire-irons and brasses dazzling, the linoleum polished and the home-made rug-mats glowing with splashes of colour. All this displayed the housewife's victory over destitution and the forces of darkness, perhaps also her affection and concern for her family. The furniture might not be very comfortable, and love was not often demonstrated by language or embrace, but the 'respectable' home spoke louder than word or deed. Hugs and cuffs, endearments and swearing, were for the disorganized, disorderly poor.

Thomas Flintoff recalls that in Preston, Lancashire, before the First World War:

In front of each house were two or three stone flags which it was the custom of the housewives to wash and clean with 'donkey stones' each weekend, and at Easter time the door-jambs and lintels over the doors and windows had to be similarly treated ... Another Easter custom was to visit the cemetery on Thursday before Good Friday and scrub the gravestones.[9]

At Todmorden, on the border of Lancashire and Yorkshire, housewives competed with each other in whiteness and artistry:

Most people in the street took great pride in the appearance of their houses, especially the outsides ... The doorsteps were scoured with donkey stone, and the more houseproud the women were the more elaborate patterns edged the steps. Some preferred to make their patterns with yellow stone, which was the colour of yellow ochre . . . On wash-days the streets were festooned with lines of washing . . . and there was fierce competition to have the cleanest washing in the street.

These were the 'respectable' families where there was 'always a great desire to better oneself, and the road to this seemd to be education'. But:

There were untidy families, even dirty families and feckless ones, and there were the respectable, upright families who knew they were the salt of the earth.[10]

In textile towns like Todmorden there was still a tradition of wives working in the mills as they had done before marriage; but it seems that by the century's end full respectability did not normally permit this, and that for a wife to work was an indication of the husband's inability to maintain his family. Apart from catastrophes such as widowhood, sickness or unemployment, the wife's role was to budget, cook, feed, clean and wash and generally keep her home and family tidy and respectable. Among the shipyard workers of Wallsend, Wilhelmina Tobias noticed that:

In all our working-class neighbourhood I never knew one mother who went out to work. However poor, they 'cut their coat according to their cloth' as my mother was fond of saying. In other words, what they couldn't have they did without, and seemed contented enough so long as their men-folk and children were kept clean and fed.[11]

Very rarely is any variation in this demarcation or roles mentioned. Husbands who worked all day and dutifully brought home their wage-packets on Saturday afternoon were not expected to share in the routine housework: they might mend shoes, repair household articles, dig their allotment and, perhaps, play with the children, but they expected their meal to be on the table, the fire to be burning brightly and their best suit ready for the weekend. Only one autobiographer records husbands contributing to regular housework, at Haworth, in Yorkshire, where it was still common for wives to work in the mill, and 'fettling' had to be crowded in on Friday evening after baking on Thursday. Here the husbands took over responsibility for the outsides of the houses:

The whole street – pavement, roadway, right across – had to be 'swilled' each week, also on Fridays. But before that could be done the outside of the windows was swilled, also by the master of the house, with bucket and brush, as long-handled in bamboo sections as a flue-brush so that the upstairs windows could be reached from ground level. Then in the old part of Haworth where we lived, which was very hilly whichever way one turned, the men had to wait until those higher up the slope had swilled their portion of road and path. And so the cleaning gradually descended the hill to the bottom, by which time the whole street was spotless on both sides – until the next horse and cart came along to sully it.[12]

This was an unusual and untypical example of shared domestic responsibility, and even here the activity was external to the house itself. The wife's pride in the perfection of her household management was mirrored by the pride of men in their gardens and allotments, where these were available. Miners were especially fond of their gardens, growing flowers as well as useful vegetables, perhaps as a reaction to the darkness of life below ground. At Dawdon the miners had

the most beautiful flowerbeds in great profusion: the colours had to be seen to be believed. Every little hole and corner was decorated with boxes or barrels . . . They were ready for the big flower show held in Seaham Hall gardens on the first weekend in August . . . That was the day of the year, for people came from all the surrounding collieries, and there was great fun.[13]

On such occasions competitions and fairground amusements were added to love of beauty and pride of creation: they were family events, putting parents and children on display as well as the flowers and vegetables.

But although husbands, as wage-earners and providers, were generally not expected to work within the home, children of both sexes in working-class households had important, even vital, functions to perform.

The organization of the household in the nineteenth and early twentieth centuries was based on reciprocal rights and responsibilities. Brought into the world by no will of their own, children had a right to be fed, clothed, sheltered and, to some degree, educated, but in return they were expected to contribute to the maintenance of the household as soon as they were old enough to be useful. In almost all working-class families, boys and girls had tasks to perform, both specific and regular and unspecific and occasional, until they graduated as full-time wage-earners and were able to make their contribution in monetary form. This concept of the child as an integral part of the domestic economy was a distinguishing feature of the working-class family, rural and urban, but was not normally found at higher social levels where servants released both mother and children from most domestic chores.

In general, the greater the number of children in the family, the more specific their tasks and the greater the differentiation by age and sex. Occasionally boys were exempted from regular household chores on the grounds that these were 'women's work'. Amy Ind, who was the eldest daughter in a family of six boys and three girls, found that 'most of the responsibility in those days was put on the eldest girl. I had three brothers older than myself, but boys weren't expected to do chores about the home.'[14] Another eldest daughter, Doris Frances, so resented the fact that both her brother and her younger sister escaped all house-work that she complained to her mother that 'I had not asked to be born.' Her unhappy childhood was burdened with a vast amount of routine housework:

From the moment I was capable of wielding a duster I was given regular weekly jobs to do, such as polishing all the brass door-handles throughout the flat with Bluebell Metal Polish, cleaning all the family's boots and shoes, and removing stains from the table-knives by rubbing them briskly on a wooden knife-board sprinkled with Bath Brick. I also had to shop for the groceries, do the washing-up, and peel all the vegetables (and for a family of five that was quite a lot of spud-bashing for one small girl). Worst of all, I was given all the family's mending to do – a most tedious and boring job which took up a whole evening of every week, and included the darning of everybody's socks and stockings.[15]

She refused to accept the logic of her mother's explanation that 'boys were not intended to perform such menial jobs, and where there was more than one daughter it was the duty of the eldest to help with the domestic work'. She was by no means the only child to feel resentment of the excessive work demanded of her. As a child of eight in Wales in the 1860s, the future Mrs Wrigley was regularly sent on a journey of two miles to gather coal and cinders, which she carried home in a basket on her head; she also had to fetch all the fresh water from a well some distance away, and once when she had forgotten to bring in the supply for next morning she was roused by her mother in the middle of the night to go and fetch it.[16]

But in most families boys and girls both had their appointed tasks, and George Mockford found that when a boy was the eldest child in a family of twelve the usual sex-role was reversed.

I had, as soon as I was old enough, to be mother's help, to amuse the baby, clean the house and do sewing like a girl, so that I was not only prevented from playing with other boys but also from going to school.[17]

Generally, boys did the heavier and dirtier jobs about the house – humping coal and water, sweeping the yard, turning the handle of the mangle, cleaning knives, running errands, and, if there was a garden, collecting manure and generally helping father. Girls' work was more home-centred, concerned with the routine activities of cleaning, washing and, sometimes, cooking. The degree of involvement varied from occasional help to almost total responsibility for the household. When Catherine McLouglin's mother died in childbirth, she had to take charge of the housework and do the baking at the age of ten, taking time off from school but making sure that her younger brothers kept up their attendance.[18] A similar responsibility fell on the children when the mother had to devote her time to wage-earning, either because the father had died or because his earnings were insufficient. With a feckless father who was frequently out of work, Alice Foley and her five brothers and sisters were brought up mainly out of their mother's wash-tub earnings; each child had its duties, but Alice remembered hers with some pleasure – the weekly sponging and polishing of the treasured aspidistra and the care of the cobbled yard and 'petty' house:

When it became my responsibility much labour was devoted to its transforma-tion. The wooden seat was scrubbed to faultless whiteness and the floor vigorously 'donkey-stoned'. The whitewashed walls were adorned with picture almanacs and scraps of verses, whilst within handy reach of the occupant I hung a neat pile of 'bum papers' culled from father's old racing handicaps.[19]

Samuel Mountford, one of eleven children of a poor Birmingham family, had a similar experience when his mother scrubbed and cleaned others' houses 'between having babies'. Here the eldest daughter went to live with her grandmother, and had good food and clothes, while the next eldest girl looked after the rest of the children; Samuel had free school breakfasts at the Church Hall (bread and jam and cocoa) and collected manure to sell to men with allotments, the proceeds always going into the family.[20]

The reaction of children to such household tasks does not seem to be generally resentful. W. G. Elliott writes that although his duties gave him little time for play, his was not a 'hard luck story' and his childhood was a happy one. Another boy, Jack Wood, distinctly remembered that Friday night in Oldham was a busy 'fettling night', when the fireplace was blackleaded, the fire-irons and fender polished, floors mopped, door-steps and window-sills donkey-stoned in preparation for the weekend, but there is no sense of injustice in his account.[21] Girls generally seem to have regarded housework as a necessary and useful preparation for married life and for the domestic service into which so many would go on leaving school. At three years old Hilda Fowler was taught to knit by her step-sisters, being made to unpick all her early efforts until there were no mistakes:

Today it would be counted cruelty to give such monotonous work to a three-year-old, but what is important is that I have been grateful to those stepsisters all my life, thankful that I learned to knit so young . . .[22]

Another kind of preparation for adult life occurred in the mining villages of Northumberland. Here the girls had an important role as hand-maidens to their father and brothers who worked in the pit. 'Daughters had to work very hard in a family of pit workers. Woe betide you if you ever forgot to fill up the boiler at the side of the fireplace.' The girls were expected to have hot water ready to fill the tin bath on the return of the miners, to wash out and dry their 'flappers' (trunks) and to beat out the dust from all the pit-clothes by dashing them against a wall, after which they were folded in a set order ready for the next shift; finally, the pit-boots were greased and softened with melted tallow.[23] In some areas daughters also scrubbed the men's backs while in the bath, apparently without embarrassment. These, and the other more usual domestic activities in which all girls took part, constituted an informal apprenticeship in preparation for the time when they would perform such tasks for their husbands. It seems that in this period such obligations were accepted as a normal part of membership of the family and, provided the tasks were not excessive, often enjoyed. The distinction which adults made between 'work' and 'play' had little meaning for children who, with limited artificial aids for amusement, could often contrive to make fun out of seemingly boring domestic tasks. Equally, parents seem to have regarded such activities not only as a useful contribution to the running of the household but as a necessary and valuable training for after-life.

2. Autobiographers often record the contents of their home in great detail, itemizing furniture and articles and the exact positions which each occupied. For some children the physical environment of the home left an indelible, photographic image as the place where consciousness first dawned. Yet the objects described – the tables and chairs, wash-tubs and fire-irons, tin tea-caddies and china dogs – are usually totally ordinary and unremarkable, hardly worthy, one would think, of recall or mention.

At the lower income levels the contents of the home were usually minimal and strictly utilitarian, especially when every room had to 'double-up' as a bedroom. 'Furniture' as such scarcely existed in some very poor homes, and was often adapted from some other purpose – children's cots made from packing-cases, dressing-tables from orange-boxes, for example.[24] Several writers record moving house by a hand-cart, indicating how few possessions they owned, but it has to be remembered that nothing like the paraphernalia of modern living existed except in wealthy families. Even in Edwardian Wealdstone, a far from poor suburb, carpets were only found among the 'very affluent'. Nevertheless, where families of several children existed in a couple of rooms the space between objects must have been very small indeed. Eleanor Hutchinson gives a good description of the two rooms in Paddington where her family of eight lived. The 'front room' contained a double bed, a chest of drawers, a square table (under which she played), a few chairs and her small iron bedstead which folded up during the day. The 'back room' was the living-room-cum-kitchen, with sideboard, range, a fitted cupboard for provisions, a table and chairs, and also a double bed where the four boys slept. 'For the times it was a clean, tidy and cosy home. How my mother managed it Heaven only knows.'[25] What this account does not include is a description of the washing arrangements which, strangely, Thomas Flintoff of Preston remembers very well.

> The back kitchen, where we had most of our meals, contained a stone sink and a brick-built washing boiler, a mangle and a 'dolly' tub. The clothes were washed in the boiler, with a coal fire underneath, taken out, put in the tub where they were possed, a posser being a long piece of wood with a handle near the top and with a round base, with which you pressed some of the dirt out of the clothes . . . When the family income increased, the brick boiler was done away with and a three-legged gas boiler installed. The old mangle was disposed of and a smaller, rubber roller mangle obtained, and a gas cooker was also installed in the back kitchen upon which we could cook meals.[26]

Although it was possible for a family to live a clean and decent life in two rooms, real respectability required something more – another living-room which could be reserved for 'best' occasions – for Sunday tea, entertaining, christenings, funerals and other ritual occasions. In working class homes this was usually referred to as the 'parlour', and was the repository of valued articles such as ornamental furniture, a piano or harmonium, pictures, family photographs, ornaments, an aspidistra and Sunday School prizes carefully displayed on a small table in the window. Women were often prepared to make great sacrifices of comfort and convenience in order to devote a room to this non-rational use of space, for the 'parlour' clearly had a social and psychological importance in announcing the status and aspirations of the occupants. Normally a parlour was only possible in a 'through' terrace house, where it was the front room facing the street, with a living-room (or 'kitchen') behind and, possibly, a scullery out-shot at the rear, but even in small flats or tenements some families preferred to set aside one room for this purpose and to crowd into the remaining space. In their Fulham flat in the 1920s, consisting of two rooms, a kitchen and scullery, Kathleen Betterton's parents gave up the largest, front room as a parlour, while all the activities of family life went on in the small back kitchen:

Yet, however crowded we were, we never dreamed of sitting in our one tolerably large room except on special occasions. The 'front room', like every other in our street, was sacrosanct. Its green venetian blinds were pulled down on sunny days to preserve the colours of the carpet, its lace curtains drawn back just enough to reveal a thriving aspidistra in an art pot . . .[27]

At the top levels of the working class there could be something more even than respectability – some pretension to style and fashion. Mary Hollinrake's father, a 'cloth looker' (inspector) in a Todmorden cotton mill, had set up his marital home with craftsman-made furniture from a local cabinet-maker; he lived into his eighties and the furniture survived perfectly. Here there was satin walnut bedroom furniture, a three-piece suite in the parlour upholstered in green velvet, walnut dining chairs, a piano.

How my father managed to save up for all this good furniture I do not know . . . I don't suppose he earned a great deal, but we were never short of anything. He was very thrifty. It was well known in the family that after his house was furnished he was able to begin his married life with a hundred golden sovereigns in hand. He did not drink or smoke, and my parents' pleasures were simple.[28]

Here, furniture was for enjoyment and display, not merely for use, and we are clearly in the region of nice social distinctions. The point is well made by Enid Stuart Scott whose middle-class parents inhabited (and owned) 'Glenfield', an 'unpretentious villa' which was 'my parents' pride and delight'. Here the 'parlour' became the 'drawing-room', decorated in the 'greenery-yallery' fashion of the day and with furniture from Maples, including a much-prized plant-stand intricately carved in Chinese style proudly displayed in the bay window.

One day a stout, pompous-looking dame called asking to see the lady of the house (it must have been one of the periods when we sported a maid). Duly ushered into the drawing-room, she immediately stated her business. She had come to offer a price for the treasured jardinière. Mother declared it was not for sale. Dame persisted, 'I always think it much too good for Devonshire Road, and I tell my husband so,' she proceeded . . .[29]

Although autobiographers rarely complain about the lack of space in their homes, they frequently criticize the amenities and the difficulties which they added to life. Particularly singled out are the cooking, washing and sanitary arrangements, or the lack of them, and writers make clear how recently arrived some basic services are. In many tenemented houses in the later nineteenth century there was no cooking-stove, and any cooking was done on an open fire or in a small Dutch oven placed in front of the grate, a fact which accounts for the use of bakers to cook the Sunday dinner and the reliance on ready-prepared foods. As late as the First World War the Mountford family of eleven children, living in a suburb of Birmingham, had no gas or electricity in the house: meat was cooked on a spit and the house lighted by paraffin lamps.[30] In the same period in Hunslet, Leeds, the Armitage family had no gas, one cold tap, and had to share an outside 'trough closet' with two other families: this was a primitive form of water-closet which disgorged its contents into the sewer once a week and was liberally sprinkled with tar oil disinfectant.[31] Even these were an improvement on the 'privy middens' or dry closets which were still common in the north and in mining and rural areas until 1914. Here, human refuse simply accumulated in a metal tank which was emptied periodically by the 'night soil' men; they were smelly, noisome, and in summer gave rise to plagues of flies and other insects which invaded the houses. Wash-day was always a laborious time and, in wet weather or when the wind blew smoke and smuts over the drying clothes, an unrewarding one too. In the absence of back gardens, washing in northern towns was often strung across the street, a prey to passing vehicles or mischievous children, while in tenement blocks the competition to secure a line on wash-day could lead to outbreaks of violence between tenants. Nora Bargate, living in the Park Buildings, Rotherhithe Street, in 1921, remembers fights between housewives to obtain the pulleys which stretched the clothes-lines between the blocks.[32]

In many cramped working-class areas in the towns, 'home' therefore extended into the street beyond the front door – the doorstep where mothers sat on warm evenings, not embarrassed to suckle their babies, the pavements where children skipped, played at marbles or hopscotch, the corner-shops and pubs which supplied the focal points of local news and gossip as well as the material needs of existence. Again, the street and its inhabitants are almost always described by autobiographers with affection bordering on nostalgia, the social aspects of community living being particularly praised. A few autobiographers are less enthusiastic, recalling the noise and smells of Victorian streets – the perpetual stink of horse manure,[33] the strange cries of street-sellers which some children found frightening, the noisy scenes and fights outside pubs on Satur-

day nights, the constant screaming of children and the queues for the
W.C. in 'The Buildings'.[34] But such comments are exceptional. The
typical view is that expressed by Edna Bold, living in a suburb of
Manchester at the beginning of the century:

Not a blade of grass, not a tree grew anywhere in the district. Rows of terraced
houses, factories, cotton mills, engineering works, belching chimneys made a
Lowryesque townscape for our beginning over a baker's shop . . . When we were
very young it was at once a terrible, beautiful, exciting place. My twin brother
and I had no sense of deprivation as we pranced and played in the labyrinth of
mean, intricate streets . . . The 'Road' was a social centre where everyone met,
stopped, talked, walked. The butcher, the baker, the grocer, the milliner, the
draper, the barber, the greengrocer, the pawnbroker, the undertaker, were
friends, confidants and mines of information. All needs from birth to death
could be supplied from these little shops . . .[35]

In such writings the sense of place, and of identity with the place, is very
powerful. Its full development clearly required some continuity of
residence, and for the very poor, constantly on the move in search of
cheaper lodgings or work opportunities, the sense of 'belonging' was
less strong. Born off the New North Road, in 1861, the son of a London
porter, Jack Goring records twelve different addresses in his first ten
years of life, though all were within a square mile of Finsbury Market.[36]

But what autobiographers most frequently stress is the sense of local
community in working-class districts and the importance of an informal
network of support composed of relatives, friends and neighbours. No
doubt this is sometimes retrospectively idealized by writers who have
subsequently moved into relatively anonymous suburban council
estates, and, as one author unsentimentally observes, the real reason
why the poor helped those in need was that they expected to be helped
when their turn came. There is no reason to suppose that the poor were
especially generous or philanthropic, but the near presence of people
who were known sufficiently well to share joys and sorrows, who could
lend sixpence or a loaf of bread or look after the baby for an hour was
evidently regarded as of great value and importance.

Such close relationships had always existed in villages, mining communities and other isolated settlements. Many rural villages continued
to be largely closed communities until opened up by improved com-
munications in the late nineteenth century, local patriotism extending to
a deep suspicion of neighbouring 'foreigners'. Henry George Lock
recalls that in Berkshire in the 1880s:

it was hardly safe to visit another village, especially for boys, unless you wanted to fight. It was the coming of the bicycle that opened up the countryside as, up to that time, unless you were rich enough to own a horse and carriage, you had to walk. It was a case of saying, 'Here is a stranger, throw a brick at him.'[37]

More surprisingly, perhaps, autobiographers describe areas of towns – even of great cities like London – in similar terms. Recalling her childhood in Paddington as late as the 1920s Eleanor Hutchinson writes:

> This, then, was our parish. This was the closed village where few outsiders dared to tread and which, as a consequence, few ever understood.[38]

In Bolton, Alice Foley observed that:

> The street in which I was nurtured as a small girl had little to boast of except that, in an odd way, we regarded it as Our Street, and rich in its own quality of community life. We were all poor of a ruck, but hardships were shared in a spirit of cheerfulness and characteristic good humour . . . If father came up on a horse we usually had a bit of a 'do'; this might stretch to buying a new suit for one of the older boys. Later it would be loaned out to neighbours on the occasions of weddings or funerals. 'Can I borrow your John's suit?' was frequently heard, and sure enough, even if it happened to be in pawn, it was cheerfully redeemed in order to maintain the dignity of our street on its big occasions.[39]

And in Oldham, where Jack Wood lived at the beginning of the century:

> In a working-class street like Nutter Street everybody knew everybody else, and if there was sickness they would gather round giving help when needed . . . During the summer evenings all the kids in the street would play games together (Catholics and Protestants). Nearly all would be barefoot, but when you went to school you had to have something on your feet. The mothers would be gathered in little groups gossiping, and maybe some of them had gone for a pint. If it was a nice evening people would be sat on their doorsteps until eleven or twelve o'clock, and then quietly go inside to bed.

There was a less attractive tail-piece:

> It was then that the fleas were most active. You could be plagued all night in summer by fleas.[40]

3. Relationships within the family – with or between parents, brothers, sisters and more distant relatives – form an important part of many of the autobiographies. Like other aspects of emotional life, they are not easy for relatively unskilled authors to understand or describe, and the historian must attempt to construct the patterns from recorded situations, oblique references and, sometimes, from what is not said as much as what is. What seems to emerge in the first place is that the degree of affection for the mother is generally much greater than that for the

father or other relatives, and that, more surprisingly, this is experienced by both daughters and sons. The simple stereotype that sons loved their mothers best and daughters their fathers is not supported by this sample of personal memoirs.

The most commonly expressed view is that it was the mother who was primarily responsible for family maintenance, for budgeting, care of children and the home, and that these duties were performed with little or no thought for self and often at the mother's sacrifice of time, pleasure and health.

As our family increased and my father's wages remained stationary, it was necessary for my mother to earn money to help to keep us in food and clothing . . . A good father and husband up to a point, he [her father] left the responsibility of the whole family to my mother . . . The worry of meeting all her liabilities, and the continual grinding away at work for her own family and working outside her home at last undermined her once splendid constitution . . . My mother was everything to me. I always thought whatever she did or said was sure to be right . . . [41]

Or Mrs Burrows, who at eight years old had to work in an agricultural gang for fourteen hours a day:

My mother's life was one long life of loving sacrifice. It might be asked how it comes about that with such a mother we, as children, should have had such a hard life of it. But the reason was not in any fault of my mother's. No woman in the world ever strove more earnestly for her children's welfare than my mother did. [42]

These are the comments of daughters, but sons write in similar vein about the sacrifices of their mothers and their own debt to them. Thus, George Healey, born in 1823:

I was blessed with a pious mother, very kind and affectionate to her family, and careful in training them in the right way. She passed through the trial of much serious illness in her family, and out of six children only three survived . . . By my mother's teaching and constant watchfulness in very early life my mind was thoroughly influenced. I loved her most dearly. [43]

This aspect of the mother's role as educator and preceptor is stressed by many writers. Thus, Leonard Ellisdon:

My mother had a stronger character than my father, who was easy-going and very popular. She ruled the roost very ably, not only making the little money which she had at her disposal go further than most, but doing her utmost to inculcate as much knowledge in her children as possible. There were twelve of us – four adults and eight children – to feed and clothe, and she saw to it that we always took a pride in our appearance. Many a time when I went out to work she has seized me firmly but kindly, and washed my ears. Dare I confess that even after my marriage she surreptitiously carried a flannel and soap with her, and when we were unobserved she would push them into my ears.[44]

In one respect, however, a sex differential is noticeable. In quarrels between mothers and fathers, sons almost always took the side of the mother, even assuming a protective role towards her at a very early age. Serious parental quarrels, not uncommonly ending in family breakdown, are frequently described by writers, especially, though not exclusively, among the poor, where money disputes and drunkenness are the most frequently cited reasons. Thus, Syd Foley conspires with his mother to deprive his drunken step-father of a few shillings from the compounded army pension, which he was quickly unloading at the local pub (pp. 313–18). Stanley Rice speaks for many when he writes:

Father was fond of his beer, and his mood would depend upon how much he had had to drink. Usually he was bad-tempered and quarrelsome, and that would mean, for certain, a row and general upset. At times, quarrels would last for hours, and I can recall how I used to lie awake in bed waiting for the last word to be said, so that I could feel it safe enough to go to sleep . . . I know, more than once, I've seen mother with a black eye. More than once she left him, and took us children with her, but always we had to return . . . The effect on my youngest sister, Jessie, was, I am sure, very bad. She would at times scream with fear when quarrels became too noisy and threatening.[45]

As a small boy, Jack Wood was regularly sent out on Friday nights to find his step-father in one of Oldham's many pubs and plead with him to come home before too much of his navvy's pay was spent. When really drunk, his father's favourite pastime was to carry all the furniture upstairs and throw it out of the bedroom window.

Of course, my mother, sister and myself would vanish until he had emptied the house, and we would creep back to find him asleep on the flags in front of the old fireplace.

One night, when he was nearly strangling his mother to death, Jack hit his step-father with a pair of pincers and knocked him out; they slept out for the next two nights in a lavatory, not daring to go home, but on their return his father thanked him, saying, 'I had saved my mother's life and saved him from being hung.'[46]

In such cases there was, at least, a high degree of affection and intimacy with one parent. As a generalization to which exceptions may immediately be cited, the level of affection appears to have diminished with increasing family size. In large families, especially in those oppressed by financial concerns, there was simply not enough time or energy to devote very much to any one child. Of her parents, Nancie Howlett remarks:

What their thoughts, hopes and aspirations were I never knew, so did I ever really know them at all? I wish I had known them as people as well as parents.[47]

And P. Marrin, one of seven surviving children of ten, wrote that they did not discuss things with their parents – 'We were told what to do, or not to do; and were not allowed to answer back.'[48] In more elevated circles the distancing of children from parents was due to other factors – the frequent absences and business preoccupations of the father, the social activities of the mother, and the belief that the upbringing of children was a specialized task which was better entrusted to nurse-maids, governesses and boarding-school teachers. Many children in wealthy households found that their most intimate relationships were with a domestic servant, and the life-long attachment of some men to their nannies is no myth. As the child of a neurotic mother who died early, Charles Esam's strongest attachment was to a fourteen-year-old maid, Clara.[49] B. E. Houle, the son of a prosperous London solicitor, wrote that 'I did not see much of my parents, except at weekends,' and that he was brought up by nurses and servants whom he 'loved dearly'; by the time he was eight he was completely out of hand and was sent to boarding-school where he at first felt 'lost and abandoned'. Later, at St George's School, Windsor, the choir school for the Castle, he was much happier, and remembers the occasions when the choristers were allowed to play cricket with the Royal Princes, Albert (later King George VI) and Henry (later Duke of Gloucester). They were still at home under a tutor:

He was a tall, forbidding-looking man with a long drooping moustache. I think he was a Dane. Parties of boys from the school used to be invited to play cricket with the Royal Boys, and this would be followed by a Strawberry and Cream Tea in their Pavilion. The Princes were kept very isolated: we were about the only boys of their own ages that they ever saw.[50]

Separation of this kind did not necessarily lead to the alienation of affection between children and parents, though it inevitably tended to formalize the relationship and to lessen the understanding which inti-mate early contact brought. As an extreme instance, after Nora Mabel Nye and her two sisters were sent from their aristocratic home, Ardleigh Court, to be educated at a convent school in Bruges, Belgium, they not unpredictably all wished to become Catholics and nuns, a decision which eventually led to a total break with their father (pp. 275–80). In the middle classes, daughters were generally kept at home and educated by a governess (sometimes shared between families) or, later in the century, at one of the day high schools which started up in most towns. In Margaret Cunningham's rectory household, in the first decade of the twentieth century, the child's day was still patterned on Victorian lines – the morning at lessons with the governess, lunch with her parents in the dining-room ('an anxious meal as Miss Trist's eagle eye was upon us') and a sedate walk, also with Miss Trist, in the afternoon.

After schoolroom tea, we went down to the drawing-room for an hour with our mother. If she had guests we were just tidied up and sent down to shake hands. Otherwise, she played with us, games like Tippit and Hunt the Thimble. Then she would read to us or tell us a story. She read 'The Fairchild Family' – a Victorian classic for children which she had had as a child herself . . . The little Fairchilds, Lucy, Emily and Henry, when they were not being punished by their stern father, were being punished by God. Henry, after fighting with one of his sisters, was taken by Papa to see the body of a murderer hanging from a gibbet to show him where evil temper might lead. Lucy, who had helped herself freely from a pot of jam in the larder, tried to wash the stains off her pinafore, got wet, and developed pneumonia and nearly died . . . Their little friend, Augusta Noble, daughter of a baronet, was so proud that she was allowed to be burnt to death.[51]

In fact, this was a far from unhappy family, the children loving their mother and the Fairchild disasters, and usually succeeding in persuading her to omit the prayers which concluded each chapter. But a significant minority of autobiographers of both sexes record unhappy relations with their mother. As a child, Syd Metcalfe was well aware that he had no normal home life like other children – that his home was always dirty, that his mother's day was spent in the pubs, and that there were constant rows between his parents in one of which his mother threw a knife at his father. First his father left home and, later, when the family was evicted, his mother was never heard of again; Syd Metcalfe himself never married.[52] Edward Punter had an almost equally unhappy childhood as the sub-title of his autobiography, 'So Often Alone', suggests: he hated his elder sister, was rejected by both mother and father, and ultimately found his consolation in religion.

So my Dad didn't want me, and now Mum didn't either . . . I had a comfort left. 'What a friend we have in Jesus . . . '. Yes, I still had religion.[53]

More frequently, unhappy relations with the mother are recorded by daughters, often because they were burdened with excessive housework and seemingly treated without love or affection. Faith Osgerby recalls that her first emotion as a child was fear, that she was never cuddled or kissed by her mother, but constantly punished for trivial offences; before her birth, her mother had taken gunpowder to try to abort her.[54] Similarly, Margaret Perry's mother had attempted to abort her by jumping from the copper; in this Nottingham household words like 'love' and 'kiss' were not used, and her parents rarely spoke directly to each other, only communicating through the dog.[55] Doris Ponton records that her relationship with her mother was one of obedience, and that there was 'little time to show affection' in this poor Southwark family where seven of the eleven children died of 'wasting' – 'we would call it malnutrition now'.[56] And Doris Frances remembers the 'constant nagging' by her mother, and that it was impossible to confide in her.

As an infant I was greatly impressed by the knowledge that she had been a 'General' before she married . . . which was a perfectly reasonable assumption in view of the way she commanded and dominated our own family affairs. I realized later, of course, that her posh title was merely an abbreviation of 'general servant' . . . Whilst my father was easy-going, kind and gentle, my mother was a strict disciplinarian, reluctant to display any kind of warmth or affection.

Once, when attending a school-friend's tea-party, she noticed that the mother affectionately kissed her daughter:

For me that was a most penetrating moment. Sensing the deep bond of affection between mother and daughter, intense feelings of envy and longing swiftly surged through me, and the missing factor in my life had been clearly revealed.[57]

A similar comment is made by Fanny O'Donnell – the only time in her childhood when anyone embraced her was when she fell downstairs and the maid put her arms round her.[58]

In many published working-class autobiographies the father emerges almost as a stereotype – frequently a drunkard, often thoughtless and uncaring of his wife and children, bad-tempered and selfish, but occasionally over-generous and sentimental. Unfortunately, this picture is mirrored in many of the unpublished accounts, especially of the poorer families, though it is far from universal. In all sections of society there were dependable, hardworking husbands devoted to their families and deeply loved by their wives and children, but for many men the harshness of their working lives seems to have blunted the emotional attachment to their families. Particularly in the earlier half of the nineteenth century fathers could exploit their own children in ways which later generations would utterly condemn – by using them as begging-boys,[59] or as chimney-boys when the dangers of suffocation were well known,[60] or by sending them into mines, factories or hard field labour at an excessively early age. Although many forms of public employment came under legislative control in the later century it remained possible for children to be exploited in their own homes by heartless parents. As late as 1888 Louise Jermy was taken from school at eleven to help with her step-mother's washing business – turning the heavy mangle for hours together, collecting and delivering the orders.

> Some days there was hardly time to get our food. I had, in addition, to fetch most of it and carry it all home, until my arms felt as if they would break, and my back ached so I could not sleep at night. If my father had any love for me he certainly didn't show it . . . There was more than money went to buy that house, my health and strength were bartered for it, and before it was quite done I laid in the London Hospital with tubercular hip disease, partially crippled, in fact, for life. What about it, I say, and all I ever say when people grumble about the school age being raised is, 'Oh well, good job for the children, they can't be driven beyond their strength like I was.'[61]

This was not a very poor family: the exploitation was not in order to buy food or pay the rent, but to buy their house (£560) through a building society, unusual among the working class at this period. But in many cases the father's apparent cruelty in sending his children to work at a very early age was due to sheer economic necessity, not to ambition or greed, and autobiographers generally seem to have understood this. Roger Langdon, sent into field labour at the age of eight, suffered agonies of persecution from a vicious employer, but afterwards wrote:

> Some people, those who have passed smoothly through their childhood and have scarcely known sorrow, may ask whether it is possible that such things could have been done in England? My answer to this is, yes. It was not the parents, but the age that was to blame . . .[62]

A similar judgement is made much later in the century by Albert Goodwin, born in 1890 at Stoke in the Potteries:

> Looking back, it would not be true to record that I realized that my parents were two of the finest people who walked the earth. On the contrary, I was of the firm opinion that they were the most obnoxious people I had ever seen, and to expect any kind treatment from them was to expect the moon to fall out of the sky. But I have since realized, and very emphatically too, that they [were] trying to fit me to [be] able to live in a world that was harsh and hard to the children of the poorer classes.[63]

Against this, a good many autobiographers whose childhoods were both rich and poor record how their fathers played with them, made toys for them, sang and told stories to them. In this connection, the affection between daughters and fathers is particularly marked. Mothers are frequently represented as over-burdened with work, irritable, nagging and demanding, but on his return home from work – unless the public-house calls him – father has time to relax with the children, even to indulge and spoil them. Nora Bargate remembers how in the Park Buildings in East London in 1920 fathers would turn a huge barge-rope from one side of the square to another so that a whole line of children could skip, but there were also some very rough watermen living there whose wives and children lived in fear of them and only spoke in whispers in their presence. Alice Foley's father, a veteran shirker and boozer, could entrance her with his store of Irish folk-lore and with scenes from Shakespeare (he had once worked as a scene-shifter at the local theatre and heard many of the great tragedians of the day), and on winter evenings when the 'White Hart' did not claim him he would read aloud to the family the novels of Dickens and George Eliot.[64] Similar memories are recorded by Harry West, son of a manager of a small paper-works, though here the father was a respectable, self-educated man, an omnivorous reader and church chorister:

My father was naturally kind and compassionate . . . Nearly all his evenings were given either to helping us with our lessons or amusing us in several ways; he was so versatile. He understood geometry, and long before jigsaw puzzles were available he cut cardboard into geometrical shapes and sizes, and coloured them for us to put together. He drew and cut out cardboard figures and objects to stand up, made folded paper figures, etc. Sometimes he would read suitable passages from Dickens and reputable authors, fairy tales, 'Alice in Wonderland', Hans Anderson, 'Uncle Remus' and others. One source of readings he had was a two-volume book entitled 'Gleanings from Popular Authors.'[65]

Among boys, respect and admiration for the father's strength, courage and knowledge is commonly expressed, and many fathers regarded it as a pleasurable duty to teach their sons manual skills and crafts, partly as a kind of game but also as a useful preparation for life, much in the way that mothers instructed girls in housework and cookery. Fred Boughton from the Forest of Dean expresses this well:

Father used to say, 'I shall not leave you much money, but I will teach you every job, then you can always get work.' He showed us every job in the garden and on the farm, including how to get stone in the quarry and trim it to build stone walls, and how to put a roof on a shed . . . He also taught us how to lay hedges. When I was a boy, for some reason I never wanted to play games with the others, but always to stroll round The Tump and the woods with the dog, and look at the sheep and the plants and the trees.[66]

Comments of this kind, however, are not the most frequently expressed verdicts of autobiographers on their fathers. The word which the majority of writers use, either expressly or by implication, is 'remoteness' in describing the much less intimate relations which they had with their fathers. This is the case at all social levels, and not only, as might be predicted, in wealthier families where the father was often absent from home or preoccupied with business or professional affairs. George Grundy, the son of a preparatory school headmaster, wrote:

Of my father I cannot say much, for the reason that I never understood him . . . Children he did not understand. They irritated him, and when we were small children we were aware of the fact. Looking back on my life as a child, I cannot help feeling that many parents under-estimate children's powers of perception, especially in respect to distinguishing what is reasonable or unreasonable in their treatment.[67]

After describing her mother's characteristics in detail, Eleanor Hewson writes:

My father, although he stood for protection and strength, was naturally a more shadowy figure. His work at the University [he was a Professor] took him from home during the day, and often in the evenings. Even when he was free to stay at home he would be immersed in books or surrounded by piles of examination papers in his study. We were used to the fact that he must not be disturbed . . .[68]

This was a far from unhappy or uncaring home: there were times when the Professor played games with her, and on the arrival of a baby brother he wisely continued to call her 'Baby' so that she would not feel displaced. But in some wealthy homes the remoteness of the father passed over the line to neglect, even cruelty. Fanny O'Donnell was the youngest of ten children in a prosperous, middle-class family; after the death of his first wife, her father had re-married, a younger woman who left him after a month. The children 'could not love' their tyrannical father; school was enjoyed because they could 'be themselves', but the holidays were hated. On father's arrival home at 6.30 in the evening, the family broke up to their separate rooms. There were constant rows over money, and when two brothers were on embarkation leave for France in the First World War, her father refused to pay the rail fare from Bromley to London so that she and another sister, aged seventeen and nineteen, could have tea with them. Both brothers were killed three months later.[69]

Similar situations can be found much further down the social scale. Sometimes the distancing of the father was due to his long hours of work, as in the case of Amy Gomm who, as a child, seldom saw her father, an assistant engineer on a great estate, who worked an eighty-hour week.[70] Violet Whale's father, a horseman on an Essex farm, was up at 4 a.m. every morning except Sunday, when he was out at 6.30; he had no holidays, but a few hours off duty on Christmas Day.[71] Of his father, George Healey comments:

> I cannot say much about my father, for he was a man who had to do much with those in high life . . . I was very little under his care.[72]

He was in service, an occupation inimical to home life, and the same applied to those in the armed forces, at sea, or on shift-work. Early death or desertion by the father were not uncommon. Winifred Relph describes her childhood as being divided into two parts by the death of her father when she was eight: with her mother left to bring up four small children the household 'changed overnight'.[73] Some fathers simply took themselves off for a few days, weeks or years, whether for a weekend's drinking or in search of work or with another woman. We cannot know the proportion of family breakdowns since few cases from working-class homes came to the courts, and legal separation, let alone divorce, was extremely rare. Edward Brown's father simply deserted his wife when Edward was a baby: his name was never mentioned and there was a total conspiracy of silence about it for forty years.[74]

But on the evidence of autobiographers drink, not romance, was the greatest single cause of family breakdown up to the First World War. Beer consumption fell slowly from its peak of 34 gallons a head per annum in the 1870s, but estimators of the national 'drink bill' concluded that between a fifth and a quarter of all working-class expenditure went on alcohol: when allowance is made for the growing number of tee-totallers this means that some households spent a third or half of their earnings on drink.[75] Though drinking was certainly not confined to men, regular heavy boozing was particularly a male phenomenon, and while many autobiographers record being sent to rescue father, or his wages, from the pub, not one mentions going to find mother. It was hard for a child to admire or respect a drunken father, and Doris Ponton expresses a typical view when she writes:

> My relationship with my father was one of love when he wasn't the worse for drink, which he was every weekend when he was on leave, and fear when he was

the worse for drink. It must be remembered that in those hungry, hard times, beer which was very cheap, and the companionship found in the pubs, were the only real recreation which the poor had after struggling to exist week after week.[76]

It was a charitable judgement, not shared by others. John James Bezer wrote:

Father was a drunkard, a great spendthrift, an awful reprobate. Home was often like a hell, and 'Quarter Days' – the days father received a small pension from Government for losing an eye in the Naval Service – were the days mother and I always dreaded most; instead of receiving little extra comforts we received extra big thumps, for the drink maddened him.[77]

In such homes the desertion of the father was scarcely a tragedy, perhaps even a blessing. Violet Jared remembers that when her father joined the army in 1914 the children were only too pleased:

Well, we all remembered the day our Dad came home – worse for drink – with a proud look holding the King's Shilling in his hand, and said, 'I was coming home and met my mate, and as we turned round we saw Lord Kitchener staring at us saying "Your King and Country Need You", so we both looked at each other and in we walked and joined the Royal Artillery.' Mum was right mad with him and had a good old row – we children made ourselves scarce! We were very pleased when he went – it was more peaceful in the house, and Maud [her eldest sister] would be a second mum while our Mum went to work.[78]

Relationships between brothers and sisters receive much shorter treatment in the autobiographies, and only rather predictable generalizations emerge – that girls often preferred their brothers to their sisters but disliked other boys, and that relationships in large families were generally happier than in small ones. Families of six to ten children, not uncommon in Victorian and Edwardian times, operated as small communities in which, as one author says, 'one was never short of playmates', and the nostalgic picture of a large family happily gathered together in reading, at play or around the piano is endorsed by several writers. Ellen Gill, one of ten children of a Leeds leather-worker, recalls that:

We almost had a family choir, and I remember on Sundays one of the family would strike up a hymn and we would all join in without any music played, as at that time we had no musical instrument.[79]

Norah Knight, one of twelve children, thought that it was very good to be one of a large family and she never needed anyone else. There was no bullying; all the children took an interest in what the others were doing:

the boys played with the girls and made necklaces for them, and on winter nights they would each do their 'pieces' – recitations, poems or hymns – or play 'Family Coach'.[80] Her autobiography is appropriately titled 'Nostalgia'. This was not a wealthy, but a comfortable, very respectable family: father was an ex-soldier, a strong advocate of 'spit and polish', who lined up his children, girls and boys, like an army squad. 'He used also to put us through our drill. We had imaginary rifles, and were taught how to slope arms, present arms and reverse arms.' Such a pattern of family life, happy but disciplined, where roles and duties were firmly fixed and observed, and where parents had the time and inclination to be with their children, required a standard of living above mere subsistence and would hardly have been possible in the poorest third of Edwardian England.

Close and devoted relationships between brothers and sisters were, of course, found in some small families as well as large. Though Kathleen Betterton had many girl-friends, her closest friend was her brother, seven years older than herself.

As for other people's brothers, I had no use for them at all. As we grew older the wide gap in our age served to cement our relationship. It produced in me an attitude of uncritical admiration, in him, a protective affection varied at times, it is true, by exasperation.[81]

Brothers, particularly elder brothers, clearly held a special place in many girls' affections and seemed to constitute a different order of existence from other boys: Kathleen Betterton had 'no use' for boys and Amy Gomm was 'brought up in the belief that boys – other than brothers and one or two selected cousins – were "disgusting"'.[82] Even where there were sisters, a girl might find her brother a closer friend and more exciting company, and even in a mid-Victorian rector's family Mary Paley Marshall was free to behave in a remarkably tomboyish fashion:

Until I was ten years old there were three of us, my sister being two years older and my brother two years younger than myself. He was my great chum: we took long walks and climbed trees and collected birds' eggs (we only took one out of each nest), and I can still feel the thrill of discovering a fresh egg to add to our collection, and the terror of thrusting my bare arm into a sand-martin's long, dark hole when there might be a peck from the bird at the end.[83]

These are majority, but not unanimous views. Not a few girls hated their brothers, regarding them as rough bullies who delighted in teasing and tormenting the weaker sex. Faith Osgerby thought her eldest brother 'always a bully and a boor' who deserved the terrible beating which his mother gave him, stripped, in the cowshed.[84] Margaret Penn

[Hilda Winstanley in her autobiography] had a similar reaction to one of her elder brothers:

> Although Hilda was always sorry afterwards for provoking her great lout of a brother, for the life of her she couldn't help doing it. With his laborious pothook writing, his slow reading and his dirty physical habits, he disgusted her. For though he washed himself just as thoroughly every night as John and her father, his clomping farm boots brought a strong smell of manure into the kitchen, and his corduroy trousers, which he tied just under the knees with a thick rope of straw, smelt of sour milk and other farm peculiarities.

Her description of relations with her younger sister is also one echoed by other writers:

> For Lily too was a dunce, as big a dunce as Jim. She was two years younger than Hilda, with a clumsy, dumpy body and a fat, sallow, stupid face with round brown button-eyes that never seemed to see anything. And she was good – born good – and a tell-tale. If, as she often did, she heard her sister, when their mother was out, trying to extract pennies out of her money-box with a knife (a feat at which Hilda was quite expert), as soon as their mother returned she would blurt out, 'Our Hilda's been taking money out of her money-box – she's taken a lot – I saw her.'[85]

4. An important theme in many autobiographies of childhood is play. Not surprisingly, many accounts are given of games, toys and holidays and, perhaps more surprisingly, of organized recreational events such as outings, Sunday School treats, church and chapel processions and the like. Some writers speak of these as 'the highlights of the year', while others record their informal play with other children as the happiest moments of their childhood. In its various forms play was an essential part of self-expression, of learning and relating to others, and of bringing fun and joy into lives which often had an undue share of unhappiness. Only one autobiographer, Norah P., says that she had 'forgotten how to play'; separated from her mother, sister and baby brother in Basford Workhouse, Nottingham, and later in a Cottage Home, she had no idea what to do when taken one Saturday to a nearby common as a treat,[86] though earlier, before the home was broken up, she had happily played dressing up a clothes peg as substitute for a doll.

In analysing writers' comments about play it is clear that geography and social class were the principal determinants. Although by the early twentieth century a common culture was emerging in which patterns of leisure and recreation were becoming increasingly universal, before that time there were still sharp distinctions between rural and urban play, and between that of working-class and middle-class children. Although most children had certain common toys and games – dolls, hoops, marbles, tops, for example – beyond these there were many regional and local leisure activities, essentially rural in origin, which persisted surprisingly long in a rapidly changing and increasingly urban society.

In the autobiographies of the early nineteenth century the connection with rural sports and festivals is naturally strongest. William Smith, born in Wellington in 1820, vividly describes the cruel, traditional sports of East Shropshire, an area where agriculture merged with the new industries of coal and iron: here cock-fighting, bull-, bear- and badger-baiting were favourite entertainments, carried on to the accompaniment of heavy drinking and gambling. At Failsworth, near Rochdale, in 1829 Ben Brierley, son of a handloom weaver, helped in the construction of a 'rush-cart', the 'king of rustic pageants', which was borne through the village as part of the 'Wakes'. About 1830 his family removed to a neighbouring village, Hollinwood, a distance of three-quarters of a mile.

My companion promised to initiate me into the usages of their boy society, which might be of a character different to what I had been accustomed to in the *country* I had left. Had I played 'chub-i'-th'-hole' with marbles? No. Had I played 'pipes'? No. Had I tossed with buttons? No. Didn't I know the difference between a 'one-ter' and 'two-ter'? No. 'Poor little feller,' his looks seemed to say, 'he knows nowt!'[87]

The isolation of rural areas before the railway age is well known, but it is still surprising to find the persistence of traditional patterns of rural recreation as late as the early twentieth century. Henry Lock's description of the village feast at Sutton Courtney in the 1880s, held on Corpus Christi Day, might almost have come from the Middle Ages. Girls in service came home on this day if the journey was not too far; there was a special church service, followed by a parade of the village Sick Benefit Society, a dinner and dancing until the bandsmen became the worse for drink. Other important events were the village steeple-chase held in May, which usually carried a day's holiday from school, and 'garlanding' ceremonies on 1 May, when girls and the younger boys displayed garlands of wild flowers and sang traditional hymns and songs.[88] At Wilton, Wiltshire, in the 1890s the village youths still acted a traditional Mummers' play on Boxing Day with characters including King Arthur, St George and the Dragon and 'Little Johnny Jack with My Wife and Family on My Back'; here, too, 'garlanding' was enacted on 1 May.[89]

In villages like this much of the recreation of children and adults centred on the church or chapel and the patronage of the local 'great

house' or wealthier farmers, and the squire's daughter, the clergyman
and the schoolteacher were often key figures in the maintenance and
organization of traditional events – harvest suppers, Sunday School
treats, concerts, 'Penny Readings' and the like. At Charlbury, Oxfordshire, the 'Big House' gave a party for the school children just after
Christmas and an estate party for employees and relatives at New Year;
there was a Sunday School treat for those who had made regular
attendances, held in a field on the outskirts of the village, and an
occasional magic lantern show in the winter. Otherwise, public entertainments here were so few that on Sunday evenings in summer everyone would walk after evening service to the local railway station to watch
the last train of the day go through.[90]

Country children, of course, were not dependent for their fun on
activities organized for them by adults, but played their own games,
indoor and outdoor, whenever they were free of domestic chores,
stone-picking, bird-scaring and other 'holiday' tasks. Despite the lack of
professional entertainment and even the scarcity of toys – Ivy Phillips of
Cranfield, Bedfordshire, had no doll until given one on going into
service in 1913, and in a village near Diss, Norfolk, in 1920 only one child
possessed a bicycle – autobiographers' accounts of rural children's play
indicate a rich variety of group games which required little beyond
improvised equipment and a good deal of imagination. Football was
played with a pig's bladder, hoops (iron for boys, wooden for girls) were
passed down the generations, never bought, marbles were made out of
baked clay and the commercial articles reserved for special tourna-
ments. There was a great variety of hiding and chasing games like 'Fox
and Hounds', 'Sheep Come Home' and 'A Night's Lodging', and some
ritualized games like 'Child Weddings' and 'Indians and Squaws'.

> On those glorious May evenings our happiness ran away with us. Having done
> our various jobs we would all go out to play on the common, where we picked
> armfuls of sheep's parsley and buttercups, and with an old piece of curtain a
> child was transformed into a bride, and a bridegroom chosen. The outline of the
> church had been made with stones . . . tins full of flowers stood everywhere, a
> child took up her position at a box as an imaginary organ, and with the strains of
> 'Here Comes the Bride' the procession began, met by the parson who con-
> ducted the service with great solemnity. Being members of the choir, we knew
> the procedure . . .[91]

Nearly a hundred years before this, Marianne Farningham and her
friends had played at child baptisms in the stream near her village
school.

Country children had the great advantage of open space – of commons, meadows and woods to play in, at least in the spring and summer months. In the dark winters there was little but the Christmas and New Year celebrations to break what must often have seemed a dreary period. This was the season when magic lantern shows, Band of Hope evenings, concerts and bazaars were concentrated and local initiative came into its own, but the picture which Ivy Phillips paints of the village boys drinking ginger beer in the local shop on wet Saturday nights is a rather melancholy one. For some of their fathers the public-house was a welcome, occasional relief, though on the wage of an agricultural labourer regular, heavy drinking was scarcely possible. By the century's end railways and bicycles were beginning to break down the isolation of centuries and to bring the bright lights and novel entertainments of the town within the aspirations of many young wage-earners, and the rural exodus rapidly gained pace.

The smaller market towns still kept their country connections, and beyond the bustle of the weekly market and the annual hiring fair had little more excitement to offer. At Berkeley, Gloucestershire, in the 1860s the great event of the year was 'Club Day' when the friendly societies paraded and had their annual share-out after sick-pay and entertainment expenses had been met.

Club Day! Who can describe what the annual occurrence of that day meant to young and old at Berkeley! The first Wednesday in May was devoted to the 'March Out' of the Clubs. There were several 'Slate Clubs' located at different public houses in the town, the most important being those at the 'Berkeley Arms', the 'White Hart' (in High Street) and the 'Mariners' Arms' . . . Headed by a brass band and a beautiful silk banner, each Club marched round the town, to the houses of the gentry and to certain farm houses not too far out . . . At the calling places they were regaled with cider and beer, in recognition of which the band played lively music and the processionists gave hearty cheers . . .

After dinner there were stalls and booths set out in the square, and dancing as long as the musicians could continue to perform.[92] Carnivals, processions and club parades played a highly important part in the communal recreations of the towns, children having their own version of them in the famous 'Whitsun Walks' when the Sunday Schools paraded in their new clothes and usually concluded the day with tea and games. At Ashton-under-Lyne in the 1870s the great events of the children's year were Pancake Tuesday, St Valentine's Day, the Whitsun Procession, Ashton Wakes Fair and the New Year Coffee Party 'which meant a whole day's enjoyment in kissing and other games, and the giving and receiving of love cheeses'.[93] In many places children had some local, ritualized event which took place on a fixed day and involved a procession or displays of some kind, often soliciting money. A typical example was the 'Grotto Night' in Hampstead in the 1880s, which took place each August:

> We would make up in pairs, collect all the oyster and scallop shells (and any other shells) we could get, with pieces of broken ornament and anything that was pretty – coloured glass, etc. Then we would pick a street where a lot of people would pass and build our Grotto up against the wall and put candles inside and light it up, and then when people passed we would hold a scallop out and ask them to 'please remember the Grotto'. Then we would recite:

> > Please remember the Grotto,
> > It is only once a year,
> > My father's gone away to sea and my
> >   mother's gone to fetch him back,
> > So please remember me.[94]

Another curious survival, 'Riding the Stang', is noted by George Ratcliffe from the slum area of 'Little Hell', Leeds, about 1870. A procession of men beating trays and cans preceded a man carried high on two poles who recited a poem levelled at 'Nick Wilbur', a notorious local drunkard and wife-beater. It promised vengeance on anyone who followed his example by neglecting his children or consorting with loose women, and is an interesting example of an attempt to enforce morality by communal control in an almost medieval form.[95]

In the larger centres of population there was obviously more opportunity of professional entertainment for those who could afford modest admission fees. Larger public-houses had long had musical evenings, comics and dancers, out of which had developed the professional music-halls of later Victorian and Edwardian days. These were generally 'out of bounds' to chapel and stricter church folk, not only for the lewdness of some of the performances but because the infamous 'promenades' were the haunts of pickpockets and prostitutes, but the same reputation did not usually attach to the smaller touring entertainments which were common by the end of the century. At Worm's Ash near Birmingham in the 1880s, Minnie Frisby enjoyed a wide variety of such entertainments – a travelling theatre, travelling circus, minstrels, 'Dyson's Gypsy Choir', the fair, and a Revival Meeting which seems to have had something of the same entertainment value.[96] In Oldham about 1910 a halfpenny admitted a child into the gallery of the Gaiety Theatre or into the new rival attraction of the moving pictures of 'Dreamland'.[97] And in the slums of Bolton on summer evenings there was sometimes free entertainment from the town's Court and Alley Concert Society which

descended upon our street with the object, I suppose, of infusing some sweetness and light into our drab environment. With unconfined joy we hailed the truck bearing the piano and cheered vociferously when it was heaved successfully into position at a convenient gable-end. The conductor, mounted on a borrowed chair, gathered the choristers around him, raised his baton, and, lo, music and soft airs that hurt not floated over the odd audience lounging at open doors, and hushed the harsher noises of the day. The street was not particularly musical, but its appreciation was generous and deafening.[98]

Like other forms of 'Rational Recreation', one of the objects of the Court and Alley Concert Society was to provide an alternative to the public-house, but to what extent it kept men from 'the demon, drink' is doubtful. For children the street itself was the principal playground and meeting-place, an extension of the home which offered the protection of a known community and was virtually free from traffic dangers. Girls and younger children usually stayed close to home, and the small ones did not play out after dark: the usual instruction was 'Stay near home, and you're to come in when I shout for you.' According to Joseph Armitage:

Mischievous antics were common, but there was little wilful damage, and delinquency and petty thieving were rare enough to be noticeable, and usually traceable quickly.[99]

Playing in the street was virtually confined to the working-class areas of towns: middle-class children played in their own gardens, were taken for walks or to the local parks, but did not share in the dirty contaminating fun of the pavement and gutter. It was here that the traditional games like marbles, five stones, whips and tops, hoops and hopscotch were played, each with their local rules and in their appointed seasons which opened and closed as if at some secret signal. Girls had their equally traditional skipping, acting and singing games, and Mrs D. Wyatt from Edwardian Wealdstone recalls two – 'Wallflowers' and 'Poor Jenny is a-Weeping' – which followed an almost identical form to those in Oxfordshire described by Flora Thompson in *Lark Rise to Candleford*.[100]

Beyond these well-known, all but universal, games, there existed a great variety of street-games which apparently had currency only in a particular town or region and were often related to local physical conditions or materials. In the 'snickets' and closet passages of Leeds, for example, a favourite game was 'Kick Out Can', a form of football played with a tin can in which the entrance to the passage served as the goal-mouth. Thomas Flintoff in Preston remembers making and flying kites ('There were very few telephone wires or electricity wires in which kites could become entangled') and playing 'Sheep, Sheep, Come Over' (elsewhere 'Home') and 'Farmer, May We Cross Your River?'[101] Elizabeth Rignall who, as a child, divided her home between Haworth in Yorkshire and London was particularly conscious of the different street-games, as well as the different language:

The games we played in London were more numerous and mostly very different from those we played in the north, where boys and girls played together much more than in the south . . . Toys and accessories were very scarce, needing money for their acquisition, whereas a piece of clothes-cord could be obtained for a copper or two, or better still, begged from one's mother, and no-one was sufficiently affluent to own a 'manufactured' rope with its polished, shaped and painted handle at each end. In any case, such a rope was short and for individual play, whereas we much preferred communal skipping games needing long ropes . . .

In London these included 'All in Together', 'Follow My Leader', 'Higher and Higher' and 'French Skipping', and street-games such as 'In and Out the Windows', 'Nuts in May' and 'Tom Tiddler's Ground'.[102] From Bolton, Alice Foley remembers 'the quaint rhymes married to old ballad tunes and handed down from generation to generation':

All go round and choose your own,
And choose my fairest daughter.

Up the streets and down the streets, the windows made of glass,
Isn't Bessie Taylor a handsome young lass?

Here's the robbers coming through, through, through,
And the baby's Ring-a-Roses, all fall down.[103]

Skipping and rhyming games were mainly, though not exclusively, for girls, boys regarding their own activities as more adventurous and manly. Footballs made from pigs' bladders seem to have been almost universal, with, in Lancashire, the added refinement of an inside made from a clogger's nail-bag. Cricket is only rarely mentioned outside school games, perhaps because the streets did not provide very suitable pitches, perhaps because the equipment was not so easily improvised. In northern mining villages boys followed their fathers' traditional games like 'Knurr and Spell' and 'Nipsy', both of which involved hitting a moving object with a pick-shaft, and required a good eye and considerable strength.[104] Here and elsewhere 'Pitch and Toss' was widely played by youths and men, often for small stakes, and some children received their introduction to gambling by 'dogging out' (i.e. watching out for the police) for adult players. But many autobiographers stress that children's street activities were very rarely criminal or delinquent, that there was considerable fear and respect for the policeman and his tightly rolled-up cape, and that parents also usually punished behaviour which could impair neighbourly relations. Deliberate damage to property or violence to the person by children was apparently rare in working-class districts, and street amusements generally stopped at the level of horse-play or 'larking around'. This was often aimed at unpopular adults such as particular neighbours, shopkeepers or schoolteachers and took various forms ranging from innocent 'pranks' to techniques of resistance to authority; it was certainly common in the poorer areas of late-nineteenth-century towns, and is mentioned by a number of autobiographers, though it is doubtful whether its scale justifies the comment of a recent researcher that 'for working-class youth larking around was an integral part of an informal, irreverent and independent street culture which profoundly influenced their identity and attitudes to authority during their passage to adulthood'.[105] What seems clear is that such activities provided an opportunity for somewhat coarse humour and personal expression at a time when they were increasingly being restrained by schooling, policing and social control.

Skylarking took many forms, including truancy from school and Sunday School, mimicry of and disobedience to teachers and the parodying of hymns, songs and poems, but the form most frequently mentioned was the practical joke, usually directed against some unpopular individual. On dark evenings, 'window-tapping' by means of a button, bent pin and long thread was a common pastime, with variations like tying two adjacent front doors together. George Ratcliffe describes the 'Long-tailed Pony', a game played in Leeds in the 1870s:

It consisted of tying a rope around a lad's body, fastening the other end to the door of any house, leaving some yards of slack rope, then giving a rat-tat-tat on the door. When the inmates tried to open it, the boy with his long leverage was as powerful as they; the door would open and shut, to the great amusement of the boys. When this see-saw had gone on long enough the rope was cut and the Long-tailed Pony was free, scampering away with the rest of us.[106]

A variant of this played in Bolton was 'Blind Horse and Skenning Driver' in which an innocent boy-victim was blindfolded, driven like a horse through the streets, and ultimately tied up to a front door to await the wrath of the occupier.[107] But larking could also involve less innocent jokes on adults, like obstacles placed strategically at night, horse-manure stuck on door-knobs or posted as a parcel through letter-boxes. Leonard Ellisdon and two friends, refused invitations to a girl's birthday party because of a previous misdemeanour, sourly observed the enjoyment of a lavish tea through a basement window and took revenge by dropping a bag of manure on to the tea-table: by sheer good fortune it fell into the teapot as Mrs Smith lifted the lid to refill it. 'It was very successful, far exceeding our expectations, but we were too frightened to stay and see what subsequently happened.'[108]

Larking was exciting, an escape from the humdrum world and the discipline of school and home. Its importance was all the greater since at this time the opportunities for extended holidays away from home were very limited, and the modern commonplace of two or three weeks at the seaside or abroad was unimaginable except to a small minority. Holidays of this kind were a clear indicator of social class. Nancie Howlett, born in Rochester, Kent, in 1906, records that 'villa people went away, cottagers did not': she was thirteen before she saw the sea, and her parents had never had a holiday.[109] For middle-class families the annual seaside holiday was well-established by mid-Victorian times[110] and had become an almost ritual event, often at the same resort year after year, where the same families would meet. Margaret Cunningham's father, the rector of Cranleigh, would let the rectory for several weeks in summer, holidaying in Southsea or Bournemouth, though some people were careful to avoid the 'Invalids' Walk' for fear of infection.[111] Another middle-class family, the Sutherland Graemes, always went for six weeks to Saundersfoot in South Wales, taking numerous trunks, cases and their own tin bath with them; only on the third day, when the children had been duly acclimatized, were they allowed into the sea.[112] Less affluent families went away for shorter periods of one or two weeks, and more often to a local than a distant resort: thus, Jean Nettleton's lower middle-class family from Harrogate always went to Whitley Bay, where they stayed in the same lodgings, buying their own food and having it cooked by the landlady.[113]

By the end of the century a good many of the 'respectable', saving working classes were able to manage a few days' holiday from home, especially where there were contributions to earnings from wife or children. The 'Wakes' holiday in Lancashire cotton towns was already developing from a long weekend into a full week, institutionalized as a communal holiday at Blackpool, Morecambe or Southport: local shops closed and the mill-town died for a week, holiday-makers taking with them as much food as possible and staying in lodgings where the landlady cooked the meals and charged for 'the cruet' of sauces, salt and vinegar.[114] When a holiday for a whole family was economically impossible, mill lads and lasses acquired a measure of independence and not a few encounters ended in romance and marriage celebrated by a honeymoon at the same resort; terms of one shilling per person per night at Morecambe in 1902 were scarcely prohibitive.[115]

But for most working-class children in the nineteenth century the equivalent of the seaside holiday was a day-trip, perhaps to a coast resort but more often to some beauty spot, woods or, simply, green fields, a few miles from home and reached by horse-drawn cart or, in one instance at least, by traction engine. Such trips were organized by Sunday Schools, Bands of Hope, church and chapel choirs, by employers for their workpeople and families, and by numerous charities such as the Poor Children's Outing Fund and the Fresh Air Fund, the last alone claiming responsibility for giving two million children a day out in 1909.[116] Although such treats now seem modest – generally some organized games and races, a tea of bread and butter, cakes and buns, and a few sweets for the homeward journey – they are lovingly recorded by many autobiographers and described by several as 'the highlight of the year'. Excursion trains made possible some more distant trips – for Samuel Mountford from Birmingham to Sutton Coldfield, for L. Taylor in 1895 from Islington to Southend-on-Sea, a trip when some of the children experienced their first train-ride. Wilhelmina Tobias of Wallsend recalls that her Sunday School outing usually took the children up-river in an old tug-boat called *The White Swan*, but affectionately known to the children as *The Dirty Duck*.[117] Sunday School and Band of Hope treats were more generally earned by regular attendance, evidenced by the issue and accumulation of so many cards, but the numerous charity outings were free to selected poor children. Jack Wood recalls that in Oldham the poorest children were picked out in school and issued with free tickets:

We walked to the yard of the Central Fire Station and lined up under a banner, the same colour as our tickets. When we were all there – and I might tell you there would be hundreds of us lined up under different coloured banners – we would march down to Clegg Street Station and board a train.

After a three-mile journey to Grasscroft they again marched up to Wharmton Moor, where there were a few swings and stalls; they were issued with sandwiches which they ate when they pleased.

It was a lovely day. I thank all the people who made it possible.[118]

Compared with the fun of working-class children – street games, Whitsun Walks, Chapel Tea and Coffee Days and occasional outings – the recreations of middle-class children were generally more private, home-based and parent-controlled. There was much less communal play, more individual amusement with books, toys, dolls (one girl owned seventeen) and a great variety of card games, many of which had a moral purpose. It was this contrast between the public play of the poor and the private recreations of the better-off which forcibly struck Mary Denison, a vicar's daughter, when she first encountered the camaraderie of Leeds slum children during her stay in a fever hospital.

You were awkward and prickly at first. You had never played with other children in your life before, but gradually you were drawn into the rough camaraderie of the streets and slums where fever flourished and where most of the children had come from . . . You came back from the Fever Hospital thin, washed-out and 'speaking like a street-child'. You weren't aware that you'd picked up an accent straight from the back streets of Leeds . . .[119]

Given free rein, the imaginative play of children was to a large extent classless and timeless. The tents made out of old sheets which poor children erected on the pavements and at gable-ends to play 'Indians and Squaws' are paralleled by 'The House in the Wood' which Camilla Campbell, her sister and brothers lovingly built out of fir branches at West Runton in Norfolk in 1916. For the girls it was a home, to be swept out, furnished and equipped with a china-shelf: for the boys it was a fort 'because the Germans are coming'.[120] The social settings were different, the fantasies the same. But a general characteristic of middle-class children's play was that it was much more controlled by parents and their surrogates – nannies, governesses, tutors and teachers – who decided where children might play, with whom and at what. Thus, street games and other vulgar pleasures were almost always denied because the contacts could not be adequately controlled. Sometimes children were not allowed to visit other children's homes for play unless their parents had written a formal invitation, and this was especially so in the case of formal parties for birthdays, Christmas and other celebrations:

Like many of her generation, my mother was inclined to be a snob, and there was always the awful business of whom we might know and whom we mightn't. And, of course, we couldn't know anyone unless our respective mothers had called on each other . . . I wasn't supposed to accept any presents from boys, but I remember being given a blue enamel brooch with roses on it for my birthday. Although I knew I could have worn it unobserved on my tie when I was away at school, my conscience wouldn't let me accept it without permission.

Organized pleasures were particularly in evidence at Christmas. Betty Sutherland Graeme continues:

There were lots of Christmas parties, both before and during the war. All families in big houses seemed to give them. There was often a conjuror or magic lantern. People in smaller houses sometimes joined with each other in giving a big 'do' in one of the local Halls. My mother combined with a friend, whose children we disliked, to give one of these. I've still got her half share of the bill of this which came to £3.16.od. for entertaining 60 children. This included hire of the hall, pathescope, invitation cards, tips, crackers, milk and all the food except the cakes which, I imagine, were made by the respective cooks. I see the pianist was paid 3s.6d. for what must have been several hours accompanying for various musical games and dancing.[121]

One family with six boys ranging in age over twenty years gave three large Christmas parties – one with a Christmas tree and games for children under nine, one a 'junior dance' from 6 p.m. until 9 p.m., and one a 'grown-up dance' from 8 p.m. until midnight.[122]

For popular children in populous places the party season lasted well into the New Year, and Florence Goddard one year found herself at a party every evening throughout the school holidays. All followed much the same pattern of tea, party games and supper, and were attended by much the same children, almost identically dressed. Maids had an important role on these occasions, accompanying their charges each way and sometimes waiting in a separate room to collect them at the end.

Kate [the Goddards' maid] liked to be allowed to accompany me into the bedrooms where we removed our Red Riding Hood cloaks (we all wore these) and changed our shoes. She would give a description of all she had been able to observe about the house to my mother on her return, and she was intensely critical of other people's maids.[123]

Behind this control of middle-class children's recreation lay the desire to protect them from contaminating influences, to develop socially acceptable behaviour and to inculcate moral principles. Children were taught to be fair and 'sporting' to others in their play, to be polite and respectful to adults and always to express their gratitude for invitations, usually in writing. Deferred gratification was preferred to immediate satisfaction of wants, evidenced by the importance placed on saving and accumulation. Several children of wealthy parents who were given a penny a week as pocket-money were required immediately to put it into a money-box where it would be saved for Christmas presents for relatives and others, and Margaret Cunningham was never allowed

to go into a shop to buy anything for herself.[124] Some children were
expected to donate half their pocket-money to the church offertory or to
a missionary society. And of the hundreds of table games invented for
children in the Victorian age many had an educational or moral purpose
in that play would be combined with 'improvement'. Leslie Missen
played 'Missionary Lotto' and read *Cautionary Tales*. Others were sub-
jected to 'The Reward of Merit', 'The Road to the Temple of Honour
and Fame', 'Every Man to His Station', and 'Virtue Rewarded and Vice
Punished', the Book of Rules describing this as 'A Race from Number 1,
the House of Correction, to Number 53, Virtue. It is designed with a
view to promoting progressive Improvement of the Juvenile Mind, and
to deter them from pursuing the dangerous Paths of Vice.'

5. Courtship properly belongs to a stage of life later than childhood,
though the line between it and adolescent flirtation is not a sharp one. In
working-class culture the pattern seems to have been that as children up
to about the age of seven or eight boys and girls played together at least
some of the time; from then on increasing segregation occurred,
emphasized by the school system which often divided boys' and girls'
playgrounds and, sometimes, classes after the Infant stage. This separation usually continued until the end of schooldays, but within a year or
two after this boys and girls, now at work and with a little money to spend
on themselves, would begin to take an interest in their appearance, their
clothes and each other. The kind of encounters that then occurred –
variously described in the vernacular as 'getting off' or 'clicking' – were
generally not serious emotional relationships but expressions of independence and searches for identity and recognition. Particularly in the
towns a distinctive 'youth culture' had developed by the end of the
century, characterized for boys by individual dress, cigarette-smoking
and attendances at places of mass entertainment. Membership of Sunday School, church or chapel, once almost universal, tended to decline
at this stage, although for some young people the opportunities which
these institutions offered of meeting the opposite sex in respectable and
approved surroundings continued to be important, and not a few autobiographers met their future marriage partners through them. 'At this
period,' [c. 1880] wrote George Ratcliffe, 'I was a regular member of St
Stephen's Sunday School, as was my companion, Joe Morgan. We each
got a sweetheart there, and after service one Sunday night the four of us
went for a short walk into the country, which was quite near by.'[125]
William Smith, born in Wellington, Shropshire, in 1820, had lived 'a
wicked and profligate life' until the age of twenty-one, when he was

converted to Primitive Methodism, and through religion met his future wife. He writes:

> I was introduced to a young lady (as was the custom in those days) by an elderly lady when going into a class meeting at the chapel. She was dressed in black, having just lost and buried two brothers. She was very dark, with long black hair and dark eyes which she modestly fixed on the ground. But she gave me such a shake of the hand that I have felt it hundreds of times since then and sometimes feel it now. I was smitten at once. It was love at first sight. But don't think I am going wrong in my head as I record this, for I am quite sane.[126]

Many years later, in 1908, Ellen Calvert met her future husband, Arthur Gill, on an Easter Monday ramble to East Keswick arranged by the Woodhouse Wesleyan Chapel in Leeds: they married six years later after an engagement sensibly cemented by a sewing-machine rather than a ring.[127] Long engagements, sometimes up to eight years, were not exceptional at a time when the average age of marriage was twenty-six, and when prudent lovers carefully saved up for the marital home at perhaps the only time in their lives when there would be earnings to spare.

But most associations between adolescent boys and girls were casual, brief affairs, the result of chance meetings at street-corners, in the park or on the 'monkey parades' – the well-established 'clicking spots' where teenagers strolled at weekends and on summer evenings in the hopes of meeting the opposite sex. Though not indulged in by those from the higher social classes or the strictest homes, 'clicking' was not usually regarded as unrespectable and could conveniently be combined with religious attendance.

> The river Ribble ran through the Park [Avenham Park in Preston] with a bridge over it. The bridge and the lane beyond it was a real 'clicking' spot for the boys and girls. We always made for there after Church on Sunday evening, but had to be home no later than 9.30 p.m. and in bed at 10 p.m. as work started each day at 6 a.m.[128]

Such meetings might or might not lead to 'dates', to 'walking out' – often, literally so, into the countryside – and to serious courtship and eventual marriage. Autobiographers are silent on the intimacies of their love-making, and we cannot know how far 'petting' practices were allowed to go, though as a generalization it seems likely that the degree of permissiveness increased with descent in the social scale. A tantalizing comment is made by Bessie Wallis about her older brother, aged fifteen, who was a pit-boy in a Yorkshire mining village. In righteous mood she one day warned him:

'You'll be in trouble with Pops if you land a lassie with a bairn!' 'I don't care' was Danny's reaction. 'The lasses egg us on. They get what they ask for. The only pleasure a lad gets is to lay a lass. Anyhow, they like it!' . . . I worried a lot about Danny and the girls. I knew just how much he hated the pit. Girls were his one escape. What I did not realize until much older was that the bodies of these undernourished boys were barely capable of achieving an orgasm, let alone making a child. To most of the boys it was play. They just enjoyed handling the girls and exhibiting their mastery over them.[129]

Her opinion that love-play did not commonly result in conception is supported by the national statistics, which show the illegitimacy rate falling from 6 per cent in the mid-nineteenth century to only 4 per cent at the end: pregnancies before marriage also declined, perhaps by as much as a half in the same period. The figures suggest a high and increasing degree of sexual self-control, all the more remarkable given the delayed age of marriage. Few autobiographers record an enforced, early marriage, and their average age of marriage – around twenty-five or twenty-six – accords closely with the national figure. Given the prevailing state of ignorance about sex it is not surprising that some girls 'fell' by mistake, but most knew enough to preserve their chastity and regarded it, as did almost all men, as a major asset in the marriage market. When, after an engagement of two years, Mrs Layton's fiancé made 'improper suggestions' to her, she was disgusted and ashamed:

From that moment I lost all respect for him, and in spite of all his protestations of regret and promises that it should not occur again, I told him I would never forgive him, and broke off the engagement there and then.[130]

John Clare comments that his relationship with Patty 'now developed dangers which marriage alone could remedy', though he was then twenty-six or twenty-seven, and his short autobiography ends with the publication of his first book of poems rather than the birth of a child.[131] The one unambiguous admission is by John James Bezer, the same who had once dressed himself in sackcloth and ashes. At eighteen he fell violently in love with a 25-year-old Sunday School teacher, the ugliest of a bevy of 'marvellously pretty girls . . . most of whom got mated while there as a reward, I suppose they thought, for their labours'. After three rejections from his 'remarkably bad-tempered' choice, Bezer's affair prospered to the point where:

About this time I unfortunately got married, and I did very wrong. Without any clinging to the unnatural Malthusian doctrines I own we did very wrong – both of us. Thank God I did not deceive her; she knew precisely my circumstances, and bitterly, very bitterly, have we suffered for our folly.[132]

Within the working class, courtship seems generally to have been limited by geography and, to a high degree, by social status. Boys and girls, men and women, generally met and ultimately married near-neighbours who lived within walking distance and whose parents followed a broadly similar occupation and standard of living. Very occasionally a successful courtship is continued by correspondence, but usually when lovers were separated by distance the difficulties of travel and the inadequacies of literary skill resulted in a breakdown of the relationship. In the 'respectable' working class at least the 'typical' pattern is a first meeting at some public but controlled place – a chapel, church, Sunday School or Band of Hope – or by introduction from brothers, sisters, friends or relatives, followed by meetings often in the company of others, 'walking out' as a couple, acceptance by the two sets of parents and, finally, a formal engagement, often of several years before marriage. What is somewhat unclear is the required degree of parental approval. In higher social circles, where succession to property was involved in a marriage, approval was normally essential and in a wealthy family, such as the Green-Prices, unions, though not 'arranged' as was the earlier landed tradition, took place within a circle of acceptable acquaintances who shared similar lineage, education and social position (pp. 269–74).

The autobiographical accounts of working people suggest a similar pattern much further down the social scale. Parental approval of an intended was almost always sought, usually at a ritual invitation to tea, after which the couple might be given the freedom of the parlour for their courting. Marriage without approval was obviously open to adults, and pregnancy was sometimes used as an inducement to a change of mind, but the threat of disowning was a powerful deterrent in a closely knit family. Several autobiographers report parental refusal of consent on the grounds of unsuitable social background, girls who worked in factories being regarded as particularly suspect in respect of morals and language. When Syd Metcalfe's father, the son of a master-builder, married a factory girl around 1880 his parents ended all connection with him,[133] and in the Betts's household it was regarded as a shameful day when the eldest son brought home a factory girl.

Skivvies were bad enough, but at least they lived sheltered lives watched over by respectable mistresses who saw that they did not get into mischief on their day out . . . The real working-class aristocrat was a shop assistant. She only worked from eight to seven, plus half an hour before and after to prepare and clear up, and she had not only a weekly half-day but all Sunday free. Furthermore, at mealtimes in the common dining-room with the shopwalker and the proprietress she could learn to use a knife and fork and even to eat peas with a fork . . .[134]

The 'civilizing' influence of shop-work, and even of domestic service with a good family, is confirmed by several writers, including Minnie Frisby who speaks of herself as becoming 'refined' after seven months in service: her parents were nail-makers at Worm's Ash, Birmingham.[135]

The length of engagements before marriage – commonly two or three years, but in several instances five, six, or more – suggests little sexual licence at a time when artificial contraception was not much known. Nor are the strictures against the low morality of factory girls borne out by other witnesses. Alice Foley, who herself worked in a cotton mill, writes:

> Most of my companions were attached, loosely or otherwise, to church or chapel; some of the younger folk had been caught up in the Moody-Sankey missions of the period, and for a time became Hot Gospellers. In our singing sessions, the strains of 'Throw out the life-line, someone is sinking today' floated in competition with the regular hum and throb of the engine. We held to a fairly conventional, if unexplored, moral code, and if anyone in the group was suspected of 'going out' with a married man she was usually due for a telling-off by her companions.[136]

The accounts confirm that sexual relations before marriage, and illegitimate births, were more common and more accepted in country districts than in towns, reflecting the survival of an older tradition in which husbands needed to be assured of the fertility of their wives and their ability to bear children who could become the family's support in old age. In her Lincolnshire village in the 1860s Mary Paley Marshall wrote that 'the villagers . . . had large families, and it was not uncommon for young couples to put off marriage till the birth of the first child was expected'.[137] So too in Moss Ferry, a semi-industrial village fourteen miles from Manchester, around 1900:

> It was accounted no shame for a child to be begotten out of wedlock – the shame was when there was no wedding to follow. That was something almost unknown – something that didn't stand thinking about.[138]

And, in direct language, Maggy Fryett from the isolated village of Gislea in the Fens recalls her courting days:

> Well, if you go a-courting they want that, don't they? He used to say, 'What you got under your apron? I got to see if you're any good. I ain't going to buy a piggy-in-a-poke.' But I wouldn't let him touch me. I were too frightened.[139]

Even in the villages it is likely that the majority of girls preserved their chastity, either from fear as in this case or from moral conviction, or because they sensed that virginity was a valuable asset in the marriage stakes and that the sort of man they wanted for a husband did not respect a girl who made herself freely available. Much depended on the local culture and the hold of religion over the people. In the Forest of Dean, a strongly Methodist region, Fred Boughton comments that the young men and girls

did not lie about like animals: they all had respect for each other. It was a terrible crime in those days if two young people lost their self-respect. The baby would be called a bastard all its life. The girl would hang her head in shame, and no man would respect her.[140]

Closed communities like this had their own moral code and sanctions, sometimes with picturesque methods of enforcement: in a mining village near Sheffield, if a girl or woman misbehaved the colliers made an effigy of her and paraded it through the streets on a barrow to be pelted.[141]

Autobiographers rarely give any extended account of their feelings for their partner or their emotional state before marriage from which we might draw general conclusions about their reasons for matrimony. In some autobiographies, marriage is discussed in a few words (James Watson, 'On the third of June I was married') or a couple of sentences (Thomas Dunning),[142] and the event which many people today would regard as the single most important in their lives apparently shrinks into insignificance. Writers in the period under review are reticent about their inner feelings, perhaps because they do not have the vocabulary to express them, but more often because they do not regard such outpourings as a proper subject for their autobiography. A few, who did possess literary skill, turned to poetry as the appropriate vehicle for emotion, but the common view is that of J. B. Leno, that 'With my home life, I am not desirous of dealing. The fact is that it would fail to prove interesting to strangers . . .'[143]

Where autobiographers do state their reasons for marriage, 'love' is specified only by a small minority. William Smith's unequivocal declaration of his feelings has already been cited, and is echoed by a few more – John Clare the poet, Thomas Cooper, John James Bezer and Christopher Thomson, all writers of considerable skill. The fact that love is not specified does not mean, of course, that it was not felt, especially at a time when the use of the word tended to be regarded as unmanly. But the words which are used to describe the virtues of a marriage partner more often suggest a solid calculation than an emotional obsession. Leno describes his wife as 'a good mother, an

affectionate partner, a wise counsellor, a model of industry'; Thomas
Carter chose a wife of 'plain good sense and of thoroughly domestic
habits';[144] John Shinn decided that 'it would be an advantage to
marry';[145] Mrs Wrigley writes that 'my young man wanted to get married
for he had no mother'[146] and the anonymous 'Cornish Waif' specifically
entered into a marriage of convenience, on her own proposal.[147] What
seems to be regarded as important in most cases is not primarily sexual
attraction, but compatability of temperament and affection based on
mutual respect – the husband's ability to work and provide for a family,
the wife's domestic skills and value as a 'helpmate' and 'wise counsellor'.
Many marriages were strengthened by common religious convictions,
by mutual economic dependence on the wife's ability to contribute to
family earnings, provided that her primary role as mother and housekeeper was not neglected. When, as happened not infrequently, a man
re-married on the early death of his first wife, the care of an existing
household, perhaps with children, often entered as an additional element in the calculation. A widower at twenty-four, John Castle found
that he 'could not get on without a woman in the house'. With an
employed housekeeper 'I soon found everything going to ruin – bad
washing, bad bread,' and, after meeting a young woman (at church)
and a courtship of a few weeks, 'as I had a house and home that
wanted looking after I thought it best to marry at once'.[148]

Working-class autobiographers rarely had any extravagant expectations of a life of marital bliss. Most seem to have hoped that the struggles
and problems of existence would be more easily born if shared, that an
economical housekeeper would be able to stretch the family income and
that, as children arrived, they would bring some joy to the earlier years
and some comfort and material help to the declining ones. Except where
a child was imminently due, marriages were normally planned for some
months or years in advance and, where possible, the man saved and the
woman prepared for the marital home. Few working men could be as
provident as Frank Marling who, around 1880, and well before his
marriage, insured his life for £100 to use for the education of his future
children and began paying £1 a month into a building society, but not a
few began married life with a nest-egg of £20–£40 which was intended
to furnish the home and provide for the vicissitudes of the early years.
Women also often saved from their meagre earnings as domestic servants or factory workers, but concentrated on accumulating a 'bottom
drawer' of linen, bed-clothes and household articles. Ellen Gill persuaded her fiancé to buy her a sewing-machine instead of an engagement ring, and when Gwen Millington's grandmother married in the

1880s she had chests of flour, tea and other groceries which, when she used, she 'bought' by putting the equivalent money into tins: in this way, she always kept a reserve.[149]

The normal, almost inevitable, outcome of marriage was a succession of children, the first usually born within a year or so, the rest following over a span of up to twenty years. The average family size in 1871 was six surviving children, though one in five marriages produced ten or more. By 1914 the birthrate was declining in the middle classes and upper levels of the working class, though the dramatic fall in average family size to between two and three children did not occur until after the First World War. The reactions of parents to family formation are again difficult to reconstruct since on this subject autobiographers are particularly reticent, but from the scattered references that are available it seems that attitudes depended primarily on income and social class. Wealthy parents generally found too many confinements and subsequent children an embarrassment to their social lives and, at least in part, disencumbered themselves by the employment of nurse-maids, governesses and boarding-school teachers; in these circles it was not uncommon for men, and sometimes women, to find sexual satisfaction outside marriage. For the poor, too many children in quick succession could be disastrous to a frail economy in that stage of the family cycle when the children were dependent and not yet contributing to family earnings. Whatever the preferred family size might have been, given adequate resources, many poorer working-class parents seem to have regarded more than three or four children as unfortunate, and more than six or seven as disastrous. Thomas Carter's ironic observation is revealing:

> On the anniversary of my birthday (July 5th) my wife made me a birthday present in the shape of a (second) son. I had not learned to consider such events as calamities . . . [150]

Many overburdened parents clearly did, as Ethel Clark's mother often heard in her little post office at Woolaston –

> We heard of the family quarrels, the skeletons in the cupboards: we knew before anyone else when women said they were 'that way again', and the joy of a miscarriage [which] helped them back to happiness again.[151]

Many mothers – though we cannot know how many – attempted to induce or procure abortion by primitive and dangerous means; some cannot have mourned too long or deeply when their baby died after a few days or weeks. Before contraceptives became widely known to the working classes in the 1920s, a woman who wanted no more children

faced the problem of her husband's natural and, in his view, enforce-
able, sexual desires, and not all were so successful as Maggy Fryett:

> I had three children. And I didn't want no more. My mother had fourteen
> children and I didn't want that. So I stayed up mending. He [would] say, 'Aren't
> you coming to bed yet?' and I would say, 'I've got to mend these before I go to
> bed. They'll want them in the morning. You can go, but these have got to be
> done tonight.' So if I stayed up mending, my husband would be asleep when I
> came to bed.[152]

The desired family size was more likely to be realized in the middle
class and 'respectable' working class, where income imposed less restraint and the generally more sympathetic relationship between husbands and wives encouraged discussion and mutual agreement on the
subject. Here, the desired family may well have been half a dozen sons
and daughters in the mid-nineteenth century and three or four at the
end of the century, when the demands of conspicuous consumption and
the availability of reliable contraceptive devices began to have effect.

Gwen Millington's grandmother, who had 'eagerly expected a family
of at least six' but contracted puerperal fever after her first child and
could have no more, must have been one of many disappointed victims
of the state of medical knowledge and practice. At all income levels
many parents enjoyed large families, regarded them with pride as a
blessing and joy, as well as a Christian duty and economic responsibility.
In that belief, wives dutifully submitted themselves to an annual pregnancy, to miscarriages, illness, premature old age and early death. Alice
Moody's mother cheerfully married a man whose first wife had died,
leaving him with four surviving children out of thirteen, and proceeded
to give him nine more;[153] at Sutton Courtney, Berkshire, in the 1880s
one labourer had twenty-five children from two marriages, and was able
to field a family cricket eleven against the rest of the village.[154] Especially
in the earlier, poorer half of the century an over-large family could bring
poverty and misery, brutalizing the relationship between man and wife
and blunting the natural affection of parents for their children, but as
real incomes rose and working hours fell in the later years, as homes
became more comfortable and less crowded, as education increased and
heavy drinking declined, the space and time available for love in family
relationships continuously expanded. The middle-class family pattern,
which elevated the home to the centre of civilized life, the refuge and the
rock on which society rested, was increasingly aspired to and achieved
by the growing proportion of the 'respectable' working-class, so that by
the end of the century it was mainly in that poorest third of the

population which Booth, Rowntree and other social investigators documented that an older family pattern survived – unwanted children, severe punishment, premature entrance to work and familial relationships poisoned by the struggle for survival. In such families the initial affection on which most marriages had always been based could quickly wither in the face of adversity: the great majority of unions endured because there was no practical alternative and because the partners found some way of continuing to live together, not because their love for each other continued and prospered over the years. But the autobiographical evidence suggests that by the century's end more working-class marriages existed on a basis of affection, respect, common goals and shared responsibilities, that children were more treasured and less exploited, that the home had grown in importance as a physical, social and moral structure, and that the family had survived the shocks of industrialization and urbanization to emerge smaller, closer and more affectionate than before.

John Castle

John Castle was born at Great Coggeshall, Essex, in 1819. His 'diary' – in fact, an autobiography – was written in 1871, eighteen years before his death; the manuscript is in Essex County Record Office, but a typewritten version of thirty-eight pages was produced by Colchester Co-operative Society for their centenary in 1961, from which these extracts are taken. I am very grateful to the Essex Record Office and Mrs L. C. Johnson for permission to publish this extract from John Castle's diary. Extensive extracts were also published in *Essex People 1750–1900* by A. F. J. Brown (Essex Record Office Publications, 1972).

In these extracts Castle describes the poverty of his childhood during the uncertainties of the silk industry on which the town largely depended, his sufferings in the workhouse under the rigours of the New Poor Law, his return to employment and the two marriages he contracted by the time he was twenty-five. Major themes in his autobiography are the importance of family connections, his moral questionings and eventual religious conviction, but Castle is also informative about the large families of his day, the ill-health and early deaths of children and adults. In later life Castle became foreman of a silk works in Colchester and manager of the Colchester Co-operative Society; like many working men of his day he was a firm supporter of the Liberal Party and a strong believer in education and self-improvement.

I was born at Great Coggeshall in the Year 1819. My father was a native of Soulbury in Buckinghamshire, my mother of Coggeshall, in Essex. When I was the age of two years and a half my father returned to his native place, taking his family, four in number, with him. After residing a little over two years at Soulbury an attack of Inflammation of the body suddenly caused my fathers death, at the age of 27. My mother and family were left quite destitute and she being near another confinement. During the short time we lived at Soulbury our two sisters, Hannah and Eliza, died, my brother William was about seven years old, myself five. At the death of our father my mothers mother walked from Coggeshall to Soulbury, about 75 miles. When she arrived with my fathers sister from a place called Walkern, in Hertfordshire, he was buried when they arrived. After a few days stay they walked back, taking me with them, leaving my mother and brother behind. One month after my fathers death my mother was confined with a son, whom she named Isaac. A few months afterwards my mother returned to Coggeshall. The parish allowed her seven shillings per week to bring us up. We were sent to the Church School on Sundays and to a womans day school. My mother, to get a living, went out as Nurse. At the age of eight I was sent to a writing school, where I filled only two copy books. At the age of nine I was sent to Messrs William and Charles Beckwiths Silk Factory to learn to be what was called a draw boy and to clean the silks ready for weaving. After a few years the Jacquard machine from France took the place of the draw boy machine. . .

Soon after this an event occurred in the silk trade which caused a great change – Messrs W. and C. Beckwith failed for a large sum, which stopped the trade, throwing nearly 100 out of employment. About this time great failures took place in America, causing the silk trade to be bad all over England. I was out some months, sometimes tramping to Halstead and then to Colchester to seek for employment. I called at the Royal Mortar, Military Road, Colchester, on Mr Pain, foreman to Mr Foot, and got a promise of employment, but the trade got so bad he could not give me any, I returned home to Coggeshall pennyless. My poor old mother would have gone without bread for me, but I had a stepfather who grudged every mouthful I ate. My brother William was married and had one son, he was at his wits end to get bread to eat. At last our mother persuaded us to go to the Board of Guardians at Witham. We went and were asked questions about the parish of our father. We were sworn to our settlement, which was Soulbury, in Bucks, near Leighton Buzzard, in Bedfordshire. We were ordered back to Coggeshall with instructions to go to one C. Smith, a baker, who was overseer at that time. We had plenty of bread for a week and then it was stopped, we were told to get work or go into the Union Workhouse at Witham. To get work was out of the question, so we packed up next morning, determined to see it out, we had nothing to lose. We arrived at Chipping Hill Union before dinner, produced our order and were admitted. We were not the first lot from Coggeshall, there were several families belonging to our shopmates. One James Cox and his wife had become bakers. As soon as they saw us they gave us a hint to put our names in as Dissenters, although he was grave-digger at Coggeshall Church and we had been brought up to the Established Church, yet we turned Dissenters because the church was close to the door of the Union. The Chapel was in Witham Street, a long way off, this gave us a good walk every Sunday.

The first day after dinner we were ordered to strip and put on the regimentals of the Union, which were composed of a pair of thick leather breeches, leather coat, low shoes, ribbed stockings, and a hairy cap with peak. I could but smile at the appearance of my brother, who was very thin, his small clothes hung about his legs. This day made me think of the words of my mother, she had often remarked – 'Ah, boy, as you make your bed so you must go to it.' This came true literally that day, we were ordered to go to work in a factory where stood two machines, one named the Devil, the other a carding machine. Old carpets were brought to us very greasy, we cut them into ribbons and fed the Devil, who tore them into a thousand pieces. We then took them to the carding machine, put them through it, and they came out first rate flocks. Whilst we were doing this some of our shopmates were set to sew up some bed-teaking and we had a capital flock bed, as we did not forget to put plenty of flocks into it. The work in this factory was very dusty.

The next day some one was wanted to clean boots, shoes, knives and so on, this situation I obtained, and thought it a promotion, to say nothing of the emoluments I obtained. I used to come in for a few nubbles, as we called them, which broke off the loaves of bread as they came out of the oven, these were a great relish to a hungry youth of 17. When work was done we had a large room with good fire, and about 30 or 40 of us sat round it, some talking of the days gone by and wondering where the end of this poverty would take us, others were singing or making a poor half-witted man sing, none of us seemed to be thinking that the cloud we so much dreaded was big with blessings, in fact it was a blessing that we could not see the roughness of the road we had got to travel. The days passed on. . .

After remaining at Chipping Hill Workhouse 14 days orders came that I and my brother, his wife and child, were to start the next morning on the Coggeshall coach for Soulbury, in Buckinghamshire. We took off our regimentals and put our own clothes on, and walked seven miles to Coggeshall. We spent the night with our relatives. The next morning which I think was the 7th of February, 1837, we all started on the coach for London, under the care of a Mr Goodey, who was a parish officer. The weather was bad – it snowed part of the way. We arrived in London after five hours ride in the cold. But our conductor was a jolly fellow when the coach arrived at the Saracens Head, Aldgate, he ordered a good beefsteak dinner. After partaking of this meal we started for Wood Street, Cheapside, to take the coach for the Shires. Whilst waiting in the street to listen to some music, of which I was very fond, who should I see but my old employer, Mr Charles Beckwith, whose house was in Wood Street, he saw us and kindly enquired our business, and gave us a shilling, which was a large sum in our estimation then . . . [After a night at Aylesbury] We were delivered up to Mr Durrant, the Guardian of Soulbury, and our guide bade us fare well. After a little refreshment we were told to walk to Leighton Buzzard Union, which was nearly three miles off. We arrived at the iron gates just at dusk, rang the bell, and were ushered into a building which appeared more like a gaol than anything I could imagine.

My brother was parted from his wife and child, and a sad night it must have been for a young woman so soon after marriage, to be so far from home and among strangers, it was not so bad for me and my brother, we slept together. The building is four square – the front was the Board Room, Relieving Officer's and Porter's houses, the back, Master's house and store rooms, left side for women and children and warehouse, right side for men and boys. On the top of the Master's house was a cistern, which had to be pumped full every few days, a stone balcony ran down left and right leading to the bedrooms, which had brick flooring. The Union was but just finished building as we arrived. We were set to work in a gravel pit to get gravel and make paths round the Union, we had to form a round hill in front and two triangles. Inside the house was an oven to bake all the bread. One evening the baker called for some one to assist him draw the bread, I and my brother went. There a Providential circumstance occurred which was a turning-point in my life. The baker hearing us talk said 'You are Essex people, I know, by your brogue, how came you here?' I told him my father was a native of Soulbury. 'What name?' he asked, I told him 'John Castle'. 'Why I knew him' he said, 'he died some years back'. He also added 'You have two first cousins living in this town, the son and daughter of Old Roger Hedgcock, who married your father's eldest sister Maria.' This sounded as a fable, for we had never heard that our father had a sister Maria. But the news was no more strange than true. He added 'I sold a side of pork and a sack of potatoes to-day to George, your cousin'. He promised to inform them. A day or two after, George Hedgcock came down to the Union and asked to see us, but could not do so without an order. He told the baker to tell us to go to the Wesleyan Chapel on Sunday, where he was a member and a class leader. Accordingly on Sunday morning, as soon as the porter let us out for Church we turned off the road leading to that building, and the porter told us we were going wrong. I told him jokingly that the Church Clergyman were such poor preachers that we were going to Chapel. We reached the Methodist Chapel and took our seats upon the gallery, on looking round I saw a man in the body of the chapel whom I pointed out, telling my brother that I thought this man might be our cousin, as I thought there was a family likeness. After the sermon was over we were passing out of the Chapel yard when this very man touched me on my shoulder and asked my name I told him, and he said 'Is that your brother and his wife?' I replied 'Yes' he asked me to go home with him to dinner, I replied 'I dare not absent myself from the Union, or I might be turned out' little did I dream that before many weeks it would be my lot to be turned out of a Workhouse. He then told us to get leave from Mr Bromley, the Master, for the afternoon and evening. Never shall I forget the joy I felt at finding so kind a relative in a strange land – one who was not above us in our low estate. We went to his house and met his wife and eight children. After a short stay of an hour he suggested that I should put on a suit of his clothes and go with him to see his sister, Sarah Grace, for that was her name. We spent a comfortable afternoon and were invited to go and see them every opportunity we could get. About a week after this we had a day's holiday with rations to go and spend the day at the village where our father was buried. The grave was pointed out to us by an old lady who knew us when children. When standing over the grave I thought what would my poor mother give to stand here? she was nearly 100 miles off. We returned back to our mansion.

The Clergyman's name who was Chairman of the Board of Guardians and Rector of Hedgerley parish and also a Justice of the Peace was *Wroth*, and as you, dear reader, shall soon know, he poured out his wrath on me. As I said before, we were set to dig up the front of the Union, which was so trodden down and hard that we had to loosen the ground with a mattock before we could use a spade. My brother, just before leaving Coggeshall had the scarlet fever badly, and was now anything but strong. Our diet, also, was not calculated to give him nor me strength. We had 7 ozs of bread and about one pint of skilley for breakfast, for dinner, about three potatoes 4 ozs of meat and 2 ozs of bread, at night, 8 ozs of bread and 2 ozs of Common Dutch cheese – making 17 ozs of bread per day. Well one afternoon as we were working outside Mr Wroth was going into the Union I suppose to preach what is called the Gospel, he stopped when he got to us 'Well, young man' he said, 'You are not gone home yet' 'No Sir' was our reply, my poor brother just at that moment was standing upright. He said to my brother, 'Go on with your work, you are lazy' my brother never spoke, not so with me, I spoke to my sorrow, I looked him in the face, feeling indignant at my brother being so unkindly treated, I said, 'We do not have food enough, Sir, to do this hard work' no doubt I spoke rather hastily. He said to me, 'Do you know who I am? I am a magistrate and will send you to gaol for insolence' I said no more, but picked away. He went into the house and told the Master. At night Mr Bromley said 'What have you been saying to Mr Wroth?' I replied 'The truth, and nothing more, I told him we did not have food enough to do the hard work outside.' He remarked 'He would send you to gaol as soon as he would look at you, the Guardians are afraid of him' I said 'I am not afraid of him or any other man when I speak the truth.' The following day a Quaker, named Reeves, Guardian for Leighton Buzzard parish, came to me and very kindly said 'thee should not have said what thee did to Mr Wroth' I told him I did not think it any harm to speak the truth. I could have eaten my own and brother's meals any day except the day I first saw my new-found cousin whose kindness was a great contrast to Mr Wroth. Well Friday came, the day for the Board of Guardians to meet. Mr Culverhouse the porter, called out 'John Castle come before the Board' I looked at my brother, expecting to be sent to gaol by this great man. Such was not the case, but something that seemed at that time even worse. I was taken by the Relieving Officer and placed in front of the table. Mr Wroth addressed me thus: 'Young man, we believe you are lazy, or you would not be in a Union' I challenged him to write to my late employer, but he would not let me speak, but like a wicked oppressor he sentenced me to be expelled the Union, at 9 o'clock next morning, with the sum of four shillings, I made an effort to ask him what I was to do, nearly 100 miles from my mother, with 4s. 'Take him out' was his reply. I was not allowed to speak, but pulled out of the room by Mr Meeton, the Relieving Officer, who told me going down the stairs to go for a soldier! My heart failed within me, and I wept at the thought of being sent adrift in a far-off country . . .

[Castle next found work in the silk industry in London, where he had an aunt.]

Soon after this one morning I met the postman he handed me a letter to say that my brother had been to Colchester at the request of my poor old mother, and engaged for a loom's work of satin for me, and had bargained for a loom and even hired two rooms. All this they had done without my knowledge or consent. They did not know but what I had work, it so happened that I was out of employment. This seemed to me strange at the time, but after my eyes became opened I could see a good Providence in it . . .

I left London on the Sunday morning by railroad the Great Eastern, as it is now called was only 12 miles long – it only reached to Romford then. I walked from Romford to Coggeshall that day, 32 miles, the next day I proceeded to Colchester and went up to the Royal Mortar to Mr Elson, Messrs Henderson and Arundles foreman, he told me where my loom was and my two rooms. In a day or two I received my cane and began to weave satin in Colchester and to be a housekeeper. I bought one chair, one table and a bed, also one saucepan all on trust. Thus I lived for two years getting on well.

I had not been in Colchester long before I became acquainted with the housemaid of Mr Newell a solicitor of Colchester. We had kept company about 15 months when she was sent into the Hospital, and the doctors pronounced her in deep decline, the physician said she must leave the Hospital – if she lived till the Thursday week it was as much as she would. I consulted her aunt, who lived at service in the town, and lodgings were taken for her by this aunt at Thomas Seaborn's over North Bridge. To this place she was removed, but was not expected to live. I went to see her every night, she was attended by Messrs Nunn and Son, surgeons, but no improvement seemed to take place, neither did she die at the time named. Doctor Nunn had a son-in-law by the name of Blyth, who took her in hand he sent a blister to be put on her left breast and ordered it to be kept on till he called, he came and asked to look at it, he turned it up at one corner, so as to get a hold, and rent it off, skin and all. This was cruel, to all outward appearance, but it set her on her legs again. The cough she was the subject of seemed to come from there, and he ordered it to be kept open. In a week or two her cough left her and she gained strength. Her friends began to get tired. She had no mother, her father was left with ten children, she was the eldest. Her name was Elizabeth Sandford, from Great Waldingfield, Suffolk, the daughter of a ploughman. She had been very kind to her father and her brothers and sisters so that she was quite destitute of money when overtaken by affliction. Her friends persuaded her to call on the parish, she consented, believing that she belonged to St Mary-at-the-Walls, Colchester, having lived at Mr Bolton Smiths, wine merchant. Mr Roger Nunn being a magistrate, she was sworn to her settlement, and it turned out she belonged to Waldingfield, Suffolk, where her father lived. One night when I went to see her, as I thought the Relieving Officer had taken her to the Sudbury Board of Guardians and they settled 3s. per week on her to go and live with her father, I was not at all sorry to think if I ever married her I must take her off the parish. She had been very high-minded and proud, not willing to marry till she had a house such as a silk weaver could not afford, but God knew how to bring down pride, and he brought her down so that she was glad to be in a low place – even the wife of a weaver. She had been home nine days when I walked over to Waldingford on the Saturday afternoon, about 16 miles, I found her improving in health but her father was far from well, I slept with him that night. He came in on the Sunday morning quite upset a farmer by the name of Vince had blown out his brains, this seemed to play very much upon poor Sandford, I returned to Colchester on the Monday morning I went again in a fortnight he was getting worse, his daughter was well enough to wait upon him, he expressed a wish to see me marry his daughter so I put in the banns of marriage at the Church I went down every week to escape being published in Colchester. The last Sunday of being published I rode down with her Aunt Chignall. I thought of marrying on the Monday week, but when I went to the bedside of poor Sandford he had death set in his face, his eye-strings seemed broken. The Clergyman advised me to stop and marry next day, as it would be better to go from a wedding to a funeral than from a funeral to a wedding. We married next day, her father died the very day we intended to marry. When we came from the Church we went up to his bedside and his daughter placed her hand with the wedding ring on to his eyes, he tried to speak, but we never knew what he said. He died and left my wife in charge of the children, the youngest being a boy about eight years old. I agreed for my wife to stay till after the funeral, but advised her to let the parish take charge of all the children. To my surprise she brought a brother and sister home to my house – the Parish Officer had persuaded her, and she had 2s. 6d. each per week to feed and clothe them, she had always had a mother's feeling for them since her mother's death, therefore I could not say anything to her. Her health continued middling for some months, but it soon got bad again during those trials, and I might say they had scarcely began . . .

My wife, Elizabeth, was taken worse about this time, and gradually sank. Her little brother Isaac I had sent to several schools, but he did not know the alphabet. I found it best to keep him at home, he learnt nothing ´at school, I undertook to teach him, I bought him a small spelling book and set him one letter per day to learn or no dinner – unless he had learnt that one letter before dinner time, then dodging him till he very soon knew the 26 letters – such a deep impression was made on my mind as to the importance of education that I should have considered it a shame on my part to have any one under my care without learning to read and write. After he had learnt his letters I put him to spelling about three words per day, and in less than twelve months he could read the New Testament, so that he learnt the first chapter of Hebrews by heart and read it to Mr Herrick and then said it without the book. The girl was the eldest, she was never well, Abscess broke out on her legs and she was in the Colchester Hospital a good while. My wife got so bad that I could scarcely work the noise of my loom in the house seemed too much for her. Some times I was at my wits end to know how to get the bread that nourisheth – but the Lord God who careth for his children often opened a way in the desert for us. Once we were reduced to the last penny, but there was one pound due from Sudbury Union for the two children. My wife was too ill to allow me to leave home, as I had done several times before I had walked from Colchester to Waldingfield and back in the day, a distance of 32 miles to fetch the money due. It was about five o'clock one morning we were talking about how we should manage, only one penny left, when someone struck the bedroom window with a whip. I opened the window and found it was Mr Sargent, the Overseer of Waldingfield, he had to come to Colchester for coal and thought we might be glad of the money, I thought of Elijah and the ravens. Many such deliverances I had which made my heart praise the goodness of the Lord. I used often to say as the Psalmist said 'Oh, that men would praise the Lord for His goodness to the children of Men.'

Laura Green-Price
our life

The author was born in 1857 in Knighton, Radnorshire, one of thirteen children of a lawyer whose family was related to the county gentry. Her unpublished memoir describes how her father became squire of Norton Manor, Presteigne, and was eventually knighted (Sir Richard Green-Price) for his services to the Liberal Party; it is as much concerned with the family's history – her parents, her sisters' marriages, the house and village in which her father took a keen paternal interest – as it is with her own life story. The dominant themes are the concerns of the estate and her love of the secure, closely knit family at Norton Manor where 'we were as happy as birds from morning till night', but she also stresses the responsibilities of the family's position and the high regard in which they were held by the local community.

The typewritten version of the manuscript is of forty-four pages, of which this extract is approximately one-third. I am grateful to Mrs Anthea Phillips for allowing me to quote from her great-aunt's memoir.

We lived many years in a very pretty Welsh town called Knighton, County Radnorshire, and twenty miles from Shrewsbury our nearest large town.

Our house was called the 'Cottage', also Frydd (pronounced 'Frith') House, from a hill of that name in front of the house. This early home of ours was a very lovely place and though rather small for ten of us, yet we were always very happy there.

My father was a lawyer and worked hard for his living, often not coming home till late at night. My sweet mother was never very strong and the cares and anxieties which her children caused her, did not improve her health.

No children could have had a dearer or fonder mother than ours and our every joy or sorrow were all alike shared with her and our darling father.

Not only was she the best of mothers but also the best of wives, always ready with a cheerful look or word to help on my father in the worries of business. Seldom was there seen such happiness in any home as in ours, for Love dwelt there and we were always taught to look to Him who is the 'Author and Giver of all good things' and to be truly thankful for the many blessings and comforts we enjoyed.

About five miles from Knighton on the Herefordshire side, an old uncle of Papa's lived in a large house called 'Norton Manor'. He was a bachelor and lived in solitary glory, quite happy in his large estate, and glorying especially in his trees of which he was very proud, and looked upon in the light of children. He was never known to cut *one* down and the Manor stood surrounded by wood, but with a large extent of ground in the front leading through a long drive to the public road. In this house our great-uncle lived leading rather a recluse life and seldom visiting anywhere, at least not in his later years. We children always looked upon him with great dread, partly because of his peculiarities and hatred of children, and partly because he never liked our dear father. So he was seldom seen at the Cottage and when he *did* pay a formal visit, we always kept well out of his way!

Years went by quickly and peacefully with no striking change except that every year another brother or sister was added to the home nest, and the cares daily increasing for our father and mother, though we knew nothing of them.

About this time my father was contemplating making sundry improvements and enlarging the Cottage, when an event happened which changed the aspect of affairs. Papa's uncle, Mr Price of Norton Manor, died! He had been ailing for some time and had had to resign his seat in Parliament. He died quite suddenly one day with only my father and brother with him. My Uncle George being the eldest brother and therefore next heir, came down from London where he lived, in order to attend the funeral and hear the will read, and found as he had expected, that all the house and property (which was a very extensive one) was left to him, with only a few hundreds to my father and his younger brother.

My Uncle George was a bachelor and a man of very quiet tastes and habits. To everyone's surprise, soon after Mr Price's death, he told Papa that he intended giving up Norton Manor and all the property to him on certain conditions etc. He declared to my father that he was never meant to live in such grandeur, and having always lived quietly in London he should only be miserable with such a large estate to manage, and not know how to do it.

So it was finally settled after many arguments on both sides (for my father was *very* loth to say yes) that we were all to leave our dear home where we had been born and where we had lived so long and so happily, and make a new home at Norton Manor.

We ever looked upon dear Uncle George (who is now dead many years) with great love and admiration for having behaved so nobly and so generously to his younger brother (to whom he was devoted as may be imagined!) and he has since gone by the name of the 'Generous Uncle'. He rented our old home from my father and had so much a year from the Norton Estate and lived there very happily and beloved by us all till his death in 1869.

But I am looking on too far into the future and must go back to our departure from Knighton. When the townspeople and friends in the neighbourhood heard of our intended move, there were many cries of regrets and sorrow. What my father did for the town will never be forgotten. Our nearest railway station, Craven Arms, being fifteen miles away, he brought a line from it to Knighton, nearly wearing himself out in the attempt, but being very much helped by his friend Sir Charles Boughton who stood by him through it all. He built shops, helped the poor, and was always ready to do any kindness to everyone. The goodbyes were many and sad from both rich and poor and having lived among them so long and knowing all so well, we were *quite* as sorry to leave as they were to part from us, although at the same time it was nice to feel our place would be missed.

On a fine Spring day of 1861 we bid goodbye to our dear house and started for Norton, which was a very pretty little village surrounded by hills, with a curious looking Welsh Church (rather like a barn!) and Vicarage opposite it, also very old and dilapidated. The Manor was a little way out of the village. The bells of the old church were ringing merrily (though they were all three cracked) on our arrival, and as we drove through the village we were greeted on all sides by well-wishers who cheered lustily 'The new Squire and his wife and children'. At the end of the village we turned off the main road and entered the drive to the Manor, winding through a beautiful park about a mile long with here and there a peep of the grey-stone, gabled house which was henceforth to be our home.

We all felt very strange at first, and it was a long time before we were reconciled to the large gloomy house, for it wanted many improvements, Mr Price having let the trees grow close up to the windows which from the inside gave a dreary look to the place. At first we used to declare we should *never* like Norton! If we could only have looked on a few years, how differently we should have thought!

At the end of our first year at the Manor my father decided we should all go abroad for a year, while another wing was added to the house and many other improvements made, in the garden etc.

We spent a summer in Boulogne, my father and mother going from there for a tour in Switzerland and joining us at Brussels where we spent a winter.

For the following year of 1864 we returned to Norton after having enjoyed our year abroad very much. On our return the house was so altered that we hardly recognized it, so much was it improved. A great many large trees had been cut down near the house, hiding the view which was now most lovely, looking straight across a wooded valley with the Malvern Hills in the far distance.

A beautiful garden had been laid out, terraces made, a large archery ground under the shade of the wood, making it a shady spot from the hot sun, and a croquet ground (Lawn Tennis had not then come into fashion).

We now came to the conclusion that this was a lovely place and one to be very proud of, and every day we grew fonder of it, with its lovely nooks and walks through the woods which we were never tired of exploring.

My eldest brother was this year married to Miss C. Powell, daughter of Rev. T. Powell of Dorstone, Herefordshire. She was a very sweet and lovely girl, who was always much loved by us for her good temper and unselfishness. Whenever she came to stay with us she kept the house alive by her bright winning ways which won all hearts.

My eldest sister (or rather half-sister, for my father was twice married), Constance Mary, was married in the following year to Mr T. Baskerville Mynors, whose family lived four miles from us in a pretty house standing on high ground and called 'Barland', where Consty and her husband afterwards lived.

It was a very large wedding, the Mynors being an old Herefordshire family and well known. We missed Constance very much but got reconciled to it in time as we do to all things, and having her within driving distance was very pleasant as we saw her frequently. I of course was in the schoolroom at this time, as also were two sisters older than myself, whose names were Milla and Edith. We had several governesses, French, German and English, and worked hard in the dear old schoolroom. We were all fond of our lessons but I can't say the same of our governesses, at least not of all.

My father's great wish about this time was to improve the village. After completing the Manor and grounds, he determined to build a new Vicarage, Church and Cottages for his labourers. The Vicarage was soon built and the new Cottages which [were] made very comfortable and were in a row by the side of the road as you drove through the village.

The Church was a more difficult thing to begin upon and a good deal of discussion and talk there was before the first stone was pulled down, and the old Welsh barn was fairly being restored. It had then high pews (very moth-eaten), a small East window, high white-washed pulpit and reading desk and also a screen white-washed! But in two years' time, Mr Gilbert Scott the architect (since made a Baronet by Her Majesty Queen Victoria), restored it so perfectly that we were really proud of our village church and it was the admiration of all visitors and strangers.

Three painted windows, a beautiful organ, two transepts, a handsome carved oak screen (which in the old church was white-washed!) leading into a large chancel, were the leading features of the church, and the tall white spire, very characteristic with the rest of the building, was seen from far, nestling among the trees. Our third sister Nettie (Henrietta Margaret), who was very musical, undertook the choir, and by dint of working hard with what village children she could find could sing, we soon had a very good choir, and few would have known it as the same that was there two years ago. So Norton became a pattern village and very proud and happy we were of all that our dear father had done, and how he had made himself beloved by all in the parish and on the estate.

I have forgotten to say that my father had, soon after our arrival at Norton, been elected Member for the Radnor borough, succeeding his uncle Mr Price who had held that honourable position for forty-eight years and only resigned on account of old age. My father generously gave up his seat to Lord Hartington (Duke of Devonshire's eldest son, in politics like Papa, viz. Liberal), who had been turned out of his seat in the county of Lancashire. My father offered it to him, thinking he, being a leading man in the country and a staunch Liberal, would do more good for the Liberal cause than my father could. After canvassing the county for votes for Lord H. and nearly wearing himself out, Lord Hartington won the day by a majority of votes, having been opposed by a Tory gentleman. The worry and anxiety of the election added to the long drives and rides to the different voters in bitter weather, brought on asthma to my dear father. The Spring following the election, he suffered terribly from it and after trying many English places without success, the London doctors advised him to winter abroad as the only means of curing it. So after much talk and consultation, it was settled that we should all leave Norton in the Autumn and go to

Cheltenham, while my father and mother with my two sisters Milla and Edith should go to Cannes in the south of France till the Spring. It was sad work breaking the news to the dear old village people, and all our friends in the neighbourhood, especially to our clergyman and his family, of whom we were very fond. Worse than all was the thought of leaving the dear Manor with all our favourite nooks and haunts which we had indeed learnt to love. But everything comes to an end and that sad day of leaving Norton came to an end, after having lived there ten happy years . . .

[For the next four years the family divided its time between Cheltenham and Norton, her father's health gradually improving. Two sisters were married during this time.]

The summer of 1873 we gave up our house in Cheltenham and came home for good, and though we had made many friends in Cheltenham who seemed really sorry at our departure, yet our hearts were at Norton and we left but *very* few regrets behind us.

All through that summer and the following winter, all England was intent on the coming General Election which was to take place in the Spring, and Radnorshire especially was in a state of ferment and division. My father opposed the Conservative Member for the county, Hon. Mr Walsh. Mr Haig, a wine merchant and a man who professed himself to be a Liberal, having come forward first to oppose Mr Walsh, Papa could not stand idly by and see all his Liberal interests fall into the hands of such a man as Haig, who was in *no* way fit to represent the Liberals of Radnorshire in Parliament. He made everything as unpleasant as he could for my father, for instead of resigning in his (Papa's) favour as he should have done, he went up to the Poll and lost the Election by polling fifty-seven votes, which was the majority my father lost by. The excitement of that Election will *never* be forgotten in Radnorshire. The feeling of the people was entirely for my father and great disappointment was shown at the results of the Poll. I remember the day perfectly well, and how beautifully my father spoke, though he was beaten, and how *tremendously* he was cheered, then and when we drove home through the town afterwards. I believe I felt sorry for Mr Walsh.

We feared much for our darling's health, but he was quite wonderful and never suffered for a single day, not at the time nor after. Indeed, everyone said how well and how young he looked, and we could not but feel thankful, even though the Election had been lost.

Soon after this an event happened which took us all much by surprise. Mr Gladstone wrote in Queen Victoria's name to offer my father a Baronetcy, saying at the same time that no man deserved a reward more than he did, for his great good and untiring services in Radnorshire, and his continual interest *in* and great good *for* the Liberal party in Radnorshire. My father accepted it, not without much true heartfelt gratitude to Her Gracious Majesty for the great honour bestowed at her hand, and as he said many a time, he looked upon it, not as a good thing for *him* only, but as an honour which would descend to his son and son's son, and remain in the family for ever . . .

That was a memorable summer [1880] for me, for I met again an old friend, and before the three months were over, was engaged to be married to Mr Henry Hill Meredith. It all took place at the Oxford and Cambridge Match at Lords. He and Chase [her brother] had been college friends, both at Eton and Oxford and he had many times spent weeks at Norton, but a certain misunderstanding or rather uncertainty of mind on my part had made it difficult for him to renew his visits until the meeting again at 39 Cumberland Place, and the renewal of old friendship ended in my showing my love and having it returned. The news soon spread to Norton, and the congratulations were a curious mixture of joy and sorrow. When we returned there in the August of 1880, I could hardly believe myself that I was really to leave them all, and my dear, dear home, but I was very happy and Harry's love was so intense and been so *tried* that my fears for the future were few. Alice felt it more than all, but always showed a bright face and was extremely contented with my choice.

The remainder of the summer and autumn was spent by us very happily at Norton. Now that I was about to leave it, the dear home seemed each day to *get dearer*, and Alice and I felt the thought of parting more and more as the days sped on, autumn changing to winter, Christmas (my last at the organ in our village church) coming and going, and the New Year, 1881, beginning with its fearful cold and snow storms, memorable still, and the third of February 1881 bringing me my wedding day. It was a great day in Norton. We had a large party in the house, twenty-two to dinner the night before, and sixty at Breakfast on the third. Everything went off well. It was said to be the brightest wedding that had been at Norton and that was my *great* wish. I struggled hard all day to be bright myself, came down as usual in the morning, and breakfasted with all our party in the large Hall. All my sisters were there with the exception of Edith, who was too poorly to leave home, and that was a bitter disappointment to me, but Powlett Milbank came, and he and my other brothers-in-law helped greatly to keep everything going, and Alice and Fanny were wonderful. I had eight bridesmaids. Harry had three college friends who were much liked, and were very jolly. My dear brother Chase [who had been ordained] married me, and a cousin and our Vicar assisted. Everyone remarked on the youthful appearance of my brother! He read the service most impressively, and many were in tears. Our little church was crowded inside and out and many were the prayers and good wishes that followed me that day. I had a hundred and forty presents, and among them a pearl necklet, pendant and earrings presented by the Knighton and Prestyn people and tenants on the Norton Manor Estate. I wore them on my wedding day which pleased the people. My wedding dress was cream satin and cream fur, and considered very pretty. The Norton choir and Villagers presented me with an oxydized silver and gilt inkstand, candlesticks, and pen tray, a gift I love and prize more than all, for the very poorest gave their mite. We left for Rugby, there being thousands of people at Knighton to witness our departure, and my husband had to make a short speech thanking them all . . .

Nora Mabel Nye
the story of my life

Nora Nye (née Cardinal) wrote an unusual autobiography in that it describes descent in the social scale from an aristocratic family background to near subsistence farming in Australia. One of seven children, she was born in 1885 at Ardleigh Court, Tendering, Essex, where her interests appear to have been mainly horses and the hunting-field. But on her mother's early death and father's re-marriage the family virtually broke up, she and two other sisters being sent away to a convent school in Bruges, Belgium. Unlike the Green-Price family, her father seems to have pursued only his own interests with very little affection or concern for his children. Surprisingly from such a sheltered back-ground, Nora Nye later adapted remarkably well to living in a farm labourer's cottage and to the rough life of an emigrant to Australia in the 1920s. On her return to England in the thirties she and her husband farmed in Sussex; she died at Cuckfield in 1973. Her brother, Alan, became Governor of the Falkland Islands. The memoir is written in a naive, almost childish style, suggesting only meagre educational attainment. I am grateful to the author's granddaughter, Alison Nye, for permission to reproduce the greater part of the unpublished autobiography.

I was born on January 4th 1885 in a lovely home called Ardleigh Court – my Father renamed it Holly Court as it had a massive hedge up the tradesmen's entrance. When I was born my Mother had scarlet fever so there had to be two nurses, one for me and one for my Mother. My sister was very ill with it when she was only four years old. My father had me christened by Canon Perry. Time went on and all was very peaceful. The home was large and we had many servants. There was cook, kitchenmaid, housemaid, house parlour-maid, parlour-maid and butler, nanny, and under-maid in the nursery. I remember we had a lovely garden and many lawns. Two head gardeners, Bush and Jaggs. I remember to this day my love for horses grew as I became older. It hurt me so as I was never allowed to go near the large stables unless someone came with me. We had a lovely pony to ride but someone always had to come with you. Life went on very peacefully and our days were very full. In the winter it was three days a week hunting with the Essex and Suffolk or the East Essex hounds. My uncle who lived at Bromley Park was Master of Hounds, so our home was always full of hunting people. My Mother being a Londoner took no interest in any sport.

Father was a real country man. Hunting, shooting and fishing were his hobbies. I was four when Mother came into the nursery and told nannie my uncle had died. This meant that Father came into the large estate of Tendering. He became lord of the manor of the Tendering hundred. Many villages were included. Mother was very pleased as Father told her he would get a town house for us if she wished. So we had after a long time searching found one in Hove which was better known then as West Brighton. I was six then. So we had two homes going, of which half the year we spent in one and the other half in the other. During the summer we made the country our home, then during the winter months we lived in our town home. Mother loved the town and it was so easy for Mother and Father to get up to London to watch the opera which Mother so dearly loved. I and my three sisters Vera, Lilian, and Violet, all older than me were growing up. We had a governess called Miss Richards. I don't think she liked the country much but when we lived in Hove she came with us for walks along the Downs.

Everything was very peaceful still. The eldest of my three brothers was at Charterhouse School, while Dick the middle brother went to a preparatory school down the road and later went on to Winchester. Meanwhile Claude the youngest was in the schoolroom with us. Then on December 4th 1899 Mother died at the very early age of 46. The house was very quiet. Two trained nurses arrived a week before Mother died. While having tea in the schoolroom one of Father's sisters arrived. She had only been in the house a short time when she came to us and said if you wish to see your Mother for the last time come at once. It was a shock, none of us had any idea she was so bad. These days of 1972 she would have had an operation and been alive today, surgery has so advanced. It took some months to sort our lives out, anyway Father's sisters helped by suggesting we three girls be sent to a convent school in Belgium. A friend of theirs had sent their daughters to Ostend. Anyhow the shock came when he told us we were all three going to Bruges and Vera, the eldest, was to take Mother's place and help with the entertaining.

Our next step was to meet an Aunt at the Army and Navy stores, London, to fit us all three in the convent dress (black). After that, which was three months after Mother died, we sailed from Dover to Ostend. Lilian and Violet were very sick. On arrival we were met by two nuns who could hardly speak English, they marched us up the cobbled streets to what looked like a prison. The great doors closed behind us and we seemed to be in another world. We were taken to the refectory where a hundred girls were sitting for an afternoon meal. They all stood up and said something we did not understand. We were then shown our sleeping quarters. There were ten curtained beds in our dormitory. Oh, how different from home. We had to get up on the bell the next day and march to church. We didn't understand a thing. We were all three very homesick.

After a time we liked the quite peaceful life; at this impressionable age we all three wanted to become nuns and catholics. When my Father got to hear about us wanting to change our religion he was furious. He wrote and told us he would take us away if we had such silly thoughts. Anyhow, three years went by and Lilian went home as she was just on twenty-one and was home for nearly three months. One early morning Sister Jane our dormitory Sister came to Violet's and mine bed and said, 'Get dressed quickly as your sister Lilian has arrived and wishes to become a nun.' So we went at 6.30 a.m. and met Lilian. She said she couldn't stay at home, her home she said was the convent. Next day my eldest brother arrived to take Violet and self home. Lilian said she was stopping. We caught the boat from Ostend feeling very unhappy leaving our convent after four years there. We got back to be greeted by Father and my eldest sister who were very pleased to see us, and so was our old butler, all he could say was you ought never have gone. After several weeks we settled down. Each had a dog so we had wonderful walks with them. Father used to go each day to town, but one day he came home with a nasty cough. He told us when he got into the train at Victoria he was late and just managed to get the last carriage in which sat an old lady who looked surprised, Father gave her his card. All went well, but the same thing occurred the next day, and it was raining and very foggy. She asked him if he was being met. He said no I never have the horses out on a dirty night, so she said would you care to share mine, dropping me first at the hotel Metropole; he accepted. Telling us at dinner that night my brother at once said to Father, 'Look out, she's after you.' Father was furious. Anyway to make my life story short it was his undoing. The house was upset. Vail our old butler gave notice. He said he would not take orders from her. He could see what she was. In the end we had nearly all new servants.

For a time we had a German butler who Father couldn't stand. It ended after a real row – the German was dismissed. Vail came back on condition Miss Vera could take over the downstairs staff. Things were more peaceful. My sister Violet who was Mother's favourite could not get on with her stepmother. One day coming in from a walk there were two men and my stepmother in the drawing room valuing the lovely ornaments (cut glass), especially the Crown Derby tea set. My sister strode up to the men and said 'You put those back, they were my Mother's, and have been in our family for years; my stepmother cannot sell them.' They were put back but Father again was cross, and told my stepmother all these valuables are to be untouched. The next upheaval was when my stepmother and Father went to stay at Luton. Violet got her chance, she took me to the post office and drew all her money, about sixty pounds. She then said, 'Here is a pound for you, I'm off tomorrow morning to Dover and then the convent'; she gave me her little dog. When Father came home he was furious and said he would leave her there for a week and then send someone for her. The week passed and Vera and friend went and saw both Lilian and Violet. Lilian was then a Novice, she said she wanted to come home but the Nuns would not let her, Violet wished to remain. The next evening the only way Lilian could escape as the doors were barred, she went into the music room and got out of the window where Vera and her friend were waiting. They put a shawl on her head and took her to the Hotel. Home next day.

The next day Lilian had to go to a hairdresser as the Nuns had cut her hair very badly. It did not take long before she settled down. Then came trying to get Violet home but she refused. She could not stand my stepmother in mother's place. She wished to remain so Father just left her there. My stepmother had a house left her at Maidenhead called Bridge House, which had previously belonged to my stepsister. Every comfort was in the house, but something was lacking. I and my sisters had four dogs which loved the garden. I loved the river and always looked for our row on the river, or rather to punt across to Cliveden, the Astor's place or Lord Desborough's place. It was such fun as they were young like us. Many times my brother, who was a Naval cadet used to come with me down to Bray.

Father by this time was very ill and so thin, my sister Lily and I decided to relieve the tension in the house (a feeling my stepmother did not want us) by going with our dogs to stay as P.G.'s with friends at Sandgate, nr Folkestone. We were with these good people for four months, then as winter was drawing near we looked for rooms near Tonbridge so we could be nearer hounds. We stayed there until the spring, having had one or two days with the Cornwallis hounds. Spring had come early so we decided to try and get either a caravan or a workman's cottage. We and a friend tossed a penny and heads came down for a cottage. So off we went – one in one direction and one in the other. I found a semi-detached cottage in Sevenoaks Weald, just one room, a scullery and two bedrooms. We took the cottage for three shillings a week. For a few shillings we bought two camp beds, two chairs, a little table, an oil stove, a lamp. Neither could cook. Vera my elder sister did that, I looked after the chickens and ducks. We bought a donkey and trap which I used to go round getting broody hens to use for hatching ducklings. Lilian my other sister got a good job teaching, she had to cycle each day about nine miles each way. It helped us for rent, etc.

My Father died before he had signed his will so my stepmother took all. We were too ignorant to discuss our plight. After a time my two cousins, both grown up, brought us a signed document which left us a bit (the signature was like Father's?). Anyhow we were able to carry on. Before we left our Brighton home I had met a young man in the hunting field, he became more than a friend. He came at Father's invitation to dinner. Father seemed to think he was serious and so was I. Father then told me he was not to come again, as it was no use as he would never give his consent to our marriage. Only because he had not had a college education, only a local one, he was an only son of a well known solicitor. Well, time went on and Father died in 1910, and as I have told you, we were in our cottage. Charles, my husband, now came to Lingfield where I met him. We spent some very happy times.

In 1912 we married in Sevenoaks Weald Church. The village turned out. My brother who was home for a time came and gave me away. We had a carriage with two white horses, everyone else had cars. I wore my great-grandmother's lovely veil. I also had a long white dress, and long white doe-skin gloves. After the ceremony we had a wedding buffet in the village hall. My dear old nannie was there, she dressed me for my going away clothes, and packed my wedding gear . . .

Things went smoothly until I discovered I was going to have a baby in the June. This baby came one year after my wedding, a wee thing. I had a private nurse who stayed with me for five weeks. After that all went well, I had many friends. We only had that house for three years and it was sold. Sir John Suscombe bought it so we hunted for a farm and found a sweet little place with thirty acres. It was at Tinsley, quite near now to Gatwick airport. We were very happy there, it was during the First World War by now and I had three sons. Charles went up to Redhill to go under a test for the Army and he was turned down as he had lung trouble so he was given a badge to wear to show he had offered his services.

I think he was pleased as we had only just started our little farm. We had only been there four years when our landlord Sir Francis Montefiore came to see us and told us he was selling all his small farms. He said he wanted £2,000 for ours. Of course we had not got that money so it meant another move. This move took us to a lovely farm and a huge house in a lovely place near Cuckfield. But like young fools we only rented it: however, we did have first refusal if the owner died. Well, we heard she had died and so applied to her agent who told us a Mr Worsley had bought it. We ought to have had her written word that we would get first refusal.

This meant yet another move, so we decided to buy and got a 30 acre farm at Danehill. My three sons were growing up and had a governess, the schools were several miles away. We sent them daily to Haywards Heath. This went on for a little while, when a friend suggested that we should emigrate to Australia. So we went up to Australia House and got all the papers etc. When we got home everybody thought it was a good idea so we sold up. Emigrating to Victoria, Australia, we sailed on the Hobsons Bay from the homeland and, after a nice trip, we arrived at Melbourne. Charles left us as he had to go to the Commonwealth office for our tickets to where we had to go. After this we caught a train to Sara, where we were met by a funny old man and a bus. Getting out of the train a porter and the station master were in a fit of laughter. It appears Charles had his bowler hat on and of course they don't wear things like that, only we had nowhere to pack it.

We were driven to a place called the Elcho Training Centre. It was a hill with many wooden bungalows dotted about. One was ours – it had two bedrooms, sitting room and a scullery. The table was laid for our meal. A Mrs — met and welcomed us saying if there was anything we wanted to come over to the house (not very far away) and she would come and see what was wanted. It was a strange feeling living on the side of a hill, we had a lovely view on to open fields. The air was lovely, warm and sunny, we got to know several people like ourselves waiting to be given land. Gelong was our nearest township, up along a straight dusty road, I only went once. At last after three months my husband with others was asked to go with the head man to view our 90 acres they called a 'block', a wooden rectangle was put up on this land and we just had a flat piece of land and a house that looked most depressing. Anyway we went up with the little furniture we had bought in Melbourne and after a time it felt like home. My husband and the boys put up wire fencing and I sorted out a piece of garden. As there was irrigation it would be easy to water any plants I had laid out in the garden. So I sent away for some plants and so did my eldest son, Ken, who also bought me a spade. No end of plants and shrubs I grew from seed, most were various. They grew to 6 feet in no time, in fact after three years I had a very pretty garden. I had to leave home in June as I was expecting my fourth child. I was taken to Shepperton June 15th and put into a dreadful place, and was told it was where expectant mothers waited.

Finding I could not sleep I only stayed there one night. It was then I remembered a lady on our ship coming out saying that she was going to live in Shepperton and to be sure to come and see her. So I put my things on and went round to her. She said 'You must not stay there', and so allowed me to stay with her. So I did and was there until 21st June. It was then that I went into hospital where my daughter was born on June 23rd. I had rather a bad time at her birth as I was in my forties and it was ten years between my last son. Anyhow I was so pleased to have a little daughter . . .

Albert Goodwin
autobiography

Although written in 1961, Albert Goodwin's autobiography has a typically Victorian flavour. He was born in 1890 at Caverswell, Stoke, in the Potteries, where his father worked on sanitary ware. The memoir is unusual in giving so much space to his parents' and grandparents' lives, from which it appears that social conditions in the Potteries had not greatly advanced since those of the early nineteenth century described by Charles Shaw in 'When I Was a Child' (1903). Goodwin had no great love for his parents ('the most obnoxious people I had ever seen') but appreciated that they were responding to the harshness of the times. His memoir is valuable for its portrayal of working conditions and for Goodwin's account of his parents' marriage and his own birth, presumably second-hand. In later life he became a keen trade unionist and was appointed Assistant Secretary of the National Society of Pottery Workers in 1947.

The unpublished memoir was kindly brought to my notice by Gladys Harris, a former Oxford Extra-Mural Tutor in north Staffordshire, one of whose classes Albert Goodwin attended and was encouraged to write his autobiography.

LIFE OF 'A POTTER'
Foreword

If, in reading this epic(?) of mine you are expecting to get some idea of how good it was to be alive, of junketings in pleasant places and a story of 'love' and 'happy ever after' please put down the book for this is just a record of the life over 70 years of a very ordinary mortal. Many times has he appeared in a Courtroom, been handed a Bible to hold in his Right Hand, and a Card in his Left from which he had to repeat 'I swear I will tell the Truth, the whole Truth and nothing but the Truth' and this I propose to do in all that follows. In many instances, I could use names, but as they have descendants still living, I do not care to cause them pain by taking away their many kind thoughts of their ancestors. I may appear a little bitter at times so I hope my readers will forgive me as my sole object is to place before them what happened to very ordinary mortals in the 'good old days'.

ALBERT GOODWIN

Introduction and background

At the age of 71 memories of one's early days seem to become more vivid and the ability to recall the years that have passed can be done with a certain amount of ease, and it seems to me that though my life has been tough, with some smooth patches, on the whole I have been allowed to live in years of great change, both good and bad.

I was born in the Parish of Caverswell which is on the S.E. perimeter of the City of Stoke. At the time of my Birth in 1890 the six Towns of the Potteries were each a separate entity, and Caverswell Parish, or the part in which I arrived in this world, to wit East Vale was administered from Longton by the Town Council. The other five of the Six Towns were North to South Tunstall, Burslem, Hanley, Stoke and Fenton.

I was the 2nd child of my working-class parents, Benjamin and Caroline Goodwin (nee Cartridge) whose 1st child a Boy had died at the age of 4 months.

Looking back it would not be true to record that I realized my parents were two of the finest people who walked the earth. On the contrary, I was of the firm opinion that they were the most obnoxious people I had ever seen and to expect any kind treatment from them was to expect the moon to fall out of the sky. But I have since realized, and very emphatically too, that they were trying to fit me to be able to live in a world that was harsh and hard to the children of the poorer classes.

My Father was the eldest legitimate son of his family, he being born 25 minutes before his Brother and therefore a twin. His Brothers and Sisters were fairly numerous, as families were at that period being seven. John, Polly, Sarah Ann, David, Millicent and Hannah. William, born out of Wedlock, was senior to my Father. Six other children had died. My fraternal Grandmother was a confirmed Drunkard and the family home in a terrace off Upper Hill St, Longton was a very squalid place. Built on a hill, with 2 Water Taps to 14 houses, two privies to the same, and very little backyard as there was only the passage at the rear of the premises to provide entrance, the conditions pertaining can be quickly imagined. There were also 2 ash middens to 7 houses each. These hovels have now been demolished. Within 80 square yards of these houses there were 8 Beer of Public Houses and 2 Off Licences so it will be very easy to appreciate that my Grandmother had ample opportunity of indulging in her favourite recreation. Incidentally these 'Pubs' were open from 6 a.m. until 11 p.m. I daresay some research would show that some of them closed down when my Grandmother died. Her biggest problem at that period was money, and she would resort to any method to obtain the same, and I shall give an example of this a little later. When I can recall that even at the age of 3 yrs, when my Father wanted to take me to see his Mother, who was on her deathbed (I didn't realize this but was told later) I objected to going because I was afraid of her and she didn't 'smell nice'. Mother told me of this in later years. My fraternal Grandfather had died before I was born from Asthma, or his Certificate said. And what of my Maternal Grandparents. I never knew either of them. My Mother was the only child of her Father's second marriage, he having three children by his 1st Wife, Mary, Eliza and Tom. The latter was bedridden at the age of 28 and being married with 2 sons had to trust to his wife's earnings as a Decorating 'Missis'. It was said that she owed her advance to a good position because she had a great friend in the Decorating Manager, but there was no doubt that even if people put the worst construction on this friendship this Aunt of mine did a wonderful job for which her children's success in after life more than repaid her for any sacrifice she had made.

Information gleaned from my Mother and our neighbours in East Vale points to the fact that my Maternal Grandfather must have been a somewhat remarkable man. He was a 'Looker to Ware' (Pottery) who suffered from Diabetes and severe Chest Trouble. To alleviate the breathing trouble he grew a beard, as it was accepted at that time that this was a way of guarding the chest and throat and so make it easier to draw breath. Whether this is so I have no means of knowing. He had been a good scholar and although he had left school at the age of nine had got hold of all sorts of literature and was a great reader. Mother told me of his Sunday afternoons spent on the step in his backyard where a lot of his fellows who could neither read nor write would sit around and listen to my Grandfather reading the Sunday Paper (it was called Lloyds News I believe) and explaining to them what was meant in his opinion. He was also a great Chapel-goer, and at times took round the collection plate at the Primitive Methodist Chapel in the near vicinity. When he attended Chapel he wore a frockcoat and Top Hat and Mother often told me 'how proud she felt walking along with him to Chapel on Sunday morning'. Her words to me were 'Albert, I thought how jealous the other girls must be of me having such a grand papa.' He died at the age of 43 from Diabetes and as his wife had died 4 years earlier my Mother went to live with her Mother's Spinster Sister at the age of seven. Her Half-Brother and Sister were married.

My Father left school at the age of 11 and became employed as a mouldrunner (maker's assistant) at Chapmans Pottery Factory. Wages for 55½ hrs was 2s. 6d. per week and if he carried out his duties satisfactorily, nay perfectly, he got 2d. for himself. Any excuse was sufficient to have the 2d., or part of, deducted.

When he was 14 he was 'put down' as an Apprentice Presser and served seven years at this trade. Immediately he became 21 and 'out of his time' he was dismissed as he would have had to be paid Journeyman Rate. At this period this was common practise and it is only over recent years that it has been abolished through Trade Union activity. This was in 1884 and after a week or two of Unemployment he got a job at his trade at another factory. After 3 years he was asked to take over the management of the Clay Dept and on the strength of this he married. But at the end of 6 months the employers asked my Father to cut the prices of almost the whole of the operatives and this he refused to do. He was asked to resign but would not do so and therefore the employers gave him a fortnights salary in lieu of notice. As a married man whose wife was pregnant with her first child one can readily appreciate how much courage he had to have to take up such a stand. Sanitary Fireclay had been improving over the years, and with the advent of heavy clay workers brought into the district from Scotland there was a 'boom' in these types of sanitary appliances. The rapid expansion necessitated the recruitment of more workers and my Father was fortunate to obtain a job in this comparatively new side of the Pottery Industry. Despite the heavy nature of the work my Father stuck to it and was eventually recognized as a good man at his job. One can understand that this was a terrific change for him. To tackle the making of these heavy and rather (at that time) crude articles after years of handling the most delicate china was indeed a very radical change. He was given a job in the Urinal Top Dept and from accounts given to me in later life he must have become a first class craftsman . . .

I suppose that now my Father was a member of the highly paid working class he and my Mother thought they could afford to start a family, which they proceeded to do and hence the entry into this world of another poor mortal, with additions at fairly regular intervals. It is essential for me to point out that the necessity for more improved sanitary appliances of every sort, and the tardy realization that it was important there should be a raising of the standards in matters of hygiene meant that those workers who were fortunate enough to be working in this side of the Industry were fully employed. Yes, if you had been lucky to get in on the ground floor at this time you could now earn enough to make you feel you could 'lash' out a bit, improve your home and even, if you were of a very saving nature, have a holiday at some salubrious seaside resort. Of course, one had to find something to do in one's spare time, because the hours at the Factory were only 7 a.m. to 6 p.m. with ½ hr for breakfast and 1 hr for dinner and 7 a.m. till 1 p.m. on Sat. As we lived 4 miles from the Factory this necessitated my Father catching a train at 6.23 a.m. and one back at 6.31 p.m., these being between Longton and Stoke with a mile walk at each end. The fare was 1s. for a Weekly Ticket equal to a ½d. per mile. After 2 miles you were glad to walk as the seats were not too well cushioned. My Father, thinking he had some spare time, took on a Part Time Assurance Book with the Royal Oak Society (which later was merged with the Liverpool Victoria Legal Friendly Society) and he was also a Collector of Dispensary for a local Doctor: he now had money coming in from 3 sources. He was also Hon Sec for the Pleasant Sunday Afternoon at the

Congregational Church in Caroline St, Longton, and Sick Visitor for the North Stafford Provident Society (still in existence and colloquially called the Old Church Club) for whom he visited claimants to Sick Benefit at night after the hour (7 p.m.) when they had to be at home or if caught not present their Benefit was stopped. My Father really enjoyed this because he would while collecting his various dues on Saturday afternoon call where the sick person lived and remind them that he hoped to see them when he called at so and so time on a certain date. The fee for visiting was 6d. per visit and he had to go up to two miles for some of them and walk all the way. Where did I get all this information from you may well ask, and my reply will be that my Mother and Father loved to impress me with what they had had to do for me, especially if I had worn my shoe fronts out with various forms of playing such as kicking an empty tin along the street or playing marbles on my hands and knees. Both my parents were good at reminiscing, Father being particularly good in a boastful manner as shewing how clever he had been and what brains could do for people.

What of my Mother? As I have recorded, she was taken over by her Aunt, a dressmaker, for whom she had nothing but praise, and often in later life she said to me 'Albert, she was too good for this world'. Mother's Aunt had a Bradbury sewing machine and this gave her a very high status as a dressmaker. But when Mother offered to give any assistance she thought she could her Aunt would be continually telling her 'No, you must be a child as long as you can and get what pleasure you can out of life, for you may have some hard times to face.' A woman of thought! Mother left school when she was twelve and got a situation as servant with some people named Bridgwood who kept a shop on the corner of Ford St and Hope St, East Vale. Mother, who died at the age of 73 always expressed the opinion that the good food she received while in service had fitted her to withstand the storms and stresses of later life, which to say the least sometimes required great courage and endurance. She also realized that the teaching she got in making cheap and nourishing meals was of the highest value when in the nature of things she had to provide for a young and growing family. She received 1s.6d. per week in money, slept at her own home, had Breakfast, Dinner, Tea and Supper found for her, but with the money she had to provide herself with everything for the job, her Aunt looking after what I suppose it would be correct to call her Civilian clothing. Her hours were 7 days per week from 7.30 a.m. to 9.30 p.m. except Wednesday when she had from 6 p.m. to 9.30 p.m. completely free, but that night was Choir Practise Night at the Congregational Chapel.

Courtship of my parents

As I have previously recorded, my Parents prior to marriage were members of a Chapel and were also Choristers. Mother must have been a fairly good singer because if there were any Soprano Solos to be given then on the Bills of the special services went the name Caroline Cartridge, Soloist. Mother was very fond of telling how she finally captured my Father. He was walking out with another young lady chorister fairly steadily, but she had the misfortune to catch a cold and Father I suppose, wishing to keep his hand in, took my Mother home from Choir Practise. On the following Sunday the Chorister having recovered taxed my Mother with the great sin of moving in to negotiate a merger, I would suggest, but Caroline poohpoohed the idea that she had any designs on this poor specimen of humanity concluding with the words 'I don't want your Benny, I wouldn't have him as a gift!' Six months later Mother and Father were married and went to live with Mother's Aunt. In this consummation the Bridgwood family were unconscious connivers. On Sunday when they went to the Congregational Church my Mother went with them at night. She returned to her job afterwards but as the Bridgwoods were 'big' people at the Chapel they had to discuss with other high-ups various things such as finance, amount of collection, trend of sermon etc., and so this gave my Mother and Father a chance to have a few words.

When my Father was sure that he was going to marry my Mother he at once began to organize his life to that end. He bought a new suit and kept it at Mother's Aunt's so that he could go down early on Sundays and change from his working clothes, go to the Chapel looking a little respectable and do credit to the woman who was to be his wife. He had previously done the same thing by going to a male friend's house and changing there for which he had to walk a distance of 1½ miles. The reason for this was that if he took anything home on which a few shillings could be obtained his Mother would have pawned them, sold the ticket and had a most glorious orgy of drinking. It had happened so many times before and as there were 5 pawnshops within easy reach of Upper Hill St one can imagine how easy it was for his Mother to get the needed money. The expression used by my father's family of 'I've got what I stand up in' was simply the truth and nothing but.

The wedding

It will be realized that this was not reported in the Press, for although it must have been a great day for my Parents it was of little interest to the World outside. There was no rehearsal as is the pattern in some cases today.

To purchase a ring, pay the fee, Father have his boots soled and heeled (the reason for this will appear) was a big drain on the Exchequer and as this was in a poor state not a lot was left on which the couple had to live the next week. Of course my Father might have had more had he refused to listen to the appeals of his younger brothers and sisters whom he had kept as decently as he possibly could, thereby giving him little chance to save. He was still a China Presser and had not moved up at this time into the moneyed (Sanitary Presser) class. That was later as recorded. Mother had been fitted out by her Aunt so that she was in the clear. No guests were expected as none had been invited. No best man, no bridesmaids because as they were to be married at Caverswell Church they had to walk 3 miles each way. Yes walk! Sunday morning 7.30 saw the start as they had to be at the Church for 9 a.m. When they got to the Church witnesses had to be found and my Father prevailed upon the Verger to be one. Mother went round the village, got a woman as the other witness 'if she could come along when she had washed her face and combed her hair'. Eventually the wedding took place and the return home began. Mother had got her 'Benny'. One reads of Champagne by the bucketful, caviare by the ton appearing at weddings but these delicacies were all missing from my Parents wedding breakfast. The truth is that the meal consisted of 3 pairs of kippers which my Mother's Aunt had procured cheaply on the Saturday just before they closed. One year later and just before the birth of their first child, named Percy, my Mother's Aunt died. As a house two doors away had become vacant my Parents decided to take up their residence there as they would have their own tap, own sink (made of sandstone) and own privy, instead of sharing with 5 others. Also there was no gap between the house and the back kitchen which during inclement weather was a great advantage . . .

Birth

Eight months after the death of my Brother Percy I was born on April 19 1890 at 2.30 a.m. and from what I learned later, weighted 7lb 4oz. Arrangements made before birth were very involved as at this period midwives for the poorer classes were conspicuous by their absence and here was where the woman from the shop next door was the person of importance. She had attended my Mother over her first child and had been 'spoken to' by my Father as to my entry. He had notified the Doctor of the approximate time of my arrival so that should he be needed he could be there as soon as possible, circumstances warranting the same. A young man nearby had also been asked to be ready at any time to fetch the Doctor, if needed, because he was a good runner. Telephones were not so prevalent as today and 'shanks pony' always had to be used. What qualification had the 'nurse' as she was always called, to take charge of a confinement? None! except that she had had four children herself, was a motherly person, and had by reason of attending so many confinements with various Doctors got a reputation for successful deliveries. She also found any money she was paid for her services very useful in bringing up her own growing family. Her charges were 10s. for the first child and 6s. 6d. for any others. But I must tell of the numerous times she did not charge anything or very little because the people were too poor to be able to pay. Others would pay on the Hire Purchase system of so much down and so much per week. It was also very often the case that she had to take with her things discarded by other people to those she had to attend because of the parlous conditions into which the new arrival was to enter. She was continually on the 'beg' and was a woman who gave selfless service to humanity. If there is a judgment day I know where I shall find Nurse Lewis. Her ante-natal attendances were strictly adhered to, and from her visits to my home to deliver various brothers and sisters I know that her great standby's were neatsfoot and goose oil to be rubbed in back and front and so help the prospective mother. Whether it did so or not I have no knowledge but the method was 'sworn by' at the particular time of which I write. Another ritual was for the pregnant woman to go about her household duties as usual but at every opportunity she *must* when sitting down put her feet up on another chair and so relieve the weight on the abdomen.

A strong wooden box, which had usually contained 'Hudson Soap' or tins of salmon had to be procured and put on one side so that it could be placed against the bottom bedrail and be a purchase for the woman to press her feet against at the time of the delivery. The bedsteads were made of steel and brass, garnished in black and gold paint with feather bed and pillows; straw mattresses were more a matter of chance than the rule. Nurse Lewis could adapt herself to any conditions and I must record we had the proper articles to ensure my safe arrival. A bath tin holding 2 gals of water was also a most important item at these times and it was the nurse's job to borrow this from people who possessed one to use at a case where it was non-existent. What sort of a uniform did Nurse Lewis wear? To be candid none! But for the ante-natal period she wore a black apron and for the delivery she wore a white one. In later years this was the sign to all and sundry (including myself) that there would be an increase in the family. Oh! Yes! she carried a little black bag, but that contained the baby or so we thought. And the preparation for the birth included the getting down of the bed from upstairs and re-erection in the 'parlour'. Preparation for a fire in the parlour grate must be made and plenty of candles (4d. per dozen) must be got in so that there could be all the light necessary. The fire in the kitchen must be banked up for the night so that if the accouchment took place at an awkward time there would be plenty of hot water at a few minutes' notice. This fire was the only means of heating and therefore a big iron kettle, if you had one (we had) placed on the hob of the grate ready to pop on the fire at a moment's notice. If you did not have a kettle, yes, you borrowed one. All these things had to be done in the hope that the delivery would be normal and straightforward because if the Doctor had to be called a bill would be presented and as it was a matter of a guinea, it became a matter of economic necessity to try and avoid this. My entry was a normal one except that I was told later I cried for 17 hrs non-stop and drove everybody up the wall . . .

And so I arrived, and was very likely thought of by my parents as the eighth wonder and the infant who was going to raise their prestige to the heights. What a shock they must have had in later years!

It was usual for the Mother to remain in bed for 10 days or a fortnight after the birth, and she was very careful not to meet anyone for 3 weeks until she had been 'churched'. Even the rentman or any other callers who had not been invited into the house had to be avoided. This was rigidly carried out and anyone who overstepped the bounds was a subject of scandalous gossip among the neighbours. The baby could be shown and praised (especially when the Father was around and there was something to 'wet the baby's head') but the mother had to suffer the pangs of isolation. Why! I really don't know.

My Mother was always looked after in re food as neighbours would slip in bringing various little dainties, a lot of which my Father had to eat. Whether the neighbours came out of kindness or curiosity I wouldn't like to say, but it is definitely true it was not the beauty of the child which attracted them . . .

Kate Taylor

Kate Taylor's memoir, of which this extract is almost the whole, tells nearly all about her, and all we need to know. Born in Pakenham, Suffolk, in 1891, the fourteenth of fifteen children of an agricultural labourer, she had a hard childhood which only seems to have strengthened her resolve never to submit to injustice. She grew up an intelligent, strong-willed 'rebel', deeply loving her family but hating her 'betters' who still exercised an almost feudal sway over village life. She left school at thirteen to become a farm-servant, later to work as a maid and cook in many different households. She married a farm labourer in 1924 when she was thirty-two and he thirty-eight, telling her employer, 'Love is for the young. Harry and I are no longer young, but we understand each other and we know what we want.' She continued to do domestic work while having a family, and only finished work at the age of seventy-nine. 'When I finally gave up charring the price had gradually risen from fourpence to five shillings an hour.' She wrote her unpublished memoir at the age of eighty-two.

I was born at Pakenham in November 1891, being the 14th member of a family of 15. My parents were both middle-aged at the time, therefore I know only what I have been told of their young life and conditions and also that of my elder sisters and brothers.

My grannies were both very old when I first knew them; both grandfathers were dead.

My father, Harry Bales, was born at Pakenham. My mother, Naomi Miller, was also born at Pakenham. My father died in August 1918 at the age of 70, which means he was born in 1848. My mother was born in the same year and they were married shortly after my mother's 21st birthday which makes it 1869.

My sisters, Alice, Jane, Lizzie, Sarah and Annie, and my brother, George, were married and away from home before my birth. Lizzie and George had children of their own before I was born. Alice hadn't any; her husband was employed by the Bury St Edmunds Water Works. To make life a trifle easier for Mother after I was born, Alice took Edith, then under five years old, to live with her.

I understand my father was brought up a strict Plymouth Brethren. The nearest meeting house was at Woolpit; his parents walked there each Sunday. He had one brother and two sisters and as they grew old enough they, too, had to walk to Woolpit and back.

At the time of my parents' marriage my father could neither read nor write. After his marriage he attended night school, paying one penny per night. As his wage was only 9s. per week, even pennies counted, so he was able to attend three nights a week only, but even that taught him to read and write sufficiently to help himself to learn more and gain the knowledge he was anxious to acquire.

Mother's father died quite young, leaving a widow with nine young children to support, of which my mother was the 8th. The 9th, and youngest, was a boy named Harry who at 18 years of age emigrated to Australia and was never again heard of. Grannie Miller supported her family by taking in washing and needlework for the families in the big houses in the parish, particularly the Vicarage where there was a large family of daughters and four maidservants. The young ladies of the time wore many petticoats, chemises, drawers, nightgowns, all made of fine linen or calico much betrimmed with tucking and fine lace. This work Grannie Miller excelled at, but one can't help wondering how, with only a small oil lamp for night work and her hands roughened by so much washing and ironing with no washing aids but yellow soap and soda.

Grannie Bales was left a widow much later in life. Her family were all married and she herself bedridden with bad legs and so she became chargeable to the parish. When I was about three weeks old my parents moved from Pakenham to the Mill Cottage on the outskirts of Ixworth.

I understand that when my sister Alice was a baby (my mother's first baby), Lady Greene of Nether Hall also had her first baby. Being unable to feed her baby, my mother was engaged as wet nurse and walked to Nether Hall three times a day to breast-feed Lady Greene's baby. She received a meal each time, and this she did for three months by which time the baby was sufficiently developed to be hand-fed by the nurse.

My earliest memory of Annie is of Mother being called for to go to London when Annie's baby was due. Her husband was serving in South Africa with the Royal Artillery, where he remained for four years, during which time his son lived for two years only. Bert never saw his first-born son.

My first memory of Rose was of a very pretty, curly fair-haired girl home for a short holiday to prepare for her wedding. She brought with her a form for my father to sign giving his consent to the marriage, and a letter from the bridegroom-to-be, also an artillery man and brother to Annie's husband. In the letter to father he mentioned that their love was mutual, a word I had never heard before. I took the earliest opportunity of asking Rose the meaning of the word 'mutual', and her face lit up as she told me 'It means Tom loves me as much as I love him.' I have every reason to believe that proved a very happy marriage.

Father was not a regular farm labourer – more a seasonal worker. He worked as a timber feller, a bark peeler, a faggot maker, a hurdle maker and a sheep shearer all in their season. At odd times he would act as a drover for a farmer. He would help with the corn threshing and also during the shooting season, but he always worked on a farm for the hay harvest and the grain harvest. On one occasion, when I carried his purses to the harvest field, I found him lying under the hedge, unable to speak and almost unable to breathe. A wasp had stung his tongue. The wasp was in his tea and he didn't see it and didn't know till it stung him. I helped him home, and Mother bathed his tongue with vinegar and water for about two hours when the swelling gradually subsided. On another occasion

I remember him being brought home in a tumbril with a badly cut leg. His axe had slipped as he was at work on a tree. District nurses or casualty wards were an unheard-of luxury, and being a pauper the local doctor couldn't be bothered with him. Mother washed, dressed and bandaged the cut, at which she was very able. Village folk, all being equally poor, tended to help each other. Mother was midwife to a number of other wives, helping too in illnesses, so with the exigencies of her own large family and helping others she was very well up in first aid.

Father was unable to work for several weeks. Then indeed life was rough and we had good cause to be grateful to the daughters in domestic service who each sent home the greater part of their small wage.

When we moved to the Mill Cottage Ethel continued attending Pakenham School as she was day girl at a farmhouse. It was a two mile walk to the farm from Mill Cottage, and Ethel left home at 6 a.m. to start work at 6.30. After doing housework and helping with the dairy work, she delivered milk, in cans, eggs, butter, cream, and sometimes prepared chickens in baskets on her arms, to at least six of the big houses in the parish, taking back the cans she delivered the previous day. Her breakfast was on the table on her return – a cup of cold tea, and two slices of bread from which the butter had been scraped not spread on – but after about four hours' work, mostly out in the fresh air, a hungry, growing girl can eat anything. Owing to this work Ethel was excused an hour's schooling, reaching school at 10 a.m. instead of 9.00. Exactly the same conditions applied to me when I was old enough to do the work after Ethel had left school and taken a full-time general servant's job. The day girl's wage was 9d. per week. On a Saturday, after the milk delivery, there was the dairy, the kitchen and the larder to be scrubbed, and the dining room to be turned out and thoroughly cleaned. Ninepence per week didn't pay for the amount of shoe leather we wore out as the roads then were rough, muddy and stony, and we frequently had our feet bound in rags which would flap in the mud.

The Mill Cottages were really four cottages under one roof. Each cottage had a living room and two bedrooms with one backhouse between two cottages. This backhouse contained one large washing copper, and a large brick oven. The women took turns in using both the copper and the oven. Father cut bush faggots each winter specially for heating the oven. After each harvest we went gleaning often in the fields from 8 a.m. till 8 p.m. We always hoped to glean sufficient wheat for bread for the winter. At the end of the gleaning season Father would thresh the corn with a flail and then take it to the mill to be ground into flour. We, the children, would go gathering acorns for the miller's pigs to pay for the grinding. In the spring and autumn when the grain was newly-drilled we would go stone-picking, sixpence a tumbril load. On Sundays we would go rook-scaring from 6 a.m. till dusk for twopence. Father made us a clapper – that is, three slabs of board, the centre piece having a handle and the two outer pieces attached to it with string through two holes. This made a real clattering noise when shaken vigorously.

After we moved to Mill Cottage Father joined the Ixworth Salvation Army and soon became a bandsman. I thought him very handsome in his uniform, but unfortunately often he would bring the bandsmen home with him to Sunday dinner. We were shut out in the backhouse whilst the bandsmen enjoyed the meal Mother had prepared for us. The bandsmen would practise most of the afternoon in preparation for the evening service. After they had gone we would scavenge for any crumbs they may have left from dinner.

Father was foolish in his generosity, but his fellow bandsmen knew he had a family. They also knew our poverty-stricken condition. They were selfish and thoughtless in taking the dinner we needed.

When I was about seven we moved back to Pakenham Street and that was the end of the Salvation Army. We children were sent to church and church Sunday School. It was after we moved back to Pakenham that I really got to know my sister, Nelly. New clothes for us were an unheard-of luxury. Mother mentioned Nelly had had a new dress made and I was so anxious to see this new dress that I walked to meet her when it was her Sunday afternoon to come home. She was allowed home one Sunday in four. It was a grey dress trimmed with black baby velvet, such a trim little figure. After a few years Nelly left the farm and went to another village to the vicarage. She wasn't able to visit home very often – it was too far away. Her wage was three shillings a week, paid monthly. However, on one occasion when she came home it was wonderful. She brought home a swiss roll that the cook had been specially told to make for Nelly to bring to us. It was the first we had ever seen, and no other has ever been as good since . . .

I remember the period when my father was a political agent; it was then I really learned to write. Father wrote beautifully, but very very slowly. I could write fairly quickly and clearly, so when he had reports or speeches to write he would dictate them to me to write out for him. Likewise, when he was made ganger of the sheep-shearing gang on the death of his cousin, I would write out his estimates to farmers and the accounts to the rest of the gang. I learned far more from my father than I ever learned at school. I not only loved my father, I admired him. He was very strict, but he never punished severely or without cause. Honesty and truthfulness had to be strictly observed.

My mother was such a good, humble little woman. Although I loved her and pitied her, I caused her much heartache because I was always a rebel but I knew I could always depend on her love and support. If I was caned at school, which very frequently happened, Mother was as hurt as if she herself had been caned, but Father would just say 'You go to school to learn and do as you're told; if you don't you must accept the consequences.' On one occasion in particular, I was on my knees scrubbing the doorstep when Lady Thornhill from the Lodge came along. Of course, I should have got up, stood to attention and curtsied. I didn't, but just kept on with my job. Lady Thornhill had to walk round my feet. Poor Mother was very concerned and said 'Kate, you should have got up and curtsied to her ladyship. You know you must show respect to your betters.' Needless to say, her ladyship reported me to the Head Master; next morning I was hauled out before the whole school for all the children to see what happened to girls who didn't respect their betters. I was given six strokes of the cane on each hand with the full weight of his arm behind each stroke, and then two strokes·across the shoulders for good measure. Then he said to me 'Perhaps that will teach you to respect your betters,' but I just resolved never ever to curtsey to Lady Thornhill again under any circumstances. I didn't mind the caning, but it hurt my sister who, like my mother, was very humble and sensitive.

Mother taught us all to sew, but as there were fewer of us at home and she had more time she taught me to knit and crochet as well. At school the Head Master's wife was in charge of the needlework class. She would never allow me to do anything worthwhile. Oddments of wool to knit, unknit and reknit – the same with needlework, just odds and ends to stitch together, unpick and restitch. One afternoon, after taking the same little piece of calico, sewn, unsewn and resewn for the sixth time, I just threw it on her desk, jumped the seat, through the door, jumped the playground wall, and was away home. I had just explained to Mother when two of the bigger boys arrived to take me back. I flatly refused to go back. Of course, Father had to be told and he just said 'Take your punishment – it's the penalty for being a bright pauper.' The Head Master kept me standing in front of the class for an hour before caning me again six severe strokes on each hand, and as I faced him he gave me a severe cut on the back of each hand saying 'Cry, damn you, cry.' I merely smiled, knowing I'd beaten him. He enjoyed inflicting pain, but I hadn't given him the satisfaction of knowing he'd caused me pain. I accepted my pauperism, but I wasn't the cause of such pauperism. Why should I cry? Margery did – she was hurt most to see me hurt. Margery left school before she was thirteen, and went as general servant at the local grocer's shop. The snobbery of those days was unbelievable. The woman couldn't afford a servant and paid only one shilling a week wage and Mother had to do Margery's washing. Poor Margery was overworked and underfed, and her living and sleeping quarters were dark and damp. Margery was allowed home for two hours once a week. One evening she came home and letting her hands fall in her lap, she said to Mother 'I feel just like that.' Mother could see she was ill. I was sent to the shop to say that Margery wasn't well and could not return that evening, to which the wretched woman replied 'Tell her to be early in the morning.' However, she was too ill to get up in the morning, and I was sent to Ixworth to the doctor. He gave me a bottle of physic for her which I am convinced was nothing but Epsom salts. He didn't come to see her, and in ten days she was dead. Father went for the certificate from the doctor and to the relieving officer for an order for a parish coffin. The doctor signed the certificate stating diphtheria as the cause of death. He hadn't seen her. Of course, it was pneumonia. Because of the doctor's statement of diphtheria, the coffin was not allowed in the church. There were just committal prayers at the graveside. After these were said Mother looked straight at the vicar and said to him 'You have kept her out of church; you can't keep her out of heaven.'

Mother was upset for a very long time over the loss of Margery (her 13th child, 13 years old, the 13th day of the Month at the 13th hour of the day), the shame of a pauper's funeral, and her own daring to speak up to one of her betters without even curtseying. I, in my impotent ignorance, thought 'What does it matter about going into church? If she hadn't had to work so hard for that stuck-up shop woman she wouldn't have died.' . . .

It was during Harry's [her brother's] residence at Mill Farm that Grannie Miller, now very old and feeble, was considered unfit to live alone. As she was living on parish relief – one shilling and sixpence per week plus half a pound of sausages – the relieving officer decided that she must be put in the workhouse. This upset Mother terribly; the workhouse was a horrible place. She had been such a good mother and worked so hard for many years that it seemed all wrong. My brother, Harry, seeing Mother so upset, offered to pay Mother five shillings a week for the rest of Grannie's life if Mother could have her and look after her. Father was willing. Mother talked it over with her two sisters and two brother's living in the village as Harry made one request – he wanted the corner cupboard from Grannie's room. The aunts and uncles readily agreed; the corner cupboard was a small price to pay to keep their mother out of the workhouse and to know that she would be well looked after for her few remaining years. She deteriorated into her second childhood, or at least to the past, as she frequently spoke of her youngest son whom she had not seen for so many years, saying that he and his little dark-haired wife had been to see her, or were coming to tea. She was ninety-eight years old when she died. Harry paid the funeral expenses so she did not have a pauper's funeral. Harry himself was only thirty-two when he died. Mother was with him. He, like Margery, died from pneumonia.

One winter while we were yet children we were ill – I had croup and Flo and Margery had bronchitis – and Mother mentioned to the vicar that she hadn't sufficient bed clothes to keep us warm. In turn he mentioned it to Lady Greene. A few days later a groom arrived at the door with some sheets of brown paper and a message from Lady Greene saying 'These will keep the children warm and when the warm weather comes they won't need washing but can be burned.'

I left school at thirteen and took a place as general servant in a farmhouse. Mother was with me when I was interviewed by the farmer and his wife. The farmer's wife stated that my wage would be a shilling a week. Mother explained that I hadn't cotton dresses, aprons or caps. The farmer then said 'Make it fifteen pence a week.' The farmer's wife had to agree. She also agreed to buy the necessary print for dresses and hessian for aprons, I could make them myself, and she would keep back my wages until the material was paid for. This was agreed. I worked without wages for six months, and each evening, Sundays included, I sat behind her chair and sewed, thankful for my Grannie's example. The farmer was fairly pleasant, but the woman constantly checked me about the extra threepence, saying she had never paid so much before. I had to help with the dairy work. If she saw me flinch when I was getting dairy utensils out of the boiling sterilizing water she would push my whole hand in saying that was the only way to get hardened. She was an elderly woman and had been doing dairy work for years. I was only a girl and although my hands were rough they weren't hardened as hers were hardened.

At school then there were no ii-plus exams or even free place exams, but a school inspector attended once a year to examine all the classes. In my last term

at school I passed in Scripture and Arithmetic. The inspector was so pleased
with my work that he gave me a penny for each subject from his own pocket. It
was wealth to me, but wealth I had to pay for during the few remaining weeks at
school. The Head Master was keenly watching for any chance for caning. My
weakest subject was map drawing so we had map drawing each day. He usually
carried a heavy pointer and any mistakes meant a blow with the pointer across
the shoulders. To give himself a better swing with his pointer arm he moved me
to a back seat. There he defeated himself because the boy he sat me beside was
good at map drawing. He quickly drew the outline of the various maps for me,
leaving me to fill in rivers, mountains, principal towns, etc.

The Head Master retired at the end of my last term. Before breaking up each
child was presented with a gift. I was the very last to be presented with such. It
was a very dirty and torn outworn cigarette card album obviously thrown out by
one of his children years before. I accepted it and thanked him very politely, then
deliberately tore it up, scattering the fragments on the school floor, defiant to the
last. Poor Mother cried. Father just said 'You reap what you sow' . . .

During my years in domestic service I have lived in various counties. Each has
a beauty of its own but none as poor or better controlled as Suffolk, even now. I
am still a rebel, an outsider, and a loner, but I have my family and my memories.
My brave little Grannie Miller, my humble hard-working mother, my father
who taught me so much, my two handsome brothers, all my lovely sisters – it's
wonderful to be a member of such a family. Although at eighty-two I have
nothing to look forward to, I have much to look back on and the good things far
outweigh the less good. For instance, the last time I saw my sister, Nelly, shortly
before her death from cancer of the breast, we enjoyed a real laugh together at
the way our foot-rags flapped in the mud, proving that even poverty can be
laughed at from a distance when it is shared with family love.

Fred Boughton
the forest in my younger days

Fred Boughton was born in a cottage on Harrow Hill in the Forest of Dean,
Gloucestershire, in 1897. His father was a miner but, like other foresters, had an
acre of land and exercised the ancient right to graze sheep in the woods and on
the grass verges. Fred Boughton describes the simple, self-sufficient life which
was still lived in this remote region at the beginning of the twentieth century, the
closeness of the family, the strength of religion, and his debt to his father who
passed on to his children the traditional knowledge and skills which enabled
them to survive in a harsh environment. In later life the author worked as a
farm-hand, a timber-feller, a butcher and a milk roundsman, but much of his

216-page manuscript, written in 1974, is devoted to the natural life of the Forest – the trees, plants, animals and, especially, the sheep. Extracts from the autobiography have been published by the Forest of Dean Newspapers Ltd, though this is taken from the original manuscript.

The way the Foresters lived in those hard days would be impossible today. They never wanted anything they could do without, and their home life was wonderful. Our home life was typical and on a winter's night the fire would be burning bright, with a pot of stew on the hob and a tin of bacon roasting in the oven, the cat on the mat and, best of all, Mother would be sitting in her wicker armchair, knitting. Father would be mending boots, and each of us kids had a job, some knitting, some making rag mats, some cooking. Mother taught us to do every job in the house. I made myself many shirts, and knitted pairs of socks. Once I made myself a pair of knee breeches out of odd pieces of cord. Then when bedtime came we had a good hot supper. Then we all knelt round Mother's knee and said the Lord's Prayer and Father would say a few words about the goodness of God. Then we sang 'The day is past and over' and with humble thankful hearts ran off to bed.

In the morning we sang 'We thank thee for another night of quiet sleep and rest.' Father and my brothers went to work at 5.30. We all got up at 7 a.m., and after a good breakfast each of us had a job to do before we went to school. At dinner time our food was always ready, and when one of us had said Grace we all sat down to dinner as quiet as mice. Mother said it was rude to talk about nothing at meal times.

After school we ran home and had a cup of tea and some home-made cake. Mother used to bake every Wednesday and there were always lots of muffins and lardy cakes with lots of currants in, and some big rice puddings we always enjoyed.

After tea we changed out of our school clothes, then off to work. One would be looking for our two little black cows, another would be feeding the pigs and hens. In the summer some would be weeding in the garden. In the winter we would be cutting chaff and pulping roots, etc., and knocking some tins to call our sheep home to feed. They would come from everywhere when they heard the tins, and we used to put about ¼lb of maize for each on the grass and that kept them going.

We all went in to tea about six. By then Father and my brothers had changed out of their pit dirt. We all sat in our places and never spoke. Mother always had plenty of good food ready for us, in winter plenty of stewed meat with potatoes, carrots, onions and suet dumplings all mixed together. Then we had a piece of suet pudding called 'Spotted Dick'. When we had finished our food Father would ask us if everything was alright.

A miner never saw his home in daylight in winter except on Sunday, and Sunday was not a working day in the Forest but a day of rest and gladness. After tea Father would get the do-re-me board, put it by the grandfather clock, and

ask us to sing a hymn one by one, then we would all sing together with Father
leading us. We always enjoyed that half hour. In the summer we all went out on
the Tump and sang a few hymns. I always loved singing but never thought that
some day I should be singing to hundreds in the Welsh valleys and in the hop
yards in Herefordshire.

I never preached to anyone, but I loved to explain to people that the best things
in life are free and the only way to live a happy contented life was to get the love of
God in your heart.

On Sunday we all went to the Methodist Chapel at Drybrook three times and
we were a happy crowd. On Sunday night the chapel was full. Most of the
families averaged six or seven, so we were a happy bunch, and when we had our
Sunday School treat we were all full of joy.

We started from the chapel, with the Drybrook Brass Band in front, then two
carrying the banner. We marched in twos, with the teacher in front of each class.
We marched down to the Cross, then up Morse Lane nearly to Ruardean, then
back down the Morse Road to Nailbridge, then back to Drybrook to Downton's
Field by the New Inn yard. We had marched about four miles and crowds of
people had lined the roadside to see us pass, and we all tried to look our best.
Mother used to make us sailors' blouses. The girls had blue skirts, and the boys
had blue knicks. The girls had two long plaits tied with ribbon and we all had
coronation mugs hanging round our necks and tied with red, white and blue
ribbon. We had plenty of sports, everyone was happy and I never remember a
wet day on treat day.

Money was always short in those days but we managed because we lived
carefully. A miner only got 5s. a day and 12 cwt of coal for 4s.6d. each month . . .

In the summer a miner was the worst off because the pits only worked three or
four days a week, so he did any job to help out. A lot of them kept a bit of livestock
on the Forest, sheep, pigs, donkeys, ponies, sometimes a cow, and all had a few
hens or ducks or geese. Some would go a few miles and work on the farms.
These men could do any job and do it tidily, and the farmers used to depend on
them for sheep shearing, hoeing, haymaking, harvesting, thatching the ricks,
threshing the corn, etc. They were not paid much money, but they could have a
bag of potatoes and swedes, some apples, some hay for the sheep. Anything they
needed the farmer would let them have, because there was that happy understanding that each one helped the other.

There were about 40 miners on Harrow Hill: 30 kept livestock free on the
Forest and each one would help the others. A man could buy two small pigs and
go to the shop and explain how he was off for money to feed them. The
shopkeeper would let him have all the meal he needed and have one of the pigs
when fat: he sold the pigmeat in the shop and cured the bacon and sold it later.
The pig paid for the meal and the miner had a fat pig to feed his family for
£1. 10. 0. and his trouble. A farmer would let you plant a row of potatoes at
2s. 6d. per 100 yards because he knew you would go and help him sometimes . . .

The children in the Forest had a full life; there were plenty of games which
cost nothing. The boys used to walk on stilts and play cat. Cat was a stick about

the size of a brush handle, nine inches long with the two ends sharpened. You knocked it on the one end and it flew in the air, sometimes 50 yards, and the farthest was the winner. The girls would swing on the trees, and sometimes skip for hours. They were happy in those days because they made their own pleasure.

When a boy left school he always went to work in the pit because no tradesman would employ a boy who had not been to the pit and learned to work. The girls went to domestic service, often to Cheltenham. They only got about £8 per year to start with, but they always sent their mothers a few shillings to help at home. A boy would give his mother his wages, and have a bit of pocket money, because when a baby was born the mother would pay a penny a week into the Co-op. Penny Bank, so she could rig them up with clothes when they started work, and they were always grateful for what she had done. I often heard the teenagers coming home at night singing, 'Mid pleasures and palaces, where e'er ye may roam; Be it ever so humble there's no place like home.'

We had a good schoolmaster and teachers. The schoolmaster would use the cane sometimes when it was needed, but he was kind and would listen to your troubles.

When Jack Johnson and Jim Driscoll fought for the world's heavyweight boxing championship the master came round every class and said Jack Johnson had won and was shouting, 'Mamey, I'm bringing home the bacon.'

When Dr Campbell had his first motor car he let all we kids go out and see. The boys stood in a line by Mr Shapcott's hedge and the girls stood in a line by the school wall. We should have had our photographs taken because the girls wore clean white pinafores and ribbon in their hair. The boys wore white india rubber collars and every kid tried to look his best, and when the Dr came racing along in his blue-grey De Dion car we all shouted 'Hip, hip, hooray'. That was about 1908 and the first motor to come to Drybrook. Then Tom Brain at White Hill Farm bought a £110 Ford. It was a lot of money in those days.

There was always somewhere for the kids to go to on a winter's night. The girls used to go to sewing classes and the band of hope and dancing lessons in a room at the back of the New Inn. Bernard Parker had a tin shack at the bottom of a lane near the Cross. There the boys used to go and play dominoes and other games. Some used to play boxing and you would see this chalked up on the shed, 'Big Contest on Tonight. Bill Wet v. Jack Frost, 10 Rounds. Sam Damp v. Harry Snow, 8 rounds. Don't be late.' It was somewhere for the kids to go. There was always a good fire and they enjoyed themselves for a penny a night.

At school our teachers sometimes lost their tempers if we did not learn, and if a boy had dirty boots she would send him out to the master for the cane. I have heard the master ask, 'Why did you not black your boots this morning?'. 'Because we had no blacking and no money to buy any, Sir. Mother spends all the money on food.' Many times I have seen the master give him a penny and say 'Go and buy a tin.'

The Head Teacher, J. B. Parker, was very smart and tidy and a very interesting teacher to listen to. He would tell us our fathers and brothers had made the British Empire on which the sun never sets, all about the Black Hole of Calcutta,

General Gordon, the relief of Lucknow, the Zulu War and the Boer War, how General Wolfe and his army climbed the heights of Abraham and won the battle of Quebec and Canada was ours, all about Nelson, the Duke of Wellington, Captain Cook and a lot more. He would teach us all the old songs, and we used to sing from our hearts because we were full of pride and joy. They included 'Hearts of Oak', 'Rule Britannia', 'Men of Harlech', 'When the mighty roast beef was the Englishman's food' and dozens more. Sometimes we would recite 'The Charge of the Light Brigade', and the 'Psalm of Life' and a few more. At 74 I can still recite 'The Psalm of Life'. There have been times when its words have helped me a lot and given me fresh hope . . .

At work in Serridge Pit

They put an endless strap about six inches wide on me with an opening for me to put my head through, then they hooked it to a hodd or box of coal, and my job was to drag it on my hands and toes. I could not stand up because the hole was only three foot six inches high in some places. The only light I had was a candle stuck on the side. You took four size 16 candles, we called comps, each day. If the air was good they would last eight hours, but if the air was foul you only burned three. You only had about ten minutes for food and all you took was a lump of bread with a hole scooped out and a lump of cheese put in, and all you had to drink was a pint of cold tea with no sugar or milk.

At 2.30 we started walking back to the cage, then up in the fresh air. I remember all the miners were very friendly and would say, 'How dist get on, butty? Thee'll soon get used to it.' I used to look at the other hodders; they looked fit and well, and I thought if they can do it I can. I had a job to walk home after the first shift, so I had my tea and went to bed, but after a few days my muscles began to form and I didn't get so tired and began to feel like the other hodders fit and well. The tears I saw in mother's eyes when I gave her my first pay packet I shall never forget. What happened to me happened to all my schoolmates; some stayed at school until 14, but we all started work hodding.

In the summer the pits only worked about three days a week, so Father used to buy a few acres of brush-wood and showed us how to handle timber. We started on the left hand side of the wood and dropped every stick the same way. When we had cut a strip, one would cut the beansticks and cloth props, then tie them in bundles and stack them tidily. Another would cut the pea sticks and stack them tidily, then we would all pick up the bits and tie them into faggots for firewood. We always left the wood clean and tidy. If there was some sapling to fell Father would show us how to do it. He would put a peg in the ground and drop an eighty-foot tree on it. This was a spare-time job but it taught us the timber trade, and a few years after I was in charge of a timber gang in South Wales.

We had good food in those days, not tinned stuff, and nearly all had some tidy clothes. Some men would wear a best suit for 20 years and never show a mark or wear. They always took care of it and changed when they came home. The young men always looked very smart. The girls made the most of their clothes and the women only wore their best clothes for special occasions. They always wore a pinafore or an apron to look tidy. The men and boys worked hard and the women and girls mended the clothes, looked after the home and did the washing at the dolly tub. They all got tired but were fit and well.

What a difference today. They are like cows waiting for a bright red apple to fall, and when it does they find out it was crab, and not what they wanted. Sixty years ago working people did not have the expense of motor-cars, televisions, washing-machines, spin-driers, etc. There were no buses, no H.P. debts and no strikes. Now they have homes they only sleep in and half the children have no home life.

Father used to say, 'I shall not leave you much money, but I will teach you every job, then you can always get work.' He showed us every job in the garden and on the farm, including how to get stone in the quarry and trim it and build stone walls . . .

My life was always very busy and from a young boy I was always working at some job. My brothers used to give me sixpence a week to run about the Forest and see their Tats [sheep], and in the football season they used to ask me to take their clothes and football togs and meet them when they came out of the pit. I had four miles to go so I took the donkey with all the clothes tied on his back because I could not carry it all. They used to come up out of Serridge pit, run down into Strip-and-at-it Green and wash the pit dirt off in a brook, take off their pit clothes, put on their other clothes, pick up their football togs and run through the wood to Brierley to catch the brake and their mates. A brake was the only transport in those days. It was a long wagon pulled with four horses. They used to play rugby and their legs were black and blue from kicks, but they enjoyed it . . .

I always felt sorry for the girls in those days. When they left school at 13 their parents could not afford to keep them at home, so they would apply to a domestic agent for a job. As soon as a job was found, the mother would draw the girl's money out of the Co-op. Penny Bank to buy her uniform and a tin box to put everything in. The only way a mother could save enough money then was to pay one penny each week into the Penny Bank from the time a baby was born.

This young girl who had never been away from home in her life was taken to the station, then she was met at the other end by someone she had never seen. She may be taken to a large house in the country, or a large house in the town. She may have a good home and she may have a crabby old housekeeper to slave for. Sometimes she started work at 6 a.m. and kept on until 10 p.m. Sometimes the food was good and sometimes she could only eat when she was hungry. I knew a woman who called herself a lady who would shout and rave the foulest words she could think of to a young servant girl because she dropped a plate. These girls could not run away. If they found another job and did not have a good reference they had no chance. They had a few hours off duty one half day each week, and a few hours off every other Sunday and about two weeks' holiday each summer which they spent at home in the Forest. The wages at first were £8 per year. If they rose to be a cook they may get £20 per year.

When these girls came home on holidays they would soon find other girls on holidays, then they would all stroll through the beeches. Sometimes they would sit under the beech trees and have a chat with a number of young men. They did not lie about like animals, they all had respect for each other. It was a terrible crime in those days if two young people lost their self respect. The baby would be called a bastard all its life. The girl would hang her head in shame and no man would respect her. The man would pay 7s. 6d. each week for 16 years. 7s. 6d. then was 1½ days' wages. He would be marked, and no woman would marry a man who was paying to a child.

But if two looked at each other and decided they were made for each other, that was when the joys of life began. The girl would feel very proud when she took her young man home to tea for her parents to see. After tea her mother would let them sit in the parlour undisturbed so they could talk about the future. The girl would go back to service and keep making something to put in the bottom drawer. The man would find a cottage and get it furnished, and when everything was ready they would get married and live together like a pair of doves and as the family came along they would thank God for his blessing . . .

James Brady
a long, long trail a-winding

James Brady was born in Rochdale, Lancashire, in 1898, one of five children of a clog-iron maker. Educated at a Board School, he became a half-timer in a cotton mill at twelve and a full-timer a year later. At seventeen he joined the army in the First World War, spending some months as a prisoner in Germany. Subsequently he worked as a youth leader in the Y.M.C.A. and as a journalist and broadcaster, being one of the pioneers of broadcasting in the West Region. He completed a 90,000-word autobiography in 1978, of which the following extract describes his parents, family life and early introduction to work. The work is unpublished.

My father was a clog-iron maker – and proud of it, though, by the wages he received for long hours of slavery, God knows why. Tall, slim, though strong as a lion, he was an honest-to-goodness sort of fellow who, like the village black-smith, always 'looked the whole world in the face, for he owed not any man'. With pride I remember him as a strong-minded character, though of limited education and somewhat shallow outlook, loyal, industrious and conscientious in all things. A proud, caring responsible family-man, he enjoyed nothing more than working hard during the week and spending an hour or two in 'The Highland Laddie' with his gill of home-brewed and his clay-pipe of a Saturday night. Though I was sad when he came home the worse for drink on occasions and was rough with Mum. For all that his qualities make him a decent, ordinary working-man, a sensible, responsible citizen of the squalid world in which he lived between the last quarter of Victoria's reign, through Edward's brief spell as sovereign to the tumultuous years of George V. So he was – but it took me, regrettably, a long time to realize it.

Of one thing I was certain – he was a damn good clog-iron maker who, in his time, must have turned out millions of little heels on his anvil in John Wilson's Penn-street foundry. Oft-times, after school, I would make my way to the foundry and stand as near as maybe to his furnace, marvelling at the lightning dexterity with which he manipulated the white-hot lengths of metal with pliers and hammer to flick yet another iron into the hot dust. Then he'd remove his pipe and spit loudly into the hissing fire before bending down on his haunches to count out his products into a large tin-bucket. Finally, he would smear a veneer of healing ointment over his blistered arms and hands before rolling down his shirt-sleeves ready to go: 'Reet, Jim, lad, let's get w'hom.'

Even with the extra earned working on piece-work, I don't think the poor chap ever took much more than thirty bob a week home, little enough for a growing family of three sons and two daughters. Small wonder he had to resort to 'moonlighting' – scene-shifting, four nights a week at the Theatre Royal, at two-bob a night, or grooming dray-horses for a local brewery, probably paid for in gills of bitter. When one spare-time job folded, he found another, acting as caretaker at St Edmund's Sunday-School, for instance, for half a crown a week. When, after a year, he asked for a rise, the Parochial Church Council awarded him sixpence a week extra. Dad resigned on the spot and took to making rugs out of swaddies' tunics, for newly-weds. Nor was he an amateur with the plane and the saw; there was scarcely a household within two hundred yards of ours which didn't have one of father's plant-stands for the aspidistra. The man was only happy when he was working.

Beginning his working-life in Bolton at the age of eleven he slaved on, year after year, for little pay and few holidays, for fifty-odd years. It took him a whole year to save up enough money for a family trip to New Brighton, which included a thrilling ferry-trip across the Mersey, eating fish and chips and black pudding – and being sick. Then I recall an exciting five days at Southport, in a cheap guest-house with newspaper table-cloths – and bring your own egg for breakfast – which must have cost Dad a fortune. Our first visit to Blackpool, when I was eight, was limited to a day-trip – scoffing corn-beef sandwiches and drinking pop on a sweltering beach, jam-packed with people smelling of cotton flocks and variegated dyes. Sometimes we went to Belle Vue, Manchester, to see the lions and tigers and witness firework displays simulating Blenheim and Waterloo. On other occasions we went to Bolton to visit my Uncle Jim, at the fire-station where he was chief engineer. Always the joke was that every time we went Aunt Mary had 'had another'. My father never ceased to chide his brother, Jim, on his marital promiscuity and the visit usually ended up in a blazing row between the two of them.

Allowing for these casual, indeed, very infrequent relaxations, my father worked on. Small wonder that before he was sixty he was completely worn out. Life never really gave him a chance. At 62 the family doctor decided Dad had had enough and advised him to 'take it easy'. He gave up his lung-destroying job in an asbestos-factory and tried to exist on his less onerous side-lines.

Why, oh why, is fate so cruel to some people? Within weeks of deciding, much against his inclination, to 'retire', my big, strong, energetic father was struck down with cancer. Christie's hospital, Manchester, did their best for him. As I sat at his bedside, his strong, muscular arms, scarred by a hundred burns, outside the bed-cover he said, sadly: 'Jim, lad, they've made a reet mess o' me this time. I shan't ever work again.' Poor chap – all he thought about was work.

They sent him home to die. But he fought to the bitter, painful end. 'I don't want to die; why should I die yet?', he screamed in his agony. By tragic irony he won five pounds on a football pool. 'What are you going to do with your fortune, Dad?', he was asked. 'I'm going to buy a new suit – and give the rest to mother,' he replied.

Just like Jack Brady – brave and arrogant with it. He never got round to buying that new suit. In sad retrospect I nurture a quiet pride and respect for this decent, ordinary man, my father, who, like scores of his contemporaries, slaved every hour God sent just to fulfil his responsibilities and preserve his self-respect. His was the stuff of which all good British workingmen were made in days long gone. I am ashamed to admit that, at that time, I possessed no real appreciation of his worth. Incidentally, in the light of subsequent knowledge, I am driven to conclude that his untimely death was not unassociated with his having worked for many years in an asbestos factory. But nobody cared in those days.

They called my mother Kitty Brady, a sweet little woman of sly humour and calm demeanour: 'A gradely lass and a fighter'. So she was – of stout heart and happy spirit – and she could sing 'When Irish eyes are smiling' ever so sweetly. That's why she was so much loved by the twenty or so housewives who were her neighbours in that neat rectangle of drab cottages, known as Shepherd's Terrace, Spotland, a mile from the Town Hall Square. The cobble-stoned cul-de-sac, with its squalid row of shared privvies in the middle, was her world from Monday to Sunday, a grey world of hard times and hard work, bringing up a family of five on a purse for ever running empty. Often, come Thursday night, she would send me to Mrs Cropper's, next door, to borrow twopence to buy a chop for Dad's evening meal.

Even now, after all these years, my heart is ready to burst with indignation when I think of the constant battles against poverty and adversity my poor mother, and others like her, had to fight. It was a social crime which took long to eradicate. No wonder Lancashire folk grew up tough, hard fighters. I can think of no other reason for the stubborn aggressiveness which has so often blighted my own mien than the common influences of my childhood. But my mother always understood my impetuosity, my enthusiasms and fantasies, my virtues and defects, and my boyish eccentricities. I was built in her mould; there was always a deep affection between us.

When war came in 1914, the absence of my brother, Billy and myself, away in France, must have increased her anxieties, yet, so I'm told, she was ever smiling, cheerful, fighting. When I was living off sauerkraut and burnt barley soup in a German prison-camp, she spared two shillings a month from her meagre purse to have British Red Cross parcels sent out to me.

Her weekly treat was to call 'in't cook-shop' in Toad Lane on her way back from shopping, for two-pen'orth of potatoe-pie, garnished with black pudding. Alternately Billy and I used to go with her to share this marvellous guzzle, so utterly, deliciously tasty.

Mum's family originated in Southern Ireland; she was Roman Catholic. Dad's stock came from Northern Ireland, a long time back, and he was a Protestant, C. of E. But never once do I remember a cross word between them that could be related to religious matters. Indeed the words 'catholic' and 'protestant' were rarely, if ever, heard in our household.

To me it is a matter of deep regret that any differences on that score were left until after they both had died. Mother survived my father by fifteen years and, on the day of her funeral, the Roman Catholic priest refused to pronounce the committal over her grave because she had chosen to be buried beside her husband on the 'protestant' side of the cemetery. After conducting a brief service in the Catholic church the 'Holyman' donned his wide black hat and departed without uttering one single word of condolence to members of the family and relatives, leaving my mother's Catholic nieces to pronounce the final words of farewell at the graveside. . .

It was the vicar's son, Francis, who interested me in the scout movement, but money was tight at home and all mother could manage towards uniform and accoutrements were a hat, a neckerchief and a belt. What Chief Scout, Sir Robert Baden-Powell, thought of the comic figure who paraded before him on Rochdale town hall square during a county rally in 1910, I wouldn't know. But he smiled kindly as he acknowledged my smart two-fingered salute. Point was Francis, away at Keble College, had left me in full command of our dozen or so tenderfoots, and when B.P.'s visit was announced I found myself marching down Yorkshire Street through cheering, giggling crowds oblivious of the clown-like figure I presented in my blue-serge suit, caught up in the middle by a scout-belt, a green and orange neckerchief hiding my collar and tie, Buffalo Bill hat perched precariously on my head and wearing canary-coloured gloves. I guess it was one way of making the bizarre look ludicrous, but I didn't care – after all canary-coloured gloves were all the rage at the time. Of course we had other diversions; every Easter saw a colourful recrudescence of Lancashire folk-lore among the simple, uninhibited mill-folk seeking innocent variants from their unexciting lives. Chief among the junketings was 'The Peace Egg', a crude mummers play enacted in the streets by boys garbed in sashes and tunics to represent St George, King of Egypt, Prince of Paradine and so on. A Doctor and Beelzebub made up the caste, and at the end of the day the spoils, collected from kerbside audiences, were divided equally among the performers and spent on a tram-ride to Hollingworth Lake, a Pennine beauty-spot three miles out, with a three-penny row on the lake and fish and chips in a newspaper for the homeward journey. . .

When 'The Peace Egg' staled a bit we formed a black and white minstrel troupe, with bone-rickers and tambourines, burnt cork faces and coon-songs like 'Swanee River' and 'Oh, I lub a lubbly girl', traversing the town with tremendous success. Our takings increased in proportion to the jealousy and animosity of the old-fashioned 'Peace-eggers' who resented our 'Avant Garde' show and tried to hound us off the streets without much success. I bought a new pair of clogs out of my share of the collections.

General elections, of which there appeared to be an inordinate number around the early part of the century, provided us with scope for aggro and self-expression as we youngsters paraded the narrow streets with placards urging folk to 'Vote for Gordon Harvey', or Tawney; or was it Ramsey Muir? – lively diversions from the boredom of school or the monotony of the mill. My father, like most working chaps in those days, was a staunch Liberal, fearful of the growth of this new, revolutionary philosophy called 'Socialism'.

I recall the glee with which he received news of the Liberal victory of 1905 which took them into office under Sir H. Campbell-Bannerman, though he was angry and alarmed that Labour had captured thirty-odd seats.

These were the days of Liberal growth with higher pensions, an eight-hour day for miners, launching of the Children's Act and the Trade Boards which swept away sweat shops and brought some humanity to industry. There were unemployment and insurance schemes – and Dad hung a portrait of the Prime Minister, Sir Henry Campbell-Bannerman, in our parlour. Exciting, ebullient times they were, full of incident and promise – and always, always the sun seemed to be shining. Even for the annual Whitsuntide processions when we all turned out in our Sunday best, me in a neat sailor-boy suit with a wide collar and Nelson-type straw boater. I always conspired to hold a blue riband attached to one of those high blue and gold banners depicting Christ on The Mount. As I got older I carried a smaller tabard of my own, fighting against the wind to keep possession of it. It was always a long foot-blistering walk through the cobbled streets between crowds of smiling relatives, and we were all glad when we turned into the playing field to queue for buns and coffee and a hunk of meat pie. Then there were races and games – and romps with the girls. What happened to this happy, happy world? Where are the bands and banners and the smiling faces of yore? All we have today are mobs of ragged jean-clad teenagers, shaking their childish fists and shouting 'We shall overcome' underneath mis-spelt slogans on crude placards. God! what a lousy, protesting violent world it is today, compared with the carefree tolerance and good friendship of sixty years ago. But then trade unions hadn't developed their power-mad muscle in pre-Mons days, had they? And, of course, we were prepared to work for our living.

The sheer force of economic necessity drove my astute mother to pre-empt my twelfth birthday by a couple of weeks and find a job for me as an alley-sweeper half-timer at Messrs Samuel Heaps and Sons' flannelette factory, at Brookside, a ruin of a place whose foundations must have been laid during the industrial revolution of a century before.

But, ruin or no ruin, the prospect of 'starting work' pleased me; the revered Heap family, born and bred in Rochdale, had employed generations of Rochdalians in their textile, dyeing and finishing mills and I was glad, and proud, that I was to be given the opportunity of starting my work-a-day life in one of their mills. And, with father bringing home less than 30-bob a week, it gave me satisfaction to know that I would soon become a breadwinner to help the family budget. Mother arranged everything. I was to be paid 3s. 6d. per week for a morning shift of twenty-six hours, and 2s. 6d. a week for the afternoon shift of twenty hours. The early morning period meant getting up at 5 a.m. to be at the mill, three miles away, before the buzzer finished wailing at six. We half-timers knocked-off at half-past twelve; then it was a race home for a quick meal, change from corduroys and scarf into knicker-bockers and collar and button-on bow, then a final dash to Spotland school at two o'clock. The afternoon shift worked in reverse; school in the morning and work in the afternoon until 5.30 p.m. Life was worth living!

Incidentally I had a small 'moonlighting' job of my own about this time, hauling coal in buckets from cellar to upstairs-rooms and keeping garden paths clean and tidy for a wealthy family in Falinge Road, for which I was paid one shilling a week, plus a cup of tea and a rock bun on Fridays. My Mum was glad of the extra bob.

I knew that when I was thirteen I would have to say goodbye to my schooling at Spotland Board School and become a full-timer at Heaps, working a fifty-five and a half hour week for ten shillings and sixpence – a fortune for mother and there was always a chance to do a bit of newspaper-work selling sports editions on Saturday nights as well . . .

Now new horizons were opening up, new thrills were in the offing in preparation for which I had to undergo the stimulating ritual of being 'lengthened', which meant changing baggy knickerbockers, long socks and elastic garters which stopped your circulation, for long, smelly corduroy trousers held up by stout leather braces. It also meant a new heavy brown cap, with a button on top and a thicker scarf to keep the icy blast out. This was the drab, but completely utilitarian attire of the traditional Lancashire working-man which transformed you in a day from boyhood to manhood. What a landmark in my life when Mum took me down to the Co-op in Toad Lane to have me rigged out at a total cost of fifteen shillings. From that moment I merged with the amenities of the scene as a working-man, a 'cotton operative'.

Bessie Wallis
yesterday

Bessie Wallis was born in the mining village of West Melton, near Wombwell, Yorkshire, in 1904. Her autobiography gives an excellent account of the family and social life of this closely knit community where coal-mining was the inevitable occupation for men and domestic service equally inescapable for girls. A highly intelligent girl, Bessie won a county scholarship which would have taken her on to secondary education, but 'it was doomed from the start' as there was no money for books, uniform and fares. She left school at thirteen to go into service, but after two years of misery went to live in Leicester where she studied shorthand and typing at evening classes and obtained clerical work; during the Second World War she became first cashier in a London bank. Bessie therefore successfully overcame her restricting background, yet concludes her autobiography, 'There was indeed something about those early Yorkshire days when this century was young, when a coal mine dominated all our lives'. Her unpublished memoir was kindly lent by her daughter, Mrs H. M. Peel.

There was no such thing as homework so, after our meal, we had to amuse ourselves. We had little in the way of toys. There was never enough money for the luxury of a toy for a child but we did have our snap and playing cards. These cards were frowned upon in most homes where the Methodist religion was closely followed.

In the Summer we took ourselves off for long walks or played a multitude of invented games. Sometimes though we were delegated to weed my father's allotment. On those long and cold Winter nights we had to amuse ourselves. My eldest brother did a lot of fretwork which was very popular then among the boys. When this bored, out would come the playing cards! Myself and my friend usually played at 'shops'. Mother always kept a huge stock of soap in the kitchen cupboard. There was a blue and white mottled soap, a green naptha variety and the ordinary white windsor. These tablets of soap did duty as lard, butter, cheese and general grocery goods. A lot of imagination was required but little girls have never lacked inventiveness!

Our meals though were nearly always the same. Sunday dinner was always a piece of undercut of beef. This only varied at Christmas when we had a chicken, or sometimes as a real treat, a goose. Monday was the cold meat day with bubble and squeak made from Sunday's left-overs. Tuesday was a hash-day which I hated! Hashed-up meat makes me shudder now! Stew appeared faithfully on each Wednesday though, I must admit, at odd times this was replaced with pig's fry or liver. Thursday was fish and chips day while on Friday we ate whatever was available. The reason for Friday being a pot-luck day was that mother helped her parents then in their shop. She also worked for them on Saturday but as I spent each weekend with my grandparents I fared quite well. Their kitchen oven nearly always had a huge stew jar which brimmed with delicious meat and vegetables. Take a bowl-full of fresh stew from such a brown pot – none of your frozen stuff – add a hunk of newly-baked bread and there is a meal fit for the Gods indeed!

Twice a week mother baked her own bread. When I was considered old enough the task of kneading became mine. At first, I had to stand on the stool to reach the bowl and it was no light task for a six-year-old to knead seven pounds of flour. I was often punished for slicing the crust off a new loaf when mother's back was turned. A heel a bread from the front with a hunk of cheese – bliss indeed!

Twice a year the butcher slaughtered a pig. A butcher's table would be brought into the yard and then the squalling pig! The animal's legs were tied, it was hoisted on to the table and the butcher slit its throat! Boiling water was poured over the carcase and then the rough, outer hairs were scraped off easily. Cutting up was the next stage and, like young ghouls, we watched without batting an eye! The boys hopefully waiting until they were given the bladder with which they played football until it wore out.

The meat then went to the butcher's shop where Mrs Butcher took charge. She blanched the chitterlings, made poloney, sausage rolls, brawn, potted meat and the tastiest pork pies we ever had. She was spotlessly clean as was the girl who helped her . . .

One thing I did hate though which made my stomach heave! We had to share a Privy! No such luxury as a flush toilet. These were earth privys and the ashes from the fires were dumped down them. Invariably the seat was covered with ash and the smell – especially in the Summer – was appalling. These nauseous privies were emptied in the middle of every Friday night. The carts were taken to a tip to be emptied which was situated near the fields where we liked to walk to get to the railway stations . . .

One of the highlights of those early Yesterdays was the Feast. This first came to West Melton for a week, then it moved to Wath. Rubys, the owners, had a good fair. There were boat swings, others – quite large – were propelled by steam and these always had nets over the top in case the swing did a somersault. This happened often too! No one ever seemed to be hurt though. There was always a very good helter-skelter, the usual steam roundabouts, small ones for toddlers as well as cocoanut shies and side stalls which sold brandy snaps, delicious flakey cocoanut toffee and roasted peanuts. We children were lucky. We were usually given money by our various uncles of whom we had fourteen which did not count the in-laws. These delights happened over sixty years ago but I still have a fluted dish and sugar basin Father won on the hoop-la. Quite valueless but nevertheless, prized possessions.

As children we had one halfpenny (old money) each and I had also one halfpenny from my grandparents every Saturday. This magnificent old penny was carefully spent. My favourite was ever-lasting toffee though sometimes I chose anniseed balls or licquorice boot-laces. An old penny could buy four ounces of delicious 'chews'. Now and again, for a change, I would split the penny and buy tiger nuts or a locust bar. This latter was a highly unusual dark brown coloured bar. It was not any type of toffee or sweet. It was the fruit of the cicadar tree shaped like a small, flat broad bean. Inside were tiny, hard stones not unlike a small seaside pebble. They were concrete-hard. The whole thing was delightfully 'chewy'!

I hated my clothes! My normal Summer dress was dreadful because, no matter the weather, I had to wear long, black wool stockings; long-legged knickers with thick elastic, 1 flannel petticoat and 1 cotton one with embroidery; 1 liberty bodice and 1 vest. In Winter, because I was 'chesty' this was increased to vest and combinations!

When I was six years old my other Grandfather committed suicide because he had cancer of the liver. All grandchildren, no matter their age, had to attend the funeral. I was put into a long, black dress made of Stuff with the most horrible long, leg-of-mutton sleeves. I looked a freak and felt it too and I have always hated black.

I also hated Monday because this was wash day and the field of operations would daunt the average housewife. All the clothes were first heavily soaked, then rubbed by hand on the rubbing board. This was repeated in fresh water before they were laboriously loaded into the large, copper boiler. From here they went into another tub where they were rinsed twice in perfectly fresh and clear water. The next stage was to fold the wet clothes by hand after they had been blued. White clothes were both blued and starched! They were mangled by hand and when I was home this was my job. It was utterly exhausting work for a little girl but it had to be done. When it rained, black Monday became worse because the clothes had to be dried indoors. Mother would string lines in the sitting room before the great, open black-leaded fire and here they would hang. Luckily, the fire dried them quite swiftly but then came another hated task; ironing. The proceedings on Mondays seemed to go on and on in a soap-suds nightmare which can never be forgotten!

Wath itself was quite a large village with some nice shops. It had a town hall which stood in delightful grounds. In the Summer we were all able to listen to music from local musicians because the town hall had a terrace at the front from which the musicians played. I never missed a concert if I could help it because music has always been my great love.

Brampton only boasted one shop which was a general grocery but West Melton not only had two off-licences but also four Cooperatives, and grocers, drapers, shoe-shop and butchers . . .

Most of the people then always shopped at a Cooperative because the dividend was very good. Every half-year this was paid out at four shillings (twenty pence) in the pound. Most people spent this on clothes for their children because such savings were a God-send to them . . .

We had to walk everywhere in those days. It was four miles to the hospital for accident treatment although the fever and diptheria hospitals were nearer.

My job every Saturday was to go to Wombwell which was about three miles away. Mother had her favourite shops there. They were no better than those in Wath but no one could tell Mother that! One particular morning I started out quite early and I happened to catch up with the lady who collected the insurance. She questioned me as to where I was going and why then said, 'Keep with me. We'll get a lift!'

She was right too! Along came a motor car! A rare and rich object. It had its canvas hood down and we got into the back. I have never been so exhilarated in all my life as on that first ride in a motor car with the wind tumbling my hair as the fresh air flicked at my cheeks. I couldn't get home quickly enough to relate this experience which, for a long time, set me apart from my fellows! . . .

Dad had a very nice baritone voice and he could also play many of the stringed musical instruments. He had never been taught and played solely 'by-ear' but he was grand to listen to. Others thought so also. I played the piano and we had many a good sing-song but Dad's gift caused trouble as well. Dad had singing engagements – in the pubs! He usually came home the worse for drink because glasses of beer were put on the piano top for him and he, of course, could not say no! His favourite role was to dress as a Minstrel and sing Foster's songs accompanying himself on his 'G' string banjo.

Mother had to make special trousers for him from a Paisley cretonne as red as possible. It used to take him a long time to black his face with burnt cork and special grease-paint. He would come home blind-drunk with his pockets full of money. He would clean himself and tumble into bed. As soon as he was fast asleep Mother would sneak out of bed, upend his trousers and help herself to exactly half of his money. She used to take this over to Grandma to keep for her. She was often warned ominously, 'Dan will find out one of these days!'

When Dad woke up he would empty his trouser pockets and always complain most bitterly that he had thought he had earned more than that! Mother was always a match for him and no one ever gave her away! We children benefited enormously because that sly nest of money gave us many a day out at Cleethorpes!

The miners had few amusements. Soccer was not the be and end all it is today. Games were home-made or those which had been faithfully handed down through the years. Two great favourites though were Knurr and Spell and Nipsy. Both of these games required a good eye and a very strong arm.

Knurr and Spell was played with a potty. This was a particularly large marble made from hard, baked clay. Its colour was always white. A pick shaft was the next essential and the third item was a board which was made in two sections about six inches by four inches. The sections were carefully joined in the centre but placed on a round piece of wood which gave the whole thing a see-saw action. A hole was carefully scooped on one side and in this rested the potty. The game consisted of banging down on the side which did not hold the potty and, as the potty rose, the player swiped it as hard as he could to see how far he could send it. This is not as easy as it sounds! The men always divided up into teams and that team which scored the longest hits were, of course, the winners.

Naturally a game like this was played in the open fields because a well-hit potty was as lethal as a bullet! Naturally also, bets were placed!

Nipsy was similar but there was no potty. Its place was taken with a small wooden peg made from box wood. It shone like crystal from constant rubbing and chammerfering.

The pick shafts were shaved down to fine points with glass; no other method was ever used. Then, in their turn, their whole length would be lovingly polished with other glass until the whole shaft glistened and winked in the sun light.

Nipsy was the more difficult of the two games. The little wooden peg, called a spell, was so light and small that great strength was needed to make it rise high enough for a hit to take place. The miners though were a tough breed with excellent muscles developed from years hewing coal on their backs with pick and shovel.

These two games were so popular that mine competed against mine and clubs and pubs against each other. There were nine pubs and two working men's clubs in the district so competition was never lacking!

Another favourite pastime was Pitch and Toss. An isolated and remote area was found and two lookouts were always posted, for the police were hot stuff on attempting to stamp out all gambling games in those stern Methodist days. They never succeeded – but – they tried!

The Mechanics Institute provided snooker and in the Winter education. Evening classes were considered vitally important. No miner who risked his life in those hazardous mining days before Nationalization wanted his son to follow him so education was always fiercely encouraged . . .

Some of the more fortunate miners saved up and purchased a fishing rod. They fished in the local canal and the River Dearne. Competition was most keen. A few men even travelled into Lincolnshire to compete in the angling competitions. My Dad even won a barrel of beer once!

The pit bosses went shooting. About a mile across the railway hump was an isolated patch of water though it could never by any stretch of the imagination be called a lake. Duck could always be found there and the bosses considered it a favourite and cherished place for them alone. Many of the miners went with the bosses; sometimes to shoot themselves but usually only to retrieve the shot birds. My father was an excellent shot whether with a gun – or catapult! He was always one of the fortunate ones chosen. Apart from his natural skill he was a lively-witted fellow, well liked and much in demand as company. We children would go long periods without seeing him, then my tiny Mother would put her size 3 foot down firmly and Dad would then be around the house for a bit until he took to roaming again! . . .

The Chapel gave magnificent teas. It was Grandpa's job to boil the great hams as well as bake the bread and teacakes. Grandma and my Mother attended to the sponges and all the other marvellous foods.

On Tea Day itself all the Chapel older ladies wore a dress almost uniform. Their bodices were black with very long black skirts. Over these they wore a starched white apron with a bib. It was their job to cut the mountain of sandwiches and to fill plate after plate with the cakes. One old lady's speciality was seed cake. We children called this Funeral cake because no one would have dreamed of having a Funeral Tea without a seed cake.

Each cake plate was dressed with a lovely d'oyley. They were crocheted by hand and every lady vied with the other to produce the nicest one.

It was the job of the men to erect the trestle tables in the Sunday School. These were covered with cloths made from white linen or damask. Every lady had one of these huge cloths and they were handled as treasures and kept solely for great occasions.

I often wondered why the tables did not collapse. The amount and weight of food placed on each table always seemed far too much but, of course, it never was. The food was made all the more wonderful by being cooked and prepared by the people themselves.

The people would pay sixpence to enter, then they would sit and wait for Grace. After this had been sung, the serious business of eating started as if each person had suffered malnutrition until the second beforehand. It was as much as the helpers could do to keep those plates filled.

The money that was taken was always used carefully for the Sunday School funds. It went on outings as well as sports and book prizes for the scholars who gave a good attendance at Sunday School.

When at last the people were eventually filled it was the helpers' turn to sit and eat. How that food would vanish! But there was always some left over to be given to the sick and old who had been unable to attend in person. This chore fell to the children. Alice and myself usually took half a dozen teas which were packed in a large, flat-bottom basket covered with another white cloth.

I liked this part very much. It was fun to visit the old people. They always gave such a welcome. Although most of them certainly could not afford sixpence they always paid. They were fiercely independent and charity was hated.

Even then there was still food left over and this was carefully divided amongst the helpers who usually had children themselves, few of which ever tasted ham or cake except on Tea Day.

The backbone of the Chapels were the old ladies. They were the organizers and administrators who knitted, sewed, crocheted and also solicited the local business men for funds. As most of these had Chapel connections it was quite impossible for them to dodge giving a contribution. Which facts were always quite well known to the old ladies!

Four Teas were given in a year. Two for the adults and two for us children. Ours were at Christmas and prize-giving. Each child received a 'star' card for attendance at Sunday School. The first Sunday in May was the time for the Sunday School Anniversary. For weeks before we had to practice and practice at those hymns which must be sung to absolute perfection on the day. Some children were soloists; others recited special poetry.

Uncle Jim was the Anniversary Organizer. He selected two of the scholars to sing solos in the afternoon and two for the evening. He never chose his sister's children though, even if we were considered the best singers. My mother used to get infuriated over this. She would say, 'His own kids can't sing and he won't let mine!'. This statement too was an Anniversary ritual dialogue!

We were a musical family. One uncle played the piano, another the violin, while a cousin managed the big bass fiddle. Together with the orchestra plus a trumpeter for the Trumpet Voluntary, made a very fine accompaniment for the singers.

The Sunday School teachers and Choir usually sang two pieces from The Messiah and the evening service always included the Hallelujah Chorus.

Every Sunday Grandpa collected Danny and myself for Sunday School both morning and afternoon and then again for Chapel in the evening. Older boys only had to attend the evening service as they worked, and soon Danny started to complain bitterly about Sunday School. He considered he was too big for such childishness.

After the evening service the old men stayed behind by themselves for a prayer meeting. Most of them had been drunken reprobates but now they let off steam with their Hell-fire-and-damnation shoutings. These could be heard a very long way off and caused much scoffing and ribaldry at the nearby local pub where, up to recently, the old men had done their drinking!

One Sunday night I suggested to Danny we should hide in the back pew and listen to what went on. In the end there were six of us hidden in the dark.

Each old man took it in turn. He would get up and start shouting and posturing and calling down God's wrath on all gamblers, drunkards and fornicators. Hell-fire-and-damnation was the one and only theme! Each old man did his level best to outdo his neighbour and some of them actually foamed at the mouth!

We were nearly in hysterics though one or two of our companions started to get very frightened. I dragged Danny out. I knew if Mother ever found out we would be in very serious trouble indeed. Neither Danny nor myself would have been capable of sitting down for a week. I remember Danny became very quiet as we walked back home. 'Do you really think they mean what they say? If so, God cannot be very forgiving!' 'They do while they're there!', I replied, 'but I don't suppose it will make the slightest difference when they get home to start their beer drinking even if it was bought on a Saturday!'

I know that evening made a big impression on Danny. He never forgot what he had heard. It worried him. In later years he did indeed escape from the pit and made hospital work his career. He passed numerous examinations until he became a top laboratory technician and he worked with children for years . . .

Syd Foley
asphalte

Syd Foley was born in 1917 in a London slum known as 'Little Ireland', one of three children of a Cockney mother and an Irish father. His father died in 1919 from chest trouble aggravated by war service, and one child also died in the flu epidemic of that year. Although the family experienced much hardship, Syd, an intelligent boy, won a place at a Roman Catholic grammar school and gained a good School Certificate and a university place which he could not afford to take up. A socialist and pacifist, he was a conscientious objector in the Second World War and was assigned to work in a sawmill, where he has continued ever since ('and I quite like it'). In 1938 he married Winifred, a miner's daughter from the Forest of Dean, then working as a waitress in London, but now well known through her own autobiography, *A Child in the Forest* published in 1974. 'Asphalte' is Syd Foley's first publication.

Nothing can be seen of it now, not a cobble. When you walk round you can hardly imagine it was there, but as the shafts of memory pierce the mists of time it all comes back in pictures. A curious rectangle of cobbled streets, so narrow you could nearly jump across; bounded by the humming, smoking power-station and the clanking, steaming coal-wharf; six blocks of withering, three-storeyed, terraced houses, with a pub on every other corner. The whole place was dying of old age. Right in the middle of it, Mum and Flo and I lived in one room, a first-floor front. The rent for this was five shillings, and Mum used to leave it under the clock for 'Dr Crippen' to collect. No-one knew his real name, but he looked like that famous folk-villain, pince-nez and all, and he was almost as ruthless, chasing his quarry even to the lavatory door. He knew some tricks, and he needed to.

One Monday he left a note under the clock to tell us that owing to shortfall in rents and to our deplorable habits of smashing up our own homes, there would be no more repairs done except by order of the sanitary, and we all knew what that meant. I asked Mum who really owned our house, and she said 'Lord Bleeding Portman'. Not only ours, but all the rest, and a lump of Edgware Road and Oxford Street as well. It was ridiculous! How could one man own a great lump of Oxford Street? He must be so rich! Why was he not king?

Mum said well, he wasn't, that's why, and we'd never see him as he was so busy, not that she wanted to anyway. Lord Bleeding Portman still lived in Marylebone, but down the posh end in a big quiet square. Somehow I felt that Mum was rather ungrateful; it was quite an honour for me. I was proud to live in

a lord's house, although the leg of Mum's bed did keep sinking through the floor
boards and Uncle Bob had to patch it up.

Fifty yards or less from the chimneys of the power station stood the school,
elementary in every sense, and dyed by the swirling sulphur smoke to a nice
shade of clerical grey just right for a church school. It was not graced with a
saint's name, none of them would have owned it; nor hallowed by tradition, nor
hampered by reputation.

But we liked it; it was warm and dry and clean. Twelve o'clock, dinner-time so
called, came all too soon. Out we had to go till two, and there were no school
dinners or milk unless you had consumption, which was hardly worth it. Hunger
sent us home hotfoot, trotting, hopping, jumping, counting the paving stones,
breathless up the stairs and through the ever-open door of our one-room home.
Mum was at work, as usual. A young war widow with two children had to be at
work anywhere she could get it. In winter she washed up and peeled in Dan's
coffee-shop, and in summer the same at Lord's Ground.

The little grate was empty but not clean, the two beds unmade, the lamp
unscrewed ready for filling, the glass chimney dirty by its side. The big china
water-jug on the wash-stand was empty. The little house was so quiet you could
hear the clock ticking. Why wasn't Mrs Mack moving about upstairs? Where had
Gran Smith gone from the back room? Why was Aunt Mag so silent downstairs?

On the table were two plates of margarine sandwiches under a tea-cloth. We
studied them for a time to be sure they were absolutely equal, then sat down and
began to munch. The meal was soon over and the last crumbs picked up with a
licked finger. Flo got up, went to the cupboard, and shut the door with a sigh.
'Wotcher reckon's fer tea, then, Flo?'. 'I dunno, s'no good askin' me, 'ave to wait
'n see, I s'pose. 'I'm still 'ungry.' 'Oh, you! You're always 'ungry! 'Ungry,
'ungry, 'ungry! I reckon you got worms. Anyway, go'n get the water. It's your
turn!'. She swung round on me fiercely, expecting resistance, so I took the other
tack. 'Alright, gi's the bloody jug, big 'ead,' and I ran downstairs to the tap in the
yard. She had the last word, shouting, 'Don't spill it all over the stairs as usual,
you big baby.'

The filled jug was heavy, and I had to carry it with one hand in the handle and
the other under the lip, and waddle up the stairs not to spill it. Flo had cleaned
out the grate and laid the fire. I grabbed the paraffin to fill the lamp, but she
leaped up at me like a gazelle. '*I'll* do that, clumsy. You wipe the glass. Oh, for
Chrissake be careful! You break that Mum'll skin yer.'

We were never reluctant to go back to school; afternoons were short, easy, and
sleepy. In the Infants, the work was done in the mornings. We had done our
sums, torn the Catechism apart, and shouted out in concert to the Almighty to
forgive us our sins. Now we could do what we pleased, and often nothing, which
was quite in order so long as we did it quietly. Sometimes we were told to lower
our heads and feign unwanted sleep while the nuns stood by the fire whispering.

After school Flo hurried home but I was diverted by my mates into a gang
fight. There was a deal of chasing and shouting, insults and stones were hurled,
but the fracas was broken up by the sight of a policeman. Disappointingly, no

blood was shed, but there was promise of another battle when it grew dark, so we all went home victorious.

Mum was in, and the place was clean and tidy. The lamp was lit, turned low for now, and Flo sat by it straining her eyes to read an old comic that we knew by heart. Two saucepans simmered on the hob. Two! Whatever was in them, I was ready for it, but it was not quite ready for me.

'Oh!', said Flo, all aggrieved, "is royal bloody 'ighness 'as turned up now, now it's all done!'.

I struggled for an answer that would absolutely crush her, but Mum interposed. 'Never mind all that, you got a treat tonight. There's neck o' mutton stew, an' boiled rice 'n jam. Only, you got to get the jam. Nip round Finucane's an' get a penn'orth o' jam in this cup. Only, 'fore you do, better get some coal off Clarky. Bucket's empty, 'ere's the fourpence, fourteen pound o' coal, an' beg a few sticks. Don't forget.'

Errands done, and back home again, and Mum had turned the lamp up and was dishing out the stew. It went round twice and a good job it did. That was really our dinner, tea and supper, and we made the most of it. We ate in silence, Flo reading her old comic while I read the newspaper table-cloth upside-down. An old paper was a good table-cloth; no-one cared if it got dirty, you could read it, and it lit the fire next day. In the sheen of the polished body of the lamp you could see the gleaming bedknobs, and again in them the lamp, and in that the bedknobs, and so infinity was present until your eyes grew tired.

The house was alive now with domestic content. Upstairs Mrs Mack was shuffling about getting something tasty for Old Mack's tea. He would come home drunk, and like as not throw it on the fire, plate and all, but she always did it just the same. In the back room Annie the ironer had come home and we could hear Gran Smith scolding her for being late and her bloater spoiling and all. Downstairs Uncle Bob had his gramophone going while Aunt Mag clattered and nagged.

Flo washed up and I went down in the dark twice to fetch water. The street was full of kids, skipping and hopscotching, swinging round the lamp-posts, fighting in the gutters, and we ran out eagerly to join them.

Bedtime, Mum went through my cropped hair with a toothcomb. 'Siddy, you got nits again,' she said wearily, cracking them with her nails, 'you better get a penn'orth o' soft soap tomorrer, an' I'll 'ave another go at 'em. Otherwise, you'll 'ave to go to the bake, an' I won't 'ave the shame of it.'

'Dirty little sod,' cried Flo, whose long dark hair never had nits. I screwed round to poke my tongue at her. I did not care anyway, as long as Mum was combing my hair. Mum turned the lamp down, threw some coal dust on the dying fire, and went into the Phoenix with Aunt Mag for a half of porter. Flo went in the back room to sit with Gran Smith. I got into the bottom end of the little bed and arranged my legs along the wall so as to leave room for Flo at the top end.

It was warm and cosy. The fire glowed red under its crust of dust, a pie of flame. Now, on top of the crust a few little pieces set up in business on their own with tiny blue flames and streaming yellow fumes. I could hear Flo's clear young voice and Gran Smith's grumpy answers. Downstairs Uncle Bob's gramophone boomed on. When I left school, I would be a dustman, too, and I would have a gramophone and sit listening to it in my socks, and smoke my woodbines. Everything was going to be alright; we were all going to live like this nearly for ever; nothing was going to change. Slowly I dozed off to sleep, nits and all.

But it did change, very soon, and that change jumped into our lives suddenly, brutally, and wearing two hobnailed boots.

Old Mack dropped dead in the street, and Uncle Bob carried the corpse upstairs on his back. He stopped on the landing by our open door to catch his breath, then he tramped on up in the dark, and we heard the bedspring squeak as he dropped his grisly burden.

As soon as the old man had been laid to rest in Kensal Green, Mum negotiated with the widow for her back room. A bargain was struck at three-and-six which gave Mrs Mack sixpence profit, and, as she kept saying, she could do with it now. Mum and I went down the market and bought an old iron folding bed for two bob. It grew heavier as we lumbered it round the coal-wharf, so we had several stops, and sat in it in turn, countering the sarcastic jests of neighbours asking where we were going camping.

Mum seemed in a hurry, and I asked her why. 'Never mind,' she said, 'Flo must have her privacy now. She's thirteen. She's a big girl now. Come on. You know what I mean.' I did not, but I banged some nails into the partition, and put a stout string across the room. Mum threw a blanket over it, and there we were, private. We took our things up, that was no burden; the moving was finished, and so was our snug childhood.

The next Saturday, the reason for Mum's urgency walked in with her. A soldier from India, on discharge leave, he wore medal ribbons from the war in Flanders. He had tea with us, talked about India, showed us his scars, and gave us a ha'penny each. We went to bed reluctantly, leaving him down there with Mum. We did not like him, although he was brown and handsome and strong. Soon he was there every evening, and on Sundays we were made to go to Sunday School so he could have his lie-down. When we came home, there he was asleep on Mum's bed, and Mum was by the fire, singing, and combing her hair. Sometimes he was there in the mornings, and I had to fetch the jugs of cold water he threw liberally over his suntanned shoulders.

Well, they got married. The wedding was a very quiet one, practically hushed. Hardly anyone but us was there, only Grand-dad who had had a shave and fat Annie who was drunk. There was no reception, no extra food, no cake, and no honeymoon, but they went into the Phoenix, and there was a grand booze-up.

On the Monday, our new Dad, Alf Sullivan, assumed his role as master, bully, judge, jury and executioner. His word was law and its instruments were his fist, his belt, and his naily boot. Mum soon realized that she had backed a loser, and she paid dearly for whatever she got out of that marriage.

Alf was a casual worker, very casual, much given to arguing with foremen. When he was out of work, Mum had to work harder than ever, and Flo and I became proper cadgers, taking pathetic notes to the Relief and the Salvation Army, lining up with the scruffs for a pennorth of soup, tramping to the West End for stale bread, going to the pawnshop for one and another, chopping sticks, running errands at cut rates, waiting around at the back of Lord's Ground for them to throw their waste food out. We plagued the butcher for bones and oddments, and begged credit from all the little shops; Mum always paid up in the end, somehow.

Eventually came the ultimate deprivation; Alf stopped our Sunday 'asphalte'. Mum had always managed to save a few pence for us to have this little treat; it was always something to look forward to, and well worth waiting for. Asphalte was Dinny Finucane's speciality, always in the middle of his shop window to make your mouth water.

They made it themselves; great big square slabs of a sort of jam tart, thick layers of fatty pastry, plenty of oozy jam in between, and topped off and clothed in white icing. The icing turned a little grey as it cooled, and the colour and the texture gave it its name. This confection was one of man's greatest achievements, nothing like it before or since. Dinny sold it more by whim than weight. If he was in a good mood, or he had a piece past its prime, you might be lucky and get a good helping for your money, though he would not sell less than a penn'orth. Kids with a ha'penny each could club together for a piece, take it round the corner and argue about it, but not in the shop.

There was spite in Alf's ban, because he kept it up when he was working and some money coming in, and we were having butter sometimes, and Mum bought a gramophone on the never-never. He still maintained it when his trouser pocket was stuffed full of notes. He had compounded his pension for eighty pounds, and we did not get a penny of it. He took it into the Phoenix, and to make sure not to lose on the deal, he set about smoking and drinking himself to death.

One day, or rather one night, we got a bit of our own back. It was one of those hot nights when no-one can really sleep, but this was no matter for tomorrow was Sunday. Flo and I lay sleepless and fidgety upstairs, waiting for the boozy singers in the pub to do 'Nellie Dean' for the last time. We heard them turned out, and soon Alf's drunken lumbering footsteps coming up, and then him and Mum having a dreadful row. Soon he was shouting for me to get up, nothing else would do; so, fearing for the lamp, I ran downstairs.

I was to get him one-and-sixpence worth of eels and mash, and hurry, but not so as to spill the gravy. I was practised at this, so not really minding I grabbed a basin and trotted off. There was a queue, and it was almost midnight when I got back. Alf had his boots off, but kept one handy to throw at me if necessary. Sitting with his feet in the coal-bucket he wolfed the lot, and washed it down with a quart bottle of brown ale. Mum leaned over to take the basin off the mantelpiece, then she stood and watched him close, like a doctor, and said, "'E's paralytic now, drunk as a lord, don't know what 'e *is* doin', an' couldn't remember nothin'. 'E can't do no 'arm till mornin'. I'm goin' down to Aunt Mag's; till I'm back you sit an' watch 'e don't tip the lamp up.'

Half-asleep I sat and watched, and soon he stirred and began to undress by habit in soldierly fashion. Jacket, waistcoat and belt were hung nice and square on the chair-back. With the control of a real boozer he teetered over to the bed, took off his trousers, and began to fold them. As he did, there was a pleasant clink of money, and he took a handful out. Looking craftily about, he unscrewed the brass knob of the bedstead, put two coins in, and they clattered quietly down to the bottom. I saw them in the dim light; they were a half-crown and a florin. He screwed the knob back, pulled out the bucket for a great long boozy piddle, fell on the bed in his long-johns, and went to sleep at once.

Next morning I told Mum all about it. 'The crafty bastard,' she said. 'You sure? Perhaps you was dreamin'!' I convinced her. 'Right,' she said, 'we'll bloody 'ave it. 'E owes it. But say nothin', not even to Flo, else we'll both cop a black eye. 'Sides, knowin' 'im, might be a trap, but I doubt it. We'll see.' Wednesday morning, Alf was flat broke because he borrowed woodbine money off her, so now she knew for sure.

Dinner-time, we stripped the bed, knocked the spring out, canted the bed-head carefully upside-down, and out slid the two coins, a half-crown and a florin, just as I had said. All Mum could say was, 'Well,' then after, 'I'll give these bloody bugs a bashin' now we got it to pieces.'

I stood there quiet, looking at her as she looked at the money. She looked at me, then she reached for a big plate. Mum was always one to make up her mind quick. "Ere,' she said, 'nip round Dinny Finucane's an' get a bob's-worth of asphalte; no, get one-and-six worth, le's make pigs of ourselves for a change.'

It was the best errand I had ever run. Dinny was most impressed by the amount and reality of the money in my palm. 'Gawd,' he said, 'your Mum backed a winner? She owes me a bit, let me think, now . . . ' I snapped him off, 'No, she don't Dinny. She cleared you up last Friday; I brought it round meself. Give us eighteenpence worth of asphalte please.'

He must have been in a good mood, or the asphalte gone a bit stale in the heat, because he cut a great big square of the lovely stuff, and the corners of the soggy pastry bent over the side of the plate. The jam dripped out, and I caught it on my finger not to waste it. We three ate the lot at once, every atom, and I felt sick.

Through the years Alf had his four-and-six back over and over again.

Margaret Perry

The author was born in a terrace house in Sneinton Dale, a working-class area of Nottingham, in 1916. Although her father was a relatively well-paid skilled engineer, her mother was not a good manager and throughout Margaret's childhood debt and poverty were her constant fears. She gives an unusual, frank account of her parents' backgrounds and married life, their solitary habits and inability to communicate, and also describes the improvements which took place in their living standards in the years immediately before the outbreak of the Second World War. Their move to a new suburban house with bathroom, garden and other amenities was an experience shared by a good many better-off working-class people in the more prosperous regions of England at this time. It seems at last to have brought her parents into a closer and happier relationship. Margaret Perry's full-length, unpublished autobiography, of which this is a small part, was written in 1975.

Writing about one's own relations is, as with all opinions, a very one-sided affair, but far more so within a family, where reactions to each other are mostly completely different from reactions to outsiders. Therefore when I say, for instance, that my Father was a miserably natured man and my Mother a happy natured woman, it could well be that the reverse was true. I rarely saw either of them in the company of their friends and doubt in fact they had any. So this, then, was my opinion of my family.

I loved my Father when I was a small child. And he loved his children, the youngest always being the favourite. He, himself, had been the third of a family of ten children, and the victim of his father, a stern Victorian, who believed, as was the tradition, that children should be seen and not heard. This paternal attitude seemed not to have had a lasting effect on the rest of his brothers and sisters, for I recollect sitting uncomfortably on horse-hair chairs for many boring hours on our occasional visits to the Grandparents, listening to the chat of these numerous aunts and uncles. My Father's voice, when he did speak, was little more than a whisper and a husky whisper at that, as he had bronchitis all his life, which heavy smoking did little to help. He married my Mother at the age of 20 years, having got her pregnant first. This seemed to be common-place at that time, with the working class, who, being extremely poor, couldn't think of marriage unless forced into it in this way. Nevertheless once married, they appeared to be extremely faithful and I never heard a breath of scandal about any relations of ours. They were a highly moral lot whom one couldn't imagine indulging in any sort of sex life whatsoever. My Father's youngest brother Arthur was the oddity of the family. No doubt these days he would have been termed 'Gay'. He was taught Ballet Dancing as a boy and had been 'on the stage'. There were one or two photographs of him in a ballet pose and dressed as a woman in a sequin-encrusted dress. On our Sunday visits I remember him sitting surrounded by miles of net, stitching on thousands of sequins . . . He was very good to his mother. My Father would never go to see his parents unless he could take them some money. In those days their pension was about ten shillings per week, so they relied upon their sons for support. Three pound notes were usually left discreetly on the table after tea. It was never mentioned. It must have been difficult for my Father to give this when he had to watch his wife and children in such need, though we were less poor than most of our neighbours in those days of mass unemployment. My Father had a regular job with a firm of

Wholesalers. He was the Chief Engineer, though he had no staff but a young boy, whom he spoke to like a dog, (but not as *he* would have spoken to a dog). I think this boy was the only creature he ever had power over in his life. Father wore overalls for his work, but never came home in them. He dressed as much like a white-collar worker as he could afford on his four pounds per week. He was an Electrical Engineer, and had served his apprenticeship at the Woolwich Arsenal, during the Great War. Thus he hadn't been called to fight in the war and was now slightly better off than most of his class as he had a trade.

His hobby was 'fiddling' with old wireless sets though I don't remember anything emitting from any except excruciating noises. He didn't talk to either my mother or we children, because he had nothing to say. He loved us but wasn't interested in us. He had his job, his wireless and his Sunday mornings in the pub with his brothers. The Sunday mornings were compulsory outings. Whatever the weather, he walked a few miles to his brothers' allotment garden, taking us children with him. In the summer, it meant a lemonade and a packet of crisps in the pub garden with my sister Beryl and any other lucky little girls. My father drank only beer, and not a great deal of that, but he seemed to need a glass of beer before he could speak. Having drunk his first half-pint, his thin-lipped face would relax and assume a constant amused smile. He was like a child trying to be polite and look as though he was enjoying himself. This expression lasted until he fell asleep in the chair after our Sunday dinner.

We were always late home from these jaunts, as we never left the pub until well after closing time at 2 p.m. Then we walked home. It didn't occur to him to take a bus. Sunday morning was for walking and drinking. During the winter months when it was too cold for us to go with him, he drank rather more. Then, the smile turned into a cheeky grin, and his trilby hat took on a rakish angle. My Mother despised him when he appeared like this and almost threw his dinner at him. We had usually had ours, and his had been kept hot in the oven. He invariably pushed it away in disgust. He didn't enjoy food at the best of times due to a stomach full of peptic ulcers and my Mother wasn't the best of cooks, but her Sunday roast was always eatable. Beer and ulcers apparently weren't conducive to eating a good meal. Every few months, however, the ulcers flared up and threw back everything he ate. He would be in terrible pain for about three weeks at a time, but the idea of either going to or calling in the doctor didn't seem to arise. Anyway the doctor had to be paid in those days and one didn't waste money on such luxuries. Nor did my Father ever take a day off from his job in his whole life. When he was ill, he had no beer, no cigarettes and lived on gruel. He suffered like this, with no medical attention whatever, for as far back as I can remember. When he was sixty, his poor stomach finally perforated and an operation saved him. For the first time, at least within my memory, I watched him eat with enjoyment. And he had a subject for conversation, for months to come.

Both my maternal Grandparents died when my Mother was very young, her Father from alcoholic poisoning and, by all accounts, her Mother from hard work. They had kept a thriving business in the form of a 'Fish and Chips' shop.

By 'they' I mean my Grandmother, for her husband contributed nothing to the business but an ability to drink away the profits. He also managed to make his wife pregnant regularly once a year, but as she was usually up and out to the fishmarket at 5 a.m. within a couple of days of each birth, not many of these babies survived, nor in fact did she herself survive her early forties. My mother spoke bitterly of the hard life her Mother had had, not for lack of money, as was the usual cause of suffering then, but for lack of help from a sober partner. My Mother remembered sleeping under the counter of the shop every night until it was closed at midnight. She remembered most the terrible poverty of customers of the St Ann's Well Road district, the barefoot ragged children and the reek of the urine-soaked babies. She told me this smell had thwarted her maternal instincts and not until she had a baby of her own did she discover they don't smell all the time. She was 16 when her Mother died, and then went to live with a married brother until, following the tradition, she became pregnant and married at twenty. This fact was never mentioned, of course, it just came home to me in later years when the wedding anniversaries came too close to my eldest sister's birthday for respectability. I found this fact extremely difficult to reconcile with my parents' attitude to sexual morality. When I heard either of them railling about 'The Youth of Today' and 'When I was young' etc. . . , as parents are apt to do, I was frequently tempted to ask in high sarcastic pitch, 'And what about you then?' But I never did. The whole question of sex was just not in my parents' vocabulary. Nor did one use words like 'love' or 'kiss'. They seemed to stick in their throats, as did any term of endearment. 'Duck', being Nottinghamese and pronounced with a strong Nottingham 'u', was the only acceptable term in our class of society . . .

In 1922, my Father was given his 'steady' job as Foreman Engineer and things began to look up. With a daughter of eight and a son of six, they thought their family complete, but when my own presence was threatening my Mother was furious. She told me she drank a lot of Gin, soaked in hot baths, and 'jumped off the copper top' every day, which was the recognized way of procuring an abortion at that time. The fact that it rarely succeeded was no deterrent it seems.

The result of this drastic attempt at abortion was to have an adverse effect upon my whole life. My birth was breech and in 1922 obstetrical knowledge did not include the skill of turning the baby before birth. Pulling a baby out feet first can cause irreparable damage. In my case it caused a squinting eye which I had to live with for fifteen years, yet another instance of medical ignorance. These days squints are corrected within the first two years. Mine was left until I had 'finished growing' and consequently was only a partial success.

However in due course I was accepted and loved as is the norm, but the damage done to me had frightened my Mother. When my sister Beryl was on the way, four years later, there was no question of 'doing anything silly' this time.

The 1930s were not called 'The Depression' without good reason. In 'our street' every other household had a father on 'the dole' which meant a few shillings a week to keep his family, but with his trade my father was one of the lucky ones. This was not to say he earned enough to keep a family of six – far from it. My poor Mother, who for the first 16 years of her life had not known poverty, could not learn to manage her housekeeping money. Dad got his wages every Friday morning and deposited £3 under the clock on the mantlepiece before returning to work in the afternoon. Immediately I was sent down the street to pay Mrs S. whatever had been borrowed from her during the week. It would be borrowed again within a few days, but no matter, this debt had to be paid first. Then my Mother sat down with a scrap of paper and pencil and wrote out the budget. It varied little, and is imprinted in my memory.

Rent	11	0d	
Club	6	0d	this was for clothes and household things
Butcher	10	0d	
Milk	5	0d	this bought 3 pints a day. We were never short of milk.
Grocery	30	0d	
	£3 2	0d	

Then she had to work out which bill to miss. Sometimes we hid from the milkman on Saturday mornings, sometimes from the clubman. We had to be quiet, when there was a familiar knock at the door and sometimes hid behind a chair. The pretence at being out saved embarrassment on both sides of admitting the inability to pay. This degrading situation was not taken philosophically by my Mother as with many women, who were brought up to it. She was shamed by it and by her own inability to 'manage' her regular income. Never having learnt as a child how to cook with cheaper meat or make filling meals out of vegetables, she spent more than her neighbours on food. Unwilling to see her children shabby, she made most of our clothes in good materials and they were passed down of course, as in the best of families, though we always had new shoes. She owed the clothes club about £30 I suppose . . . And everything we ever acquired other than food was bought from this same store. This was a continual source of embarrassment to me with my slightly better-off friends whose mothers bought things from different shops. I never knew the answer when asked 'Why do you get everything from the "Star Stores"?' I knew they suspected it was for credit trading only, and hated being put in this situation. Some weeks we didn't pay the rent of eleven shillings but this was cleared up once a year out of my Father's holiday pay. Hence we never had a holiday. Our fuel bills must have been quite small. A gas cooker and gas mantles for light which were paid by a penny meter were no problem. We were the first people in the street to have electricity installed after the main cable was laid, as my Dad did it himself. This was a shilling meter, but as there were no gadgets to run at that time, a shilling went a long way . . .

A neighbour, Mrs Brown, with whom I spent more time than with my own family, began to teach me the piano. 'She is getting on like a house on fire,' she told my parents, so Dad, proud as a peacock, bought me a second-hand piano. On H.P. of course, and another weekly item to add to my Mother's list. I got home from school one day to find her in tears, a rare occurrence. She'd been skipping the payments, and they were taking back the piano the next day unless she could find the money. My Dad found it, somewhere, but ever after this, I took no pleasure playing. I knew it was a burden, but it was eventually paid off and I am grateful to this day for the sacrifice. I was badly taught and had little talent, but could make a lot of satisfying noise.

This was not the only time my poor Mother was in trouble over money. She had borrowed a few pounds from a money-lender without telling Father, and couldn't pay it back. She was threatened with the courts and had to sink her pride once more and tell Father. I don't know why she was so afraid to do this. She had not squandered the money, she had no luxuries herself and I remember hating my Father at this time for letting her get into this situation, and I hated his wasting money on cigarettes. It seemed to me very wicked and self-indulgent for him to spend a shilling every day on cigarettes, when there were so many other things we needed. Sometimes I would refuse to fetch them for him, but on the few occasions when he did try to give it up, it was my Mother who would fetch him another packet to sweeten his mood. We children didn't notice how sulky he could be with her, as even when in the best of moods, he didn't talk to her. She had acquired the habit of singing to herself to break the silences and didn't know she was singing for much of the time. Many times I begged her to be quiet while I was trying to read or write something for school. It was a constant distraction to me, as I'd learnt all the words of her songs, and couldn't shut them out of my mind, but she sang on through her life almost to her dying day. From early rising, she sang through her morning's work till she sat down regularly at 2 p.m. every day with her book. Then, with a short break to get the tea ready, she read through the evening till bedtime. The public library was her salvation. She read four or five books a week all her life but had no-one to discuss them with. She had read all the classics several times over in her youth and again in later years, and the library had a job to keep her supplied with current publications. Married to a different man, she could have been an intelligent and interesting woman. She suffered frequently with severe migraine headaches, which I often thought in later years were caused by the frustration of living with my Father. Her debts and money worries she shared with me, not suspecting that I took them as seriously as I did. They made my whole childhood a misery, for I visualized us being turned out of the house one day and my parents put in gaol. I reckoned that her debts amounted to about £100 and prayed regularly for ways of making this money so that my poor Mother could start afresh with a clean slate . . .

By 1936 the financial situation seemed to improve. My brother was earning enough to keep himself and pay my Mother a few shillings, and when I got a job at fourteen, it was decided that we could afford a better house in a 'nicer' neighbourhood. We moved a couple of miles out of Nottingham to a detached modern house with a garden. We rented it for £1 per week. We were all thrilled with it and took on a new lease of life. The joy of a bathroom can only be appreciated when you've lived without one. The ritual of lighting the copper, dragging the zinc bath up the cellar steps, emptying the dirty water every time anyone had a bath, was at last over.

The new house was only a few minutes walk from the woods so very soon we acquired a dog, a Springer Spaniel which of course had to be exercised. My parents started to take him for walks together, and through him began to communicate with each other. A strange new relationship developed. Dad would say, 'Ask your Mum if she wants to go for a walk' or 'Tell your mum we're going for a drink.' And when they were out, the dog was asked which way he wanted to go and whether he was ready to go home yet . . .

Within a year we moved house yet again to a 'very desirable property', still rented of course, as no money was ever put by, but my Father seemed to have more ready money at that time though his job hadn't changed. We had new furniture and carpets and things were paid for as they were acquired now. My mother began to have an easier life. She loved the garden and the greenhouse. She joined the Women's Institute and Old Time Dancing and went on outings with them, but within another year the Second World War started. I found her weeping when making the black-out curtains one evening. I was seventeen years old and the war to me was exciting. Far from consoling her, I laughed at her worries, innocent of what was to come . . .

REFERENCES

PREFACE

1. David Vincent, 'The Growth of Working-Class Consciousness in the First Half of the Nineteenth Century: A study of the autobiographies of working men', Cambridge Ph.D. Thesis, 1975.
2. William Matthews, *British Autobiographies: Bibliography of British Autobiographies Published or Written before 1951*, 1955, reprinted 1968.
3. An example of this form of autobiography is that of George Mockford. See this volume pp.72–7.
4. Recent republications have added to their number, e.g. *Testaments of Radicalism: Memoirs of Working-Class Politicians 1790–1885*, ed. with an Introduction by David Vincent, 1977; John Wilson, *Memories of a Labour Leader*, ed. John Burnett, 1980.
5. Peter Laslett, *The World We Have Lost*, 2nd edn, 1971, pp.109–10.
6. Philippe Ariès, *Centuries of Childhood*, 1962.
7. Lloyd de Mause (ed.), *The History of Childhood*, 1974. Further contributions from the psychohistorical school are to be found in the *Journal of Family History* and the *Journal of Interdisciplinary History*.
8. Ivy Pinchbeck and Margaret Hewitt, *Children in English Society*, Vol. II, 1973.
9. Lawrence Stone, *The Family, Sex and Marriage in England 1500–1800*, 1971.
10. Michael Anderson, *Family Structure in Nineteenth Century Lancashire*, 1971.
11. Edward Shorter, *The Making of the Modern Family*, 1977.
12. Joan Scott, Louise Tilly and Miriam Cohen, 'Women's Work and European Fertility Patterns', *Journal of Interdisciplinary History*, Vol. VI, 1976.

PART ONE – CHILDHOOD

1. Margaret Cunningham, 'End of Exploring: An Autobiography', unpublished autobiography (199 pp. typescript), p.4. The author was born in 1900, the daughter of the vicar of Wonersh, Surrey.
2. Averil Edith Thomas, 'Me', unpublished autobiography, privately communicated by Averil Harper Smith (26 pp. ms.), p.2. The author was born in 1893 in Melton Mowbray.
3. Charles Esam, unpublished autobiography (96 pp. ms.), p.2. The author was born in Thornton Heath, Surrey, in 1899.
4. James Carter, *Memoirs of a Working Man*, 1845, p.18. Carter was born in Colchester in 1792 and wrote his autobiography at the age of fifty-two; a continuation of the memoirs was published in 1850.
5. Christopher Thomson, *The Autobiography of an Artisan*, 1847, pp.31–3. Thomson was born on Christmas Day 1799, at Kingston-upon-Hull.

6. W. J. Linton, *Memories*, 1895, p.2. Linton was born in 1812 in the Mile End Road, London.

7. Mary Paley Marshall, *What I Remember*, with an Introduction by G. M. Trevelyan, 1947, p.1. Mary Marshall was born in 1850, the daughter of a country rector, near Stamford, Lincolnshire; she was one of the first students at Newnham College, Cambridge, and later married the famous economist, Arthur Marshall. She lived until 1944.

8. Jack McQuoid, 'One Man in his Time', unpublished autobiography (55 pp. typescript), p.22. The author was born in West Derby, Liverpool, in 1910.

9. Samuel Mountford, 'A Memoir', unpublished autobiography (28 pp. typescript), p.4. The author was born in 1907 in a suburb of Birmingham.

10. Charles Esam, op. cit. (see n.3), p.6.

11. James Dawson Burn, *The Autobiography of a Beggar Boy*, 1st edn, 1855; new edn with an introduction by David Vincent, 1978, p.40. Burn was probably born in Dumfries between 1805 and 1806; the murder to which he refers took place in 1807.

12. Frank Wensley, 'My Memories 1890–1914', unpublished autobiography, p.1. The author was born in 1887 in Higher Venn, north Devon.

13. Thomas Cooper, *The Life of Thomas Cooper, Written by Himself*, 1872, republished with an Introduction by John Saville, 1971, pp.4–5. Cooper began attending school in 1810 at Gainsborough, Lincolnshire.

14. James Hopkinson, *Memoirs of a Victorian Cabinet Maker 1819–1894*, ed. Jocelyne Baty Goodman, 1968, p.5. Hopkinson was born at Cropwell Butler, Nottinghamshire in 1819.

15. Eleanor Hewson, 'An Edwardian Childhood', unpublished autobiography (115 pp. typescript), pp.16–17. The author was born in 1905, the daughter of a professor living in Barnes.

16. Jack Goring, 'Autobiographical Notes', unpublished autobiography (321 pp. ms.), p.14. The author was born in 1861 in Wenlock Street, off New North Road, London and his memoirs were written in 1938. They were kindly provided by his daughter, Elsa Houghton.

17. Averil Edith Thomas, op. cit. (see n.2), pp.2–3.

18. George Grundy, *Fifty-Five Years at Oxford: An Unconventional Autobiography*, 1945, pp.17–19. The author was born in 1861 in Wallasey, Cheshire, the son of a private school proprietor and grandson of a clergyman.

19. Jack McQuoid, op. cit. (see n.8), p.8.

20. J. H. Ingram, 'A Wartime Childhood', unpublished autobiography (21 pp. typescript), pp.1–2. The author was born in Manchester but spent his childhood in the village of Barnardiston, Suffolk.

21. Thomas Cooper, op. cit. (see n.13), pp.5–6.

22. Eleanor Hewson, op. cit. (see n.15), p.24.

23. Margaret Cunningham, op. cit. (see n.1), pp.10–11.

24. Marianne Farningham, *A Working Woman's Life: An Autobiography*, c. 1900, pp.20–22. The author was born in Farningham, Kent, in 1834, and took her pseudonym from her place of birth. Her father was Joseph Hearn, a small tradesman.

25. Margaret Cunningham, op. cit. (see n.1), p.13.

26. Ethel Davidson, 'Without My Brother', unpublished autobiography (246 pp. typescript), pp.49–50. The author was born in 1907 in a Thameside Essex town, where her parents kept a small shop.

27. Thomas Carter, op. cit. (see n.4), pp.37–8.

28. Mercy Collisson, 'Memories of a Country Rectory', unpublished autobiography, ch.3, p.4. The author was born in 1900 at Gravenhurst, Bedfordshire, where her father was rector.

29. Stella Entwistle, 'Web of Sunny Air', unpublished autobiography (175 pp. typescript), p.91. See this volume pp.108–13.

30. Ellen Nesbitt, 'Gemini Child', unpublished autobiography (127 pp. typescript), p.25 et seq. The author was born in a Yorkshire mining village in 1930.

31. Eleanor Hutchinson, 'The Bells of St Mary's', unpublished autobiography (100 pp. typescript), pp.22–3. The author was born in Paddington, London, in 1915.

32. Winifred Griffiths, *One Woman's Story*, privately printed, 1979, p.31. The author became the wife of the Rt Hon. James Griffiths, Minister of National Insurance, 1945–50, and deputy to Hugh Gaitskell in 1956.

33. Jack Goring, op. cit. (see n.16), pp.28–9.

34. James Dawson Burn, op. cit. (see n.11), p.67. Burn was referring particularly to a wild moorland region in north Cumberland.

35. Charles Shaw, *When I Was a Child, by An Old Potter*, 1st edn, 1903; facsimile edn, 1977, p.54. The author was born in Tunstall in 1832.

36. John Clare, *Sketches in the Life of John Clare, Written by Himself and Addressed to His Friend John Taylor Esq.*, 1821; first published, ed. with an Introduction by Edmund Blunden, 1931, pp.56, 70. Clare was born in Helpstone, Northamptonshire, in 1793.

37. Reginald Gowshall, *With the Turn of the Traveller*, privately printed, 1971, p.8. The author was born at Theddlethorpe All Saints, Lincolnshire in 1906.

38. Margaret Cunningham, op. cit. (see n.1), p.70.

39. Eleanor Hewson, op. cit. (see n.15), p.54.

40. Harry Alfred West, unpublished autobiography (50 pp. typescript), p.10. The author was born in Upper Stanton, Somerset, in 1888; his memoir was kindly supplied by his daughter, Mrs E. de Kluiver.

41. Beatrice Stallan, 'Childhood Recollections', unpublished autobiography. The author was born in 1873 in Sawston, Cambridgeshire; her memoir was supplied by her grandson, Mr C. E. Tongue.

42. Enid K. F. Stuart Scott, 'I Wear a Hat: A Cambridge Childhood 1900–1916', unpublished autobiography (117 pp. typescript), pp.4–5. The author was born in 1900.

43. Leonard W. Ellisdon, 'Starting from Victoria', unpublished autobiography (118 pp. typescript), p.1. The author was born in 1885 in Brixton, London.

44. *A Cornish Waif's Story: An Autobiography*, with a Foreword by A. L. Rowse, 1954.

45. Wilfred Middlebrook, 'Trumpet Voluntary', unpublished autobiography, p.50. The author was born in Lancashire, c. 1900.

46. Kathleen Betterton, 'White Pinnies, Black Aprons', unpublished autobiography (143 pp. typescript), p.3. See this volume pp.204–11.

47. Ethel M. Clark, 'Their Small Corner', unpublished autobiography, privately communicated (109 pp. typescript), p.21. The author was born at Wollaston, Gloucestershire, in 1904.

48. ibid., pp.56–7.

49. Ruth Howe, 'A Twenties Childhood', unpublished autobiography, p.3.

50. Albert Ellis, 'As It Was', unpublished autobiography (16 pp. typescript), p.7. The author was born in Bolton in 1897.

51. Syd Metcalfe, unpublished autobiography, (83 pp. typescript), pp.2–3. The author was born in London in 1908.

52. Daisy Cowper, 'De Nobis', unpublished autobiography (109 pp. typescript), p.42. See this volume pp.198–204.

53. Kathleen Hilton-Foord, 'The Survivor: Memories of a Little Dover Girl' (6 pp. typescript), p.3. The author was born in Dover in 1903.

54. Edward Punter, 'So Often Alone', unpublished autobiography (Part I, Childhood, 114 pp. typescript), p.70. The author was born in 1897; his memoir was kindly supplied by his widow, Mrs H. M. Punter.

55. Leonard W. Ellisdon, op. cit. (see n.43), p.4.

56. Patrick MacGill, *Children of the Dead End: The Autobiography of a Navvy*, 1914, p.19.

57. Arthur Frederick Goffin, 'A Grey Life', unpublished autobiography (96 pp. typescript), pp.10–34. The author was born in Beccles in 1879; his memoir was supplied by his son, Mr J. R. Goffin.

58. Katherine Henderson '(née Dudley), 'Had I But Known', unpublished autobiography (7 pp. typescript), p.2. The author was born in Ruckinge, Romney Marsh, in 1908, the youngest of fourteen children.

59. Benjamin Taylor, 'A Sketch of the Author's Experience', p.2. This autobiography, of thirty pages, forms an introduction to a collection of Taylor's sermons, which were published in 1861. It was kindly brought to my notice by his great-granddaughter, Mrs P. Cant.

60. James Hopkinson, op. cit. (see n.14), p.6.

61. Mercy Collisson, op. cit. (see n.28), ch.3.

62. Margaret Cunningham, op. cit. (see n.1), pp.44–5.

63. Marianne Farningham, op. cit. (see n.24), pp.51–3.

64. Beatrice Stallan, op. cit. (see n.41), p.32.

65. Winifred Griffiths, op. cit., (see n. 32) pp.33–4.

66. James Griffiths, *Pages from Memory*, 1969, p.11.

67. Thomas Cooper, op. cit. (see n.13), pp.37–9.

68. John James Bezer, 'The Autobiography of One of the Chartist Rebels of 1848', first published in the *Christian Socialist*, September–December 1851; republished in *Testaments of Radicalism: Memoirs of Working-Class Politicians 1790–1885*, ed. with an Introduction by David Vincent, 1977, p.166 et seq. Bezer was born in Spitalfields, London, in 1816, the son of a barber.

69. Adeline Hodges, 'I Remember', unpublished autobiography (160 pp. ms.), pp.75–6. The author was born in the mining village of Dawdon, near Seaham Colliery, Durham, in 1899; her memoir was kindly supplied by her daughter, Mrs J. Pace.

70. Lottie Barker, 'My Life as I Remember It 1899–1920', unpublished auto-

biography (70 pp. typescript), p.12. The author was born in Nottingham in 1899; her memoir was kindly supplied by her granddaughter, Mrs P. Hill.

71. Arthur Frederick Goffin, op. cit. (see n.57), p.34.

72. Leonard W. Ellisdon, op. cit. (see n.43), p.3.

73. Eleanor Hutchinson, op. cit. (see n.31), p.19.

74. Winifred Relph, 'Through Rough Ways', unpublished autobiography (62 pp. typescript), p.19. The author was born in 1912.

75. Alice Foley, *A Bolton Childhood*, 1973, p.23. See this volume pp. 100–107.

76. Stella Entwistle, op. cit. (see n.29), pp.47, 108.

77. Gwen Millington, unpublished autobiography, privately communicated (19 pp. typescript), pp.7–9. The author was born in the Finchley Road, London, in 1914, but had a Victorian upbringing as she lived with her grandparents.

78. Leslie R. Missen, unpublished autobiography (61 pp. typescript), pp.10–12. The author was born in Cambridge in 1897, graduated from the university there, and ultimately became Chief Education Officer for East Suffolk.

79. George Grundy, op. cit. (see n.18), p.27.

80. Thomas Walter Laqueur, *Religion and Respectability: Sunday Schools and Working-Class Culture 1780–1850*, 1976, p.246.

81. Averil Edith Thomas, op. cit. (see n.2), p.4.

82. Paul Thompson, *The Edwardians: The Remaking of British Society*, 1977, p.292.

83. Edward Shorter, *The Making of the Modern Family*, 1977, p.89 et seq.

84. Margaret Cunningham, op. cit. (see n.1), p.53.

85. Mary Denison, Church Bells and Tram Cars: A Vicarage Childhood', unpublished autobiography, ch.7, p.6. The author, born in 1906, was the daughter of the vicar of St Chad's, Leeds.

86. Florence M. Goddard, 'Stays and Woollen Stockings', unpublished autobiography (57 pp. typescript), p.47. The author was born in London in 1904.

87. Evelyn M. Glyn Powell, unpublished autobiography, p.9. The author was born in 1901 at Westcliffe-on-Sea, the daughter of a stockbroker. The family included titled relatives, but her father had made some unfortunate speculations and they lived modestly with only one to three maids.

88. Bessie Wallis, 'Yesterday', unpublished autobiography. See this volume pp.306–12.

89. Ernest Richard Shotton, 'Personal History and Memoirs', unpublished autobiography, privately communicated by Mrs Veronica Leach (42 pp. typescript) p.4. The author was born in Birmingham in 1878 and wrote his memoirs in 1963.

90. Charlotte Dorothy Meadowcroft, 'Bygones', unpublished autobiography (35 pp. ms.), p.8. The author was born in 1901, the daughter of a Derbyshire navvy.

91. Winifred Relph, op. cit., (see n.74), p.16.

92. Mrs Layton, 'Memories of Seventy Years', in *Life As We Have Known It* by Co-operative Working Women, ed. Margaret Llewelyn Davies, 1977, p.25. The author was born in Bethnal Green in 1855, the seventh of fourteen children.

93. Eric F. Powell, 'Forest Memories: The Autobiography of a Dean Forester', unpublished autobiography, privately communicated (107 pp. typescript), p.37. The author was born at Blakeney in the Forest of Dean, c. 1900.

94. Ellen Nesbitt, op. cit. (see n.30), p.13.
95. Harry Dorrell, unpublished autobiography, privately communicated (15 pp. typescript), p.7. The author was born in Plaistow, London, in 1903.
96. Betty Sutherland Graeme, *Truly Thankful: Some Memories of Childhood*, privately printed, 1976, p.22. The author was born in 1904 in St Leonards-on-Sea.
97. Leslie R. Missen, op. cit. (see n.78), pp.54–5.
98. Elizabeth Harrison, unpublished autobiography, p.19. The author was born in Preston, Lancashire, in 1902, the daughter of a small shopkeeper.
99. Anita Elizabeth Hughes, 'My Autobiography', unpublished autobiography (15 pp. typescript), p.1. The author was born at Cotesbach, near Lutterworth, Leicestershire, in 1892, the daughter of an estate gardener. Her memoir was written at the age of eighty-four and kindly supplied by her daughter, Mrs Evelyn Wilde.
100. R. W. Morris, unpublished autobiography, p.56. The author was born at Pelton Fell, Co. Durham, in 1895. Sections of the autobiography have been edited by George Patterson, Resident Tutor for Sunderland in the University of Durham Department of Extra-Mural Studies, and published in the *Bulletin of Durham County Local History Society*, October 1977 and April 1978. I am grateful to Mr Patterson for bringing the autobiography to my notice.
101. Edward Punter, op. cit. (see n.54), p.56.
102. Jack McQuoid, op. cit. (see n.8), pp.29–31.
103. Margaret Cunningham, op. cit. (see n.1), p.50.
104. Ludivina Jackson, unpublished autobiography, p.16. The author was born at Thorp Arch, Yorkshire in 1879; her memoir was kindly supplied by her niece, Mrs E. Gibb.
105. Jean Nettleton, unpublished autobiography, p.3.
106. Charles Esam, op. cit. (see n.3), p.16.
107. Gwen Millington, op. cit. (see n.77), p.16.
108. Mercy Collisson, op. cit. (see n.28), ch.4, p.10.
109. Elizabeth Harrison, op. cit. (see n.98), ch. 'Starting School', p.1.
110. Bessie Wallis, op. cit. (see n.88), ch.2, p.4.
111. Albert Pugh, 'I Helped to Build Railroads', published in *Pilot Papers*, November 1946, pp.75–98. The author was born at Pemberton in 1867; his short autobiography was kindly brought to my notice by his son, Roger Pugh.
112. James Dawson Burn, op. cit. (see n.11), p.61.
113. William Esam, unpublished autobiography (22 pp. ms.), pp.4–5. The author was born in Norwich in 1826; his memoir was kindly supplied by his grandson, Charles Esam.
114. William Wright, *From Chimney-Boy to Councillor: The Story of My Life*, privately printed, pp.10–11. The author was born in 1846 at Alton, Hampshire; he began to be employed as a climbing-boy by his father at the age of eight.
115. Ethel M. Clark, op. cit. (see n.47), p.25.
116. Thomas Yates, 'My Memoirs', unpublished autobiography, p.2. The author was born in 1893 at Bamfurlong, a small mining village, near Hindley, Lancashire.
117. Margaret Cunningham, op. cit. (see n.1), p.46.

118. Beatrice Stallan, op. cit. (see n.41), p.23 et seq. The incident referred to occurred c. 1880.

119. Mary Denison, op. cit. (see n.85), ch.2, p.1.

120. Sybil Pearce, *An Edwardian Childhood in Bedford Park*, privately printed, 1978, pp.3–5. I am grateful to Miss E. M. Smith of Brunel University who brought this memoir to my notice.

121. Lilian Slater, unpublished autobiography (228 pp. typescript), p.33. The author was born in Bradford in 1907.

122. Timothy Mountjoy, *Sixty-two Years in the Life of a Forest of Dean Collier*, pp.2–3. Mountjoy's memoirs were first published in 1887 and have been republished by the Forest of Dean Newspapers Ltd, 1971.

123. Roger Langdon, *The Life of Roger Langdon, Told by Himself*, 1909, pp.14–17. Langdon's memoir was published posthumously; he was born in 1825 and died in 1894.

124. Frank George Marling, 'Reminiscences', unpublished autobiography, privately communicated (21 pp. typescript), p.14. The author was born in Berkeley, Gloucestershire, in 1863; his memoir was kindly supplied by his son, Mr K. G. Marling.

125. Abel J. Jones, *From an Inspector's Bag*, 1944, pp.4–5.

126. Kate Taylor, unpublished autobiography (16 pp. typescript), p.8. See this volume pp.288–94.

127. Elizabeth Grace Ranson, unpublished autobiography (60 pp. ms.), p.4. The author was born at Boosbeck, near Saltburn, Yorkshire, in 1899. Her memoir was kindly supplied by her daughter, Mrs M. Gibbons.

128. Mary Paley Marshall, op. cit. (see n.7), p.5.

129. Verbena Brighton, 'Memories of Carefree Days', unpublished autobiography, pp.28–30.

130. Alice M. Collis, 'From Paper Blankets to Central Heating', brief autobiographical sketch. The author was born in 1895.

131. Hannah Mitchell, *The Hard Way Up: Autobiography of Hannah Mitchell, Suffragette and Rebel*, ed. Geoffrey Mitchell, Preface by Sheila Rowbotham, 1977, p.39. The author was born in 1871 on a Derbyshire farm, wrote her autobiography c. 1945 and died in 1956.

132. Mrs Layton, op. cit. (see n.92), p.4.

133. Jack Lanigan, 'Incidents in the Life of a Citizen'. See this volume pp.95–99.

134. Kay Garrett, unpublished autobiography, p.3. The author was born in Hammersmith in 1899.

135. Adeline Hodges, op. cit. (see n.69), pp.7–8.

136. Mrs Layton, op. cit. (see n.92), p.9.

137. Thomas Carter, op. cit. (see n.4), pp.42–3.

138. John Castle, 'The Diary of John Castle'. See this volume pp.262–8.

139. Mrs Burrows, 'A Childhood in the Fens about 1850–60', in *Life As We Have Known It* by Co-operative Working Women, ed. Margaret Llewelyn Davies, 1977, p.111.

140. J. B. Cumberlidge, unpublished autobiography. The author was born in Manchester in 1889.

141. Anita Elizabeth Hughes (b. 1892, Lutterworth, Leicestershire) and Alice Foley (b. 1891, Bolton, Lancashire).

142. J. C. Tait, unpublished autobiography, p.4. The author was born in Newcastle in 1899.

143. Arthur Seymour, 'Childhood Memories', unpublished autobiography (38 pp. ms.), p.9. The author was born in 1879 in a cottage in New End Square, Hampstead; his memoir was kindly supplied by his daughter-in-law, Mrs A. Seymour.

144. Kathleen Hilton-Foord, op. cit. (see n.53), p.2.

145. Jack Wood, 'The Good Old Days', articles in the *Oldham Chronicle*, 20 January, 3, 10 February 1973; 5 January 1974. The author was born in Oldham in 1899.

146. Adeline Hodges, op. cit. (see n.69), p.16.

147. Averil Edith Thomas, op. cit. (see n.2), pp.19–20.

148. W. G. Elliott, 'An Octogenarian's Life Story', unpublished autobiography, p.4.

149. Kay Garrett, op. cit. (see n.134), p.1.

150. Jack Wood, op. cit. (see n.145), 27 January, 1973.

151. James Griffiths, op. cit. (see n.66), p.9.

152. William Cobbett, *The Progress of a Ploughboy to a Seat in Parliament*, ed. William Reitzel, 1933, p.4.

153. Roger Langdon, op. cit. (see n.123), pp.28–9; ch.3, from which this is quoted, is titled 'Starting in Life'.

154. Charles Shaw, op. cit. (see n.35), pp.10–11.

155. Mrs Burrows, op. cit. (see n.139), p.109.

156. Mrs Wrigley, 'A Plate-Layer's Wife', in *Life As We Have Known It* by Co-operative Working Women, ed. Margaret Llewelyn Davies, 1977, p.58. The author was born in Cefn Mawr in 1858, the daughter of a shoemaker.

157. Violet M. Whale, unpublished autobiography, pp.20–22. The author was born at Shoeburyness, Essex, in 1898.

158. Winifred Foley, *A Child in the Forest*, 1974, pp.141–6. The author was born at Brierley in the Forest of Dean in 1914.

159. Patrick MacGill, op. cit. (see n.56), p.26.

160. Marianne Farningham, op. cit. (see n.24), p.43.

161. Jack Lanigan, op. cit. (see n.133).

162. James Griffiths, op. cit. (see n.66), p.8.

163. Hannah Mitchell, op. cit. (see n.131), pp.62–3.

164. Joseph H. Armitage, 'The Late Way of Life and Living', unpublished autobiography (210 pp. typescript), pp.4, 87. The author was born in Hunslet, Leeds, in 1907.

165. William F. Belcher, unpublished autobiography, privately communicated by Miss E. M. Smith of Brunel University. The author was born in Wells Street, off Oxford Street, London, about 1886.

166. W. G. Elliott, op. cit. (see n.148), p.8.

167. Edward Cain, 'Memories', unpublished autobiography, p.4.

168. Anita Elizabeth Hughes, op. cit. (see n.141), p.4.

169. Doris Hunt, unpublished autobiography, privately communicated (14 pp. typescript), p.9. The author was born in Manchester in 1900.

PART TWO – EDUCATION

1. Standard accounts of the development of education include Frank Smith, *A History of English Elementary Education*, 1931; G. A. N. Lowndes, *The Silent Social Revolution*, 2nd edn, 1969; W. H. G. Armytage, *Four Hundred Years of English Education*, 1964; H. C. Barnard, *A History of English Education from 1760*, 2nd edn, 1961; David Wardle, *The Rise of the Schooled Society*, 1974. Also valuable is J. Stuart Maclure, *Educational Documents, 1816–1967*, 2nd edn, 1968.

2. On child labour in the nineteenth century, see P. Jocelyn Dunlop, *English Apprenticeship and Child Labour: A History*, 1912; Ivy Pinchbeck, *Women Workers and the Industrial Revolution*, 1930; Ivy Pinchbeck and Margaret Hewitt, *Children in English Society*, Vol. II, 1973.

3. Thomas Wood, *Autobiography 1822–1880*, privately published, 1956, p.7. Copyright Miss Dorothy Wood, Bronte Hall, Beckett Park, Leeds 6. A substantial extract is published in *Useful Toil: Autobiographies of working people from the 1820s to the 1920s*, ed. John Burnett, 1974, pp.304–12.

4. Charles Shaw, *When I Was a Child, by An Old Potter*, 1st edn, 1903; (facsimile edn, 1977, p.21. The author was born in Tunstall in 1832.

5. David Vincent, 'The Growth of Working-Class Consciousness in the First Half of the Nineteenth Century: A study of the autobiographies of working men', Cambridge Ph.D. thesis, 1975, p. 148.

6. John Clare, '*Sketches in the Life of John Clare, Written by Himself and Addressed to His Friend John Taylor Esq.*, 1821, first published, ed. with an Introduction by Edmund Blunden, 1931, p.48. Clare was born in Helpstone, Northamptonshire, in 1793.

7. Frank Smith, op. cit. (see n.1), p.220.

8. Thomas Carter, *Memoirs of a Working Man*, 1845. Carter was born in Colchester in 1792 and wrote his autobiography at the age of fifty-two; a continuation of the memoirs was published in 1850.

9. James Watson, 'The Reminiscences of James Watson 1799–1874', republished in *Testaments of Radicalism: Memoirs of Working-Class Politicians 1790–1885*, ed. with an Introduction by David Vincent 1977, p.105 et seq.

10. W. J. Linton, *Memories*, 1895, p.5. Linton was born in 1812 in the Mile End Road, London.

11. The first Public Libraries' Acts of 1845 and 1850 permitted local authorities to levy rates for the establishment of libraries, but only about sixty had used these powers by 1875. Geoffrey Best, *Mid-Victorian Britain 1851–1875*, 1971, pp.212–13.

12. Roger Langdon, *The Life of Roger Langdon, Told by Himself*, 1909. Langdon's memoir was published posthumously; he was born in 1825 and died in 1894.

13. George Jacob Holyoake, *Sixty Years of an Agitator's Life*, (2 Vols), 1892.

14. James Nasmyth, *James Nasmyth, Engineer: An Autobiography*, ed. Samuel Smiles, 1883.

15. John Hodge, *Workman's Cottage to Windsor Castle*, 1931, Thomas Burt, M.P., D.C.L., *Pitman to Privy Councillor*, 1924; George Barnes, *From Workshop to War Cabinet*, 1923; William Wright, *From Chimney-Boy to Councillor: The Story of My Life*, privately printed, c. 1931.

16. James Griffiths, *Pages from Memory*, 1969, pp.14–24.

17. Doris Hunt, unpublished autobiography, privately communicated (14 pp. typescript). The author was born in Manchester in 1900.
18. Hannah Mitchell, *The Hard Way Up: Autobiography of Hannah Mitchell, Suffragette and Rebel*, ed. Geoffrey Mitchell, Preface by Sheila Rowbotham, 1977. The author was born in 1871 on a Derbyshire farm, wrote her autobiography c. 1945 and died in 1956.
19. Thomas Walter Laqueur, *Religion and Respectability: Sunday Schools and Working-Class Culture 1780–1850*, 1976, pp.244–5.
20. Frank Smith, op. cit. (see n.1), p.220.
21. David Wardle, *Education and Society in Nineteenth Century Nottingham*, 1971, p.42.
22. Thomas Walter Laqueur, op. cit. (see n.19), p.246.
23. John James Bezer, 'The Autobiography of One of the Chartist Rebels of 1848', first published in the *Christian Socialist*, September–December 1851; republished in *Testaments of Radicalism: Memoirs of Working-Class Politicians 1790–1885*, ed. with an Introduction by David Vincent, 1977, p.157. Bezer was born in Spitalfields, London, in 1816, the son of a barber.
24. Marianne Farningham, *A Working Woman's Life: An Autobiography*, c. 1900, pp.28–9. The author was born in Farningham, Kent in 1834, and took her pseudonym from her place of birth. Her father was Joseph Hearn, a small tradesman.
25. Ben Brierley *Home Memories and Recollections of a Life*, c. 1886, p.12.
26. Faith Dorothy Osgerby, 'My Memoirs', unpublished autobiography, privately communicated (2 Vols ms.). See this volume pp.88–94.
27. Gwen Millington, unpublished autobiography, privately communicated (19 pp. typescript), p.7. The author was born in the Finchley Road, London, in 1914, but had a Victorian upbringing as she lived with her grandparents.
28. J. Smetham, 'Sunday for a Six-Year-Old in 1912', unpublished memoir, privately communicated.
29. Alice Maud Chase (née Moody), 'The Memoirs of Alice Maud Chase', unpublished autobiography, privately communicated (56 pp. typescript), p.23. I am grateful to Mrs P. M. Hallifax for permission to quote from her great-aunt's memoir. The author was born in Portsmouth in 1880 and died in 1968.
30. *A Cornish Waif's Story: An Autobiography*, with a Foreword by A. L. Rowse 1954, p.45.
31. See Samuel Bamford, *Passages in the Life of a Radical and Early Days*, (2 Vols), 1893, Vol. I, p.101, describing the Methodist Sunday School at Middleton so crowded that the teachers 'had to wade, as it were, through the close-ranked youngsters'.
32. Christopher Thomson, *The Autobiography of an Artisan*, 1847, pp.64–5.
33. Edward Brown, unpublished autobiography, privately communicated (185 pp. typescript), p.11. The author was born at Great Marlow, Buckinghamshire, in 1880.
34. Report of the Royal Commission on the State of Popular Education in England, XXI, 1861, Part I, Vol. I, pp.28–9.
35. For example, in Crabbe's poem 'The Borough', and in Charles Kingsley's novel *The Water Babies*, 1863.

36. *The School Board Chronicle*, 11 May 1872. Quoted in H. C. Barnard, *A History of English Education from 1760*, 1969, p.3.

37. James Hopkinson, *Memoirs of a Victorian Cabinet Maker 1819–1894*, ed. Jocelyne Baty Goodman 1968, p.6. Hopkinson was born at Cropwell Butler, Nottinghamshire, in 1819.

38. Joseph Gutteridge, 'The Autobiography of Joseph Gutteridge 1816–1899', in *Master and Artisan in Victorian England*, ed. with an Introduction by Valerie Chancellor, 1969, pp.84–5.

39. Thomas Cooper, *The Life of Thomas Cooper, Written by Himself*, 1872, republished with an Introduction by John Saville, 1971, p.7. Cooper began attending school in 1810 at Gainsborough, Lincolnshire.

40. William Esam, unpublished autobiography (22 pp. ms.), pp.11–12. The author was born in Norwich in 1826; his memoir was kindly supplied by his grandson, Charles Esam.

41. Frederick Hobley (b.1833), unpublished autobiography, privately communicated (95 pp. ms.), pp.1–2. Sections of this autobiography, which was written in 1905, were published in *Alta*, the University of Birmingham Review, No 6, Summer 1968. See this volume pp.177–82.

42. Leslie R. Missen, unpublished autobiography, privately communicated (61 pp. typescript), pp.5–6. The author was born in Cambridge in 1897, graduated from the university there, and ultimately became Chief Education Officer for East Suffolk.

43. Good accounts of the monitorial system are given in Frank Smith, op. cit. (see n.1), and in Mary Sturt, *The Education of the People: A History of Primary Education in England and Wales in the Nineteenth Century*, 1967.

44. *Educational Expositor*, March 1853, quoted in Asher Tropp, *The Schoolteachers: The Growth of the Teaching Profession in England and Wales from 1800 to the Present Day*, 1957, p.7.

45. Thomas Dunning, 'Reminiscences of Thomas Dunning 1813–1894', republished in *Testaments of Radicalism: Memoirs of Working-Class Politicians 1790–1885*, ed. with an Introduction by David Vincent, 1977, pp.119–20.

46. James Bonwick, *An Octogenarian's Reminiscences*. See this volume pp.171–176.

47. John Kerr, *Memories Grave and Gay: Forty Years of School Inspection*, 1902, p.48.

48. The complete syllabus (Revised Code, 1862) is quoted in Marion Johnson, *Derbyshire Village Schools in the Nineteenth Century*, 1970, p.98.

49. As in the autobiography of Margaret Penn, *Manchester Fourteen Miles*, 1947 republished with an Introduction by John Burnett, 1979, p.123.

50. F. Storr, ed., *The Life and Remains of the Rev. R. H. Quick*, 1899, p.134.

51. For a detailed account of the operation of 'Payment by Results' see Frank Smith, op. cit. (see n.1), chs. VIII, IX, X.

52. Alfred Percival Graves, *To Return To All That: An Autobiography*, 1930, p.219 et seq.

53. Report of the Education Department for 1895, evidence of Mr King, H.M.I., p.103.

54. Jim Tait, unpublished autobiography, privately communicated by P. N.

Farrar, Hull College of Higher Education, pp.1–4. The author was born in 1899 in Newcastle-on-Tyne.

55. Harry Dorrell, unpublished autobiography, privately communicated, (15 pp. typescript), p.1. The author was born in Plaistow, London, in 1903.

56. Arthur Allwood, 'The Turn of the Century', unpublished autobiography, privately communicated, p.1. The author was born in Whitchurch, Shropshire, in 1893.

57. W. E. Palmer, 'Memories of Long Ago', unpublished autobiography, privately communicated, p.12. The author was born in 1907 at Harting Coombe, a hamlet near Rogate, Sussex.

58. *A Cornish Waif's Story: An Autobiography*, op. cit. (see n.30), p.21.

59. F. H. Spencer, *An Inspector's Testament*, 1938, p.73. Dr Spencer began as a pupil-teacher, rising to Chief Inspector for the L.C.C. and H.M. Divisional Inspector of Schools.

60. Edward Brown, op. cit. (see n.33), pp.7–8.

61. Daisy Cowper, 'De Nobis', unpublished autobiography, (109 pp. typescript), p.71. See this volume pp.198–204.

62. Emily Gertrude Lea, 'Reflections in the Setting Sun', or 'I Remember after Fifty Years commencing 1902', unpublished autobiography, privately communicated by Mrs D. Waughman, (15 pp. typescript), p.4. The author was born in Wellingborough, Northamptonshire, in 1899.

63. Eric F. Powell, 'Forest Memories: The Autobiography of a Dean Forester', unpublished autobiography, privately communicated (107 pp. typescript), p.10. The author was born at Blakeney in the Forest of Dean, c. 1900.

64. Henry George Lock, 'An Old Man Tries to Remember', unpublished autobiography, privately communicated by Mrs A. S. Mayers (15 pp. typescript), p.2. The author was born in Abingdon, Berkshire, in 1876, but spent his childhood in the village of Sutton Courtney.

65. Reginald Gowshall, *With the Turn of the Traveller*, privately printed, 1971, p.12. The author was born at Theddlethorpe All Saints, Lincolnshire, in 1906.

66. Jack Wood, 'The Good Old Days', article in the *Oldham Chronicle*, 31 March 1973. The author was born in Oldham in 1899.

67. Harry Dorrell, op. cit. (see n.55).

68. George Rowles, 'Chaps Among the Caps', unpublished autobiography, privately communicated, (210 pp. typescript), pp.5–6. The author was born off the Edgware Road, London, c. 1890.

69. Edward Brown, op. cit. (see n.33), p.22.

70. Maud M. Clarke, unpublished autobiography, privately communicated. The author was born in West Bromwich in 1887.

71. Rev. George Gregory, 'An Old Man's Recollections of Childhood 1894–1907', unpublished autobiography, privately communicated, p.2. The author was born in a mining village in Somerset in 1888.

72. Minnie Frisby, 'Memories', unpublished autobiography, privately communicated (27 pp. typescript), p.16. The author was born at Worm's Ash, near Birmingham, in 1876; her memoir was kindly supplied by her daughter-in-law, Mrs Barbara Frisby.

73. Alfred Ireson, 'Reminiscences', unpublished autobiography, privately

communicated by Mrs A. Hoskins (175 pp. typescript), p.22. See this volume pp.82–8.

74. Mary Hollinrake, 'Lancashire Lass', unpublished autobiography, privately communicated (73 pp. ms.), p.11. The author was born in Todmorden, Lancashire, 1912. Her autobiography begins with the words 'I came from extremely respectable working-class parents.'

75. Abel J. Jones, *From an Inspector's Bag*, 1944, pp.5–6.

76. William F. Belcher, unpublished autobiography, privately communicated by Miss E. M. Smith of Brunel University. The author was born in Wells Street, off Oxford Street, London, in 1886.

77. Edward Punter, 'So Often Alone', unpublished autobiography (Part I, Childhood, 114 pp. typescript), p.86. The author was born in 1897; his memoir was kindly supplied by his widow, Mrs H. M. Punter.

78. Jessie Ravenna Sharman, 'Recollections', unpublished autobiography, privately communicated, (7 pp. typescript), p.2. The author was born in Norwich in 1892.

79. Fred Boughton, 'The Forest in My Younger Days', unpublished autobiography, privately communicated (216 pp. ms.), p.10. See this volume pp.294–300.

80. M. Jones, unpublished autobiography, privately communicated (44 pp.), pp.13–14. The author was born in a Cheshire village in 1893.

81. Ernest Richard Shotton, 'Personal History and Memoirs', unpublished autobiography, privately communicated by Mrs Veronica Leach (42 pp. typescript), p.14. The author was born at Coalbrookdale in 1878 and wrote his memoirs in 1963.

82. Edward Brown, op. cit. (see n.33), p.8.

83. F. H. Spencer, op. cit. (see n.59), p.59 et seq.

84. Arthur Allwood, op. cit. (see n.56).

85. Ethel M. Clark, 'Their Small Corner', unpublished autobiography, privately communicated (109 pp. typescript), p.64. The author was born in Woolaston, Gloucestershire, in 1904.

86. Ruth Brooker, 'Journal of Memoirs', unpublished autobiography, privately communicated by Mrs Anne Freeston, p.4.

87. W. E. Palmer, op. cit. (see n.57), p.17.

88. Faith Dorothy Osgerby, op. cit. (see n.26).

89. Michael Gareth Llewelyn, *Sand in the Glass*, 1943, p.175 et seq.

90. G. A. N. Lowndes, op. cit. (see n.1), p.80.

91. G. A. N. Lowndes, op. cit. (see n.1), p.89.

92. Thomas Wood, op. cit. (see n.3), pp.4–7.

93. William Esam, op. cit. (see n.40), p.13.

94. George Grundy, *Fifty-Five Years at Oxford: An Unconventional Autobiography*, 1945, pp.22–4. Another useful account of the small, old-fashioned Boteler Grammar School, Warrington, at the beginning of the twentieth century, is given in F. O. Stansfield, *The Early Life of an Old Warringtonian*, p.37 et seq.

95. Reginald Farndon, unpublished autobiography, privately communicated. The author was born in Ealing in 1904.

96. Nora Lumb, 'Childhood Memories', unpublished autobiography, privately communicated, p.12. The author was born in Sunderland in 1912.

97. Bim Andrews, 'Making Do', unpublished autobiography, privately communicated (14pp. typescript), p.2. See this volume pp.126–31.
98. Edith A. Williams, unpublished autobiography, privately communicated (13pp. typescript), p.7. The author was born in Aberfan, Merthyr Tydfil, in 1899.
99. Eric F. Powell, op. cit. (see n.63), pp.48–50.
100. Arthur Allwood, op. cit. (see n.56).
101. Averil Edith Thomas, 'Me', unpublished autobiography, privately communicated by Averil Harper Smith, (26 pp. ms.), p.19. The author was born in Melton Mowbray.
102. Doris Frances, unpublished autobiography, privately communicated (32 pp. typescript), pp.27–8. The author was born in Putney, London, in 1908.
103. Mary Hollinrake, op. cit. (see n.74), pp. 53–9.
104. Leslie R. Missen, op. cit. (see n.42), p.23 et seq.
105. E. Balne, 'The Autobiography of an ex-Workhouse and Poor Law Schoolboy', unpublished autobiography, privately communicated (12 pp. typescript), p.11. The author was born in Southwark, London, in 1895, and was first an inmate of Southwark Workhouse before removal to Hanwell.
106. Nora Isobel Adnams, 'My Memoirs of Dr Barnardo's Home, Barkingside, Essex, 1904–1911', unpublished autobiography, privately communicated (26 pp. typescript). The author was born in Hampstead, London, in 1901.

PART THREE – HOME AND FAMILY

1. Amy Frances Gomm, 'Water Under the Bridge', unpublished autobiography (140 pp. typescript), pp.4, 30, 49, 50. The author was born in Charlbury, Oxfordshire, in 1899.
2. Eleanor Hutchinson, 'The Bells of St Mary's', unpublished autobiography (100 pp. typescript), pp.8–13. The author was born in Paddington, London, in 1915.
3. R. W. Morris, unpublished autobiography, pp.41–2. The author was born at Pelton Fell, Co. Durham, in 1895. Sections of the autobiography have been edited by George Patterson, Resident Tutor for Sunderland in the University of Durham Department of Extra-Mural Studies, and published in the *Bulletin of Durham County Local History Society*, October 1977, April 1978. I am grateful to Mr Patterson for bringing the autobiography to my notice.
4. Mrs F. H. Smith, 'In a Mining Village', in *Life As We Have Known It* by Co-operative Working Women, ed. Margaret Llewelyn Davies, 1977, p.67. The author married in 1903 at the age of nineteen.
5. Mrs Layton, 'Memories of Seventy Years', in *Life As We Have Known It* by Co-operative Working Women, ed. Margaret Llewelyn Davies, 1977, p.1.
6. Jack Wood, 'The Good Old Days', articles in the *Oldham Chronicle*, 20 January 1973 and 5 January 1974. The author was born in Oldham in 1899.
7. Audrey Prior, 'My Memoirs', unpublished autobiography (69 pp. typescript), pp.5–8.
8. Joan Rhodes, 'A Lancashire Childhood', unpublished autobiography, pp.3–5.

9. Thomas R. Flintoff, 'Friday the Thirteenth of May', unpublished autobiography (11 pp. typescript), pp. 5–6. The author was born in Preston in 1904.

10. Mary Hollinrake, 'Lancashire Lass', unpublished autobiography privately communicated (73 pp. ms.), pp.2, 11. The author was born in Todmorden, Lancashire, in 1912. Her autobiography begins with the words 'I came from extremely respectable working-class parents.'

11. Wilhelmina Tobias, 'Childhood Memories', unpublished autobiography (22 pp. ms.), p.8. The author was born at Wallsend in 1904.

12. Elizabeth Rignall, 'All So Long Ago', unpublished autobiography (140 pp. typescript), p.7. The author was born in London in 1894, but spent much of her childhood with her grandparents in Haworth, Yorkshire.

13. Adeline Hodges, 'I Remember', unpublished autobiography (160 pp. ms.), pp.9–10. The author was born in the mining village of Dawdon, near Seaham Colliery, Durham, in 1899; her memoir was kindly supplied by her daughter, Mrs J. Pace.

14. Amy Emma Ind, autobiographical letter, p.1. The author was born in 1899 at Matfield, Kent, the daughter of an estate gardener.

15. Doris Frances, unpublished autobiography, privately communicated (32 pp. typescript), pp.19–20. The author was born in Putney, London, in 1908.

16. Mrs Wrigley, A Plate-Layer's Wife', in *Life As We Have Known It* by Co-operative Working Women, ed. Margaret Llewelyn Davies, 1977, pp.56–7. The author was born in Cefn Mawr in 1858, the daughter of a shoemaker

17. George Mockford, 'Wilderness Journeyings and Gracious Deliverances: The Autobiography of George Mockford, (for forty years Minister of the Gospel at Broad Oak, Heathfield).' See this volume pp.72–7.

18. Catherine McLouglin, unpublished autobiography, p.7. The author was born in Oswaldtwistle, Lancashire, in 1889; her memoir was kindly supplied by her daughter Mrs Kathleen Nugent.

19. Alice Foley, 'A Bolton Childhood', 1973, pp.24–5. See this volume pp.100–107.

20. Samuel Mountford, 'A Memoir', unpublished autobiography (28 pp. typescript), pp.5–6. The author was born in 1907 in a suburb of Birmingham.

21. Jack Wood, op. cit. (see n.6), 5 January 1974.

22. Hilda Rose Fowler, 'Look After the Little Ones', unpublished autobiography (20 pp. typescript), p.9. The author was born in Cheltenham in 1890; her memoir was kindly supplied by Mr G. Robson of Westhill College, Selly Oak, Birmingham.

23. Adeline Hodges, op. cit. (see n.13), pp.19–21.

24. Anita Elizabeth Hughes, 'My Autobiography', unpublished autobiography (15 pp. typescript), p.3. The author was born in Cotesbach, near Lutterworth, Leicestershire, in 1892, the daughter of an estate gardener. Her memoir was written at the age of eighty-four and kindly supplied by her daughter, Mrs Evelyn Wilde.

25. Eleanor Hutchinson, op. cit. (see n.2), p.15.

26. Thomas R. Flintoff, op. cit. (see n.9), pp.7–8.

27. Kathleen Betterton, 'White Pinnies, Black Aprons', unpublished autobiography (143 pp. typescript), pp.4–5. See this volume pp.204–11.

28. Mary Hollinrake, op. cit. (see n.10), pp.33–4.

29. Enid K. F. Stuart Scott, 'I Wear A Hat: A Cambridge Childhood 1900–1916, unpublished autobiography (117 pp. typescript), pp.7–8.

30. Samuel Mountford, op. cit. (see n.20), p.8.

31. Joseph H. Armitage, 'The Late Way of Life and Living', unpublished autobiography (210 pp. typescript), p.16. The author was born in Hunslet, Leeds, in 1907.

32. Nora Bargate, unpublished autobiography. The author was born in 1912 in East London.

33. William F. Belcher, unpublished autobiography, privately communicated by Miss E. M. Smith of Brunel University, p.10. The author was born in Wells Street, off Oxford Street, London, about 1886.

34. George Rowles, 'Chaps Among the Caps', unpublished autobiography, privately communicated (210 pp. typescript), p.5. The author was born off the Edgware Road, London, c. 1890.

35. Edna Bold, 'The Long and Short of It', unpublished autobiography (36 pp. typescript), pp.1–2. See this volume pp.113–20.

36. Jack Goring, 'Autobiographical Notes', unpublished autobiography (321 pp. ms.). The author was born in 1861 in Wenlock Street, off New North Road, London and his memoirs were written in 1938. They were kindly supplied by his daughter, Elsa Houghton.

37. Henry George Lock, 'An Old Man Tries to Remember', unpublished autobiography, privately communicated by Mrs A. S. Mayers (15 pp. typescript), p.10. The author was born in Abingdon, Berkshire, in 1876, but spent his childhood in the village of Sutton Courtney.

38. Eleanor Hutchinson, op. cit. (see n.2), p.18.

39. Alice Foley, op. cit. (see n.19), p.15.

40. Jack Wood, op. cit. (see n.6), 14 April 1973.

41. Mrs Layton, op. cit. (see n.5), pp.7–8.

42. Mrs Burrows, 'A Childhood in the Fens about 1850–60', in *Life As We Have Known It* by Co-operative Working Women, ed. Margaret Llewelyn Davies, 1977, pp.112–13.

43. George Healey, *Life and Remarkable Career*, p.1. The author was born in St Albans in 1823.

44. Leonard W. Ellisdon, 'Starting From Victoria', unpublished autobiography (118 pp. typescript), p.15. The author was born in 1885 in Brixton, London.

45. Stanley Rice, 'The Memories of a Rolling Stone', unpublished autobiography (68 pp. typescript), p.6. The author was born in Kennington, London, in 1905.

46. Jack Wood, op. cit. (see n.6), 13 January and 24 February 1973.

47. Nancie Lou Joyce Howlett, 'The Life and Times of the Howlett Family 1860–1922', unpublished memoir, p.9. The author was born in 1906 near Rochester, Kent; her memoir was kindly supplied by her daughter, Mrs C. Allard.

48. P. Marrin, unpublished autobiography (6 pp. typescript), p.1. The author was born in Walworth, London, in 1890.

49. Charles Esam, unpublished autobiography (96 pp. ms.). The author was born in Thornton Heath, Surrey, in 1899.

50. B. E. Houle, 'Up, Down and Roundabout', unpublished autobiography, ch.1, p.2, and ch.2, p.7. The author was born in London in 1897.

51. Margaret Cunningham, 'End of Exploring: An Autobiography' unpublished autobiography (119 pp. typescript) pp.47–8. The author was born in 1900, the daughter of the vicar of Wonersh, Surrey.

52. Syd Metcalfe, unpublished autobiography (83 pp. typescript). The author was born in London in 1908.

53. Edward Punter, 'So Often Alone', unpublished autobiography (Part I, Childhood, 114 pp. typescript), p.57. The author was born in 1897; his memoir was kindly supplied by his widow, Mrs H. M. Punter.

54. Faith Dorothy Osgerby, 'My Memoirs', unpublished autobiography, privately communicated (2 Vols ms.). See this volume pp.88–94.

55. Margaret Perry, unpublished autobiography (29 pp. typescript). See this volume pp.318–24.

56. Doris Ponton, autobiographical letter, pp.2, 5. The author was born in Southwark, London, in 1909.

57. Doris Frances, op. cit. (see n.15).

58. Fanny O'Donnell, unpublished autobiography. The author was born in Grove Park, near Bromley, in 1898.

59. James Dawson Burn, *The Autobiography of a Beggar Boy*, 1st edn, 1855; new edn with an Introduction by David Vincent, 1978. Burn was probably born in Dumfries between 1804 and 1806.

60. William Wright, *From Chimney-Boy to Councillor: The Story of My Life*, privately printed, c. 1931. The author was born in 1846 at Alton, Hampshire; he began to be employed as a climbing boy by his father at the age of eight.

61. Louise Jermy, *The Memories of a Working Woman*, 1934, pp.28–9. The author was born at Howe, Hampshire, in 1877, the daughter of a stonemason; they moved to Bow, London, on her father's re-marriage.

62. Roger Langdon, *The Life of Roger Langdon, Told by Himself*, 1909, p.34. Langdon's memoir was published posthumously; he was born in 1825 and died in 1894.

63. Albert Goodwin, unpublished autobiography (37 pp. ms.), pp.2–3. See this volume pp.280–87.

64. Alice Foley, op. cit. (see n.19), pp.11–12.

65. Harry Alfred West, unpublished autobiography (50 pp. typescript), pp.6, 8. The author was born in Upper Stanton, Somerset, in 1888; his memoir was kindly supplied by his daughter, Mrs E. de Kluiver.

66. Fred Boughton, 'The Forest In My Younger Days', unpublished autobiography, privately communicated (216 pp. ms.), p.31. See this volume pp.294–300.

67. George Grundy, *Fifty-Five Years at Oxford: An Unconventional Autobiography*, 1945, pp.12–13. The author was born in 1861 in Wallasey, Cheshire, the son of a private school proprietor and grandson of a clergyman.

68. Eleanor Hewson, 'An Edwardian Childhood', unpublished autobiography (115 pp. typescript), p.17. The author was born in 1905, the daughter of a professor living in Barnes.

69. Fanny O'Donnell, op. cit. (see n.58).

70. Amy Frances Gomm, 'Water Under the Bridge', op. cit. (see n.1).

71. Violet M. Whale, unpublished autobiography, pp.6–7. The author was born at Shoeburyness, Essex, in 1898.
72. George Healey, op. cit. (see n.43), p.1.
73. Winifred Relph, 'Through Rough Ways', unpublished autobiography, (62 pp. typescript), ch. Childhood, p.1. The author was born in 1912.
74. Edward Brown, unpublished autobiography, privately communicated (185 pp. typescript), p.3. The author was born at Great Marlow, Buckinghamshire in 1880.
75. John Burnett, *Plenty and Want: A Social History of Diet in England from 1815 to the Present Day*, revised edn, 1979, p.199.
76. Doris Ponton, op. cit. (see n.56), p.5.
77. John James Bezer, 'The Autobiography of One of the Chartist Rebels of 1848', first published in the *Christian Socialist* September–December 1851; re-published in *Testaments of Radicalism: Memoirs of Working-Class Politicians, 1790–1885*, ed. with an Introduction by David Vincent, 1977, p.159. Bezer was born in Spitalfields, London, in 1816, the son of a barber.
78. Violet E. Jared, a series of illustrated autobiographical scenes with explanatory text. The author was born in 1908.
79. Ellen Gill, unpublished autobiography, p.6. The author was born in Woodhouse, Leeds, in 1888.
80. Norah Knight, 'Nostalgia', unpublished autobiography (73 pp. ms.), pp.18, 25, 39. The author was born in Seacombe, on the Wirral, in 1910.
81. Kathleen Betterton, op. cit. (see n.27).
82. Amy Frances Gomm, op. cit. (see n.1), p.108.
83. Mary Paley Marshall, *What I Remember*, with an Introduction by G. M. Trevelyan, 1947, pp.1–2. Mary Marshall was born in 1850, the daughter of a country rector, near Stamford, Lincolnshire; she was one of the first students at Newnham College, Cambridge, and later married the famous economist, Arthur Marshall. She lived until 1944.
84. Faith Dorothy Osgerby, op. cit. (see n.54), p.17.
85. Margaret Penn, *Manchester Fourteen Miles*, 1st edn, 1947; facsimile edn, with an Introduction by John Burnett, 1979, pp.15–16.
86. Norah P. unpublished autobiography. The author was born in Nottingham in 1901.
87. Ben Brierley, *Home Memories and Recollections of a Life*, c. 1886, pp.3–9.
88. Henry George Lock, op. cit. (see n.37), pp.6–7.
89. Miss E. Tabor's sister, 'Wiltshire Memories', unpublished autobiography (9 pp. typescript). The author was born in Wilton, Wiltshire, in 1888; her memoir was kindly supplied by her sister, Miss E. Tabor.
90. Amy Frances Gomm, op. cit. (see n.1), pp.45,61,75.
91. Verbena Brighton, 'Memories of Carefree Days', unpublished autobiography (125 pp. typescript), p.56. The author was born in Scole, near Diss, Norfolk, in 1915.
92. Frank George Marling, 'Reminiscences', unpublished autobiography, privately communicated (21 pp. typescript), pp.3–4. The author was born in Berkeley, Gloucestershire, in 1863; his memoir was kindly supplied by his son, Mr K. G. Marling.

93. George Lomas, unpublished autobiography (6 pp. ms.), p.3. The author was born in Ashton-under-Lyne, Lancashire, in 1867; his memoir was kindly supplied by his granddaughter, Mrs D. Foreman.

94. Arthur Seymour, 'Childhood Memories', unpublished autobiography (38 pp. ms.), p.20. The author was born in 1879 in a cottage in New End Square, Hampstead; his memoir was kindly supplied by his daughter-in-law, Mrs A. Seymour.

95. George Ratcliffe, *Sixty Years Of It: Being the Story of My Life and Public Career*, c. 1925, pp.1–3. The author was born in a slum area in the East End of Leeds in 1863.

96. Minnie Frisby, 'Memories', unpublished autobiography, privately communicated (27 pp. typescript). The author was born at Worm's Ash, near Birmingham, in 1876; her memoir was kindly supplied by her daughter-in-law, Mrs Barbara Frisby.

97. Jack Wood, op. cit. (see n.6), 27 January and 10 February 1973.

98. Alice Foley, op. cit. (see n.19), p.21.

99. Joseph H. Armitage, op. cit. (see n.31), p.46.

100. Mrs D. Wyatt, 'Edwardian Wealdstone', unpublished memoir, appendix on 'Children's Play in the Edwardian Era'.

101. Thomas R. Flintoff, op. cit. (see n.9), p.4.

102. Elizabeth Rignall, op. cit. (see n.12), ch.4.

103. Alice Foley, op. cit. (see n.19), p.18.

104. Bessie Wallis, 'Yesterday', unpublished autobiography, p.1. See this volume pp.306–12.

105. Oral historians are currently studying this phenomenon as an aspect of late-nineteenth-century youth culture. See paper by Stephen Humphries given at Oral History Conference, 1978.

106. George Ratcliffe, op. cit. (see n.95), p.11.

107. Albert Ellis, 'As It Was', unpublished autobiography (16 pp. typescript), pp. 13–14. The author was born in Bolton in 1897.

108. Leonard W. Ellisdon, op. cit. (see n.44), pp.10–11.

109. Nancie Lou Joyce Howlett, op. cit. (see n.47), p.8.

110. J. A. R. Pimlott, *The Englishman's Holiday: A Social History*, 1947.

111. Margaret Cunningham, op. cit. (see n.51), pp.52–3.

112. Betty Sutherland Graeme, 'Truly Thankful: Some Memories of Childhood', privately printed, 1976, pp.37–9. The author was born in 1904 in St Leonards-on-Sea.

113. Jean Nettleton, unpublished autobiography. The author was born in Harrogate, Yorkshire, in 1916.

114. John K. Walton, *The Blackpool Landlady: A Social History*, 1978.

115. Alice Foley, op. cit. (see n.19), p.39.

116. Alan Delgado, *The Annual Outing and Other Excursions*, 1977, p.80.

117. Wilhelmina Tobias, op. cit. (see n.11), p.13.

118. Jack Wood, op. cit. (see n.6), 17 February 1973.

119. Mary Denison, 'Church Bells and Tram Cars: A Vicarage Childhood', unpublished autobiography, ch.3, pp.3–4. The author, born in 1906, was the daughter of the vicar of St Chad's, Leeds.

120. Camilla Campbell, *The Peewit's Cry: A Norfolk Childhood*, 1980, pp.26–28.
121. Betty Sutherland Graeme, op. cit (see n.112), pp.9, 44.
122. Mercy Collisson, 'Memories of a Country Rectory,' unpublished autobiography, ch.3, p.8. The author was born at Gravenhurst, Bedfordshire, where her father was rector.
123. Florence M. Goddard, 'Stays and Woollen Stockings', unpublished autobiography (57 pp. typescript), p.31. The author was born in London in 1904.
124. Margaret Cunningham, op. cit. (see n.51), p.56.
125. George Ratcliffe, op. cit. (see n.95), p.22.
126. William Smith, 'The Memoir of William Smith', ed. B. S. Trinder, *Shropshire Archaeological Society Transactions*, Vol. LVIII, Part 2, 1965–8, pp.182–3.
127. Ellen Calvert, unpublished autobiography. The author was born in Woodhouse, Leeds, in 1888, one of ten children of a leather-worker. An extract from her husband Arthur Gill's autobiography was published in *Useful Toil: Autobiographies of working people from the 1820s to the 1920s*, ed. John Burnett, 1974, p.340 et seq.
128. Anita Elizabeth Hughes, op. cit. (see n.24), p.6.
129. Bessie Wallis, op. cit. (see n.104), ch.2, pp.2–3.
130. Mrs Layton, op. cit. (see n.5), p.33.
131. John Clare, *Sketches in the Life of John Clare, Written by Himself and Addressed to His Friend John Taylor Esq.*, 1821, first published, ed. with an Introduction by Edmund Blunden, 1931, p.85. The author was born in Helpstone, Northamptonshire, in 1793.
132. John James Bezer, op. cit. (see n.77), pp.177–8.
133. Syd Metcalfe, op. cit. (see n.52), p.8.
134. Frank F. Betts, unpublished autobiography (12 pp. typescript), p.7. The author was born in Norwich in 1885; his memoir was kindly supplied by his widow.
135. Minnie Frisby, op. cit. (see n.96), p.21.
136. Alice Foley, op. cit. (see n.19), p.58.
137. Mary Paley Marshall, op. cit. (see n.83), p.3.
138. Margaret Penn, *Manchester Fourteen Miles*, 1st edn, 1947; facsimile edn, with an introduction by John Burnett, 1979, p.23.
139. Mary Chamberlain (ed.), *Fenswomen: A Portrait of Women in an English Village*, 1977, p.72. The evidence of Maggy Fryett relates to c. 1910.
140. Fred Boughton, op. cit. (see n.66), p.87.
141. M. Owen, autobiographical letter, p.5. The author was born in Fulham, London, in 1898, but moved to Yorkshire when a girl.
142. James Watson and Thomas Dunning, in *Testaments of Radicalism: Memoirs of Working-Class Politicians 1790–1885*, ed. with an Introduction by David Vincent, 1977, pp.113, 140.
143. J. B. Leno, *The Aftermath: With Autobiography of the Author*, 1892, p.29. Leno was born in Uxbridge, Middlesex, in 1826.
144. Thomas Carter, *Memoirs of a Working Man*, 1845, p.206. Carter was born in Colchester in 1792 and wrote his autobiography at the age of fifty-two; a continuation of the memoirs was published in 1850.
145. John Shinn. See this volume pp.186–92.

146. Mrs Wrigley, op. cit. (see n.16), p.60.
147. *A Cornish Waif's Story: An Autobiography*, with a Foreword by A. L. Rowse, 1954, pp.152–3.
148. John Castle. See this volume pp. 262–8.
149. Gwen Millington, unpublished autobiography, privately communicated (19 pp. typescript), p.2. The author was born in the Finchley Road, London in 1914, but had a Victorian upbringing as she lived with her grandparents.
150. Thomas Carter, op. cit. (see n.144), p.209.
151. Ethel M. Clark, 'Their Small Corner', unpublished autobiography, privately communicated (109 pp. typescript), p.14. The author was born at Woolaston, Gloucestershire, in 1904.
152. Maggy Fryett, in *Fenwomen: A Portrait of Women in an English Village*, ed. Mary Chamberlain, 1977, p.77.
153. Alice Maud Chase (née Moody), 'The Memoirs of Alice Maud Chase', unpublished autobiography privately communicated (56 pp. typescript), p.11. I am grateful to Mrs P. M. Hallifax for permission to quote from her great-aunt's memoirs. The author was born in Portsmouth in 1880 and died in 1968.
154. Henry George Lock, op. cit. (see n.37), p.8.